CHILTON'S
REPAIR & TUNE-UP GUIDE

CHAMP ARROW SAPPORO 1977-83

All Champ/Arrow/Sapporo models

President LAWRENCE A. FORNASIERI
Vice President and General Manager JOHN P. KUSHNERICK
Executive Editor KERRY A. FREEMAN, S.A.E.
Senior Editor RICHARD J. RIVELE, S.A.E.
Editor RON WEBB

CHILTON BOOK COMPANY
Radnor, Pennsylvania
19089

SAFETY NOTICE

Proper service and repair procedures are vital to the safe, reliable operation of all motor vehicles, as well as the personal safety of those performing repairs. This book outlines procedures for servicing and repairing vehicles using safe, effective methods. The procedures contain many NOTES, CAUTIONS and WARNINGS which should be followed along with standard safety procedures to eliminate the possibility of personal injury or improper service which could damage the vehicle or compromise its safety.

It is important to note that repair procedures and techniques, tools and parts for servicing motor vehicles, as well as the skill and experience of the individual performing the work vary widely. It is not possible to anticipate all of the conceivable ways or conditions under which vehicles may be serviced, or to provide cautions as to all of the possible hazards that may result. Standard and accepted safety precautions and equipment should be used when handling toxic or flammable fluids, and safety goggles or other protection should be used during cutting, grinding, chiseling, prying, or any other process that can cause material removal or projectiles.

Some procedures require the use of tools specially designed for a specific purpose. Before substituting another tool or procedure, you must be completely satisfied that neither your personal safety, nor the performance of the vehicle will be endangered.

Although information in this guide is based on industry sources and is as complete as possible at the time of publication, the possibility exists that the manufacturer made later changes which could not be included here. While striving for total accuracy, Chilton Book Company cannot assume responsibility for any errors, changes, or omissions that may occur in the compilation of this data.

PART NUMBERS

Part numbers listed in this reference are not recommendations by Chilton for any product by brand name. They are references that can be used with interchange manuals and aftermarket supplier catalogs to locate each brand supplier's discrete part number.

ACKNOWLEDGMENTS

The Chilton Book Company expresses its appreciation to the Chrysler-Plymouth Division, Chrysler Corporation for their generous assistance.

Published in Radnor, Pennsylvania 19089 by Chilton Book Company

Manufactured in the United States of America
4567890 2109876

Chilton's Repair & Tune-Up Guide: Champ, Arrow and Sapporo 1977–83
ISBN 0-8019-7344-9 pbk.
Library of Congress Catalog Card No. 82-72939

CONTENTS

Quick Reference Specifications For Your Vehicle

Fill in this chart with the most commonly used specifications for your vehicle. Specifications can be found in Chapters 1 through 3 or on the tune-up decal under the hood of the vehicle.

Tune-Up

Firing Order ____________

Spark Plugs:

Type ____________

Gap (in.) ____________

Point Gap (in.) ____________

Dwell Angle (°) ____________

Ignition Timing (°) ____________

Vacuum (Connected/Disconnected) ____________

Valve Clearance (in.)

Intake ____________ Exhaust ____________

Capacities

Engine Oil (qts)

With Filter Change ____________

Without Filter Change ____________

Cooling System (qts) ____________

Manual Transmission (pts) ____________

Type ____________

Automatic Transmission (pts) ____________

Type ____________

Front Differential (pts) ____________

Type ____________

Rear Differential (pts) ____________

Type ____________

Transfer Case (pts) ____________

Type ____________

FREQUENTLY REPLACED PARTS

Use these spaces to record the part numbers of frequently replaced parts.

PCV VALVE	OIL FILTER	AIR FILTER
Manufacturer ________	Manufacturer ________	Manufacturer ________
Part No. ________	Part No. ________	Part No. ________

General Information and Maintenance

HOW TO USE THIS BOOK

Chilton's Repair and Tune-Up Guide for the Champ, Arrow and Sapporo is intended to help you learn more about your car and save you money on its upkeep and operation.

The first two chapters will be the most used, since they contain basic maintenance procedures and tune-up information. Later chapters deal with the more complex systems of your car. Systems from the engine through the brakes are covered to the extent that the average do-it-yourselfer can perform seemingly difficult operations with confidence. It will give you detailed instructions to help you change your own brake pads and shoes, replace points and plugs, and do many more jobs that will save you money and help you avoid expensive problems. Such things as rebuilding the differential are not covered for the simple reason that the expertise required and the investment in special tools make such tasks uneconomical.

This book can also be used as a reference for owners who want to understand their car and/or their mechanics better.

Before undertaking any repair, read through the entire procedure. This will give you the overall view of what tools and supplies will be required. Read ahead and plan ahead.

When overhauling a defective part is not considered practical, we tell you how to remove the part and how to install a new or rebuilt part. Rebuilt parts of excellent quality are, in many cases, readily available. These generally carry a guarantee similar to that of a new part. Since the price of these parts is usually much lower than that of a new part and the quality is often comparable, the option to purchase a rebuilt part should never be overlooked.

When working on your car, remember that whenever the left side of the car or engine is referred to, it is meant to specify the driver's side. Conversely, the right side refers to the passenger's side.

Safety is always the most important rule. Constantly be aware of the dangers involved in working on or underneath any automobile and always take the proper precautions. (See the section in this chapter on "Servicing Your Vehicle Safely" and the SAFETY NOTICE on the acknowledgement page.)

Pay attention to the instructions provided. There are 3 common mistakes in mechanical work:

1. *Incorrect order of assembly, disassembly or adjustment.* When taking something apart or putting it together, doing things in the wrong order usually just costs you extra time; however, it can break something. Read the entire procedure before beginning disassembly. Do everything in the order in which the instructions say you should do it, even if you can't immediately see a reason for it. When you're taking apart something that is very intricate (for example, a carburetor), you might want to draw a picture of how it looks when assembled at one point in order to make sure you get everything back in its proper position. We will supply exploded views whenever possible. When making adjustments, especially tune-up adjustments, do them in order. Occasionally one adjustment affects another and you cannot expect satisfactory results unless each adjustment is made only when it cannot be changed by any other.

2. *Overtorquing (or undertorquing).* While it is more common for overtorquing to cause damage, undertorquing can cause a fastener to vibrate loose causing serious damage. Especially when dealing with aluminum parts, pay attention to torque specifications and utilize a torque wrench in assembly. If a torque figure is not available, remember that if you are using the right tool to do the job, you will probably not have to strain yourself to get a fastener tight enough. The pitch of most threads

is so slight that the tension you put on the wrench will be multiplied many, many times in actual force on what you are tightening. A good example of how critical torque is can be seen in the case of spark plug installation, especially where you are putting the plug into an aluminum cylinder head. Too little torque can fail to crush the gasket, causing leakage of combustion gases and consequent loss of power and overheating of the plug and engine parts. Too much torque can damage the threads or distort the plug, which changes the spark gap.

There are many commercial products available for ensuring that fasteners won't come loose, even if they are not torqued just right (a very common brand is "Loktite®"). If you're worried about getting something together tight enough to hold, but loose enough to avoid mechanical damage during assembly, one of these products might offer substantial insurance. Read the label on the package and make sure the product is compatible with the materials, fluids, etc. involved before choosing one.

3. *Crossthreading*. This occurs when a part such as a bolt is screwed into a nut or casting at the wrong angle and forced. Cross threading is more likely to occur if access is difficult. It helps to clean and lubricate fasteners, and to start threading with the part to be installed going straight in. Start the bolt, spark plug, etc. with your fingers. If you encounter resistance, unscrew the part and start over again at a different angle until it can be inserted and turned several turns without much effort. Keep in mind that many parts, especially spark plugs, use tapered threads so that gentle turning will automatically bring the part you're threading to the proper angle if you don't force it or resist a change in angle. Don't put a wrench on the part until it's been turned a couple of turns by hand. If you suddenly encounter resistance, and the part has not seated fully, *don't force it*. Pull it back out and make sure it's clean and threading properly.

Always take your time and be patient; once you have some experience, working on your car can become an enjoyable hobby.

TOOLS AND EQUIPMENT

The last thing you want to do is to rush out and buy an enormous set of tools on the theory that you may need one of them some day. The best approach is to proceed slowly, gathering together a set of those tools that are used most frequently. Don't be misled by the low cost of bargain tools. It is far better to spend the extra money and use quality, name brand tools than to mangle your knuckles when one of your bargain sockets cracks and loses its grip. Some tools are guaranteed for life (that's right, life) which means you buy them once and only once, unless you lose them. Forged wrenches, 10 to 12 point sockets and fine tooth ratchets are far preferable than their less expensive counterparts.

Begin accumulating those tools that are used most frequently; those associated with routine maintenance and tune-up. In addition to the usual assortment of pliers and screwdrivers, you should have the following tools for routine maintenance jobs:

1. Metric and SAE wrenches—sockets and combination open end/box end wrenches;
2. Jackstands—for safety and support;
3. Oil filter wrench;
4. Oil filler spout or funnel;
5. Grease gun—for chassis lubrication;
6. A low flat pan for draining oil.

The second list of tools is for tune-ups. While the tools involved here are slightly more sophisticated, they need not be outrageously expensive. There are several inexpensive tach/dwell meters on the market that are every bit as good as the expensive professional model. Just be sure that it goes to at least 1500 rpm on the tach scale and that it can be used on 4, 6 or 8 cylinder engines. Basic tune-up equipment should include;

1. Tach-dwell meter;
2. Spark plug wrench;
3. An inductive type DC timing light that works from the car's battery;
4. A set of flat feeler gauges;
5. A set of round wire spark plug gauges.

In addition to these basic tools there are a few other tools and gauges you may find useful but don't go out and buy them until you need them. These include:

1. A compression gauge. The screw in type is slower to use but it eliminates the possibility of a faulty reading due to escaping pressure;
2. A manifold vacuum gauge;
3. A test light;
4. An induction meter. This is used for determining whether or not there is current in a wire. These are handy for use if a wire is broken somewhere in a wiring harness.

As a final note, you will probably find a torque wrench necessary for all but the most basic work. The beam type models are perfectly adequate although the newer click types are more precise.

Special Tools

Some repair procedures in this book call for the use of special factory tools. Although every effort is made to explain the repair job using

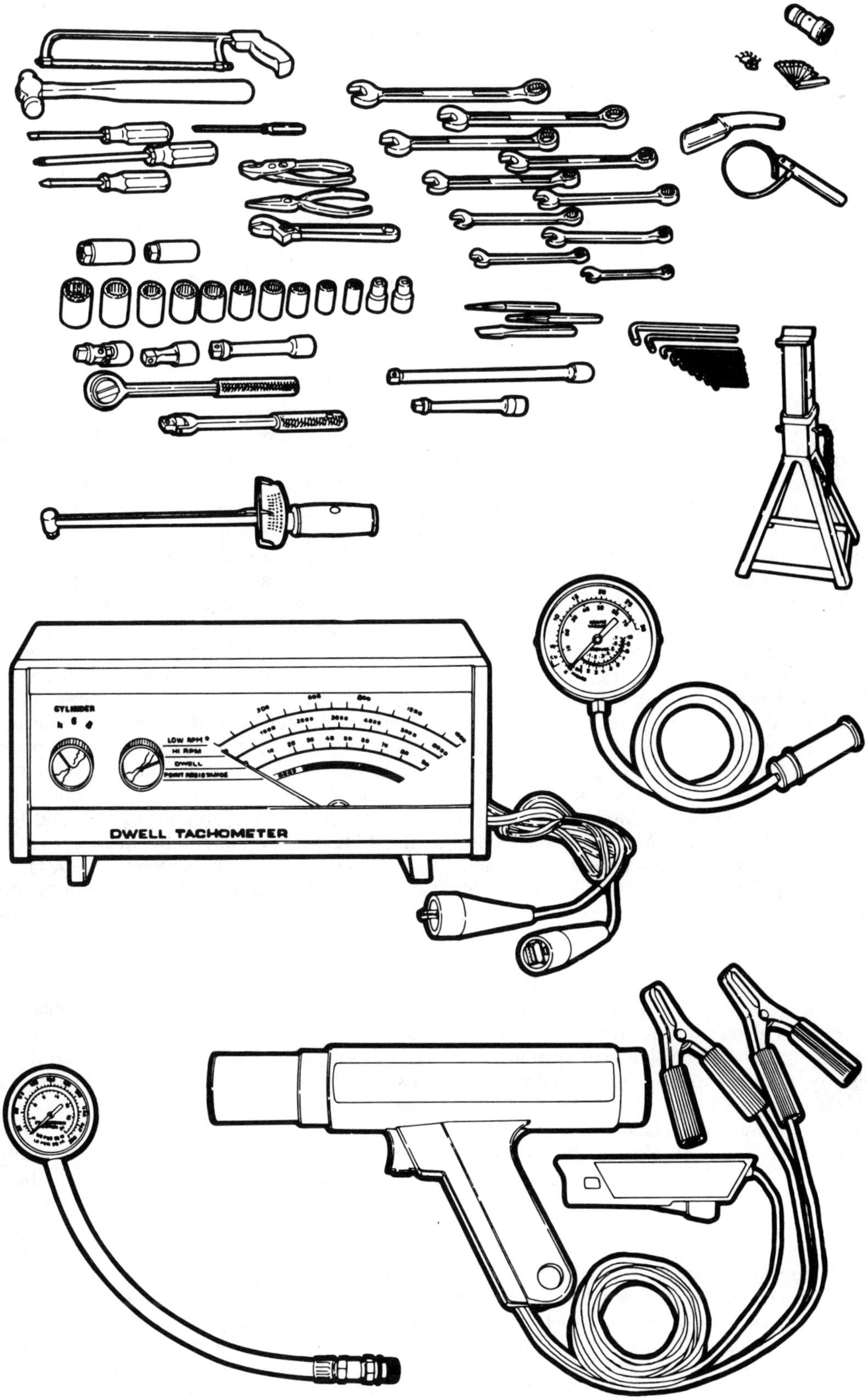

The tools and equipment shown here will handle the majority of the maintenance on a car

your regular set of tools, sometimes the use of a special tool cannot be avoided.

SERVICING YOUR VEHICLE SAFELY

It is virtually impossible to anticipate all of the hazards involved with automotive maintenance and service but care and common sense will prevent most accidents.

The rules of safety for mechanics range from "don't smoke around gasoline," to "use the proper tool for the job." The trick to avoiding injuries is to develop safe work habits and take every possible precaution.

Do's

- Do keep a fire extinguisher and first aid kit within easy reach.
- Do wear safety glasses or goggles when cutting, drilling, grinding or prying. If you wear glasses for the sake of vision, then they should be made of hardened glass that can serve also as safety glasses, or wear safety goggles over your regular glasses.
- Do shield your eyes whenever you work around the battery. Batteries contain sulphuric acid; in case of contact with the eyes or skin, flush the area with water or a mixture of water and baking soda and get medical attention immediately.
- Do use safety stands for any under-car service. Jacks are for raising vehicles; safety stands are for making sure the vehicle stays raised until you want it to come down. Whenever the vehicle is raised, block the wheels remaining on the ground and set the parking brake.
- Do use adequate ventilation when working with any chemicals. Asbestos dust resulting from brake lining wear can cause cancer.
- Do disconnect the negative battery cable when working on the electrical system. The primary ignition system can contain up to 40,000 volts.
- Do follow manufacturer's directions whenever working with potentially hazardous materials. Both brake fluid and antifreeze are poisonous if taken internally.
- Do properly maintain your tools. Loose hammerheads, mushroomed punches and chisels, frayed or poorly grounded electrical cords, excessively worn screwdrivers, spread wrenches (open end), cracked sockets, slipping ratchets, or faulty droplight sockets can cause accidents.
- Do use the proper size and type of tool for the job being done.
- Do when possible, pull on a wrench handle rather than push on it, and adjust your stance to prevent a fall.
- Do be sure that adjustable wrenches are tightly adjusted on the nut or bolt and pulled so that the face is on the side of the fixed jaw.
- Do select a wrench or socket that fits the nut or bolt. The wrench or socket should sit straight, not cocked.
- Do strike squarely with a hammer to avoid glancing blows.
- Do set the parking brake and block the drive wheels if the work requires that the engine be running.

Dont's

- Don't run an engine in a garage or anywhere else without proper ventilation—EVER! Carbon monoxide is poisonous; it is absorbed by the body 400 times faster than oxygen; it takes a long time to leave the human body and you can build up a deadly supply of it in your system by simply breathing in a little every day. You may not realize you are slowly poisoning yourself. Always use power vents, windows, fans or open the garage doors.
- Don't work around moving parts while wearing a necktie or other loose clothing. Short sleeves are much safer than long, loose sleves. Hard-toed shoes with neoprene soles protect your toes and give a better grip on slippery surfaces. Jewelry such as watches, fancy belt buckles, beads or body adornment of any kind is not safe working around a car. Long hair should be hidden under a hat or cap.
- Don't use pockets for toolboxes. A fall or bump can drive a screwdriver deep into your body. Even a wiping cloth hanging from the back pocket can wrap around a spinning shaft or fan.
- Don't smoke when working around gasoline, cleaning solvent or other flammable material.
- Don't smoke when working around the battery. When the battery is being charged, it gives off explosive hydrogen gas.
- Don't use gasoline to wash your hands; there are excellent soaps available. Gasoline may contain lead, and lead can enter the body through a cut, accumulating in the body until you are very ill. Gasoline also removes all the natural oils from the skin so that bone dry hands will suck up oil and grease.
- Don't service the air conditioning system unless you are equipped with the necessary tools and training. The refrigerant, R-12, is extremely cold and when exposed to the air, will instantly freeze any surface it comes in contact with, including your eyes. Although the re-

frigerant is normally non-toxic, R-12 becomes a deadly poisonous gas in the presence of an open flame. One good whiff of the vapors from burning refrigerant can be fatal.

HISTORY

Your car is manufactured by Mitsubishi Motors Corporation: A separate corporate entity of Mitsubishi Heavy Industries, Japan.

Mitsubishi has a long tradition of automotive excellence and was the first Japanese company to mass produce a passenger car (the Model "A," in 1917).

A reciprocal agreement, signed in 1971, with Chrysler Corporation provided for the importation, sales and service of Arrows and Sapporos in the United States.

The sales of your car model has risen dramatically; reflecting customer recognition of quality of workmanship, vehicle economy, performance and reliability.

SERIAL NUMBER IDENTIFICATION

Vehicle Identification Number

The vehicle identification number plate is mounted on the instrument panel, adjacent to the lower corner of the windshield on the driver's side, and is visible through the windshield. The thirteen digit vehicle number is composed of a seven or eight digit identification number and a five or six digit serial number. The seventeen digit number introduced in 1981 reflects the same information.

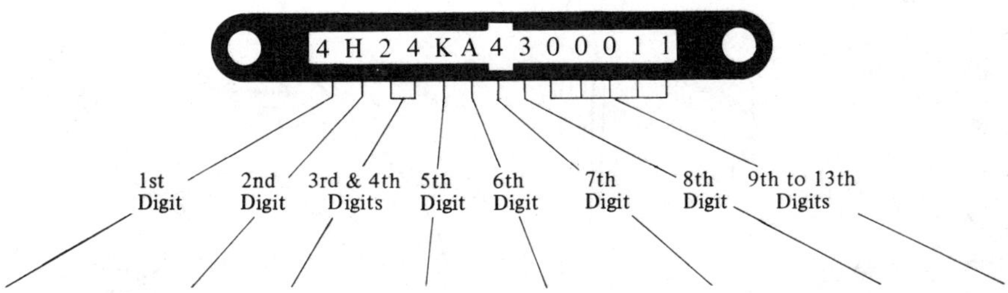

Car line	Price class	Body type	Engine displacement	Model year	Transmission code	Trim code	Sequence number
4–Dodge 1–Plymouth (for U.S.A., Puerto Rico) 5–Plymouth (for Canada)	M–Medium H–High	24–2 door hatch back	J–1400 c.c. (86.0 CID) K–1600 c.c. (97.5 CID)	A–1980	49 States 1–4 speed M/T 4–4x2 Speed M/T 7–3 speed A/T California 5–4x2 speed M/T 8–3 speed A/T Canada 3–4 speed M/T 6–4x2 speed M/T 9–3 speed A/T	2–Medium Dodge 3–High 1 Dodge 4–High 1 Plymouth 5–High 2 Dodge 8–High 2 Plymouth 9–Medium Plymouth	00011
2–Dodge Challenger 3–Plymouth Sapporo 5–Plymouth Lancer Station Wagon 6–Dodge Colt Station Wagon 7–Plymouth Arrow/ Dodge Celeste for Puerto Rico 8–Dodge Arrow for Canada	H–High P–Premium	24–2 door Hatchback 29–2 door Coupe 45–Station Wagon	K–1.6 Liter (97.5 CID) F–2.6 Liter (155.9 CID)	A–1980	49 states 4–5 speed M/T 7–Automatic California 5–5 speed M/T 8–Automatic Canada 6–5 speed M/T 9–Automatic	Arrow 1–High 3–Premium Challenger & Sapporo 3–High Dodge 4–High Plymouth Colt Station Wagon 3–High	00011

* M/T : Manual Transmission

Vehicle identification through 1980

1st Digit	2nd Digit	3rd Digit	4th Digit	5th Digit	6th Digit	7th Digit	8th Digit	9th Digit	10th Digit	11th Digit	12th Digit	13th to 17th Digits
Manufacturing country	Sales channel	Vehicle type	Other	Vehicle line	Trim code	Body type	Engine displacement	*Check digit	Model year	Assembly plant	Transmission code	Sequence number
J–Japan	B–Dodge P–Plymouth	3–Passenger car	B–Manual seat belt	E–Colt/ Champ	2–Low 3–Medium 4–High, High (RS, LS)	4–2 door hatchback	2–1.4 litre (86.0 CID) 3–1.6 litre (97.5 CID)	1 2 . . . 9 X	C–1982	U–MIZUSHIMA Plant	1–4 speed M/T Federal 2–4 speed M/T California 3–4 speed M/T Canada 4–4 x 2 speed M/T Federal 5–4 x 2 speed M/T California 6–4 x 2 speed M/T Canada 7–3 speed A/T Federal 8–3 speed A/T California 9–3 speed A/T Canada	00001 to 99999

NOTE: *"Check Digit" means a single number or letter X used to verify the accuracy of transcription of vehicle identification number.
M/T is an abbreviation for manual transaxle.
A/T is an abbreviation for automatic transaxle.
RS is an abbreviation for "Rally Sports".
LS is an abbreviation for "Luxury Sports".

Vehicle identification—from 1981

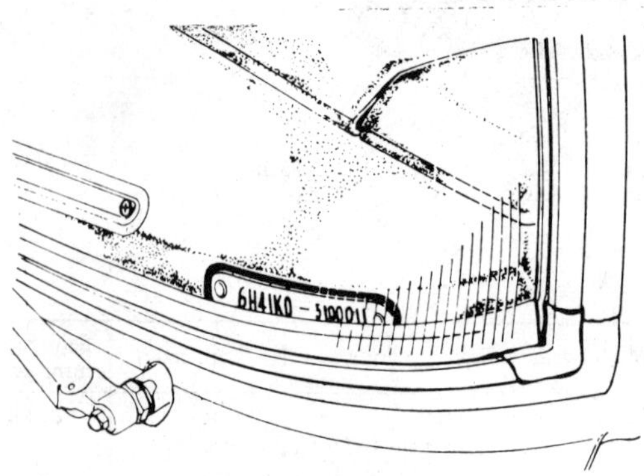

Vehicle serial number location

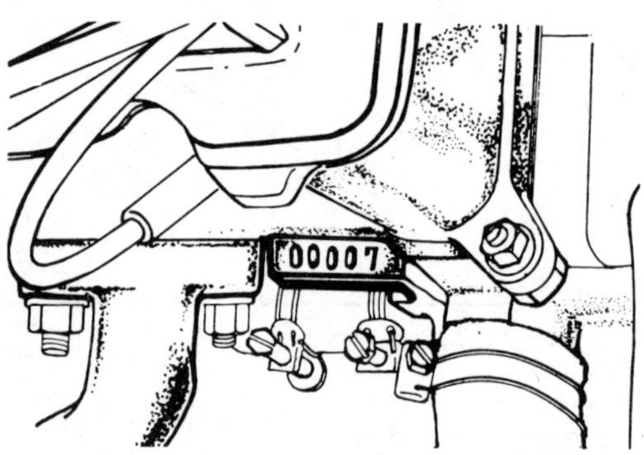

Engine serial number location

Engine Model Number

The engine model number is cast on the lower left side of the engine block or stamped near the engine serial number on the upper front side of the engine block.

Engine Serial Number

The engine serial number is stamped on a boss usually located on the right front top edge of the cylinder block.

Vehicle Body Number Location

The body number is located on the top center of the fire wall in the engine compartment.

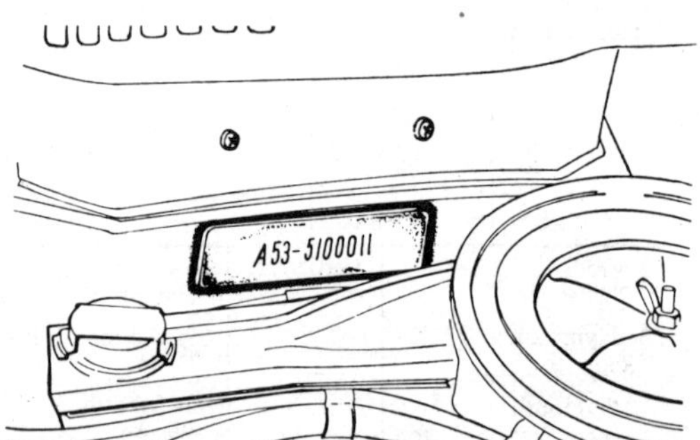

Body serial number location

Transmission/Transaxle Serial Number

The transmission serial number is stamped on the left side of the transmission case or on the clutch housing.

Front Wheel Drive

The manual transaxle serial number is stamped on the clutch housing of the transaxle case.

On automatic transaxle models, the number is on a plate attached to the side of the transmission, or stamped on the boss of the oil pan flange.

ROUTINE MAINTENANCE

Routine maintenance and driver's preventive maintenance are the most important steps that can be taken to extend the life of your car and avoid many expensive repairs.

Driver's preventive maintenance consists of taking only a minute every day (or so) to check the various fluid levels, hoses, belts, tire pressures and general visual condition of the engine and car body.

Routine maintenance calls for periodical service or replacement of parts and systems according to a schedule. The following pages will tell you what, when and how to perform routine maintenance on your car.

Air Cleaner

The air cleaner contains a dry filter element that keeps most dirt and dust from entering the engine via the carburetor. Never run the engine (other than for adjusting) without a filter element. The dirt and dust entering the engine can cause expensive damage to the pistons, bearings, etc.

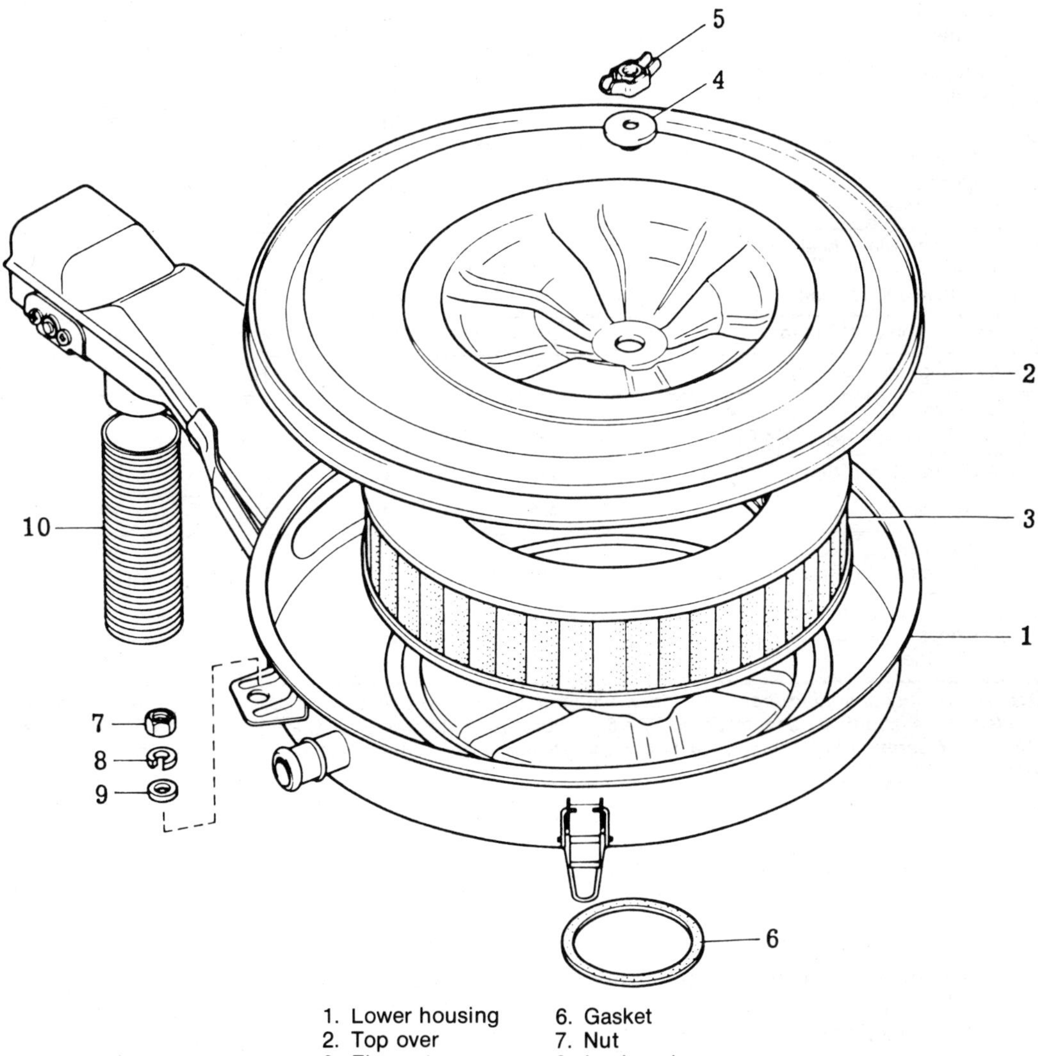

1. Lower housing
2. Top over
3. Element
4. Washer
5. Wing nut
6. Gasket
7. Nut
8. Lockwasher
9. Washer
10. Preheating hose

Typical late model engine air cleaner

Maintenance Intervals Chart

Intervals are for numbers of months or thousands of miles, whichever comes first.

Maintenance	1977–78	1979	1980	1981–83
Air cleaner (Replace)	24	24	30	30
Orifice or PCV valve				
Check	12	12	12	12
Replace	24	24	①	①
Carbon canister filter (Replace)	24	24	①	①
Belt tension (Adjust)	12	12	12	12
Engine oil (Change)	6	6	6	6
Engine oil filter (Change)	6	6	6	6
Fuel filter (Replace)	24	24	24	24
Manual transmission/transaxle				
Check	6	15	15	15
Change	24	30	30	30
Automatic transmission/transaxle				
Check	6	6	12	12
Change	—	30	30	30
Differential				
Check	6	6	15	15
Change	24	48	30	30
Front and rear wheel bearings (Clean and repack)	24	24	24	24
Engine coolant (Change)	24	24	24	24
Steering gear (Check)	12	12	12	12
Chassis lubrication Linkage and suspension	24	24	24	24
Axle shaft lubrication	24	24	24	24
Rotate tires	12	12	12	12
Valve lash (Check and adjust)	12	24	24	15
Brake and clutch fluid				
Check	6	12	12	12
Change	12	24	24	24

NOTE: *Heavy-duty operation (trailer towing, prolonged idling, severe stop and start driving, winter operation on salted roads) should be accompanied by a 50% increase in maintenance. Cut the interval in half for these conditions. Operation in extremely dusty conditions may require immediate changes of engine oil and all filters.*

① As necessary.

Proper maintenance of the cleaner element is vital. A clogged filter element will fail to supply sufficient fresh air to the carburetor, causing an over-rich fuel/air mixture. Such a condition will result in poor engine performance and economy.

Periodical cleaning or replacing of the filter element (refer to the maintenance chart) will help your car last longer and run better.

To clean or replace the air cleaner filter element; remove the top wing nut/nuts and loosen the side mounted spring clip (if equipped). Lift off the top of the air cleaner and remove the filter element. On 1981 and later models a charcoal filter is also located in the air cleaner; this is for vapor control and is not to be disturbed. If the element is not too clogged by dirt—use compressed air and clean the element. Hold the air nozzle at least two inches from the inside screen (of the element). Replace the filter element if mileage or extreme dirt clogging is indicated.

Crankcase Ventilation and PCV Valve

A closed crankcase ventilation system is used on your car. The purpose of the closed system is to prevent blow-by gases, created by the engine, from escaping into the air.

MODELS WITHOUT PCV VALVE

Blow-by gases are passed through a hose from the front of the valve cover to the air cleaner, and through another hose from the rear of the valve cover into the intake manifold. At part throttle, the blow-by gases are drawn from the rear of the valve cover into the intake manifold. At wide opened throttle, the blow-by gases are drawn through both the front and rear hoses and returned to the engine.

Servicing the closed crankcase ventilation system on models without a PCV valve amounts to a periodic check of the hoses (cracked or hard hoses should be replaced) and the cleaning of the wire mesh in the air cleaner and the fixed orifice on the intake manifold. The wire mesh (resembles steel wool) acts as a filter for the crankcase ventilation system.

MODELS WITH PCV VALVE

The PCV system supplies fresh air to the crankcase through the air cleaner. Inside the crankcase, the fresh air mixes with the blow-by gases. The mixture of fresh air and blow-by gases is then passed through the PCV valve and into the intake manifold. The PCV valve (mounted on the top end of the valve cover) is a metered orifice and reacts to intake manifold vacuum, and has an adequate capacity for all normal driving conditions. However, under heavy engine loads or high speed driving there is less intake manifold vacuum and the blow-by gases exceed the PCV valve's capacity. When this happens, the blow-by gases back up into the air cleaner through the front hose, mix with fresh air and are reburned in the engine.

To test the operation of the PCV valve; Apply the parking brake, start the engine and allow it to operate at a normal idle speed. Remove the PCV valve from the valve cover mounting. A hissing noise should be heard as air passes through the valve and a strong vacuum should be felt if you place a finger over the opened end of the valve. To check the PCV valve with the engine not running; Remove the PCV valve from the valve cover mounting, blow air through the threaded end of the valve. If air is not felt passing through the valve, it is clogged. Clean the valve and hose in solvent, recheck for air flow. Replace valve and/or hose if necessary.

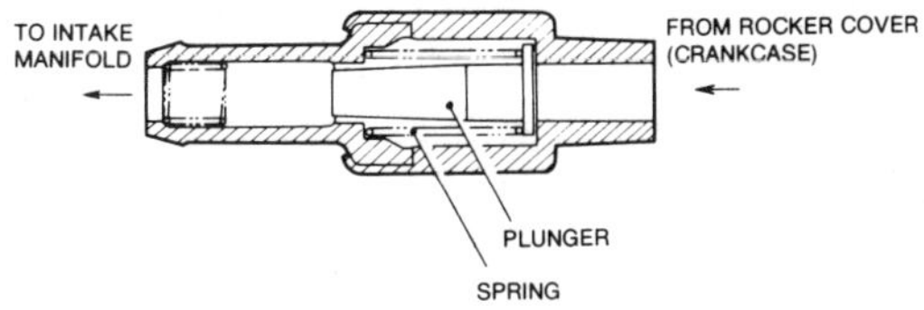

PCV valve

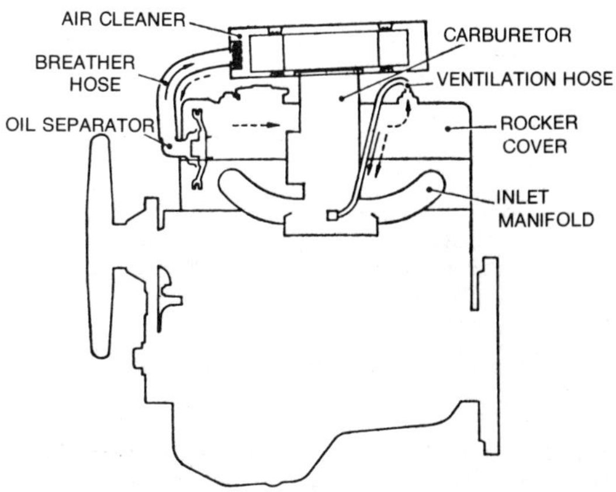

Crankcase ventilation system—without PCV valve

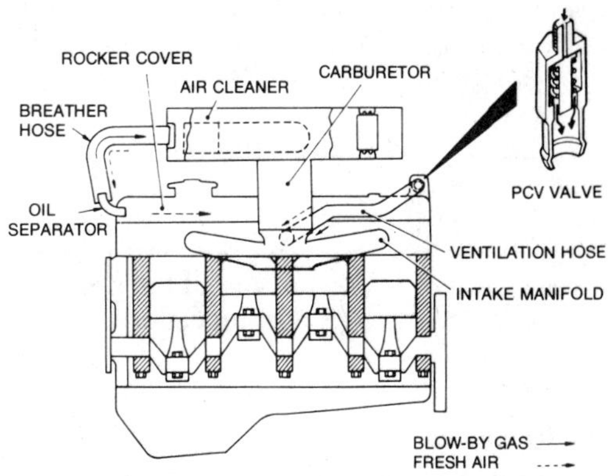

Crankcase ventilation system—with PCV valve

Evaporative Emission Canister

Fuel vapors from the gas tank and carburetor (created by changes in temperatures) are absorbed by a charcoal filled canister. When the engine is operating, the stored vapors are sucked out of the canister and fed back to, and burned in the combustion chambers. Some canisters are sealed, others contain a filter that must be cleaned.

The canister or canisters should be replaced at specified intervals as shown on the maintenance chart in this chapter. Make sure all hoses are clamped and not dry rotted or broken. The canister filter (if equipped) should be in-

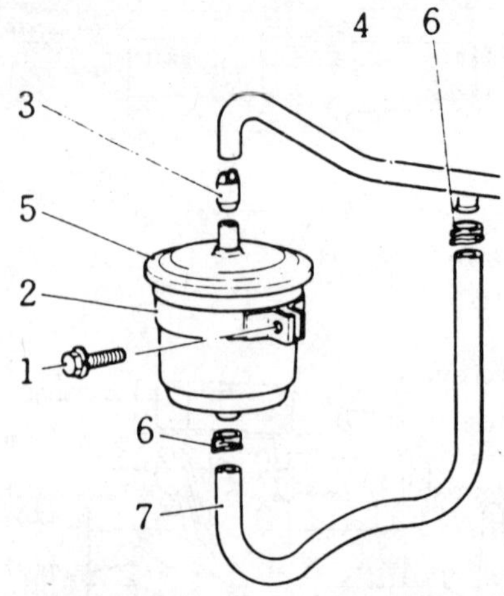

1. Bolt
2. Retaining band
3. Check valve
4. Hose
5. Canister
6. Clamp
7. Hose

Typical evaporative emission canister

spected, cleaned or replaced at least every two years. Any clogging of the filter will inhibit air flow through the canister. Two different types of valves were used in the canister lines—refer to the Emissions chapter for a detailed description of their function and necessary servicing. To replace the canister:

1. Remove the two connecting hoses from the canister.
2. Loosen and remove the canister retaining band bolt.
3. Remove the canister.
4. Check the hoses, replace any that are cracked, soft or collapsed. Install the new canister reversing the removal procedure.

Battery

FLUID LEVEL

Check the battery electrolyte level at least once a month, or more often in hot weather or during periods of extended car operation. The level can be checked through the case on translucent polypropylene batteries; the cell caps must be removed on other models. The electrolyte level in each cell should be kept filled to the split ring inside, or the line marked on the outside of the case.

If the level is low, add only distilled water, or colorless, odorless drinking water, through the opening until the level is correct. Each cell is completely separate from the others, so each must be checked and filled individually.

If water is added in freezing weather, the car should be driven several miles to allow the water to mix with the electrolyte. Otherwise, the battery could freeze.

SPECIFIC GRAVITY

At least once a year, check the specific gravity of the battery. It should be between 1.20 and 1.26 at room temperature.

The specific gravity can be checked with the use of an hydrometer, an inexpensive instrument available from many sources, including auto parts stores. The hydrometer has a squeeze bulb at one end and a nozzle at the other. Battery electrolyte is sucked into the hydrometer until the float is lifted from its seat. The specific gravity is then read by noting the position of the float. Generally, if after charging, the specific gravity between any two cells varies more than 50 points (.050), the battery is bad and should be replaced.

It is not possible to check the specific gravity in this manner on sealed ("maintenance free") batteries. Instead, the indicator built into the top of the case must be relied on to display any signs of battery deterioration. If the indicator is dark, the battery can be assumed to be OK. If the indicator is light, the specific gravity is low, and the battery should be charged or replaced.

CABLES AND CLAMPS

Once a year, the battery terminals and the cable clamps should be cleaned. Loosen the clamps and remove the cables, negative cables first. On batteries with posts on top, the use of a puller specially made for the purpose is recommended. These are inexpensive, and available in auto parts stores.

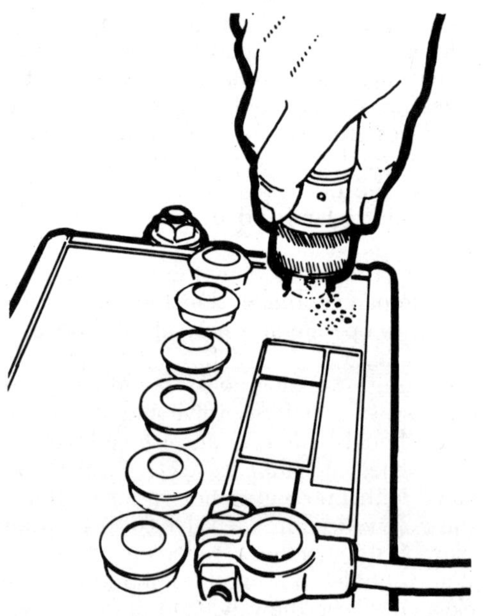

Cleaning the battery terminals with a special cleaning brush

Clean the cable clamps and the battery terminal with a wire brush, until all corrosion, grease, etc. is removed and the metal is shiny. It is especially important to clean the inside of the clamp thoroughly, since a small deposit of foreign material or oxidation there will prevent a sound electrical connection and inhibit either starting or charging. Special tools are available for cleaning these parts, one type for conventional batteries and another type for side terminal batteries.

Before installing the cables, loosen the battery hold-down clmp or strap, remove the battery and check the battery tray. Clear it of any debris, and check it for soundness. Rust should be wire brushed away, and the metal given a coat of anti-rust paint. Replace the battery and tighten the hold-down clamp or strap securely, but be careful not to overtighten, which will crack the battery case.

After the clamps and terminals are clean, reinstall the cables, negative cable last; do not hammer on the clamps to install. Tighten the clamps securely, but do not distort them. Give the clamps and terminals a thin external coat of grease after installation, to retard corrosion.

Check the cables at the same time that the terminals are cleaned. If the cable insulation is cracked or broken, or if the ends are frayed the cable should be replaced with a new cable of the same length and gauge.

Belts

As engine tune-up, or at least once a year, check the condition of the drive belts and check and adjust belt tension as below:

1. Inspect belts for signs of glazing or cracking. A glazed belt will be perfectly smooth from slippage, while a good belt will have a slight texture of fabric visible. Cracks will usually start at the inner edge of the belt and run outward. Replace the belt at the first sign of cracking or if glazing is severe.
2. Belt tension does not refer to play or droop. By placing your thumb midway between two pulleys, it should be possible to depress each belt about .4 in. (10 mm) with about 20 lbs (10 Kg) pressure. The air pump belt runs looser than this. You should be able to depress it about .6 in. (7 mm). If the belt can be depressed more than this, or cannot be depressed this much, adjust the tension. Inadequate tension will result in slippage and wear, while excessive tension will damage bearings and cause belts to fray and crack.

To adjust the tension on components, loosen the pivot and mounting bolts of the component or idler pulley, which the belt is driving. Use a soft wooden hammer handle, a broom-

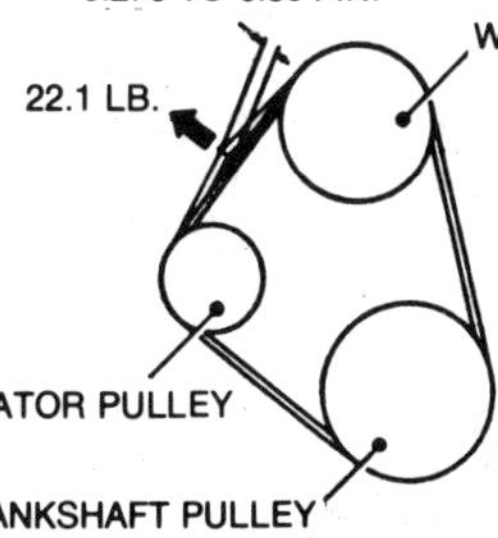

Drive belt tension adjustment

stick, or the like to pry the component toward or away from the engine until the proper tension is achieved.

CAUTION: *Do not use a screwdriver or other metal device, such as a prybar, as a lever.*

Tighten the component mounting bolts securely. If a new belt has been installed, recheck the tension after about 200 miles of driving.

If belt tension is adjusted at the idler pulley bracket. Loosen the locknut, then turn the adjusting bolt to move the idler pulley up or down until the belt tension is correct. Tighten the locknut securely and reckeck the adjustment.

Hoses

REPLACEMENT

1. Remove the radiator cap.
2. Open the radiator petcock to drain the coolant. To replace the bottom hose drain all the radiator coolant. If only the top hose is to be replaced drain just enough fluid to bring the level down below the level of the top hose. If the coolant is over a year old discard it.
3. Remove the hose clamps and remove the hose.
4. Use new hose clamps if the old ones are badly rusted or damaged. Slide the hose clamps over each end of the new hose then slide the hose over the hose connections.
5. Position each clamp about ¼" from the end of the hose and tighten.
6. Close the petcock and refill with the old fluid if it is less than a year old or with a new mixture of 50/50, coolant/water.
7. Start the engine and idle it for 15 minutes with the radiator cap off and check for leaks. Add coolant if necessary and install the radiator cap.

Cooling System

At least once very 2 years, the engine cooling system should be inspected, flushed, and re-

HOW TO SPOT WORN V-BELTS

V-Belts are vital to efficient engine operation—they drive the fan, water pump and other accessories. They require little maintenance (occasional tightening) but they will not last forever. Slipping or failure of the V-belt will lead to overheating. If your V-belt looks like any of these, it should be replaced.

Cracking or weathering

This belt has deep cracks, which cause it to flex. Too much flexing leads to heat build-up and premature failure. These cracks can be caused by using the belt on a pulley that is too small. Notched belts are available for small diameter pulleys.

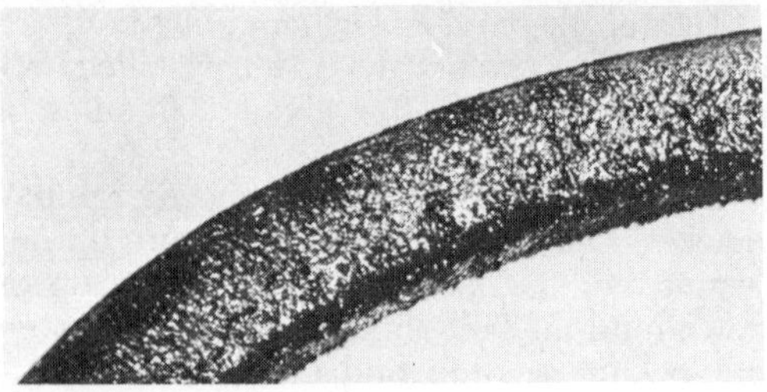

Softening (grease and oil)

Oil and grease on a belt can cause the belt's rubber compounds to soften and separate from the reinforcing cords that hold the belt together. The belt will first slip, then finally fail altogether.

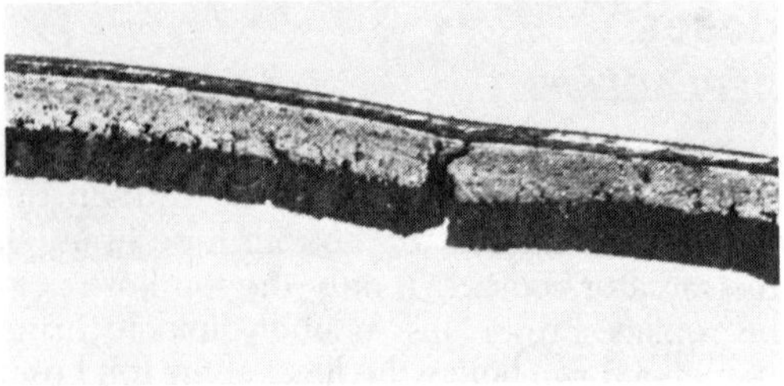

Glazing

Glazing is caused by a belt that is slipping. A slipping belt can cause a run-down battery, erratic power steering, overheating or poor accessory performance. The more the belt slips, the more glazing will be built up on the surface of the belt. The more the belt is glazed, the more it will slip. If the glazing is light, tighten the belt.

Worn cover

The cover of this belt is worn off and is peeling away. The reinforcing cords will begin to wear and the belt will shortly break. When the belt cover wears in spots or has a rough jagged appearance, check the pulley grooves for roughness.

Separation

This belt is on the verge of breaking and leaving you stranded. The layers of the belt are separating and the reinforcing cords are exposed. It's just a matter of time before it breaks completely.

HOW TO SPOT BAD HOSES

Both the upper and lower radiator hoses are called upon to perform difficult jobs in an inhospitable environment. They are subject to nearly 18 psi at under hood temperatures often over 280°F., and must circulate nearly 7500 gallons of coolant an hour—3 good reasons to have good hoses.

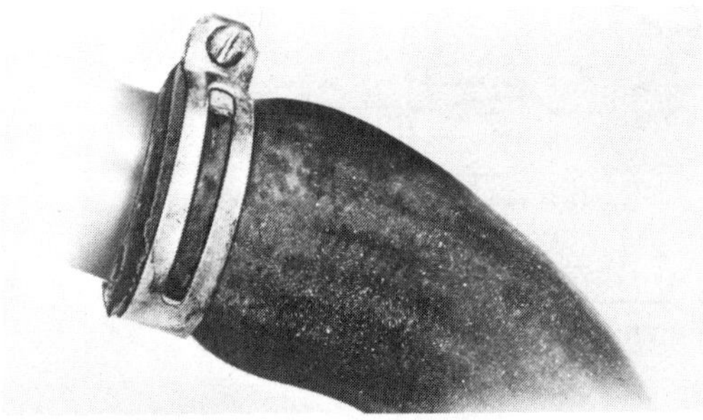

Swollen hose

A good test for any hose is to feel it for soft or spongy spots. Frequently these will appear as swollen areas of the hose. The most likely cause is oil soaking. This hose could burst at any time, when hot or under pressure.

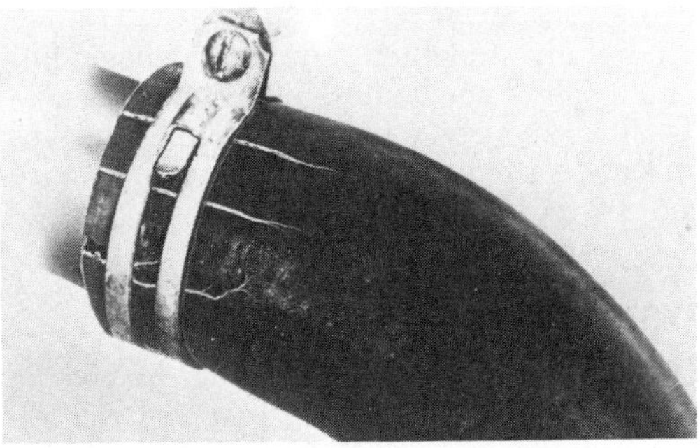

Cracked hose

Cracked hoses can usually be seen but feel the hoses to be sure they have not hardened; a prime cause of cracking. This hose has cracked down to the reinforcing cords and could split at any of the cracks.

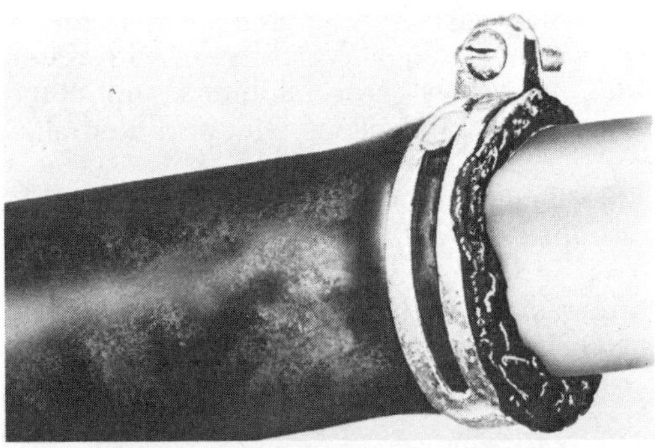

Frayed hose end (due to weak clamp)

Weakened clamps frequently are the cause of hose and cooling system failure. The connection between the pipe and hose has deteriorated enough to allow coolant to escape when the engine is hot.

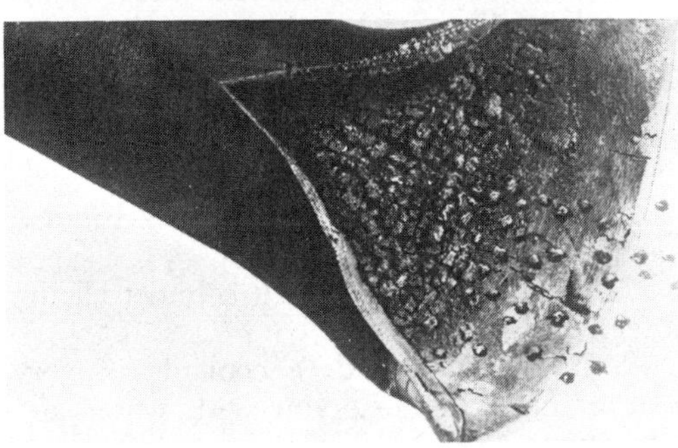

Debris in cooling system

Debris, rust and scale in the cooling system can cause the inside of a hose to weaken. This can usually be felt on the outside of the hose as soft or thinner areas.

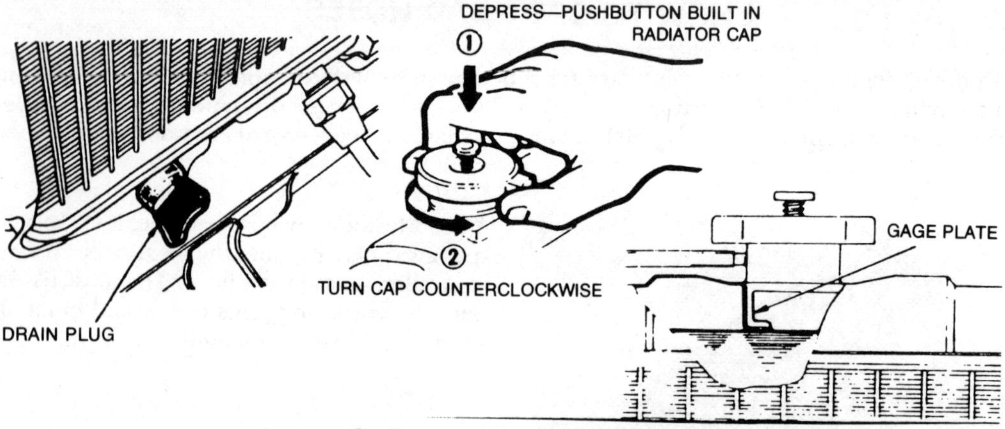

Cooling system maintenance

filled with fresh coolant. If the coolant is left in the system too long, it loses its ability to prevent rust and corrosion. If the coolant has too much water, it won't protect against freezing.

The pressure cap should be looked at for signs of age or deterioration. Fan belt and other drive belts should be inspected and adjusted to the proper tension. (See checking belt tension).

Hose clamps should be tightened, and soft or cracked hoses replaced. Damp spots, or accumulations of rust or dye near hoses, water pump or other areas, indicate possible leakage, which must be corrected before filling the system with fresh coolant.

CHECK THE RADIATOR CAP

While you are checking the coolant level, check the radiator cap for a worn or cracked gasket. If the cap doesn't seal properly, fluid will be lost and the engine will overheat.

Worn caps should be replaced with a new one.

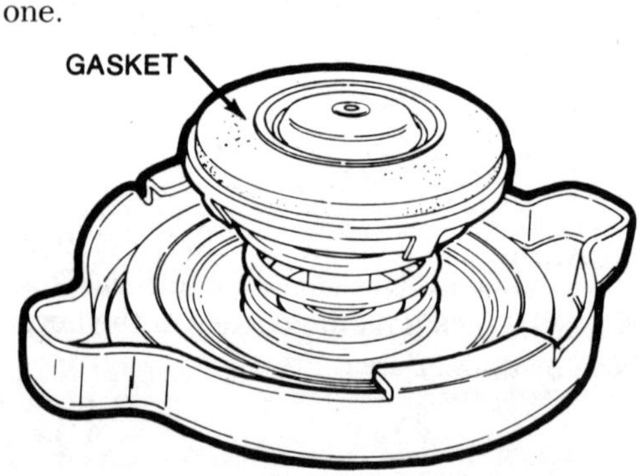

Check the sealing gasket on the radiator cap

CLEAN RADIATOR OF DEBRIS

Periodically clean any debris—leaves, paper, insects, etc.—from the radiator fins. Pick the largest pieces off by hand. The smaller pieces can be washed away with water pressure from a hose.

Carefully straighten any bent radiator fins with a pair of needle nose pliers. Be careful—the fins are very soft. Don't wiggle the fins back and forth too much. Straighten them once and try not to move them again.

DRAIN AND REFILL THE COOLING SYSTEM

Completely draining and refilling the cooling system every two years at least will remove accumulated rust, scale and other deposits. Coolant in late model cars is a 50–50 mixture of ethylene glycol and water for year round use. Use a good quality antifreeze with water pump lubricants, rust inhibitors and other corrosion inhibitors along with acid neutralizers.

1. Drain the existing antifreeze and coolant. Open the radiator and engine drain petcocks, or disconnect the bottom radiator hose, at the radiator outlet.

   NOTE: *Before opening the radiator petcock, spray it with some penetrating lubricant.*

2. Close the petcock or re-connect the lower hose and fill the system with water. Move the dash control to the hot position.
3. Add a can of quality radiator flush.
4. Idle the engine until the upper radiator hose gets hot.
5. Drain the system again.
6. Repeat this process until the drained water is clear and free of scale.
7. Close all petcocks and connect all the hoses.
8. If equipped with a coolant recovery system, flush the reservoir with water and leave empty.
9. Determine the capacity of your cooling

system (see capacities specifications). Add a 50/50 mix of quality antifreeze (ethylene glycol) and water to provide the desired protection.

10. Run the engine to operating temperature.

11. Stop the engine and check the coolant level.

12. Check the level of protection with an anti-freeze tester, replace the cap and check for leaks.

Air-Conditioning Safety Precautions

There are two particular hazards associated with air conditioning systems and they both relate to the refrigerant gas.

First, the refrigerant gas is an extremely cold substance. When exposed to air, it will instantly freeze any surface it comes in contact with, including your eyes. The other hazard relates to fire. Although normally non-toxic, refrigerant gas becomes highly poisonous in the presence of an open flame. One good whiff of the vapor formed by burning refrigerant can be fatal. Keep all forms of fire (including cigarettes) well clear of the air-conditioning system.

Any repair work to an air conditioning system should be left to a professional. Do not, under any circumstances, attempt to loosen or tighten any fittings or perform any work other than that outlined here.

CHECKING FOR OIL LEAKS

Refrigerant leaks show up as oily areas on the various components because the compressor oil is transported around the entire system along with the refrigerant. Look for oily spots on all the hoses and lines, and especially on the hose and tubing connections. If there are oily deposits, the system may have a leak, and you should have it checked by a qualified repairman.

NOTE: *A small area of oil on the front of the compressor is normal and no cause for alarm.*

CHECK THE COMPRESSOR BELT

Refer to the section in this chapter on "Drive Belts."

KEEP THE CONDENSER CLEAR

Periodically inspect the front of the condenser for bent fins or foreign material (dirt, bugs, leaves, etc.) If any cooling fins are bent, straighten them carefully with needlenosed pliers. You can remove any debris with a stiff bristle brush or hose.

OPERATE THE A/C SYSTEM PERIODICALLY

A lot of A/C problems can be avoided by simply running the air conditioner at least once a week, regardless of the season. Simply let the system run for at least 5 minutes a week (even in the winter, and you'll keep the internal parts lubricated as well as preventing the hoses from hardening.

SIGHT GLASS CHECK

You can safely make a few simple checks to determine if your air conditioning system needs service. The tests work best if the temperature is warm (about 70°F).

1. Place the automatic transmission in Park or the manual transmission in Neutral. Set the parking brake.

2. Run the engine at a fast idle (about 1,500 rpm) either with the help of a friend, or by temporarily readjusting the idle speed screw.

3. Set the controls for maximum cold with the blower on high.

4. Locate the sight glass in the head of the receiver/drier. Usually it is on the left alongside the top of the radiator.

5. If you see bubbles, the system must be recharged. Very likely there is a leak at some point.

6. If there are no bubbles, there is either no refrigerant at all or the system is fully charged. Feel the two hoses going to the belt-driven compressor. If they are both at the same temperature, the system is empty and must be recharged.

7. If one hose (high-pressure) is warm and the other (low-pressure) is cold, the system may be alright. However, you are probably making these tests because you think there is something wrong, so proceed to the next Step.

8. Have an assistant in the car turn the fan control on and off to operate the compressor clutch. Watch the sight glass.

9. If bubbles appear when the clutch is disengaged and disappear when it is engaged, the system is properly charged.

10. If the refrigerant takes more than 45 seconds to bubble when the clutch is disengaged, the system is overcharged. This usually causes poor cooling at low speeds.

Windshield Wipers

For maximum effectiveness and longest element life, the windshield and wiper blades should be kept clean. Dirt, tree sap, road tar and so on will cause streaking, smearing and blade deterioration if left on the glass. It is advisable to wash the windshield carefully with a commercial glass cleaner at least once a

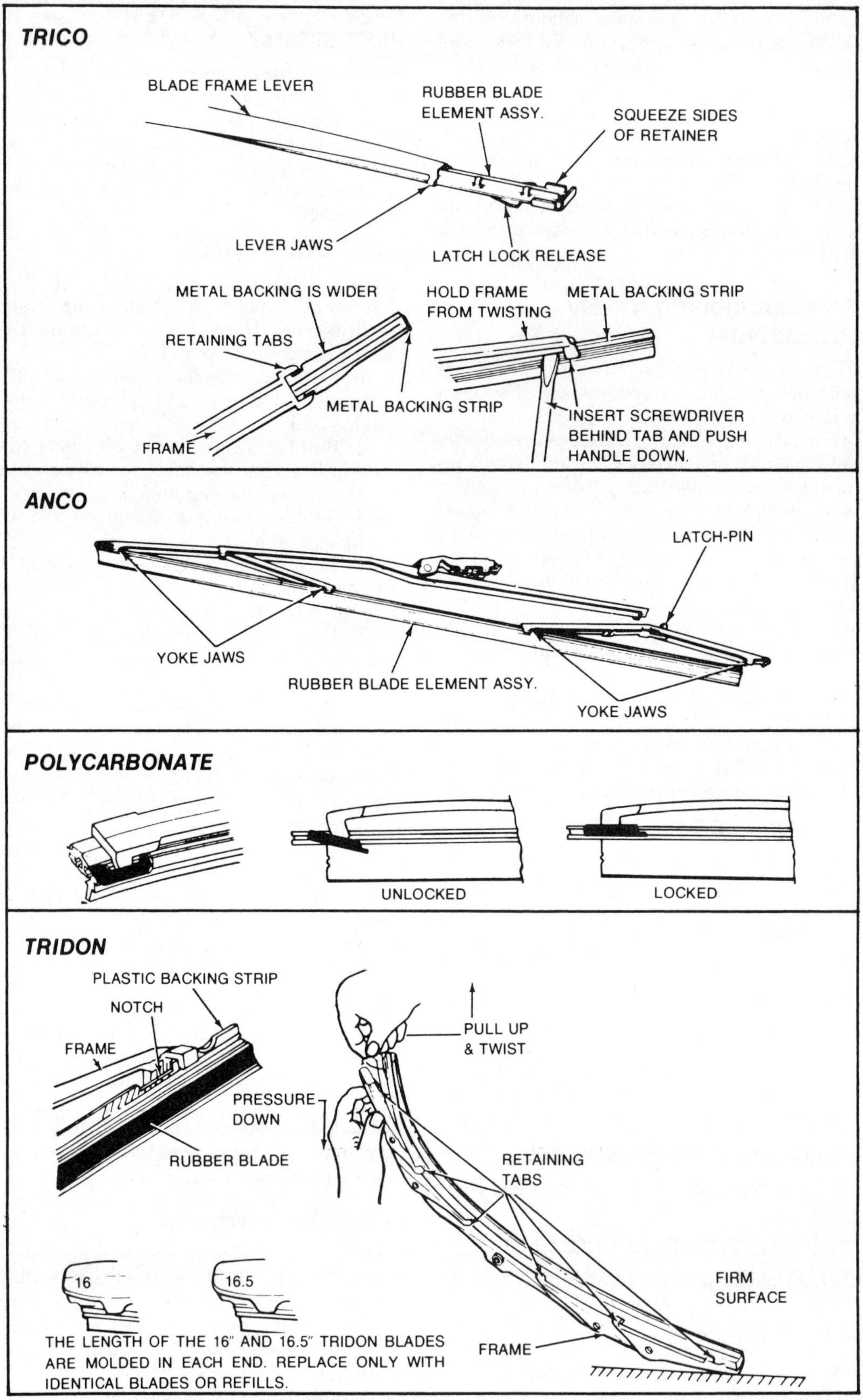

Wiper blade replacement

month. Wipe off the rubber blades with the wet rag afterwards. Do not attempt to move the wipers by hand; damage to the motor and drive mechanism will result.

If the blades are found to be cracked, broken or torn, they should be replaced immediately. Replacement intervals will vary with usage, although ozone deterioration usually limits blade life to about one year. If the wiper pattern is smeared or streaked, or if the blade chatters across the glass, the elements should be replaced. It is easiest and most sensible to replace the elements in pairs.

There are basically three different types of refills, which differ in their method or replacement. One type has two release buttons, approximately one-third of the way up from the ends of the blade frame. Pushing the buttons down releases a lock and allows the rubber filler to be removed from the frame. The new filler slides back into the frame and locks in place.

The second type of refill has two metal tabs which are unlocked by squeezing them together. The rubber filler can then be withdrawn from the frame jaws. A new refill is installed by inserting the refill into the front frame jaws and sliding it rearward to engage the remaining frame jaws. There are usually four jaws; be certain when installing that the refill is engaged in all of them. At the end of its travel, the tabs will lock into place on the front jaws of the wiper blade frame.

The third type is a refill made from polycarbonate. The refill has a simple locking device at one end which flexes downward out of the groove into which the jaws of the holder fit, allowing easy release. By sliding the new refill through all the jaws and pushing through the sight resistance when it reaches the end of its travel, the refill will lock into position.

Regardless of the type of refill used, make sure that all of the frame jaws are engaged as the refill is pushed into place and locked. The metal blade holder and frame will scratch the glass if allowed to touch it.

WIPER ARMS

The wiper arm is retained by a lock nut. Lift up the cover (where the arm meets the drive spindle), remove the nut and lift off the arm. Reverse procedure to install.

Fluid Level Checks

ENGINE OIL

At every stop for fuel, check the engine oil as follows:

1. Park the car on the level.
2. The engine may be either hot or cold when checking oil level. However, if it is hot, wait a few minutes after the engine has been shut off to allow the oil to drain back into the crankcase. If the engine is cold, do not start it before checking the oil level.
3. Open the hood and locate the dipstick, which is on the right side (passenger's side) of the engine. Pull the dipstick from its tube, wipe it clean, and reinsert it.
4. Pull the dipstick again and, holding it horizontally, read the oil level. The oil should be between the top and lower mark. If the oil is below the add mark, add oil of the proper viscosity through the capped opening of the valve cover. See the "Oil and Fuel Recommendations" section in this chapter for the proper viscosity and rating of oil to use.
5. Replace the dipstick, and check the level again after adding any oil. Be careful not to overfill the crankcase. Approximately one quart of oil will raise the level from the low mark to the high mark. Excess oil will generally be consumed at an accelerated rate even if no damage to the engine seals occurs.

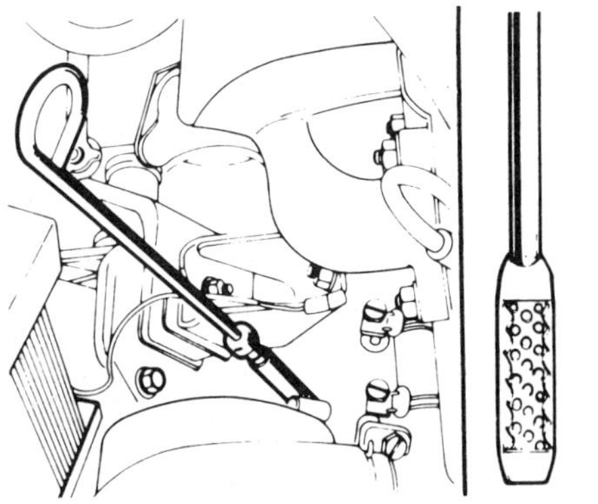

Engine oil dipstick

RADIATOR COOLANT

On models without an expansion tank, if the engine is hot, allow it to cool for several minutes to reduce the pressure in the system. Using a rag, turn the radiator cap ¼ turn to the stop and allow all pressure to escape. Then, remove the cap. On models equipped with an expansion tank, check the level visually in the tank. It should be above the low mark. Never fill the tank over the upper mark.

Fill the radiator until the level is within 1 in. (25 mm) of the radiator cap. It is best to add a 50–50 mix of antifreeze and water to avoid diluting the coolant in the system. Use permanent type antifreeze only.

BRAKE MASTER CYLINDER

Check the levels of brake fluid in the brake master cylinder reservoir(s) every 3,000 miles. The fluid should be maintained to a level not

Capacities
Rear Wheel Drive Cars

Year	Model	Engine Displacement Cu In. (cc)	Engine Crankcase (qts)		Transmission (qts)			Drive Axle	Gasoline Tank (gals)	Cooling System (qts)	
			With Filter	Without Filter	Manual 4-spd	Manual Twin-Stick	Automatic			W/ AC	W/O AC
1977	All	1600	4.2	3.7	1.8	2.4	6.8	1.2	①	7.7	7.7
		2000	4.5	4.0	—	2.1	6.8	1.2	①	9.5	9.5
1978	All	1600	4.2	3.7	1.8	2.1	6.8	1.2	15.8	7.7	7.7
		2000	4.5	4.0	—	2.4	6.8	1.2	15.8	9.5	9.5
		2600	4.5	4.0	—	2.4	6.8	1.2	15.8	9.7	9.7
1979–83	All	1600	4.2	3.7	—	2.1	7.2	1.2	③	7.7	7.7
		2000	4.5	4.0	—	2.4	7.2	1.2	③	9.5	9.5
		2600	4.5	4.0	—	2.4	7.2	1.4②	③④	9.5	9.5

① Coupe, Sedan and Hatchback: 13.2 gallons
Hardtop: 13.5 gallons
② 1981–83: 2.7
③ Coupe, Sedan: 13.2 gallons
Sapporo: 15.8 gallons, Station Wagon: 14.0 (1979) 13.2 (1980)
④ 1981–83: 15.8

below the bottom line on the reservoirs and not above the top line. Any sudden decrease in the level in any of the reservoirs indicates a probable leak in that particular system and should be checked out immediately.

When making additions of fluid, use only fresh, uncontaminated brake fluid meeting or exceeding DOT 3 standards. Be careful not to spill any brake fluid on painted surfaces, because it eats paint. Do not allow the fluid container or master cylinder reservoirs to remain open any longer than necessary; brake fluid absorbs moisture from the air, reducing its effectiveness and causing brake and clutch line corrosion.

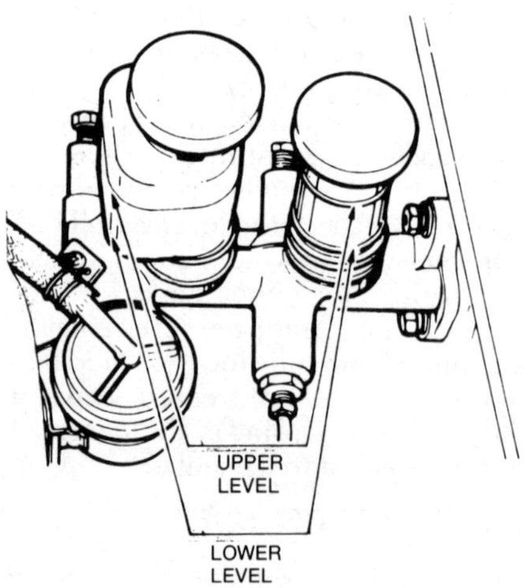

Master cylinder fluid level, single reservoir similar

TRANSMISSION/TRANSAXLE

Manual

Check the lubricant level at the interval specified in the maintenance chart.

1. With the car parked on a level surface, remove the filler plug from the left side of the transmission case; right front on front wheel drivemodels.
2. If lubricant begins to trickle out the hole, there is enough. Otherwise, carefully insert a finger (watch out for sharp threads) and check to see if the oil is up to the edge of the hole.
3. If not, add lubricant through the hole to raise the level to the edge of the filler hole. Most gear lubricants come in a plastic squeeze bottle with a nozzle, making additions easy. You can also use a squeeze bulb. Add gear oil GL4, Hypoid gear oil.
4. Replace the plug and check for leaks.

Automatic

Check the level of the automatic transmission fluid every 2,000 miles. There is a dipstick at the right side of the engine or transaxle.

CAUTION: *The electric cooling fan (front wheeldrive) may operate when the engine is off. Keep hands away.*

The dipstick has a high and low mark, which

Capacities
Front-Wheel Drive Cars

Year	Model	Engine Displacement Cu In. (cc)	Engine Crankcase (qts) With Filter	Engine Crankcase (qts) Without Filter	Transmission (qts) Manual 4-spd	Transmission (qts) Manual Twin-Stick	Transmission (qts) Automatic	Gasoline Tank (gals)	Cooling System (qts) W/ AC	Cooling System (qts) W/O AC
1979	All	1400	3.7	3.17	2.2	2.2	—	10.6	—	5.2
		1600	4.2	3.67	2.2	2.2	—	10.6	6.9	6.9
1980	All	1400	3.7	3.17	2.3	2.3	—	10.6	—	4.7
		1600	4.2	3.67	2.3	2.3	6.0	10.6	4.7	4.7
1981–83	All	1400	3.7	3.17	2.4	2.4	—	10.6 ①	—	4.7
		1600	4.2	3.67	2.4	2.4	6.0	10.6 ①	4.7	4.7

① RS, LS: 13.2

are accurate for level indications only when the transmission is hot (normal operating temperature). The transmission is considered hot after 15 miles of highway driving.

1. Park the car on a level surface with the engine idling. Apply the parking brake.
2. Shift the transmission to Park.
3. Remove the dipstick, wipe it clean, then reinsert it firmly. Be certain that it has been pushed fully home. Remove the dipstick and check the fluid level while holding the dipstick horizontally. The level should be at or near the high mark.
4. If the fluid level is below the "low" mark, add Dexron II® type automatic transmission fluid through the dipstick tube. This is more easily accomplished with the aid of a funnel and hose. Check the level often between additions, being careful not to overfill the transmission. Overfilling will cause slippage, seal damage, and overheating. Approximately one quart of fluid will raise the level from "low" to "high".

NOTE: *The fluid on the dipstick should be a bright red color. If it is discolored (brown or black), or smells burnt, serious transmission troubles, probably due to overheating, should be suspected. The transmission should be inspected by a qualified mechanic to locate the cause of the burnt fluid.*

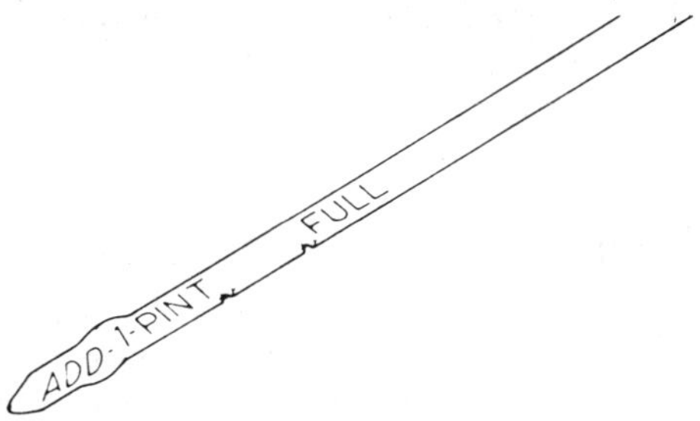

Typical Torqueflite automatic transmission fluid dipstick

REAR AXLE

Rear axle lubricant level is checked at the filler plug in the rear of the differential housing. Using a 15/16 in. box wrench, remove the filler plug. Insert your finger into the hole; the gear oil level should be right at the plug opening. Use an SAE 80 or 90 gear oil to bring up the differential oil level.

STEERING GEAR

Except Rack and Pinion and Power Steering

Remove the lower right bolt on the steering box cover and make sure that the oil level is approximately 0.7 in. from the bolt hole. You can use a phillips screwdriver inserted through the hole to gauge the oil level. Add SAE 90 gear oil if the steering box needs filling.

BATTERY

Routinely check the battery electrolyte level and specific gravity. A few minutes occasionally spent monitoring battery condition is worth saving hours of frustration when your car won't start due to a dead battery. Only distilled water should be used to top up the battery, as tap water, in many areas, contains harmful minerals. Two tools which will facilitate battery maintenance are a hydrometer and a squeeze bulb filler. These are cheap and widely available at automotive parts stores, hardware stores, etc. The specific gravity of the electrolyte should be between 1.26 and 1.20. Keep the top of the battery clean, as a film of dirt can sometimes completely discharge a battery. A solution of baking soda and water may be used to clean the top surface, but be careful to flush this off with clear water and that none of the solution enters the filler holes. Clean the battery posts and clamps with a wire brush to eliminate corrosion deposits. Special clamp and terminal cleaning brushes are available for just this purpose. Lightly coat the posts and clamps with petroleum jelly or chassis grease after cleaning them.

Tires and Wheels

Buy a tire pressure gauge and keep it in the glovebox of your car. Service station air gauges are generally either not working or inaccurate and should not be relied upon. The decal on the back of the glove-box door or on the door frame panel gives the recommended air pressures for the standard tires. If you are driving on replacement tires of a different type, follow the inflation recommendations of the manufacturer and never exceed the maximum pressure stated on the sidewall. Always check tire pressure when the tires are cool because air pressure increases with heat and readings will be 4–6 psi higher after the tire has been run. For continued expressway driving, increase the tire pressure by a few pounds in each tire. Never mix tires of different construction on your car. When replacing tires, ensure that the new tire(s) are the same size and type as those which will be remaining on the car. Intermixing bias ply tires with radial or bias belted can result in unpredictable and treacherous handling.

Rotate the tires on your car every 8,000 miles or as recommended in your owners manual. The rotation pattern shown will result in all five tires wearing out at about the same time. If you plan on replacing the original equipment tires with duplicate types, don't use the spare and rotate only the four road wheels in the correct pattern according to tire type. When you buy new tires, you'll only require three—the spare will be fresh and you can use a worn tire as the spare. The tire size chart can be used for selecting replacement tires of a different size or construction.

When removing studded snow tires in the Spring, mark them left or right with chalk so that they can be returned to the same side. Studded tires take a "set" and noise and wear will increase if they are installed on the opposite side from which they were removed, in addition to the possibility of losing studs. Always tighten the wheel nuts in a criss-cross pattern. Tightening torque is 50–58 ft. lbs.

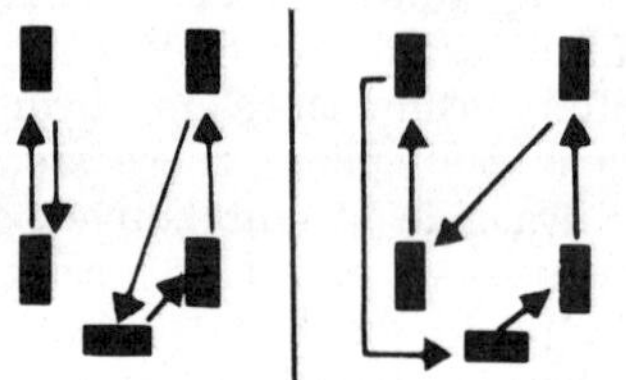

Tire rotation

Fuel Filter

The fuel filter should be replaced, or at least checked for clogging every 12,000 miles. The fuel filter is of the in-line type and is located on the left side inner fender panel or low center of the firewall, on mechanical fuel pump equipped cars. On models equipped with electric fuel pumps, the fuel filter is located in the trunk, on sedan models, or in the left rear wheelhouse, on station wagons. Removal of the air cleaner assembly or battery and battery tray may be necessary, depending on year and model. To remove the filter; loosen the hose clamps at both ends of the filter and remove the fuel lines from the filter ends. Unclip the filter from the mounting bracket. Install a new filter in the reverse order of removal. Start the engine and check for leaks. If a clogged filter is suspected, remove the filter and blow compressed air through the inlet and outlet fittings, reinstall the filter. Replace the old filter as soon as possible.

LUBRICATION

Fuel and Oil Recommendations

Your car will operate on regular, low lead gasoline of 91 octane unless it is equipped with a catalytic converter—in that case only unleaded is to be used.

Oil must be selected with regard to the anticipated temperatures during the period before the next oil change. Using the chart, select the oil viscosity for the lowest expected temperature and you will be assured of easy cold starting and sufficient engine protection. The oil you pour into your car's engine should have the designation "SE" or "SF" marked on the top of its container.

Oil Changes

ENGINE

Oil changes should be performed at the intervals as described in your owners manual or maintenance interval chart. However, it is a good idea to change the oil and oil filter at least twice a year. If your car is being used under

Oil Viscosity Selection Chart

	Anticipated Temperature Range	SAE Viscosity
Multi-grade	Above 32°F	10W-40
		10W-50
		20W-40
		20W-50
		10W-30
	May be used as low as −10°F	10W-30
		10W-40
	Consistently below 10°F	5W-20
		5W-30
Single-grade	Above 32°F	30
	Temperature between +32°F and −10°F	10W

dusty conditions, change the oil and filter sooner. The same thing goes for cars being driven in stop and go city traffic, where acid and sludge buildup is a problem. The oil should also be changed more frequently in cars which are constantly driven at high speeds on expressways. The relatively high engine speeds associated with turnpike driving mean higher operating temperatures and a greater instance of oil foaming.

Always drain the oil after the engine has been run long enough to bring it to the normal operating temperature. Hot oil will flow easier and more contaminants will be removed with the oil than if it were drained cold. A large capacity drain pan, which can be purchased at any automotive supply store, will be more than paid back by savings from do-it-yourself oil changes. Another necessity is containers for the used oil. You will find that plastic bleach containers make excellent storage bottles. Two ecologically desirable solutions to the used oil disposal problem are to take it to a service station and ask to dump it into their sump tank or keep it and use it as a preservative for exposed wood around your home.

CAUTION: *Prolonged and repeated skin contact with used engine oil, with no effort to remove the oil, may be harmful. Follow these simple precautions when handling used motor oil.*

1. *Avoid prolonged skin contact with used motor oil.*
2. *Remove oil from skin by washing thoroughly with soap and water or waterless hand cleaner. Do not use gasoline, thinners or solvents.*
3. *Avoid prolonged skin contact with oil-soaked clothing.* To change the oil:

1. Run the engine until it reaches the normal operating temperature. Raise and safely support the front of the car.
2. Remove the splash shield on front wheel drive models. Slide a drain pan under the oil pan drain plug.
3. Loosen the drain plug with a socket or box wrench, and then remove it by hand. Push in on the plug as you turn it out, so that no oil escapes until the plug is completely removed.
4. Allow the oil to drain into the pan.
5. Install the drain plug, making sure that the gasket is still on the plug.
6. Refill the engine with oil. Start the engine and check for leaks.

OIL FILTER CHANGES

The car manufacturer recommends changing the oil filter at every other oil change, but it is more beneficial to replace the filter every time the oil is changed.

To change the oil filter:

1. Drain the oil as already described.
2. Remove the lower splash shield (if equipped), which is held on with six bolts.
3. Slide a drain pan under the oil filter. Slowly turn the filter off with an oil filter wrench.

   NOTE: *Due to clearance problems on front wheel drive models, removing the alternator and replacing the filter from the top may be easier.*
4. Clean the oil filter adapter on the engine with a clean rag.
5. Oil the rubber seal on the replacement filter and install it. Tighten it until the seal is flush and then give it an additional ½ to ¾ turn.
6. Install the splash pan. Start the engine and check for leaks.

Lightly coat the filter gasket with engine oil before installation

CHASSIS GREASING

Your car requires no regular chassis greasing. The lower ball joints are provided with plugged, threaded holes. A grease nipple can be installed and the ball joints lubricated, if necessary. No other lubrication points are provided or necessary.

WHEEL BEARINGS

Due to the complexity of disc brakes, see Chapter 9 for this procedure.

MANUAL TRANSMISSION/TRANSAXLE AND REAR AXLE

It is relatively easy to change your own transmission and rear axle gear oil. The oil level should be checked twice a year and changed every 36,000 miles or three years, whichever comes first. The only equipment required is a drain pan, a wrench to fit the filler and drain plugs, and an oil suction gun. Gear oil can be purchased in quarts or gallon cans at the larger automotive supply stores.

To change the oil:

1. Jack up the front or rear of the car and support it safely on stands.
2. Slide a drain pan under the transmission or rear axle.
3. Remove the filler plug and then the drain plug.
4. When the oil has been completely drained, install the drain plug.
5. Using the suction gun, refill the gearbox or rear axle up to the level of the filler plug. Both the manual transmission and the rear axle use an SAE 80 or 90 gear oil.
6. Install and tighten the filler plug.

AUTOMATIC TRANSMISSION—EXCEPT FRONT WHEEL DRIVE MODELS

The oil pan must be removed, since no drain plug is provided. Purchase a sufficient quantity of Dexron II® automatic transmission fluid and a pan gasket before starting this project.

To change the fluid:

1. Jack up the front of the car and support it safely on stands.
2. Slide a drain pan under the transmission. Loosen the rear oil pan bolts first, to allow most of the fluid to drain off without making a mess of your garage floor.
3. Remove the remaining bolts and drop the pan.
4. Discard the old gasket, clean the pan, and reinstall the pan with the new gasket.

   CAUTION: *Tightening torque for the pan bolts is 8 to 13 ft. lbs. Tighten the bolts in a criss-cross pattern. Don't overdo it, as the transmission case is aluminum.*

5. Refill the transmission through the dipstick tube. Check the level as previously described.

AUTOMATIC TRANSAXLE—FRONT WHEEL DRIVE MODELS

1. Jack up the front of the car and support it on jackstands.
2. Slide a drain pan under the differential and remove the drain plug. When the differential is completely drained, move the pan under the transmission, remove the plug and drain.
3. Reinstall the two drain plugs. Fill the transmission with 4.2 qts of Dexron II fluid. Start the engine and allow to idle for at least two minutes. With the parking brake applied, move the selector to each position ending in Neutral.
4. Add sufficient fluid to bring the level to the lower dipstick mark. Recheck the fluid level after the transmission is up to normal operating temperature.

PUSHING AND TOWING

Manual transmission equipped cars may be started by pushing, in the event of a dead battery. Ensure that the push car bumper doesn't override the bumper of your car. Depress the clutch pedal. Select Second or Third gear. Switch the ignition ON. When the car reaches a speed of approximately 10 mph, release the clutch to start the engine.

CAUTION: *Do not attempt to push start an automatic transmission equipped car.*

Your car may be towed short distances with all four wheels on the ground only if it has a manual transmission. Always disconnect the driveshaft on automatic transmission cars or if rear axle or transmission problems are suspected.

The ignition key should be left in the lock in the "Off" position. If the car is towed on the front wheels with the ignition key removed (steering column locked), damage to the steering column or lock will result.

JACKING AND HOISTING

The vehicle is supplied with a scissors jack for emergency road repairs. The scissors jack may be used to raise the car via the notches on either side at the front and rear of the doors. *Do not attempt to use the jack in any other places.* Always block the diagonally opposite wheel when using a jack. When using a garage jack, support the car at the center of the front suspension member or at the differential carrier. Block both wheels at the opposite end of the car.

When using stands, use the side members at the front and the differential front mounting crossmember at the back for placement points.

Whenever you plan to work under the car, you must support it on jackstands or ramps.

JUMP STARTING A DEAD BATTERY

The chemical reaction in a battery produces explosive hydrogen gas. This is the safe way to jump start a dead battery, reducing the chances of an accidental spark that could cause an explosion.

Jump Starting Precautions

1. Be sure both batteries are of the same voltage.
2. Be sure both batteries are of the same polarity (have the same grounded terminal).
3. Be sure the vehicles are not touching.
4. Be sure the vent cap holes are not obstructed.
5. Do not smoke or allow sparks around the battery.
6. In cold weather, check for frozen electrolyte in the battery.
7. Do not allow electrolyte on your skin or clothing.
8. Be sure the electrolyte is not frozen.

Jump Starting Procedure

1. Determine voltages of the two batteries; they must be the same.
2. Bring the starting vehicle close (they must not touch) so that the batteries can be reached easily.
3. Turn off all accessories and both engines. Put both cars in Neutral or Park and set the handbrake.
4. Cover the cell caps with a rag—do not cover terminals.
5. If the terminals on the run-down battery are heavily corroded, clean them.
6. Identify the positive and negative posts on both batteries and connect the cables in the order shown.
7. Start the engine of the starting vehicle and run it at fast idle. Try to start the car with the dead battery. Crank it for no more than 10 seconds at a time and let it cool off for 20 seconds in between tries.
8. If it doesn't start in 3 tries, there is something else wrong.
9. Disconnect the cables in the reverse order.
10. Replace the cell covers and dispose of the rags.

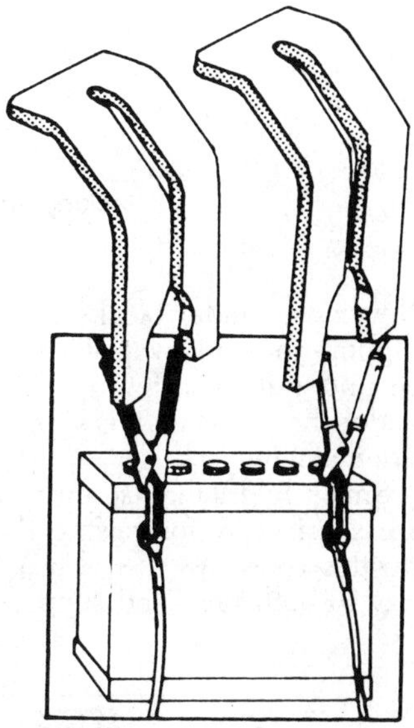

Side terminal batteries occasionally pose a problem when connecting jumper cables. There frequently isn't enough room to clamp the cables without touching sheet metal. Side terminal adaptors are available to alleviate this problem and should be removed after use.

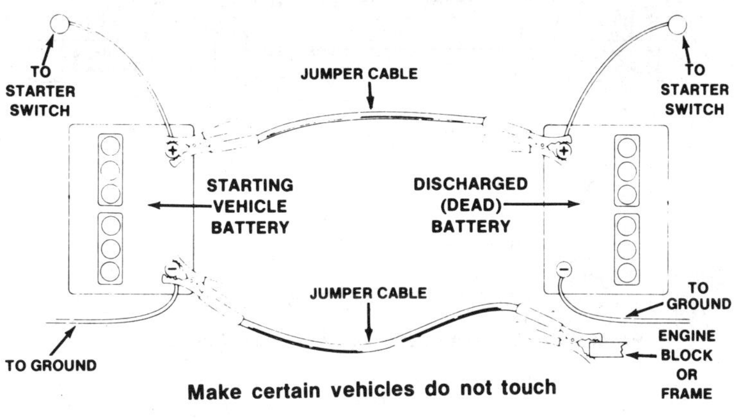

Make certain vehicles do not touch

This hook-up for negative ground cars only

LIFTING JACKING SUPPORT LOCATIONS

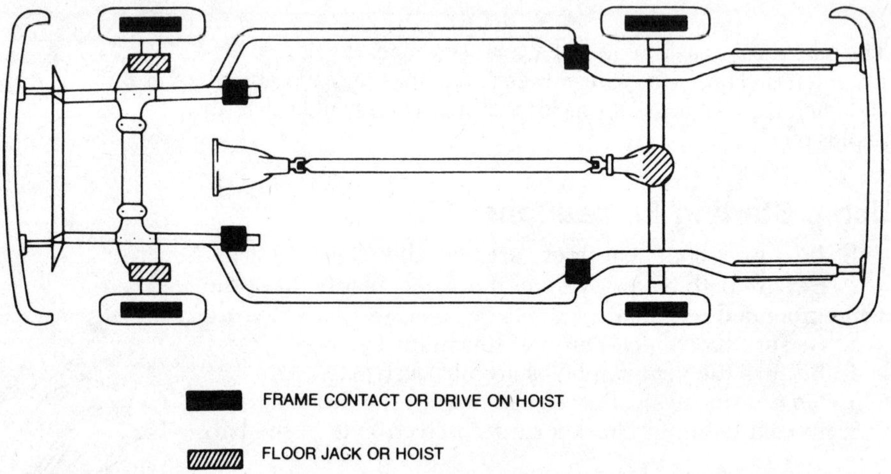

Jacking and lifting points—except front wheel drive models

Never use cinder blocks or stacks of wood to support the car, even if you're only going to be under it for a few minutes. Never crawl under the car when it is supported only by the tire-changing jack.

Small hydraulic, screw, or scissors jacks are satisfactory for raising the car. Drive-on trestles or ramps are also a handy and safe way to both raise and support the car. These can be brought or constructed from wood or steel.

If your car is to be raised with a hoist such as the type used in service stations, the pads of the hoist should be positioned on the frame rails of the car, or at the points indicated for jackstand support in the illustrations. Never support the car on any suspension member or underbody panel.

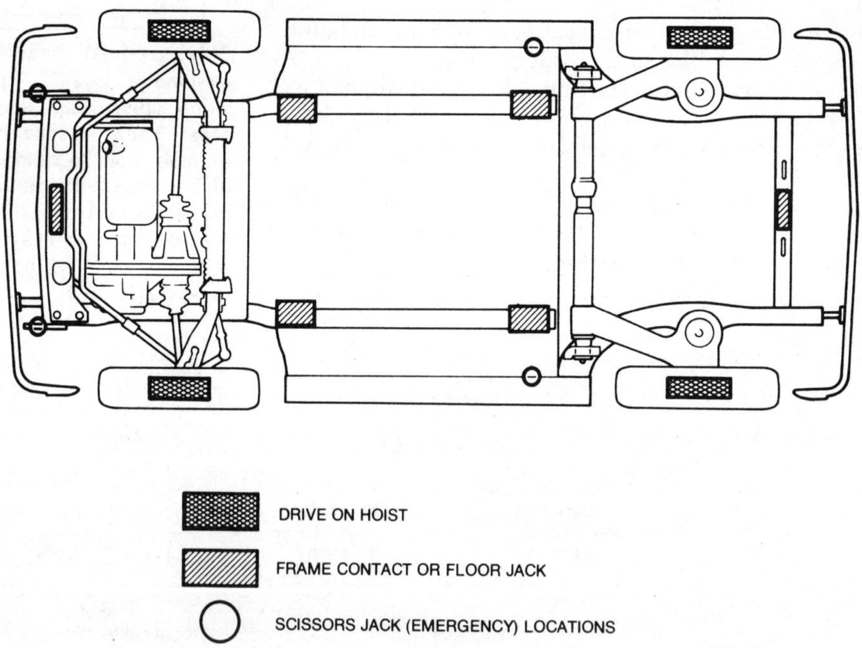

Front wheel drive models—jacking and lifting points

Tune-Up and Performance Maintenance

2

TUNE-UP PROCEDURES

A tune-up is performed periodically to make a complete check of the operation of the engine and several associated systems, to bring various minor adjustments to the best possible position, and to replace fast-wearing ignition parts. The tune-up is a good time to perform a general preventive maintenance check-out on everything in the engine compartment. Look for things like loose or damaged wiring, fuel leaks, frayed drive belts, etc.

Refer to the maintenance interval chart (chapter one) for the recommended intervals between tune-ups. After one or two tune-ups, according to the vehicle's performance, you can determine your own tune-up interval. Whether it is 8,000, 13,000, 24,000 miles, or once every year; set up a definite schedule for your car and follow it religiously. Regular tuning will head off disappointing performance and help prevent roadside breakdowns.

Spark Plugs

In addition to their basic task of igniting the air/fuel mixture, spark plugs can also serve as a very useful tool in telling you about the condition of your car's engine.

Remove the spark plug (one at a time) and compare them with the illustrations contained in the Troubleshooting chapter and the "color insert". Typical plugs conditions are shown along with their causes and remedies. Plugs which exhibit only normal wear and deposits can be cleaned, gapped and reinstalled. However, it is a good idea to replace them at every major tune-up or as recommended on the maintenance chart (see chapter one).

REMOVAL

1. If the spark plug wires are not numbered (by cylinder) place a piece of masking tape on each wire and number it.

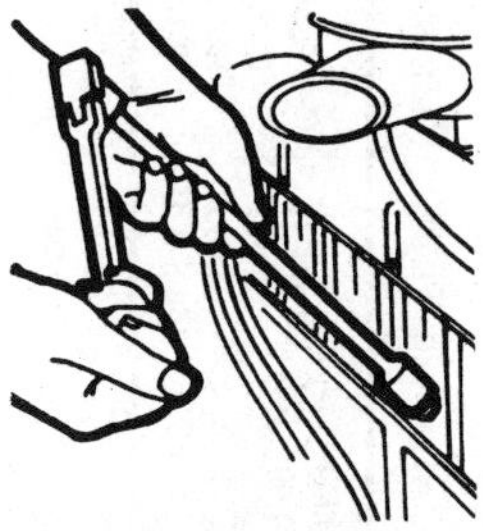

Remove the spark plugs with a ratchet and long extension

2. Grasp each wire by the rubber boot. Twist and pull the boot and wire from the spark plug.

CAUTION: *Never pull on the plug wire alone you may damage the conductor inside.*

3. Use a spark plug socket, loosen the plugs slightly and wipe or blow all dirt away from around the plug base.

4. Unscrew and remove the spark plugs from the engine. Clean, regap or replace as necessary.

TIPS

If you do not number the plug wires and get mixed up on their correct location, refer to the firing order illustrations in chapter three.

If, after removing and examining the spark plugs you feel that cleaning and regapping them is all that is necessary; use a stiff wire brush and clean all the carbon deposits from the electrodes and insulator or take the plugs to a service center and have them cleaned in a plug cleaning machine.

New spark plugs come pre-gapped, however different model cars require different size gaps. Always check the gap and reset if necessary.

To set the gap on new or cleaned spark plugs; use a spark plug wire feeler gauge, the wire gauge should pass through the electrodes

Tune-Up Specifications

When analyzing compression test, look for uniformity among cylinders, rather than specific pressures.

Year	Engine Displacement (cc.)	Spark Plugs		Distributor		Ignition Timing (deg.)		Intake Valve Opens (deg. BTDC)	Fuel Pump Pressure (psi)	Idle Speed (rpm)	Valve Clearance (in.)	
		Type	Gap (in.)	Dwell (deg.)	Gap (in.)	MT	AT				In.	Ex.
1977	1600	BPR6ES	.028–.031	52±3	.018–.021	5B ①	5B ①	24M 19A	3.7–5.1	950M ② 850A	.006	.010
	2000	BRP6ES	.028–.031	52±3	.018–.021	5B ①	5B ①	24	4.6–6.0	950M ② 850A	.006	.010
1978	1600	BPR6ES-11 ③	.039–③ .043	52±3	.018–.021	5B ④	5B	24M 19A	3.7–5.1	650M ② 700A	.006 ⑥	.010
	2000	BPR6ES-11 ③	.039–③ .043	52±3	.018–.021	5B	5B	24	4.6–6.0	650M ② 700A	.006 ⑥	.010
	2600	BPR5ES-11 ③	.039–③ .043	52±3	.018–.021	7B ⑦	7B	25	4.6–6.0	850 ⑤	.006 ⑥	.010
1979	1400	BPR6ES-11 ③	.039–③ .043	52±3	.018–.021	5B	—	18	3.7–5.1	850 ⑧	.006 ⑥	.010
	1600	BPR6ES-11 ③	.039–③ .043	52±3	.018–.021	5B	5B	20	3.7–5.1	650 ⑧	.006 ⑥	.010
	2000 ⑨	BPR6ES	.028–.031	Electronic		5B	5B	25	4.6–6.0	850	.006 ⑥	.010
	2600	BPR5ES-11 ③	.039–③ .043	Electronic		7B	7B	25	4.6–6.0	850	.006 ⑥	.010
1980	1400	BPR6ES-11 ③	.039–③ .043	52±3	.018–⑩ .021	5B	—	18	3.7–5.1	700 ②	.006 ⑥	.010
	1600	BPR6ES-11 ③	.039–③ .043	52±3	.018–⑩ .021	5B ⑪	5B ⑪	20	3.7–5.1	700M ② 750A	.006 ⑥	.010
	2600	BPR5ES-11 ③	.039–③ .043	Electronic		7B	7B	25	4.6–6.0	750 ②	.006 ⑥	.010

1981	1400	BPR6ES-11 ③	.039–.043 ③	Electronic ⑫	5B	—	18	3.7–5.1	650 ②	.006 ⑥	.010
	1600	BPR6ES-11 ③	.039–.043 ③	Electronic ⑫	5B	5B	20	3.7–5.1	650M ② 700A	.006 ⑥	.010
	2600	BPR5ES-11 ③	.039–.043 ③	Electronic	7B	7B	25	4.6–6.0	800 ②	.006 ⑥	.010
1982	1400	BPR6ES-11 ③	.039–.043 ③ ⑬	Electronic ⑫	5B	—	18	3.7–5.1	650 ②	.006 ⑥	.010
	1600	BPR6ES-11 ③	.039–.043 ③ ⑬	Electronic ⑫	5B	5B	20	3.7–5.1	700M ② 750A	.006 ⑥	.010
	2600	BPR5ES-11 ③	.039–.043 ③ ⑬	Electronic ⑫	7B	7B	25	4.6–6.0	750 ②	.006 ⑥	.010
1983	2600	BPR5ES-11 ③	.039–.043 ③	Electronic	7B	7B	25	4.6–6.0	750M ② 800A	.006 ⑥	.010

① California-dual diaphragm: 5B
High altitude-dual diaphragm: TDC 3
② Canada: 850
③ Canada: 1400-BPR6ES: .028–.031
1600-BPR6ES: .028–.031
2000-BPR6ES: .028–.031
2600-BPR5ES: .028–.031
④ High altitude: 10B
⑤ California: 700M, 750A
Canada: 850
⑥ Jet valve (USA): .006
⑦ High altitude: 12B
⑧ California-1600 w/AT: 700
Front wheel drive models: 700 USA, 850 Canada
⑨ Canadian cars only
⑩ California models are equipped with electronic ignition. Air gap: .008–.024
⑪ California models: 7B
⑫ Canadian models-point gap: .018–.021 Dwell; 52± 3
⑬ If equipped with Nippondenso plugs: Gap .035–.039

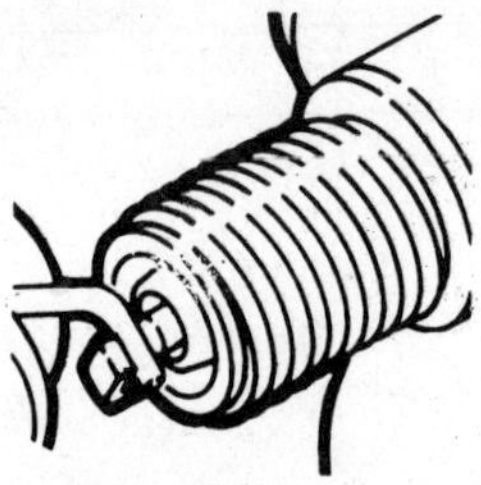

Check the spark plug gap with a wire feeler gauge

with just a slight drag. Use the electrode bending tool on the end of the gauge to adjust the gap. Never attempt to adjust the center electrode.

CHECKING AND REPLACING SPARK PLUG CABLES

Visually inspect the spark plug cables for burns, cuts, or breaks in the insulation. Check the spark plug boots and the nipples on the distributor cap and coil. Replace any damaged wiring. If no physical damage is obvious, the wires can be checked with an ohmmeter for excessive resistance. See the Troubleshooting chapter for detailed information.

When installing a new set of spark plug cables, replace the cables one at a time so there will be no mixup. Start by replacing the longest cable first. Install the boot firmly over the spark plug. Route the wire exactly the same as the original. Insert the nipple into the tower on the distributor cap. Repeat the process for each cable.

FIRING ORDER

To avoid confusion, replace spark plug wires one at a time.

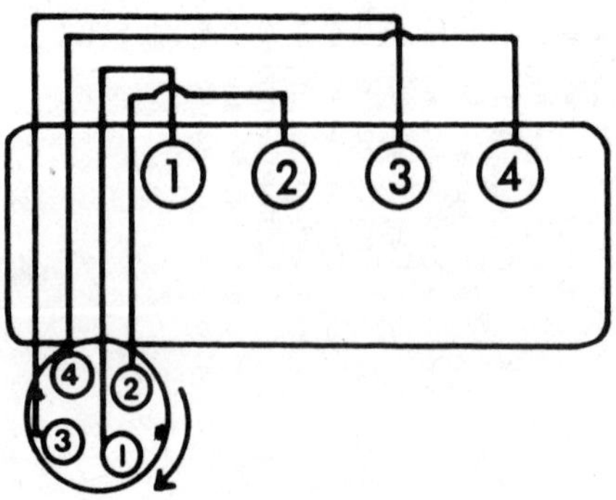

Firing order—1400 and 1600cc engines

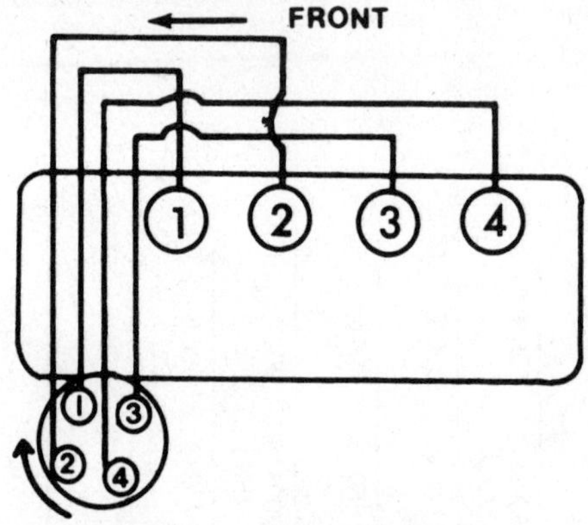

Firing order—2000 and 2600cc engines

Breaker Points and Condenser

The points function as a circuit breaker for the primary circuit of the ignition system. The ignition coil must boost the 12 bolts of electrical pressure supplied by the battery to as much as 25,000 volts in order to fire the spark plugs. To do this, the coil depends on the points and condenser to make a clean break in the primary circuit.

The coil has both primary and secondary circuits. When the ignition is turned on, the battery supplies voltage through the coil and on to the points. The points are connected to ground, completing the primary circuit. As the current passes through the coil, a magnetic field is created in the iron center core of the coil. As the cam in the distributor turns, the points open and the primary circuit is interrupted. The magnetic field in the primary cir-

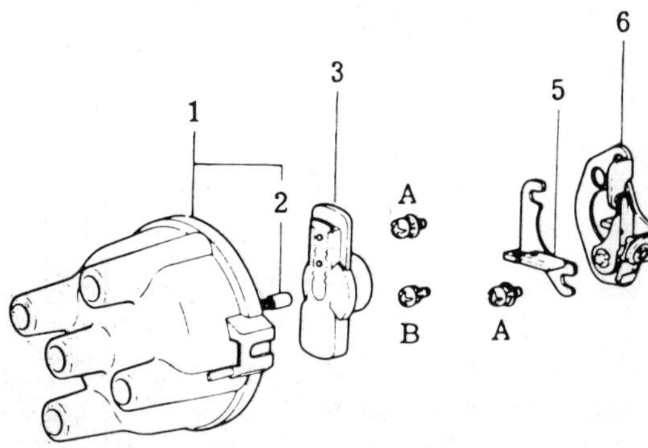

1. Distributor cap
2. Carbon button (1 and 2 and an assembly)
3. Rotor
5. Lubricator wick plate
6. Point set

A. Point and wick plate retaining screws
B. Eccentric adjusting screw (1971–74 models only)

Exploded view of tune-up related parts for a breaker point ignition

cuit of the coil collapses and cuts through the secondary circuit windings around the iron core. Because of the scientific phenomenon called "electromagnetic induction," the battery voltage is at this point increased to a level sufficient to fire the spark plugs.

When the points open, the electrical charge in the primary circuit jumps the gap created between the two opened contacts of the points. If this charge were not transferred elsewhere, the metal contacts of the points would melt and the gap between the points would start to change rapidly. If the gap is not maintained, the points will not break the primary circuit. If the primary circuit is not broken, the secondary circuit will not have enough voltage to fire the spark plugs.

The function of the condenser is to absorb excessive voltage from the points when they open and thus prevent the points from becoming pitted or burned.

There are two ways to check the breaker point gap: It can be done with a feeler gauge or a dwell meter. Either way you set the points, you are basically adjusting the amount of time that the points remain open. The time is measured in degrees of distributor rotation. When you measure the gap between the breaker points with a feeler gauge, you are setting the maximum amount the points will open when the rubbing block on the points is on the high point of the distributor cam. When you adjust the points with a dwell meter, you are adjusting the number of degrees that the points will remain closed before they start to open as a high point of the distributor cam approaches the rubbing block of the points.

When you replace a set of points, always replace the condenser at the same time.

When you change the point gap or dwell, you will also have changed the ignition timing. So, if the point gap or dwell is changed, the ignition timing must be adjusted also. Changing the ignition timing, however, does not affect the dwell of the breaker points.

REPLACING POINTS AND CONDENSER

Snap off the two spring clips that hold the distributor cap to the distributor. Remove the cap and examine it for cracks, deterioration, or carbon tracking. Replace the cap if necessary; transfer one wire at a time from the old cap to the new one. Examine the rotor for corrosion or wear and replace it if it's at all questionable.

To replace the breaker points:

1. Turn the engine with the crankshaft pulley until the rubbing block on the points is on the high point of the distributor cam. (Rotor removed).
2. Observe which screws retain the ground and primary wires. Remove the two retaining screws.

NOTE: *We suggest a magnetic screwdriver, a screw start or some kind of screwholding device so you will not drop the retaining screws into the distributor or onto the ground.*

3. Remove the distributor breaker points.
4. Install the new set of points; make sure that the pin on the bottom of the points engages the hole in the breaker plate.
5. Install the lubricator wink, primary and ground wires and two retaining screws. Tighten the screws slightly snug.
6. Check to be sure that the rubbing block on the points is on the high part of the distributor cam.
7. Point adjustment is made by using a screwdriver in the slot provided and pivoting it to open or close the gap. Refer to the underhood decal or the Tune-Up specifications in this chapter for the correct point setting.
8. When gap is correct tighten the retaining screws.
9. Install the rotor and distributor cap.
10. The condenser is mounted on the outside of the distributor. Undo the mounting screw and the terminal screw or slide connector to replace the condenser.

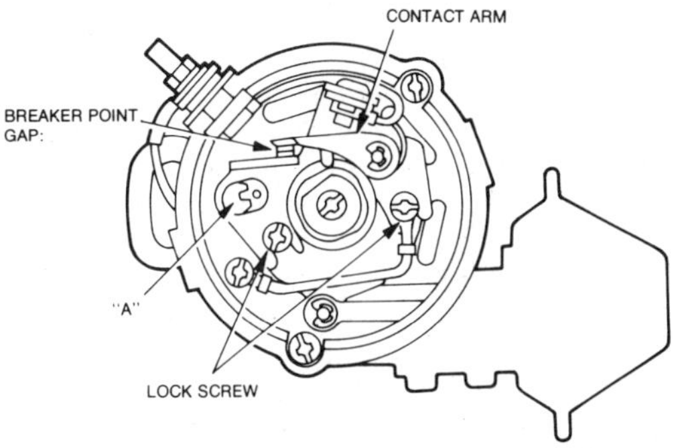

Point gap adjustment is made by twisting a flat bladed screwdriver in "slot A".

DWELL ANGLE

1. Adjust the points with a feeler gauge as described.
2. Follow the directions that come with the dwell meter and connect it to your ignition circuit. One lead of the meter is connected to a ground and the other lead is to be connected to the distributor post on the coil. An adapter is usually provided for this purpose.
3. If the dwell meter has a zero set adjustment on it, make sure to zero the meter.
4. Start the engine and allow it to idle.

CAUTION: *Be careful when working on any vehicle while the engine is running. Make sure that the transmission is in Neutral or*

Park and that the parking brake is applied. Keep hands, clothing, tools, and meter wires clear of the fan blades and drive belts.

5. Observe the reading on the dwell meter. If the reading is within the specified range, turn off the engine and remove the dwell meter.

6. If the reading is above the specified range, the breaker point gap is too small. If the reading is below the specified range, the gap is too large. In either case, the engine must be stopped and the gap adjusted. After making the adjustment, start the engine and recheck the reading on the dwell meter. When the correct reading is obtained, disconnect the dwell meter.

7. Check and adjust the ignition timing.

Electronic Ignition System (EIS)

There are two major differences between the electronic ignition system and the point type system. First, the points and condenser are replaced by an induction type impulse sender. Second, an electronic ignition control unit has been added to amplify the electrical impulses between the distributor and the coil. The impulse sender is located inside the distributor where the points used to be. Instead of opening and closing an electrical circuit, the sender opens and closes a magnetic circuit. This induces impulses in a magnetic pick-up. The sender consists of a stator, pick-up, rotor signal (reluctor), and permanent magnet. The stator and reluctor each have the same number of teeth as there are cylinders. The permanent magnet creates a magnetic field which goes through the stator. The circuit is closed when the teeth are opposite each other. The means that the reluctor opens and closes the magnetic field while rotating. This generates current pulses in the magnetic pick-up. The electronic ignition control unit (located on the side of the distributor 1979–80 and on the inside of the distributor from 1981) consists of a power transmitter chip and a ceramic board containing a monolithic IC (integrated circuit), several passive components and a thick film circuit. The electronic ignition control unit amplifies the impulses from the sender and controls the dwell angle.

Refer to chapter three for testing and troubleshooting the electronic ignition system.

Ignition Timing

Ignition timing is the measurement, in degrees of crankshaft rotation, of the point at which the spark plugs fire in each of the cylinders. It is measured in degrees before or after Top Dead Center (TDC) of the compression stroke. Ignition timing is controlled by turning the distributor body in the engine.

Ideally, the air/fuel mixture in the cylinder will be ignited by the spark plug just as the piston passes TDC of the compression stroke. If this happens, the piston will be beginning the power stroke just as the compressed and ignited air/fuel mixture starts to expand. The expansion of the air/fuel mixture then forces the piston down on the power stroke and turns the crankshaft.

Because it takes a fraction of a second for the spark plug to ignite the mixture in the cylinder, the spark plug must fire a little before the piston reaches TDC. Otherwise, the mixture will not be completely ignited as the piston passes TDC and the full power of the explosion will not be used by the engine.

The timing measurement is given in degrees of crankshaft rotation before the piston reaches TDC (BTDC). If the setting for the ignition timing is 5° BTDC, each spark plug must fire 5° before each piston reaches TDC. This only holds true, however, when the engine is at idle speed.

As the engine speed increases, the pistons go faster. The spark plugs have to ignite the fuel even sooner if it is to be completly ignited when the piston reaches TDC. To do this, the distributor has a means to advance the timing of the spark as the engine speed increases. This is accomplished by centrifugal weights within the distributor and a vacuum diaphragm mounted on the side of the distributor.

If the ignition is set too far advanced (BTDC), the ignition and expansion of the fuel in the cylinder will occur too soon and tend to force the piston down while it is still traveling up. This causes engine ping. If the ignition spark is set too far retarded after TDC (ATDC), the piston will have already passed TDC and started on its way down when the fuel is ignited. This will cause the piston to be forced down for only a portion of its travel. This will result in poor engine performance and lack of power.

The timing is best checked with a timing light. This device is connected in series with the No. 1 spark plug or the coilwire, depending on type of timing light. The current that fires the spark plug also causes the timing light to flash.

CAUTION: *When making any adjustments with the engine running, be careful of the fan blades and drive belts.*

Ignition timing should always be checked as a part of any tune-up. Timing is checked after the points have been adjusted or replaced.

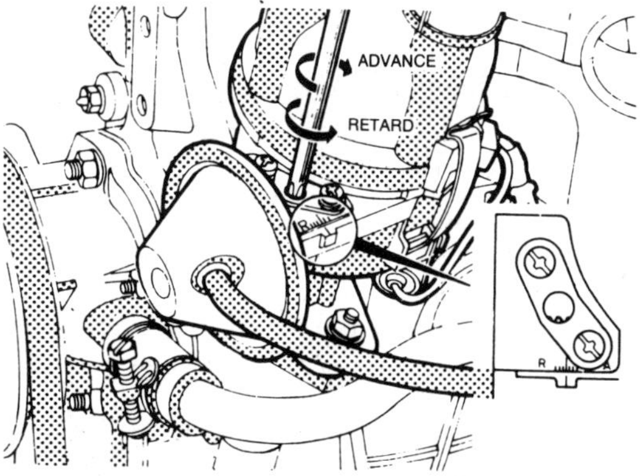

Remove the rubber plug and fine tune the timing

1977–78

The distributor used from 1977–78 is equipped with either a single or dual-diaphragm vacuum advance unit, depending upon the locale in which the car is sold, due to emission control regulations.

The retard section of the dual-diaphragm unit is located on the distributor side, with the advance section located on the opposite side of the advance mechanism. The retard section is activated during the engine idle and deceleration cycles.

At idle the basic ignition timing is retarded to 5 degrees ATDC by the vacuum retard unit. Basic timing is checked with the rubber plug removed from the advance/retard unit, the vacuum lines are *not* removed and plugged as on the single unit diaphragm equipped distributor.

To adjust the timing:

1. Attach the timing light and tachometer according to the instructions that came with the light or tachometer.
2. Locate the timing tabline on the front of the engine and the notch on the crankshaft pulley. Mark them with chalk.

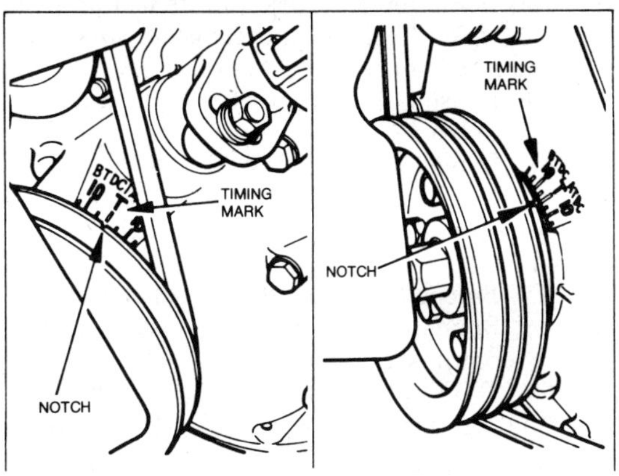

Typical timing marks

3. Remove the rubber plug on dual diaphragm unit, or remove and plug the line on single units.
4. Start the engine and allow it to reach operating temperature, adjust idle speed if necessary.
5. Shine the timing light at the crankshaft pulley marks. The marked line should align with the pulley notch.
6. If the marks do not align, loosen the distributor mounting nut and rotate the distributor slowly in either direction to align the timing marks.
7. Tighten the mounting nut when the ignition timing is correct, adjust idle speed is necessary.
8. Replace the rubber plug (dual diaphragm) and check the retarded timing. Adjustment is made by loosening the two diaphragm mounting screws and turning the phillips adjusting screw as necessary to bring timing into specs. Shut off engine and remove timing light and tachometer

1979 AND LATER

Point fired or electronic ignition:

1. Attach the timing light and tachometer according to the instructions that came with the light or tachometer.
2. Locate the timing tabline on the front of the engine and the notch of the crankshaft pulley. Mark them with chalk.
3. Start the engine and allow it to reach operating temperature, adjust idle speed if necessary.
4. Shine the timing light at the crankshaft pulley marks. The marked line should align with the pulley notch.
5. If the marks do not align, loosen the distributor mounting nut and rotate the distributor slowly in either direction to align the timing marks.
6. Tighten the mounting nut when the ignition timing is correct, adjust idle speed if necessary. Shut off engine and remove timing light and tachometer.

Valve Lash

Valve adjustment determines how far the valves enter the cylinder and how long they stay open and closed.

If the valve clearance is too large, part of the lift of the camshaft will be used in removing the excessive clearance. Consequently, the valve will not be opening as far as it should. This condition has two effects: the valve train components will emit a tapping sound as they take up the excessive clearance and the engine will perform poorly because the valves don't open fully and allow the proper amount of gases to flow into and out of the engine.

If the valve clearance is too small, the intake valve and the exhaust valves will open too far and they will not fully seat on the cylinder head when they close. When a valve seats itself on the cylinder head, it does two things: it seals the combustion chamber so that none of the gases in the cylinder escape and it cools itself by transferring some of the heat it absorbs from the combustion in the cylinder to the cylinder head and to the engine's cooling system. If the valve clearance is too small, the engine will run poorly because of the gases escaping from the combustion chamber. The valves will also become overheated and will warp, since they cannot transfer heat unless they are touching the valve seat in the cylinder head.

NOTE: *While all valve adjustments must be made as accurately as possible, it is better to have the valve adjustment slightly loose than slightly tight as a burned valve may result from overly tight adjustments.*

VALVE ADJUSTMENT

Valve clearance is adjusted with the engine stopped. When adjusting the valves cold, after the engine has been rebuilt or a valve job done on the cylinder head, proceed as follows:

1. Adjust the valves in order as shown in hot adjustment—step 8.
2. Turn the crankshaft pulley to bring the piston to top dead center (TDC) of the compression stroke of the cylinder being adjusted.
3. Loosen the two rocker adjusting screw locknuts.
4. Using a .003 in. feeler gauge for the intake and a .007 in. gauge for the exhaust, turn the adjusting screw until the clearance is correct.
5. Tighten the lock nuts to 7–9 ft. lbs.

The normal valve clearance adjustment, or final adjustment after the above initial cold adjustment, is performed as follows.

Adjusting the valve clearance—models without Jet valve

To adjust the valves:

1. Run the engine until it reaches normal operating temperature and then turn it off.
2. Undo the wing nut and remove the air cleaner. Pull the large crankcase ventilation hose off the front of the air cleaner. Disconnect the two smaller hoses, one goes to the rear of the rocker arm cover and the other to the intake manifold.
3. Loosen and remove the nuts and one bracket which attach the air cleaner to the rocker arm cover.
4. Lift the bottom housing of the air cleaner off of the carburetor and, with it, the hose coming up from the exhaust manifold heat stove.
5. Unsnap the spark plug wires from their clips on the rocker arm cover.
6. Loosen and remove the two rocker arm cover volts. The rear bolt is a crankcase ventilation fitting, so you will have to use a deep socket or a box wrench.
7. Carefully lift the rocker arm cover off the cylinder head. Using a 5/16 in. allen socket (1600 cc) or a regular socket (2000 cc) and a torque wrench, make sure that the cylinder head bolts are all tightened to 58–62 ft. lbs. on 1600 cc engines, 72–79 ft. lbs. on 2000 cc engines.
8. Hot valve clearance is .006 in. for the intake valves and .010 in. for the exhaust.

Exhaust Valve Closing	Adjust
No. 1 Cylinder	No. 4 Cylinder Valves
No. 2 Cylinder	No. 3 Cylinder Valves
No. 3 Cylinder	No. 2 Cylinder Valves
No. 4 Cylinder	No. 1 Cylinder Valves

9. Turn the crankshaft pulley to bring the piston to top dead center (TDC) of the compression stroke on the cylinder being adjusted. See step 8. Both valves will be closed at this point and the rocker arms will be resting on the "heel" of the camshaft lobe (the round side, not the egg-shaped side).
10. Loosen the two rocker arm adjusting screw lock nuts.
11. Using the correct thickness feeler gauge, turn the adjusting screw until the gauge just snaps through the valve stem and the rocker arm.
12. Proceed to adjust the valves of each cylinder. Remember to bring each piston to TDC of its compression stroke.

CAUTION: *The importance of correctly setting the valve clearance cannot be overemphasized. The clearance must be right or peak performance and efficiency will never*

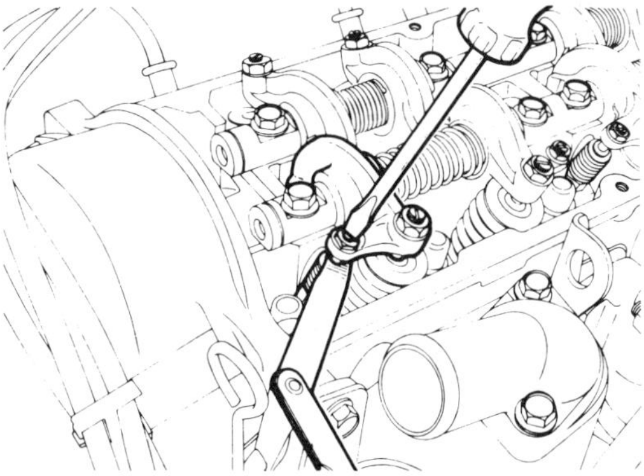

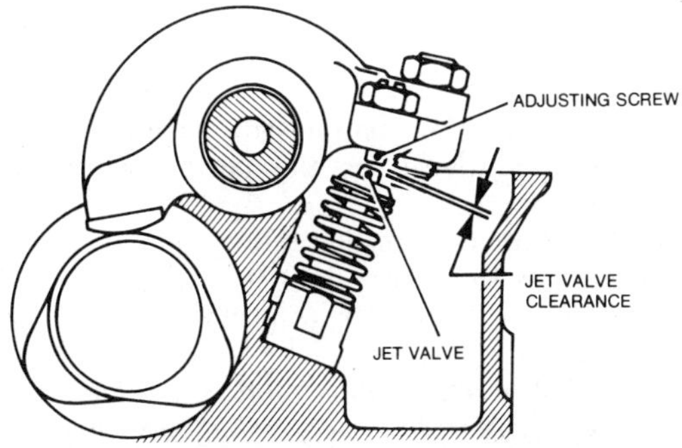

Adjusting the Jet valve clearance

be realized. Loose valve clearances will result in excessive wear and valve train chatter; tight valve clearance will result in burnt valve seats.

13. Apply non-hardening sealer to the rocker arm cover gasket. Always use a new gasket.

14. Install the cover, hoses, spark plug wires and the air cleaner in the reverse order of removal. Tighten the rocker arm cover bolts to 4–5 ft. lbs.

15. Start the engine and check for leaks.

1978 AND LATER WITH JET VALVE

A jet valve has been added to the combustion chamber (US models) its adjuster is located on the intake valve rocker arm. The jet valve must be adjusted before the intake valve adjustment is done.

1. Start engine and allow it to reach normal operating temperature.

NOTE: *Do not run engine with rocker arm cover removed, oil will be sprayed on to the hot exhaust manifold.*

2. Shut off engine and remove the rocker arm cover.

3. Watch the valve operation on No. 1 cylinder while turning the crankshaft to close the exhaust valve and have the intake valve just begin to open. This places the No. 4 cylinder on TDC of its firing stroke and permits the adjustment of the valves.

Exhaust Valve Closing	Adjust
No. 1 Cylinder	No. 4 Cylinder Valves
No. 2 Cylinder	No. 3 Cylinder Valves
No. 3 Cylinder	No. 2 Cylinder Valves
No. 4 Cylinder	No. 1 Cylinder Valves

NOTE: *On 1980 and later front wheel drive models with the "K" engine (1600 cc) a crankshaft pulley access hole is located on the left side fender shield. Remove the covering plug and use a ratchet extension to turn the crankshaft when adjusting the valves.*

4. Jet valves must be adjusted before the intake valve.

To adjust the jet valves:

4a. Loosen the intake valve lock nut and back off the adjustment screw two or more turns.

4b. Loosen the lock nut on the jet valve adjusting screw. Turn the jet valve adjusting screw counter clockwise and insert a .006 in. feeler gauge between the valve stem and the adjusting screw.

4c. Tighten the adjusting screw until it touches the feeler gauge.

NOTE: *The jet valve spring is weak, be careful not to force the jet valve in.*

4d. After adjustment is made, hold the adjusting screw with a screwdriver and tighten the lock nut.

5. Proceed to adjust the intake and the exhaust valves on the same cylinder as the jet valve you finished adjusting and move on to the next cylinder. See chart step 3.

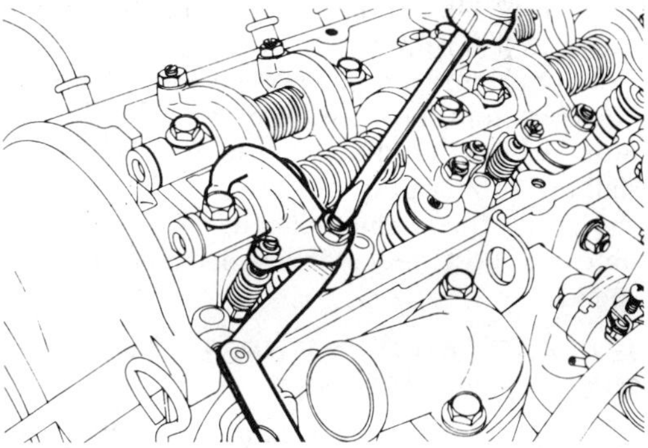

Adjusting the valve clearance—models with Jet valve

Idle Speed Adjustment

1977 IDLE SPEED ADJUSTMENT

1. Warm the engine to normal operating temperature.

2. Disconnect the air shut-off solenoid electrical plug. This is located under the air control valve which is on the left-side of the en-

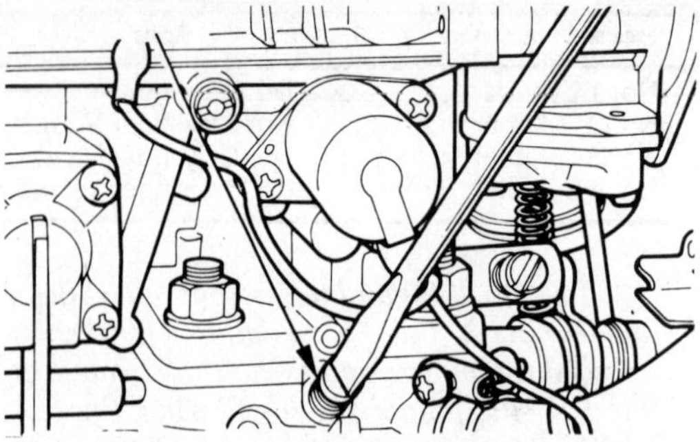

Typical mixture screw adjustment

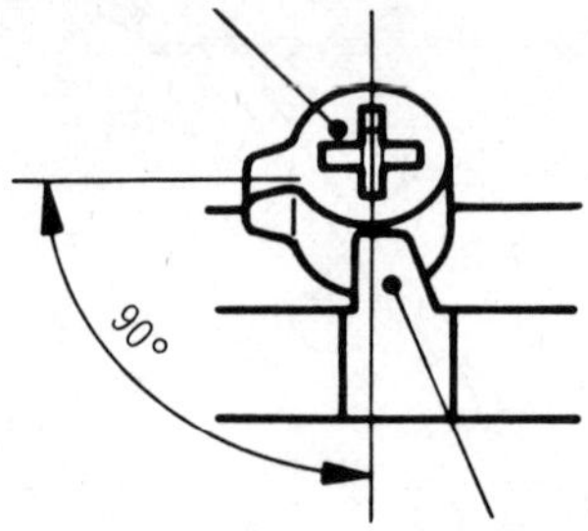

Idle limiter adjustment arc

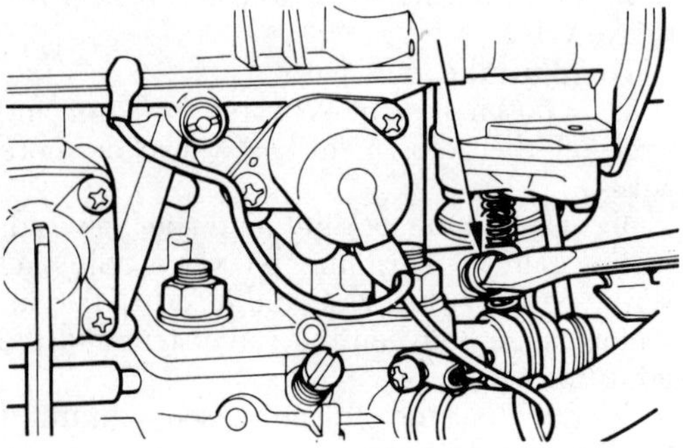

Typical idle speed screw adjustment

gine. This equipment is part of the air injection system.

3. Adjust the idle speed to 900 rpm on manual transmission cars or 800 rpm on automatic transmission cars. Do this with the carburetor idle speed adjusting screw.

4. Connect the air shut-off solenoid.

5. On manual cars, adjust engine speed to 1000 rpm. On automatic cars, set the engine speed to 900 rpm.

6. On automatic cars only, remove the rubber plug from the vacuum unit on the distributor. Adjust the idle speed to 800 rpm, reinstall the rubber plug.

7. Race the engine to about 2500 rpm a few times and observe that it returns to normal idle speed.

1978 AND LATER IDLE SPEED AND MIXTURE ADJUSTMENT

1. Start and run the engine at idle until normal operating temperature is reached.

2. Check the chart in this chapter or the underhood decal for the correct curb idle speed.

3. Connect a tachometer (follow the instructions that came with the meter) and adjust the idle speed screw until the correct rpm is reached.

4. *Idle mixture adjustments should be made by an authorized garage using a CO meter.* However, a small amount of adjustment is possible (within the limits of the idle mixture screw limiter cap—which must not be removed).

NOTE: *Some late model carburetors have a tamperproof, sealed idle mixture screw—these cannot be adjusted, except by an authorized garage.*

5. To adjust the idle mixture; first, adjust carb to correct curb idle speed. Next, watch the tachometer scale, listen to the engine and slowly turn the idle mixture screw clockwise. A drop in engine rpm or engine roughness will tell you when to stop. Then, slowly turn the mixture screw counter-clock-wise until once again you encounter rpm drop or engine roughness. A point in-between the clockwise or counter-clockwise positions, that gives you the highest rpm or smoothest running engine, is the best setting.

6. Check and readjust the curb idle speed, if necessary.

7. Have your adjustment checked with a CO meter as soon as possible.

Engine and Engine Rebuilding

3

ENGINE ELECTRICAL

Electronic Ignition System (EIS)

Your cars performance and economy depend on a number of things, one of which is the ignition system. Most people are familiar with breaker point ignition systems; their problems and repairs. If you are not, please refer to the "Tune-Up" and "Troubleshooting" chapters in this book.

The electronic ignition system (EIS) requires a different "troubleshooting" technique. (For a description of the EIS refer to chapter two).

When you suspect that an ignition problem is causing hard starting or poor performance do the follow checks and tests.

NOTE: *If engine will not start, go to test 1 or test 2, depending on the year of your car.*

If the engine will run:

1. Start the engine, allow to idle until the normal operating temperature is reached.
2. Check the ignition timing, adjust if necessary.
3. Visually check electrical connections for frayed insulation or bare wires. Make sure all plug-in connectors are clean and tight. Check the spark plug and coil wires for cracking, crossfiring, corroded terminals, continuity and resistance.

Check the distributor cap for cracks or carbon tracking. Check any suspect parts. Check the spark plugs for foiling, nonfiring and correct gap.

4. If none of the checks have solved the problem, or the car fails to start, proceed to the following tests.

1979–80 TEST 1

1. Remove the distributor cap by inserting a screwdriver in the ends of the two retaining

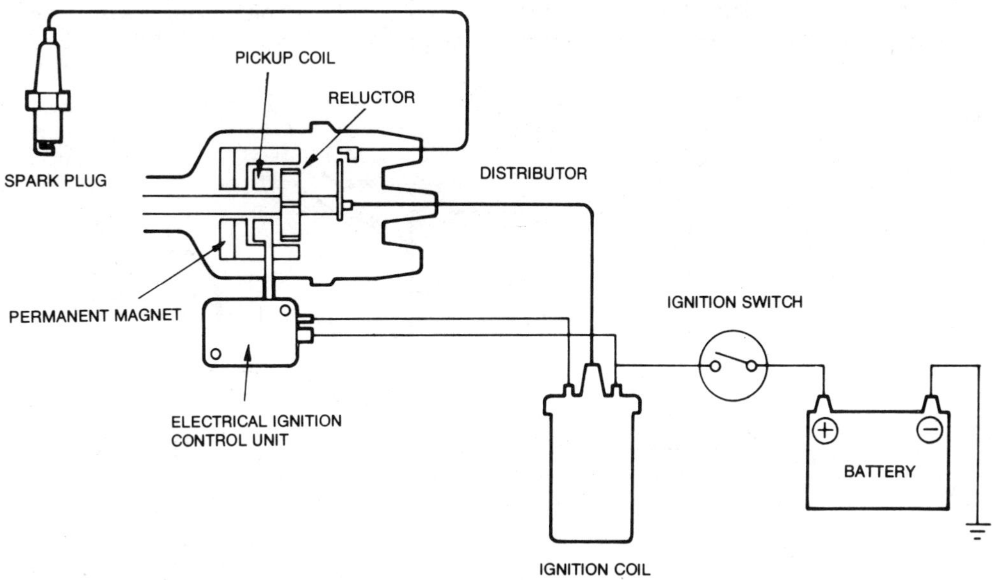

Typical electronic ignition system circuit

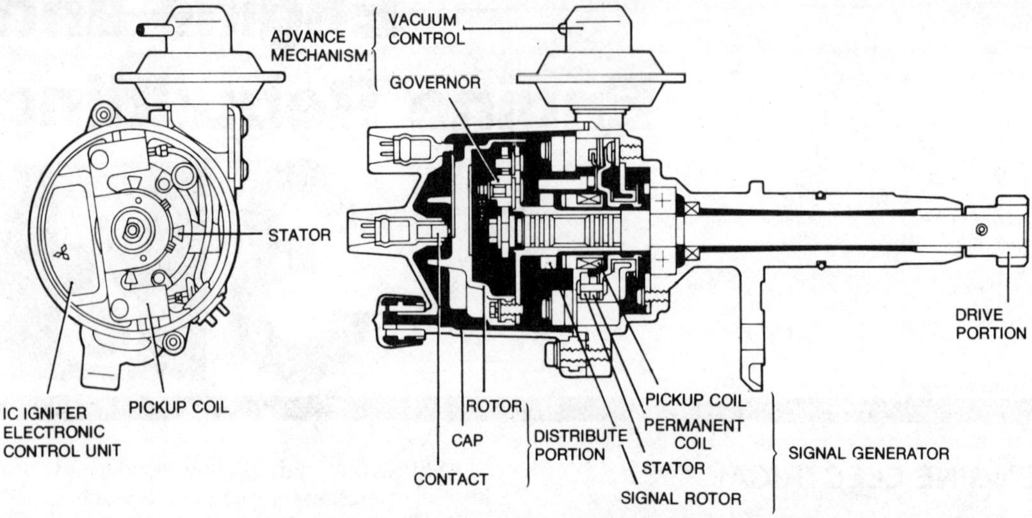

Cross section of an electronic distributor (1981 shown)

screws, pushing in and turning the screws clockwise.

2. Remove the screws holding the rotor assembly and lift out the rotor.

3. Turn the ignition switch to the ON position.

4. Disconnect the high tension cable (coil wire) from the center terminal of the distributor cap and hold its end about a quarter of an inch away from a ground (cylinder block etc.).

NOTE: *Use insulated pliers to hold the cable.*

Insert a flatblade screwdriver between the reluctor and the stator (see illustration). A spark should jump from the high tension wire to the ground. If a spark is not produced, a defective control unit, pick-up coil, ignition coil or faulty wiring may be the problem. Further service should be left to a qualified service technician. However, in the paragraphs that follow further tests are described.

1981 AND LATER TEST 2

Remove the coil wire from the distributor cap tower. Hold the end of the wire with insulated pliers (prevents you from getting a shock). Locate the end of the wire about a quarter of an inch away from the cylinder head and have a friend crank the engine with the starter. Observe the spark or no spark condition. If a spark is produced, the IC igniter and ignition coil may be considered in good condition. Remove the distributor cap and check it for cracks, carbon tracking or dirt. Check the rotor for wear. Replace as necessary. If no sparks are produced a defective control unit (internal), pick-up coil, ignition coil or faulty wiring may be the problem. Further service should be left to

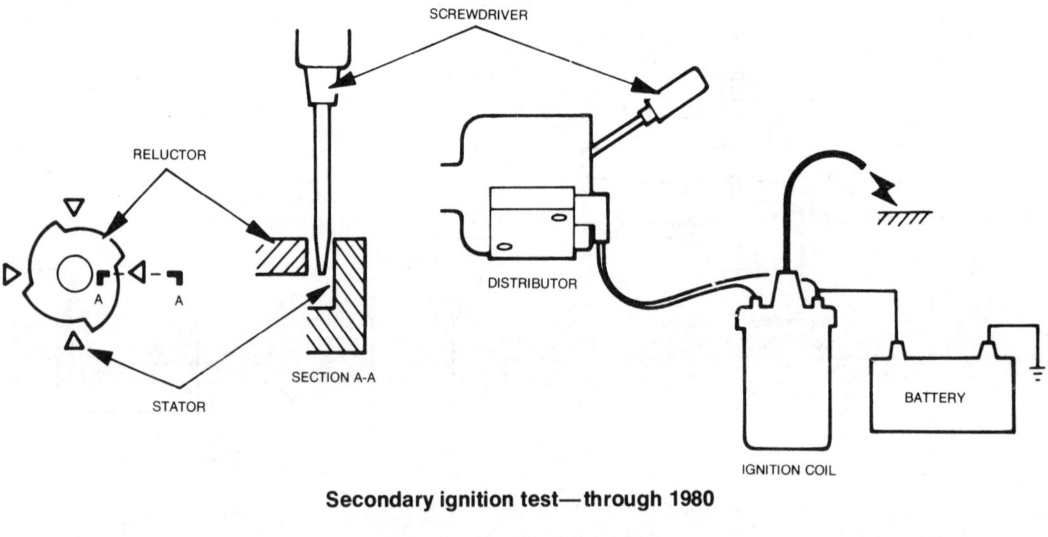

Secondary ignition test—through 1980

a qualified service technician. However, in the paragraphs that follow, further tests are described.

IGNITION COIL

If either test one or test two produces no spark, the ignition coil could be at fault. The fastest way to check is by substituting a known good coil. If a coil is not on hand, proceed with one or more of the following tests.

1. With the ignition switch in the ON position measure the voltage at the negative terminal of the ignition coil. If zero volts are shown, there is an open circuit in the coil.

2. Check the ignition coil resistance. If the engine will run allow it to reach normal operating temperature (the ignition coil should be hot). Shut off the engine and disconnect the high tension lead (coil wire) from the coil tower.

2a. Measure primary resistance with an ohmmeter, connecting the coil minus and plus primary terminals. Resistance should be; 0.7–0.85 ohms (through 1982) 1.04–1.27 ohms (from 1983).

2b. Measure the secondary resistance by connecting the ohmmeter between the contacts in the coil tower and the plus primary terminal. Resistance should be; 9–11 k ohms (through 1982), 7.10–9.60 k ohms (from 1983).

3. Replace the coil if the voltage tests show zero volts or the resistances are not within "specs."

TESTING THE EXTERNAL RESISTOR

1. With the ignition switch off: connect an ohmmeter between the terminals of the external resistor.

2. Obtain a reading from the ohmmeter. Resistance should be 1.22–1.49 ohms.

3. If the reading on the ohmmeter is zero or not within specs, replace the resistor.

TESTING THE PICK-UP COIL

The pick-up coil may be tested while mounted in the distributor. Remove the cap and rotor and connect an ohmmeter between the two terminals of the pick-up coil. If the resistance is not within the limits; (1980) 1,050 plus or minus 50 ohms: (1981 and later) 920–1.120 ohms; replace the pick-up coil.

PICK-UP COIL REPLACEMENT

Distributor must be removed from the engine, (see distributor removal procedure).

1. Remove the distributor cap and rotor.

2. Remove the center mounting bolt (screw) and remove the governor assembly. Take care not to mix up the governor springs they must be installed in the same position. Remove the reluctor.

3. Remove the two mounting screws and take out the pick-up coil (79–80) or the pick-up coil and IC Igniter (from 1981). Carefully pull the Igniter from the pick-up coil.

4. Installation of the new pick-up coil is the reverse of the removal.

CONTROL UNIT TEST

The control unit is mounted on the side of the distributor (1979–80) and internally mounted (in the distributor) on 1981 and later models.

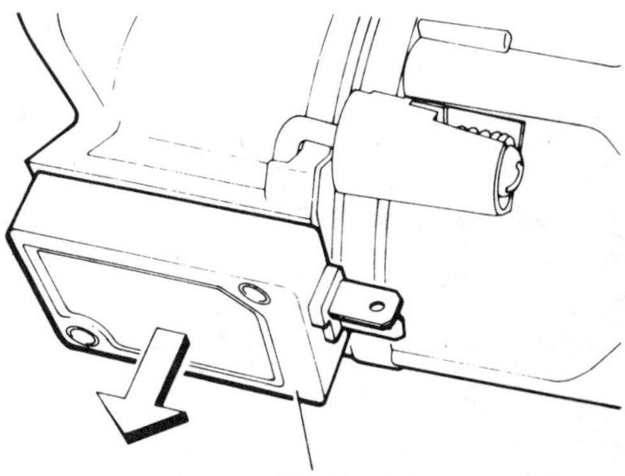

Removing the control unit

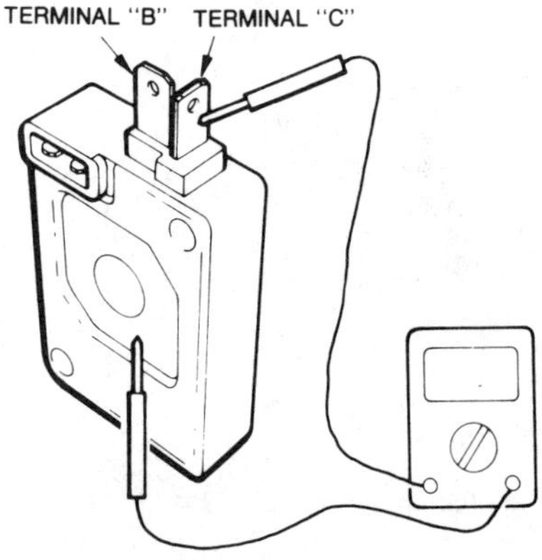

Control unit test—through 1980

TO TEST THE 1979 AND 1980 CONTROL UNIT

With the control unit still mounted on the distributor: check for continuity between terminal "C" and the distributor housing. If the control unit is not mounted: check for continuity between terminal "C" and the metallic side of the unit. (See illustration) Alternately switch the leads of the meter; if there is continuity or an open circuit in both directions, the control unit is defective.

NOTE: *Only the transistors in the switching*

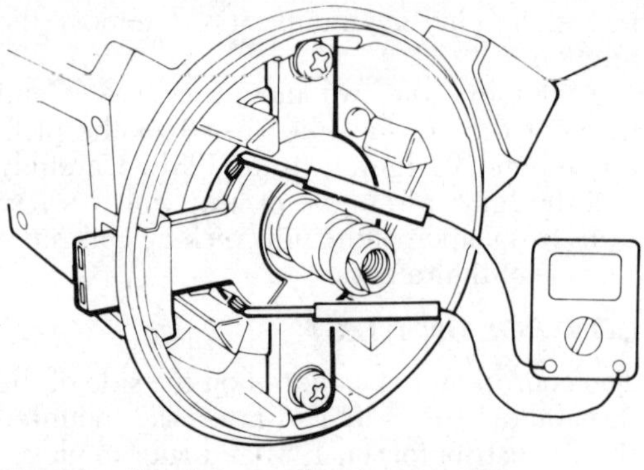

Checking the pickup coil—through 1980

section of the control unit are checked by this test.

Even if they test as good, the unit could still be defective.

TO TEST THE CONTROL UNIT FROM 1981

Connect the igniter unit, battery, lamp or ohmmeter as shown in the illustration. Apply signal voltage. If the lamp lights or ohms are read when voltage is applied, and goes out or reads no ohms when the voltage signal is removed, the igniter may be considered good.

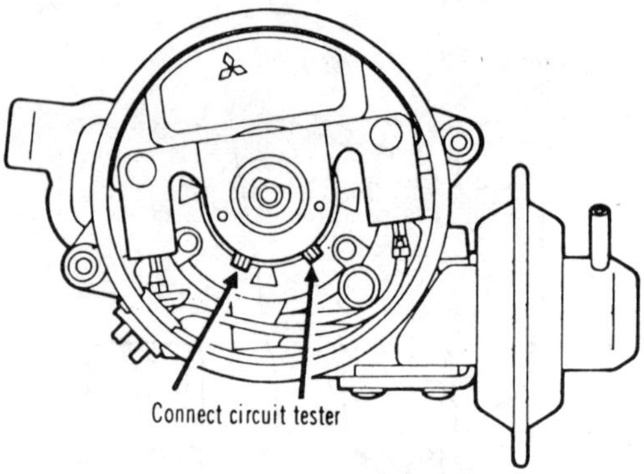

Checking pick-up coil—from 1981

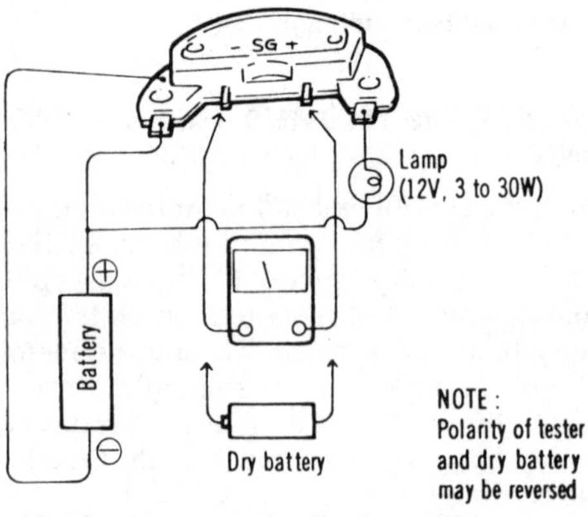

Test hook-up for control unit—from 1981

NOTE: *Only the switching section of the control unit is checked with this test. Even if the unit tests as good, it could still be defective.*

Distributor

REMOVAL

Although the distributor can be removed from the engine no matter which cylinder is about to fire, it is a good idea to have number one cylinder at TDC before distributor removal.

1. Unsnap the two clips or unfasten (press down and turn clockwise) the two screws that hold on the distributor cap. Position the cap out of the way or remove the spark plug wires from the spark plugs (twist and pull on the boots), the coil wire from the coil and remove the cap and wires from the car.
2. Turn the engine (use a wrench on the crank pulley or bump the starter) until the rotor points to number one cylinder position and the timing marks on the crankshaft pulley and the timing tab (refer to chapter two) are aligned at TDC.
3. Mark the distributor body to the exact place the rotor points. Matchmark both the distributor mounting flange and the engine block.
4. Disconnect the negative battery cable from the battery.
5. Disconnect the distributor primary wire or wiring harness. Remove the vacuum line (lines) from the advance unit. Loosen and remove the retaining nut from the mounting stud. Lift the distributor straight from the engine. The rotor may turn away slightly from your mark on the distributor body, make note of how far. When you reinstall the distributor this is the point to position the rotor.

INSTALLATION

If the engine has not been disturbed, i.e. the crankshaft was not turned, then reinstall the distributor in the reverse order of removal. Carefully align the matchmarks. Always check the ignition timing whenever the distributor has been removed.

If the engine has been disturbed, i.e. rotated while the distributor was out, proceed as follows:

1. Turn the crankshaft so that the No. 1 piston is on the compression stroke and the timing marks are aligned (see chapter two).
2. Turn the distributor shaft so that the rotor points approximately 15 degrees before the rotor position that you marked on the distributor. If you did not mark the distributor, line up the factory marks on the shaft and housing.
3. Insert the distributor into the engine. On

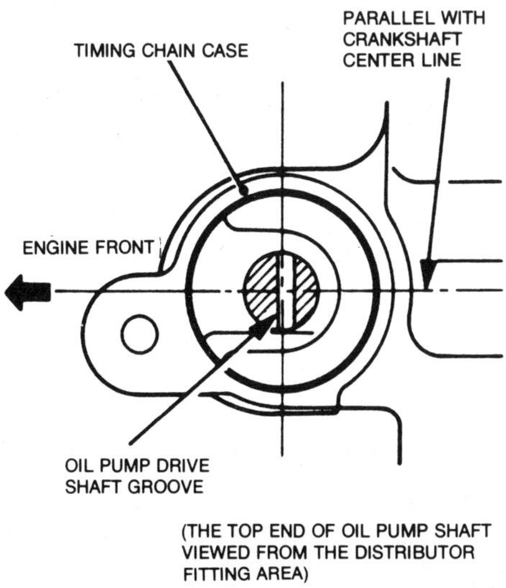

1600cc engine block mounted distributor, oil pump gear alignment

block mounted distributors, if you meet resistance and slight wiggling of the rotor shaft does not help seat the distributor; the oil pump gear is probably out of alignment.

NOTE: *Do not force the distributor.*

Remove the distributor, and using a long screwdriver, turn the oil pump shaft so that it is vertical to the centerline of the crankshaft on 1600 cc engines; parallel on 2000 cc engines (see illustrations).

When the distributor seats against the engine block or head, align the matchmarks and install the retaining nut. Do not tighten the retaining nut all the way, you still have to check the timing. Reinstall the rotor, cap, plug wires,

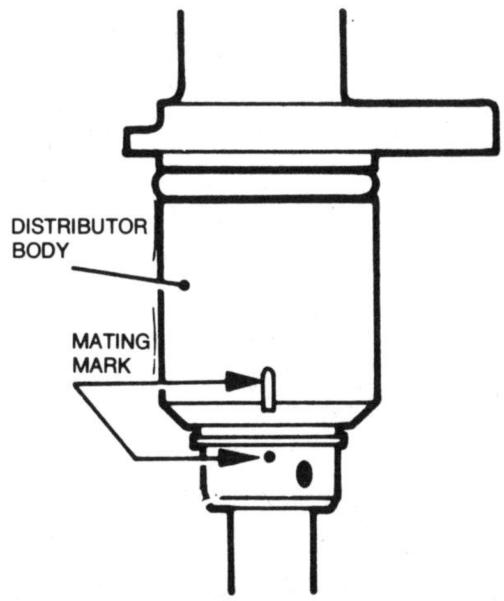

Alignment of factory markings—distributor housing and drive shaft spacer

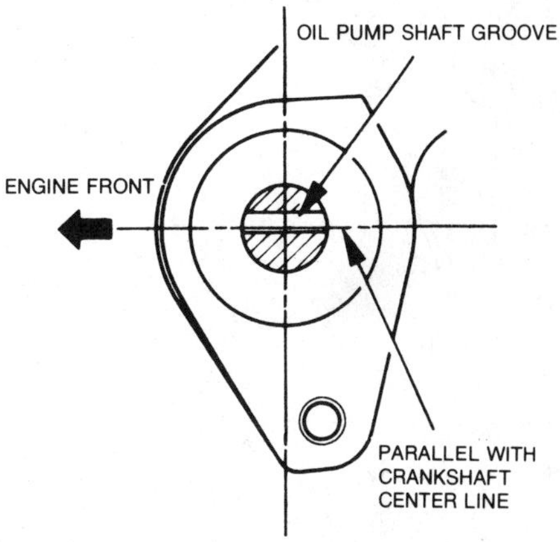

2000cc engine block mounted distributor, oil pump gear alignment

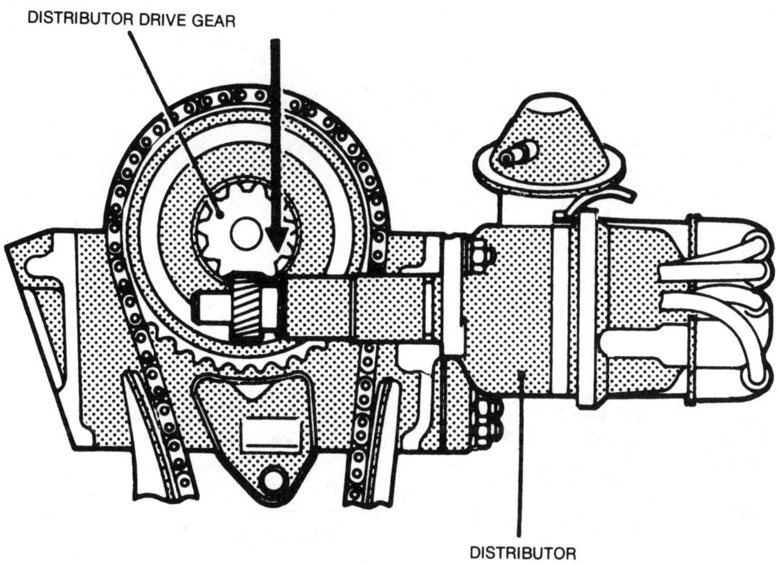

Cylinder head mounted distributor (typical)

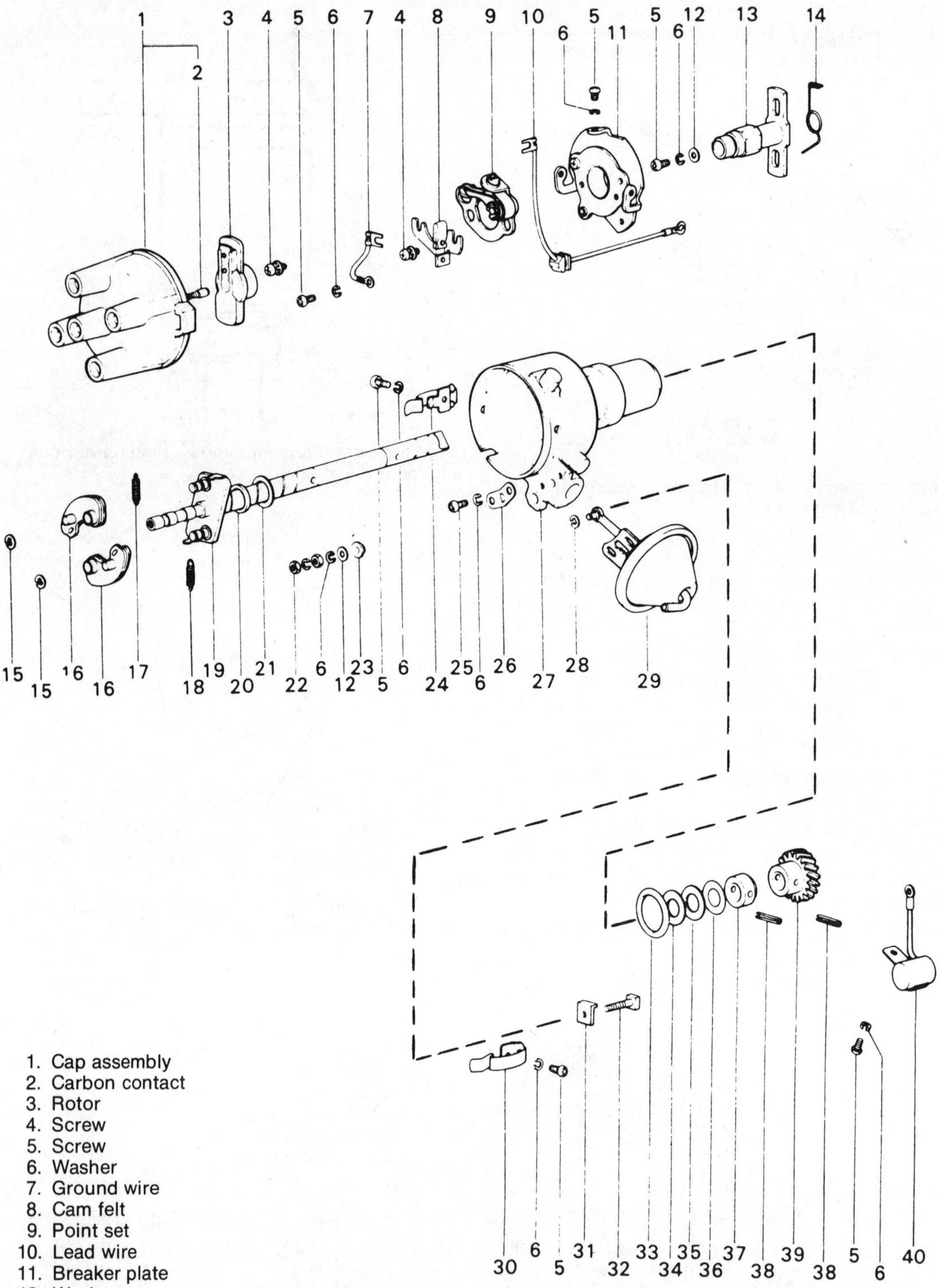

1. Cap assembly
2. Carbon contact
3. Rotor
4. Screw
5. Screw
6. Washer
7. Ground wire
8. Cam felt
9. Point set
10. Lead wire
11. Breaker plate
12. Washer
13. Cam assembly
14. Spring
15. Retaining washer
16. Governor weight
17. Governor spring
18. Governor spring
19. Shaft assembly
20. Spacer
21. Washer
22. Nut
23. Insulator
24. Cap clamp assembly
25. Screw
26. Plate
27. Housing assembly
28. Retaining washer
29. Vacuum unit
30. Cap clamp assembly
31. Insulator
32. Bolt
33. O-ring
34. Washer
35. Washer
36. Washer
37. Thrust collar
38. Pin
39. Gear
40. Condenser

Exploded view of a typical distributor

coil lead, primary lead (or harness) and connect the vacuum hoses. Connect the negative battery cable. Start the engine, allow it to reach operating temperature and check the ignition timing (outlined in chapter two).

Alternator

ALTERNATOR PRECAUTIONS

Your car is equipped with an alternator. Unlike the direct current (DC) generators used on many older cars, there are several precautions which must be strictly observed in order to avoid damaging the unit. They are:

1. Always observe proper polarity of the battery connections) be especially careful when jump starting the car (see chapter one).
2. Never ground or short out alternator or alternator regulator terminals.
3. Never operate the alternator with any of its or the battery's lead wires disconnected.
4. Always remove the battery or at least disconnect the ground cable while charging.
5. Always disconnect the battery ground cable while repairing or replacing an electrical component.
6. Never use a "fast" battery charger to "jump" start a dead battery.
7. Never attempt to "polarize" an alternator.
8. Never subject the alternator to excessive heat or dampness (for instance, steam cleaning the engine).
9. Never use arc-welding equipment on the car with the alternator connected.

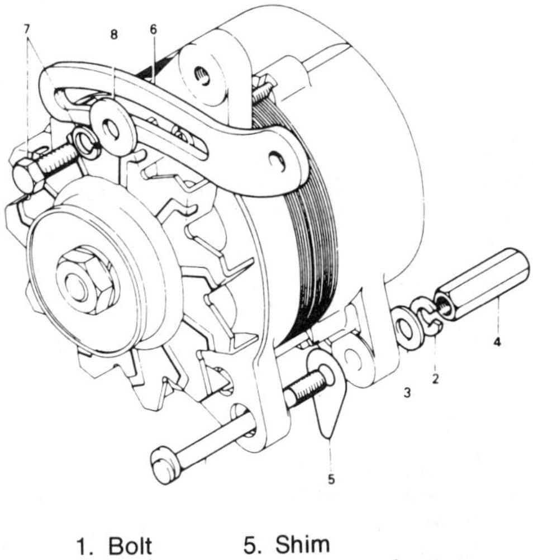

1. Bolt
2. Washer
3. Washer
4. Nut
5. Shim
6. Generator brace
7. Bolt
8. Washer

Alternator mounting (typical)

REMOVAL

1. Disconnect the battery ground (negative) cable. Tag (location) and remove the wires connected to the alternator.
2. Loosen and remove the top mounting nut and bolt. Loosen the bottom mounting nut and bolt. Push the alternator towards the engine and remove the drive belt.
3. Remove the bottom mounting nut and bolt; remove the alternator.

NOTE: *When removing the bottom mounting bolt do not loose any of the adjustment shims.*

INSTALLATION

1. Align the hole in the lower alternator leg with the hole on the mounting and insert the lower bolt. Remember to install any adjustment shims you removed. Install mounting nut but do not tighten at this time.
2. Install top mounting bolt and nut but do not tighten. Install drive belt and pull the alternator away from the engine to put pressure on the belt.
3. Adjust the drive belt to the proper tension and tighten top mounting bolt. Tighten lower mounting nut and bolt. (See chapter one for proper belt adjustment).

REGULATOR

NOTE: *A transistorized (electronic) voltage regulator was introduced in 1979. The regulator is either built into the alternator, or mounted on top. Repairs to the alternator/regulator should be done by a qualified repair shop or dealer.*

REMOVAL AND INSTALLATION—1977–78

1. Disconnect the ground cable from the battery.
2. Disconnect the electrical connector plug.
3. Loosen and remove the two mounting screws. Remove the regulator.
4. Clean the attaching area for proper grounding of the regulator.
5. Install the regulator. Do not overtighten the mounting screws or you will distort the case.
6. Connect the electrical plug and the battery cable.

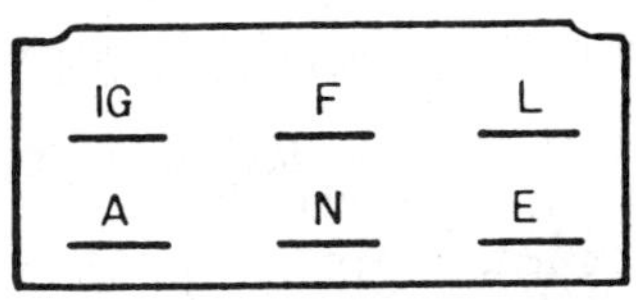

Regulator connector plug showing test terminal locations

CAUTION: *Never operate the engine with the regulator disconnected.*

VOLTAGE CHECK AND ADJUSTMENT

NOTE: *Check the voltage in a garage or other enclosed area if the outside temperature is lower than 68°F.*

1. Connect a voltmeter by inserting clips into the (A) and (E) terminals of the regulator connector plug.

NOTE: *Do not disconnect the plug.*

2. Disconnect one of the battery terminals while the engine is idling to unload the alternator.

3. Increase the alternator speed to approximately 4000 rpm (engine speed of 2000 rpm). The voltmeter should show a value of 14.3–15.8 V at room temperature.

If the reading is not within specifications, adjust the regulator as follows:

1. Carefully remove the two retaining screws and remove the regulator cover.

2. Adjust the constant voltage relay (located on the left) by bending the end of the coil side plate up or down as shown in the figure.

3. Bending the plate down reduces the voltage; bending it up increases the voltage.

4. The field (lamp) relay is adjusted in the same manner as the voltage relay.

5. After adjustment, recheck the voltage with the meter.

6. Install the cover, making sure that the seal is evenly compressed.

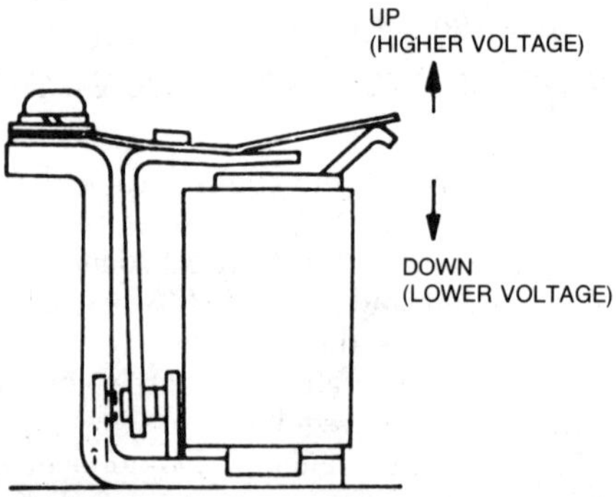

Voltage regulator adjustment (except built-in or alternator mounted

Starter

REMOVAL AND INSTALLATION

1. Disconnect the battery ground (negative) cable from the battery.

2. Jack up and support (use a jackstand) the driver's side of the car.

3. Tag and remove the wires connected to the starter motor. Tagging the wires helps when reinstalling the starter motor.

4. Loosen and remove the two mounting bolts, make sure to support the weight of the starter motor.

5. Before reinstallation of the motor, be sure to clean the mating surfaces of both the starter and the engine block.

6. Reverse the removal procedures to reinstall the starter motor.

STARTER OVERHAUL

Direct Drive Starter

NOTE: *Starter removed from car.*

1. Remove the wire connecting the starter solenoid to the starter.

2. Remove the two screws holding the starter solenoid on the starter-drive housing and remove the solenoid.

3. Remove the two long through bolts at the rear of the starter and separate the armature yoke from the armature.

4. Carefully remove the armature and the starter drive engagement lever from the front bracket, after making a mental note of the way they are positioned along with the attendant spring and spring retainer.

5. Loosen the two screws and remove the rear bracket.

6. Tap the stopper ring at the end of the drive gear engagement shaft in towards the drive gear to expose the snap ring. Remove the snap ring.

7. Pull the stopper, drive gear and overrunning clutch from the end of the shaft. For 1979 models with automatic transmissions, remove the center bracket, spring and spring retainer.

Inspect the pinion and spline teeth for wear or damage. If the engagement teeth are damaged, visually check the flywheel ring gear through the starter hole to insure that it is not damaged. It will be necessary to turn the engine over by hand to completely inspect the ring gear.

Check the brushes for wear. Their service limit length is 0.453 in. Replace if necessary.

Assembly is performed in the following manner. For 1979 models with automatic transmissions, fit the spring retainer, spring and center bracket on the shaft.

8. Install the spring retainer, and spring on the armature shaft.

9. Install the overrunning clutch assembly on the armature shaft.

10. Fit the stopper ring with its open side facing out on the shaft.

11. Install a new snap ring and, using a gear

Alternator, Regulator and Battery Specifications

	Alternator			Regulator ③				
						Charging Light Relay		
Year	Engine	Rated Output	Rotation (Viewed from Pulley)	No Load Adjusted Voltage	Cover Temperature	Off Voltage	On Voltage	Battery Capacity Ampere-Hour
1977	All	45A @ 12V	Clockwise	14.5 to 15.3V	68°F–20°C	4.2 to 5.2V ②	0.5 to 3.0V ②	60
1978–83	1400, 1600	45A @ 12V	Clockwise	14.5 to 15.3V	68°F–20°C	4.0 to 5.8V	0.5 to 3.5V	①④
	2000, 2600	50A @ 12V ⑤	Clockwise	14.5 to 15.3V	68°F–20°C	4.2 to 5.2V	0.5 to 3.0V	①④

① Coupe 1600 MT: 45 A.H.
AT: 60 A.H.
Sedan all models 60 A.H.
Hatchback 1600 MT, AT 60 A.H.
2000 MT 45 A.H.
AT 60 A.H.
② 1600 W/SS, off voltage 4.0 to 5.8V
on voltage 0.5 to 3.5V
③ All models are equipped with sealed voltage regulators which cannot be adjusted if the readings vary from the specifications.
④ '82 USA: Champ-45 amp
Sapporo-50 amp
'82 Canada: Champ-60 amp
Sapporo-55 amp
⑤ '83: 55A @ 12V

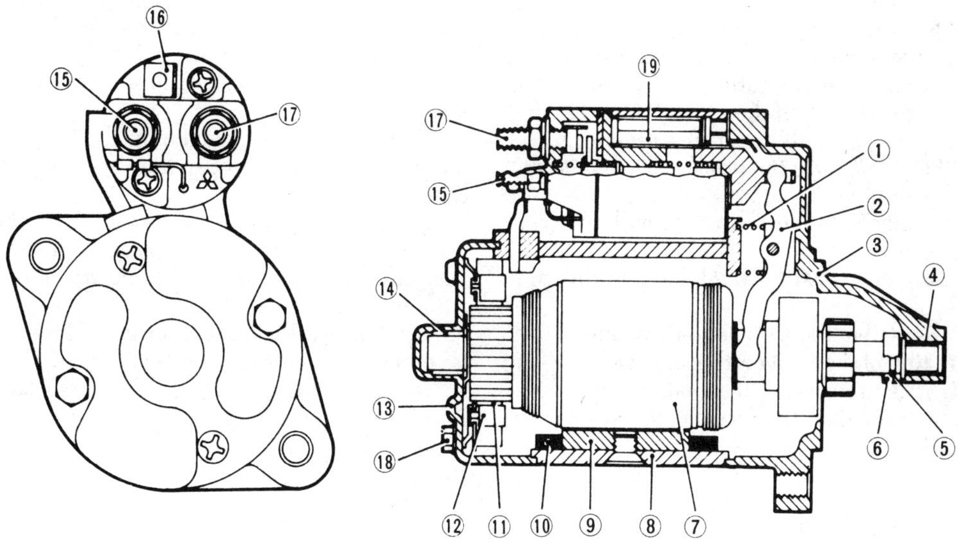

1. Spring
2. Lever
3. Front bracket
4. Bearing
5. Ring
6. Stopper
7. Armature
8. Yoke
9. Pole
10. Field coil
11. Brush
12. Brush holder
13. Rear bracket
14. Bearing
15. Terminal "M"
16. Terminal "S"
17. Terminal "B"
18. Through bolt
19. Magnetic switch

Starter motor—direct drive type

Starter Specifications

Year	Engine (cc) and Transmission	No Load Test			Load Test ⑤				Stall Test			Brush Spring Tension (lbs.)
		Amp ①	Volts	rpm ②	Amp ①	Volts	Torque ②③	rpm ②	Amp ①	Volts	Torque ③	
1977	1600 MT	53	10.5	5000	150	8.6	2.53	1600	400	6.0	6.73	2.4④
	1600 AT 2000 MT	55	11.0	6500	150	9.6	2.24	2200	560	6.0	10.85	2.4④
	2000 AT	62	11.0	4500	200	9.2	3.83	1600	730	6.0	18.08	2.4④
1978–83	1400, 1600 MT	53	10.5	5000	150	8.6	2.53	1600	400	6.0	6.73	3.3
	1600 AT 2000 MT	55	11.0	6500	150	9.6	2.24	2200	560	6.0	10.85	3.3
	2000 AT 2600 All	62	11.0	4500	200	9.2	3.83	1600	730	6.0	18.08	3.3

① Less than
② More than
③ Ft. lbs.
④ 1977—3.3 lbs.
MT: Manual transmission
AT: Automatic transmission
Brush length, all
Max.: .669 in.
Min.: .453 in.
Pinion drive to stopper gap, all: 0 to .079 in.
⑤ 1982–83 no load test:
1600 M/T, 2000 A/T, 2600 M/T = 60 amps, 11.5 volts, 6500 rpm.
2600 A/T = 90 amp, 11.5 volts, 3,300 rpm

puller, pull the stopper ring into place over the snap ring.

12. Fit the small washer on the front end of the armature shaft.

13. Fit the engagement lever into the overrunning clutch and refit the armature into the front housing.

14. Fit the engagement lever spring and spring retainer into place and slide the armature yoke over the armature. Make sure you position the yoke with the spring retainer cutout space in line with the spring retainer.

NOTE: *Make sure the brushes are seated on the commutator.*

15. Replace the rear bracket and two retainer screws.

16. Install the two through bolts in the end of the yoke.

17. Refit the starter solenoid, making sure you fit the plunger over the engagement lever. Install the screws and connect the wire running from the starter yoke to the starter solenoid.

Gear Reduction Type

1. Remove the wire connecting the starter solenoid to the starter.

2. Remove the two screws holding the solenoid and, pulling out, unhook it from the engagement lever.

3. Remove the two through bolts in the end of the starter and remove the two bracket screws. Pull off the rear bracket.

NOTE: *Since the conical spring washer is contained in the rear bracket, be sure to take it out.*

4. Remove the yoke and brush holder assembly while pulling the brush upward.

5. Pull the armature assembly out of the mounting bracket.

6. On the side of the armature mounting bracket there is a small dust shield held on by two screws; remove the shield. Remove the snap ring and washer located under the shield.

7. Remove the remaining bolts in the mounting bracket and separate the reduction case.

NOTE: *Several washers will come out of the reduction case when you separate it. These adjust the armature end play; do not lose them.*

8. Remove the reduction gear, lever and lever spring from the front bracket.

9. Use a brass drift or a deep socket to knock the stopper ring on the end of the shaft in toward the pinion. Remove the snap ring. Remove the stopper, pinion and pinion shaft assembly.

10. Remove the ball bearings at both ends of the armature.

NOTE: *The ball bearings are pressed into the front bracket and are not replaceable. Replace them together with the bracket.*

Inspect the pinion teeth for wear or damage. If the pinion drive teeth are damaged, visually check the engine flywheel ring gear. Check the flywheel ring gear by looking through the starter motor mounting hole. It

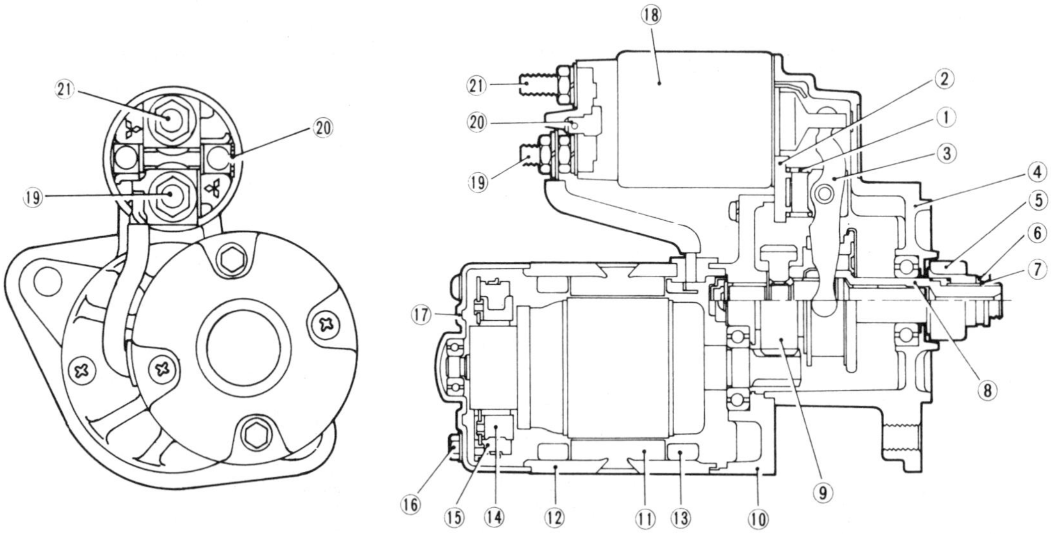

1. Lever spring
2. Packing
3. Lever
4. Front bracket
5. Pinion
6. Stopper
7. Ring
8. Pinion shaft assembly
9. Gear
10. Center bracket
11. Pole
12. Yoke
13. Field coil
14. Brush
15. Brush holder
16. Through Bolt
17. Rear bracket
18. Magnetic switch
19. Terminal "M"
20. Terminal "S"
21. Terminal "B"

Starter motor—gear reduction type

will be necessary to turn the engine over by hand to completely inspect the ring gear.

Check the starter brushes for wear. Their service limit length is .453 in. Replace if necessary.

Assembly is the reverse of disassembly procedure. Be sure to replace all the adjusting and thrust washers that you removed. When replacing the rear bracket, fit the conical spring pinion washer with its convex side facing out. Make sure that the brushes seat themselves on the commutator.

Battery

REMOVAL AND INSTALLATION

1. Loosen the battery cable clamping nuts, negative (ground) cable first. Spread the battery cable terminals (or use a cable terminal puller). Remove the negative cable and then the positive cable.
2. Remove the battery hold-down frame nuts and the frame.
3. Put on work gloves or use a battery carrier and lift the battery from the engine compartment.

CAUTION: *Be careful not to tip the battery and spill acid on yourself or the car during removal. Automotive batteries contain a sulphuric acid electrolyte which is harmful to skin, clothing and paint finishes.*

4. To install the battery, carefully fit the battery into the engine compartment holder. Install the hold-down frame and tighten the retaining nuts.
5. Lightly coat the battery cables with petroleum jelly. Install the positive cable first, then the negative cable.

ENGINE MECHANICAL

Design

Your car engine is a compact, in-line four-cylinder powerplant. The engine block is a special cast iron alloy; the cylinder head and timing case cover are aluminum alloy. The engine is "undersquare" i.e., the stroke is larger than the bore. With the design, the surface area-to-volume ratio is smaller, which helps minimize hydrocarbons emissions. Five main bearings support the forged steel crankshaft. Forged connecting rods attach the aluminum pistons to the crankshaft. Full floating pistons pins are used and are offset on the thrust side to minimize piston slap. Later model engines, in the United States, have the "MCA-Jet" system which allows better combustion (less emissions) and improved fuel economy through the use of a "jet" valve in each of the cylinders (see chapter four for details).

General Engine Specifications

Year	Engine Displacement Cu. In. (cc)	Carburetor Type	Horsepower @ rpm	Torque @ rpm (ft. lbs.)	Bore x Stroke (In.)	Compression Ratio	Oil Pressure (psi)
1977–78 ①	97.5 (1600)	1 x 2 bbl	83 @ 5500	89 @ 3500	3.03 x 3.39	8.5:1	57–71
	97.5 (1600) ②	1 x 2 bbl	83 @ 5500	89 @ 3500	3.03 x 3.39	8.5:1	50–64
	121.7 (2000) ②	1 x 2 bbl	96 @ 5500	109 @ 3500	3.31 x 3.54	8.5:1	50–64
1979–83	86.0 (1400)	1 x 2 bbl	70 @ 5200	78 @ 3000	2.91 x 3.23	8.8:1	50–64
	97.5 (1600)	1 x 2 bbl	77 @ 5200	87 @ 3000	3.03 x 3.39	8.5:1	50–64
	121.7 (2000)	1 x 2 bbl	93 @ 5200	108 @ 3000	3.31 x 3.54	8.5:1	50–64
	155.9 (2600)	1 x 2 bbl	105 @ ③ 5000	139 @ ③ 2500	3.59 x 3.86	8.2:1	50–64

① California emission:
97.5 (1600) MT: 80 @ 5500 HP
87 @ 3500 torque
AT: 78 @ 5500 HP
83 @ 3500 torque
121.7 (2000) All: 93 @ 5500 HP
106 @ 3500 torque

MT—Manual transmission
AT—Automatic transmission
② silent shaft
③ 1983: 100 @ 5000; 137 @ 2500

Crankshaft and Connecting Rod Specifications

All measurements are given in inches

Year	Engine Displacement (cc)	Crankshaft: Main Brg Journal Dia	Crankshaft: Main Brg Oil Clearance	Crankshaft: Shaft End-Play	Crankshaft: Thrust on No.	Connecting Rod: Journal Diameter	Connecting Rod: Oil Clearance	Connecting Rod: Side Clearance
1977–83	1400	1.8898	0.0008–0.0028	0.002–0.007	3	1.6535	0.0004–0.0024	0.004–0.010
	1600	2.2441	0.0008–0.0028	0.002–0.007	3	1.7717	0.0004–0.0028	0.004–0.010
	2000	2.5984	0.0008–0.0028	0.002–0.007	3	2.0866	0.0008–0.0028	0.004–0.010
	2600	①	0.0008–0.0028	0.002–0.007	3	2.0866	0.0008–0.0028	0.004–0.010

① 1977–79: 2.5984
From 1980: 2.3622

Piston and Ring Specifications

All measurements in inches

Year	Engine Displacement (cc)	Piston Clearance	Ring Gap: Top Compression	Ring Gap: Bottom Compression	Ring Gap: Oil Control	Ring Side Clearance: Top Compression	Ring Side Clearance: Bottom Compression	Ring Side Clearance: Oil Control
1977–83	1400, 1600	0.0008–0.0016	0.008–0.016	0.008–0.016	0.008–0.020	0.0012–0.0028	0.0008–0.0024	—
	2000 2600	0.0008–0.0016	0.010–0.017 ①	0.010–0.017 ①	0.008–0.035	0.0024–0.0039	0.0008–0.0024	—

① 1982–83; (2600): 0.010–0.018

Torque Specifications

All readings in ft. lbs.

Year	Engine Displacement (cc)	Cylinder Head Bolts	Rod Bearing Bolts	Main Bearing Bolts	Crankshaft Pulley Bolt	Flywheel to Crankshaft Bolts	Manifold	
							Intake	Exhaust
1977–83	1400 1600	51–54 (cold)	24–25	37–39	44–50 ②	94–101 ①	11–14	11–14
	2000	65–72 (cold)	33–34	55–61	80–94	94–101 ①	11–14	11–14
	2600	65–72 (cold)	33–34	55–61	80–94	94–101 ①	11–14	11–14

① AT drive plate—84–90 ft. lbs.
② 1400: 37–43

Valve Specifications

Year	Engine Displacement (cc)	Seat Angle (deg)	Face Angle (deg)	Spring Test Pressure (lbs. @ in.)	Spring Installed Height (in.)	Stem to Guide Clearance (in.)		Stem Diameter (in.)	
						Intake	Exhaust	Intake	Exhaust
1977–83	1400	45	45	69 @ 1.417	1.417	0.0012–0.0024	0.0020–0.0035	0.315	0.315
	1600	45	45	61 @ 1.470	1.470	0.0010–0.0022	0.002–0.0033	0.315	0.315
	2000	45	45	61 @ 1.590	1.590	0.0010–0.0022	0.002–0.0033	0.315	0.315
	2600	45	45	61 @ 1.590	1.590	0.0012–0.0024	0.002–0.0035	0.315	0.315
1978–83	Jet valve	45	45	5.5 @ .846	.846	—	—	0.1693	

The overhead camshaft is driven (depending on the year or engine) by the crank through a double-row, roller chain or a "cogged" rubber timing belt. The cam runs in five bearings (three on the 1400cc engine) and operates directly on the rocker arms. Intake and exhaust rockers are mounted on separate shafts. The rockers act directly on the valves, which open and close in a hemispherical combustion chamber formed by a "domed" combustion chamber and a flat topped piston. The cylinder head is a cross-flow design. The carburetor feeds into the intake manifold on one side of the engine and the exhaust gases are exited through the exhaust manifold on the opposite side of the engine. This design permits much more efficient cylinder head porting (breathing).

A "silent shaft" engine is also offered. The "silent shaft" engine incorporates two chain or belt driven counterbalance shafts mounted in the cylinder block. The counterbalance shafts rotate at twice crankshaft speed and in opposite directions to balance out the usual vibration associated with a four-cylinder engine.

REMOVAL AND INSTALLATION

Except Front-Wheel Drive Models

The factory recommends removing the engine and transmission as a unit.

1. Drain the cooling system. Open the radiator petcock and the engine drain plug.
2. Disconnect and remove the battery.
3. Disconnect the coil, throttle positioner solenoid, fuel cut-off solenoid, alternator, starter, transmission switch, back-up light switch, and temperature and oil pressure gauge sending units.
4. Remove all air cleaner hoses. Remove the wing nut (and snap clips) and the air cleaner top cover.
5. Remove the two retaining nuts and bracket and remove the air cleaner housing.
6. Disconnect the accelerator cable.
7. Remove and plug the heater hose.
8. Remove the exhaust manifold nuts and drop the pipe down and out of the way.
9. Disconnect the inlet and return fuel lines at the pump. Plug them so that foreign matter is kept out of the fuel system.
10. Disconnect the vacuum hose from the canister purge valve located on the passenger aide firewall. Remove the purge hose which runs from the valve to the intake manifold.
11. Scribe a line around the hood hinges and then remove the hood. Place it away from the work area or it will invariably become scratched or dented.
12. Remove the grille, radiator cross panel, and the radiator. Disconnect and plug the oil

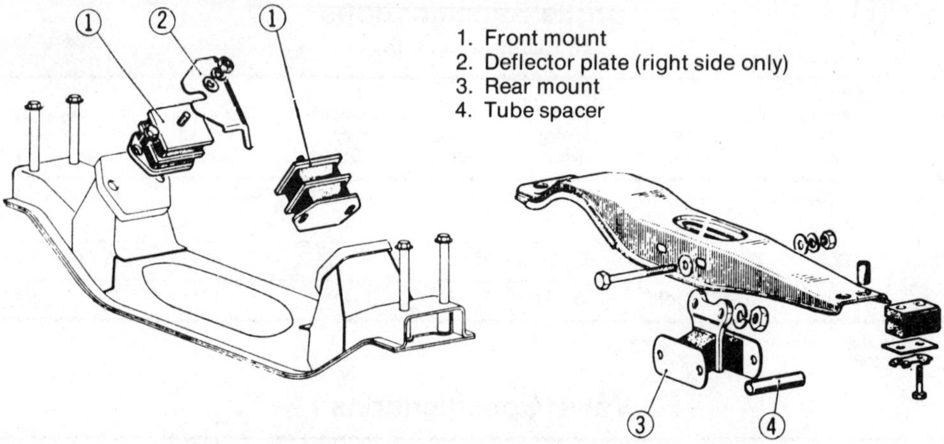

1. Front mount
2. Deflector plate (right side only)
3. Rear mount
4. Tube spacer

Engine mounting (typical) except front wheel drive models

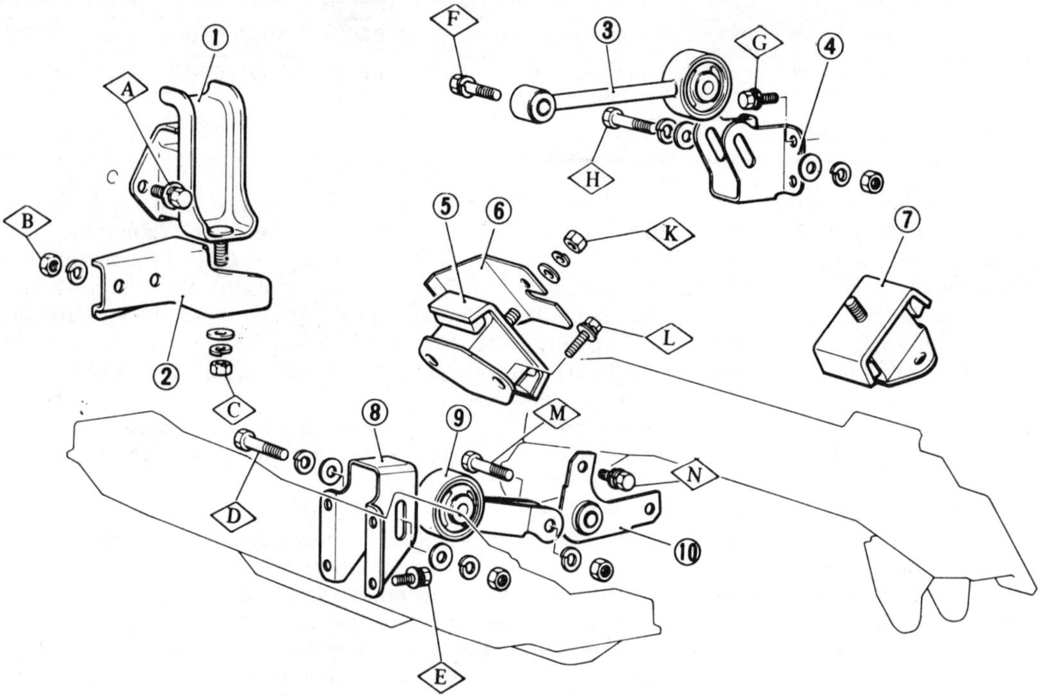

1. Transaxle mount insulator
2. Transaxle mount bracket
3. Roll rod, rear
4. Roll rod bracket
5. Engine mount front insulator
6. Heat protector
7. Engine mount rear insulator
8. Roll rod bracket
9. Roll rod, front
10. Roll rod bracket

Tightening torque NM (ft-lb)

(A) 29 to 41 (22 to 30)
(B) 18 to 25 (13 to 18)
(C) 29 to 34 (22 to 25)
(D) 29 to 41 (22 to 30)
(E) 15 to 22 (11 to 16)
(F) 29 to 41 (22 to 30)
(G) 15 to 22 (11 to 16)
(H) 29 to 41 (22 to 30)
(K) 18 to 25 (13 to 18)
(L) 29 to 41 (22 to 30)
(M) 29 to 41 (22 to 30)
(N) 15 to 22 (11 to 16)

Front wheel drive engine and transaxle mounting through 1980

cooler lines on automatic transmission equipped cars.

13. Jack up the front of the car and support it on jackstands. Remove the splash shield.

14. Drain the engine oil and the transmission oil or fluid. Remove the driveshaft as outlined in Chapter Seven.

15. Disconnect the speedometer cable and back-up switch wire. Remove the neutral switch wire on automatic cars.

On manual cars:

16. Disconnect the clutch cable from the clutch lever.

17. Remove the control rod and the cross-shaft that are located under the transmission.

18. Untie and open the leather shift boot. Pull the rug back. Remove the four retaining bolts and remove the shift lever.

On automatic cars:

19. Disconnect the transmission control rod from the shift linkage.

Then on all models:

20. Attach the lifting device to the two engine brackets provided by the factory, one near the water neck at the front and the other on the passenger's side at the rear.

21. Raise the engine a slight amount and remove the retaining nuts on the side mounts and the rear crossmember mount.

22. Lift the engine out of the compartment by tilting it at approximately a 45° angle.

23. Check the condition of the engine mounts. There are three: left front, right front, and rear. If they are at all questionable, now is the time to replace them.

24. Installing the engine is basically a reverse of the removal procedure, noting the following:

a. Drape heavy rags over the rear of the cylinder head to prevent damaging the firewall when lowering the engine into place.

b. Tighten the two front mounts first and then the rear crossmember mount. All tightening torques are listed in the chart below.

Engine Mounting Torques

Bolt	Torque (ft. lbs.)
Front mount-to-crossmember	15–17 (22–29 for 2000 cc)
Front mount-to-engine bracket nut	15–17
Front engine block-to-bracket bolt	29–36
Rear mount-to-support bracket	7–8.5
Rear mount-to-frame bolt	15–17 (Manual) 9–11.5 (Automatic)
Crossmember-to-body bolt	7–8.5

c. Refill the cooling system, engine crankcase, and the transmission with the proper fluids.

d. Double check everything: fuel lines, coolant lines, electrical connections, and bolt torques. Then, and only then, start the engine and check for correct operation and leaks.

Front-Wheel Drive Models

The factory recommends that the engine and transaxle be removed as a unit.

REMOVAL

1. Disconnect the battery cables (ground cable first) remove battery holddown and battery. Remove the battery tray.

2. Remove the air cleaner assembly. Disconnect the purge control vacuum hose from the purge valve. Remove the purge control valve mounting bracket. Remove the windshield washer reservoir, radiator tank and carbon canister.

3. Drain the coolant from the radiator. Remove the radiator assembly with the electric cooling fan attached. Be sure to disconnect the fan wiring harness and the transmission cooler lines (if equipped).

4. Disconnect the following cables, hoses and wires from the engine and transaxle: Clutch, Accelerator, Speedometer, Heater Hose, Fuel lines, PCV vacuum line, High-altitude compensator vacuum hose (Calif. Models), Bowl vent valve purge hose (U.S.A. Models), Inhibitor switch (Auto Trans), Control Cable (Auto Trans), Starter, Engine Ground Cable, Alternator, Water Temperature, Ignition Coil, Water Temperature Sensor, Back-up Light (Man. Trans), and Oil Pressure Wires.

5. Remove the ignition coil. The next step will be to jack up the car. Before you do this, look around and make sure all wires and hoses are disconnected.

6. Jack up the front of the car after you block the rear wheels. Support the car on jackstands. Remove the splash shield (if equipped).

7. Drain the lubricant out of the transaxle.

8. Remove the right and left drive shafts (see chapter six) from the transaxle and support them with wire. Plug the transaxle case holes so dirt cannot enter.

CAUTION: *The drive shaft retainer ring should be replaced whenever the shaft is removed.*

9. Disconnect the assist rod and the control rod from the transaxle. If the car is equipped with a range selector, disconnect the selector cable.

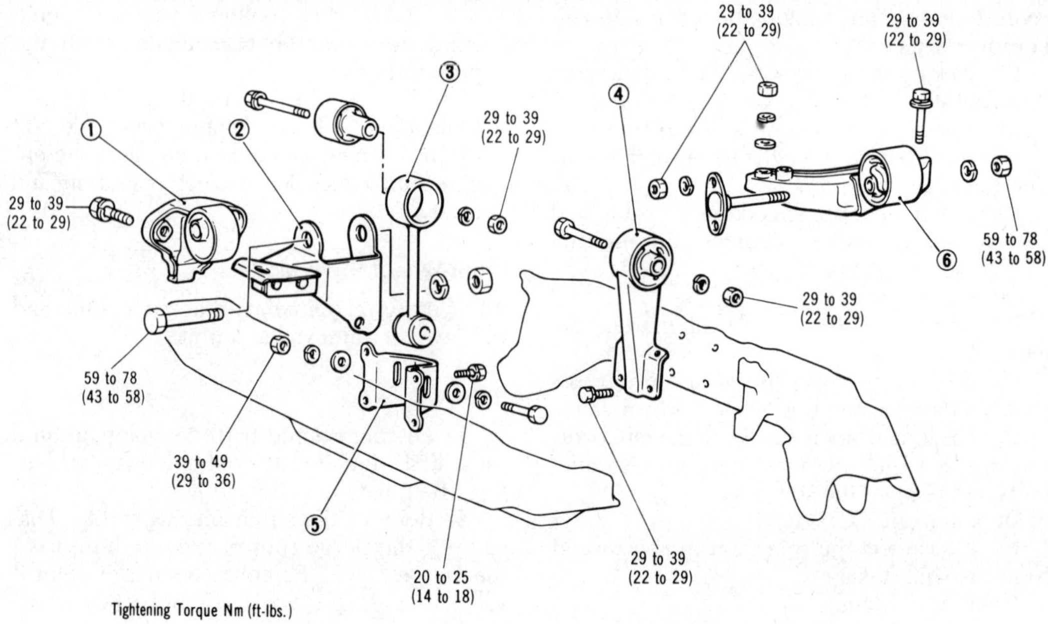

1. Transaxle mount insulator
2. Transaxle mount bracket
3. Front roll rod
4. Rear roll stopper
5. Front roll rod bracket
6. Engine mount bracket

Typical front wheel drive engine and manual transaxle mounting—1981 and later

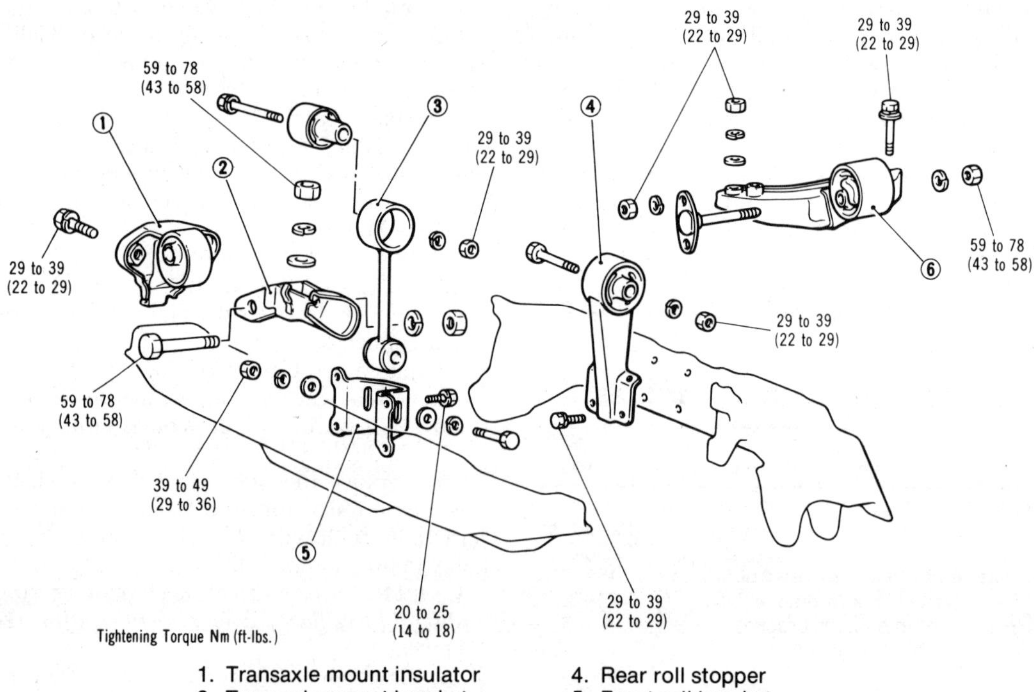

1. Transaxle mount insulator
2. Transaxle mount bracket
3. Front roll rod
4. Rear roll stopper
5. Front roll bracket
6. Engine mount bracket

Typical front wheel drive engine and automatic transaxle mounting—1981 and later

10. Remove the mounting bolts/bolt from the front and rear roll control rods.

11. Disconnect the exhaust pipe from the engine and secure it with wire.

12. Loosen the engine and transaxle mounting bracket nuts.

13. Lower the car.

14. Attach a lifting device and a shop crane or chain hoist to the engine. Apply slight lifting pressure to the engine. Remove the engine and transaxle mounting nuts and bolts.

15. Make sure the rear roll control rod is disconnected. Lift the engine and transaxle from the car.

CAUTION: *Make sure the transaxle does not hit the battery bracket when the engine and transaxle are lifted.*

INSTALLATION

1. Lower the engine and transaxle carefully into position and loosely install the mounting bolts. Temporarily tighten the front and rear roll control rods mounting bolts. Lower the full weight of the engine and transaxle onto the mounts and tighten the nuts and bolts. Loosen and retighten the roll control rods.

2. The rest of the engine installation is the reverse of the removal. Make sure all cables, hoses and wires are connected. Fill the radiator with coolant, the transaxle with lubricant. Adjust the clutch cable and accelerator cable. Adjust the transaxle control rod. Take another check on everything you have done, start the engine and check for leaks.

Rocker Arm (Valve) Cover

REMOVAL AND INSTALLATION

1. Remove air cleaner, air cleaner snorkel, mounting brackets and remove plug wires from mounting clip if necessary. Label vacuum hoses that are disconnected for reinstallation identification.

3. Disconnect breather hoses and remove cover mounting bolts. Remove valve cover.

4. Clean all mounting surfaces. Inspect the breather seal, camshaft end seal and valve cover end seals that are mounted on the cylinder head. Replace as necessary.

5. Install a new valve cover gasket into the mounting slot. Apply RTV sealant to the end seals and install the valve cover. Run engine until normal operating temperature is reached. Shut the engine off and check for oil leaks.

Camshaft and Rocker Arm

To service the rocker arms or camshaft while the cylinder head is still mounted on the cylinder block and in the car.

1. Remove the breather hoses, purge hose and air cleaner. Disconnect the spark plug cables.

2. Turn the crankshaft until number 1 piston is on TDC (refer to chapter two).

3. Refer to the cylinder head removal section in this chapter. Locate the engine size and year of your car as listed between steps 7 and 11. Proceed with the steps pertaining to your

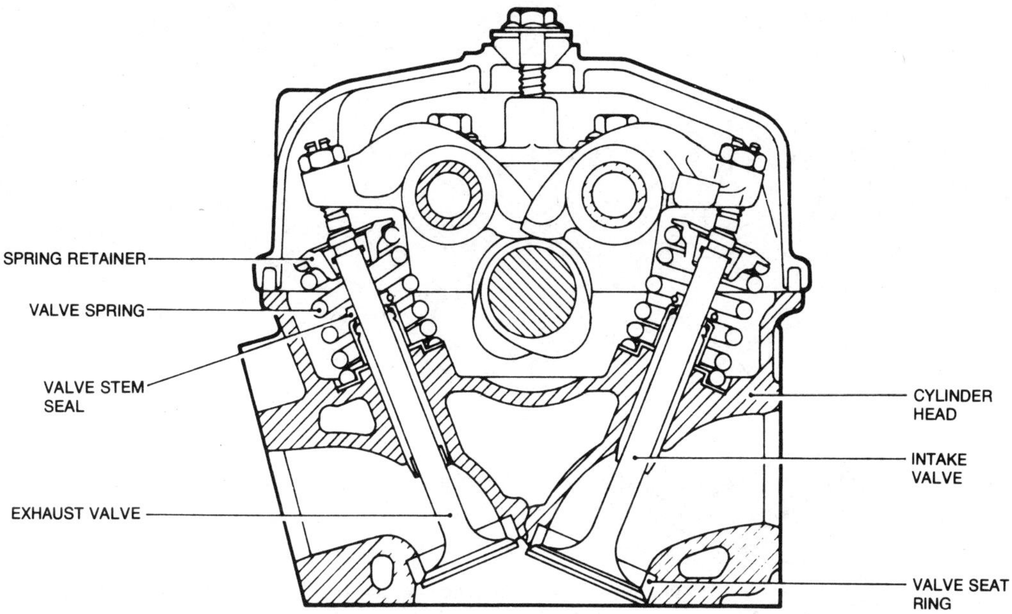

Typical valve arrangement

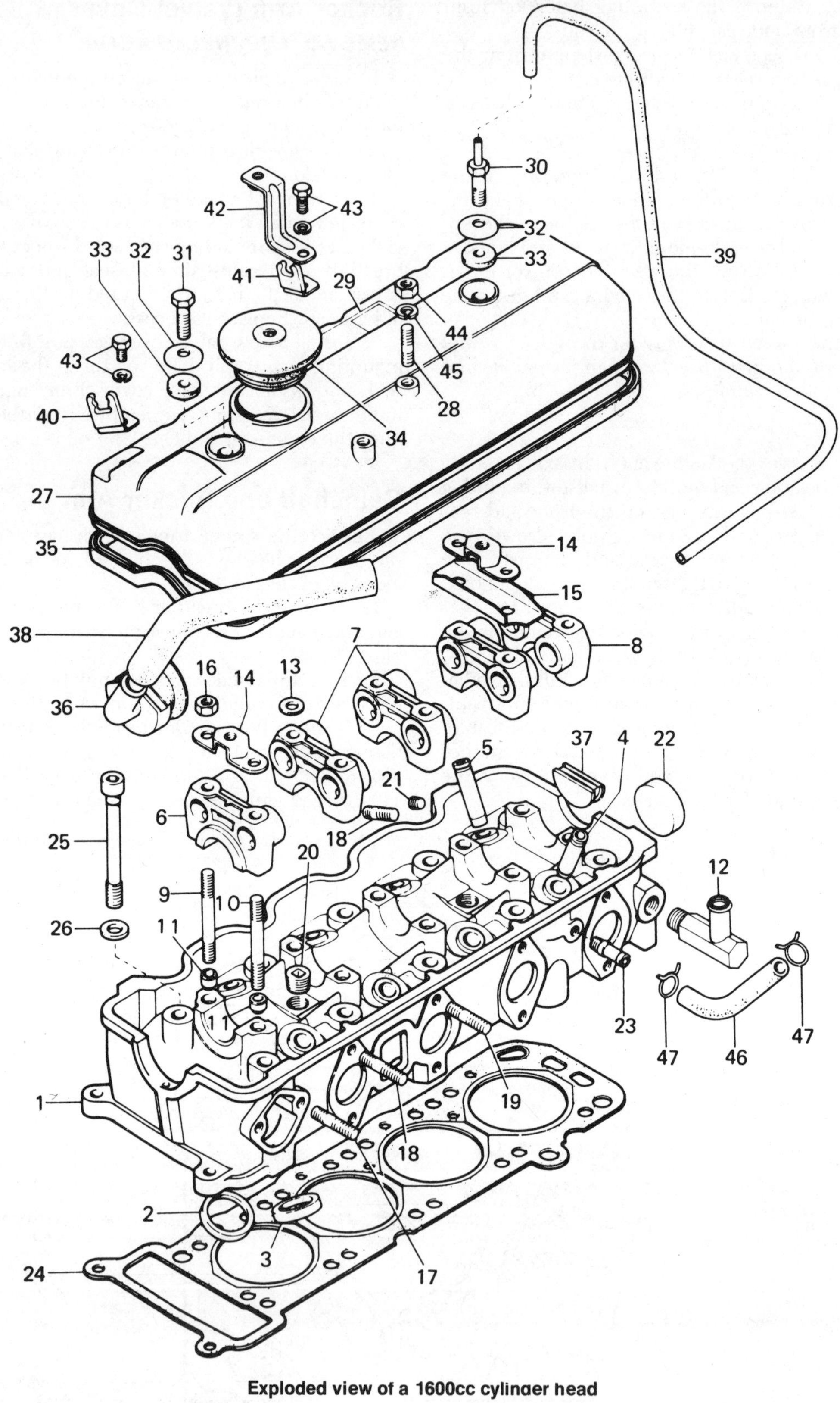

Exploded view of a 1600cc cylinder head

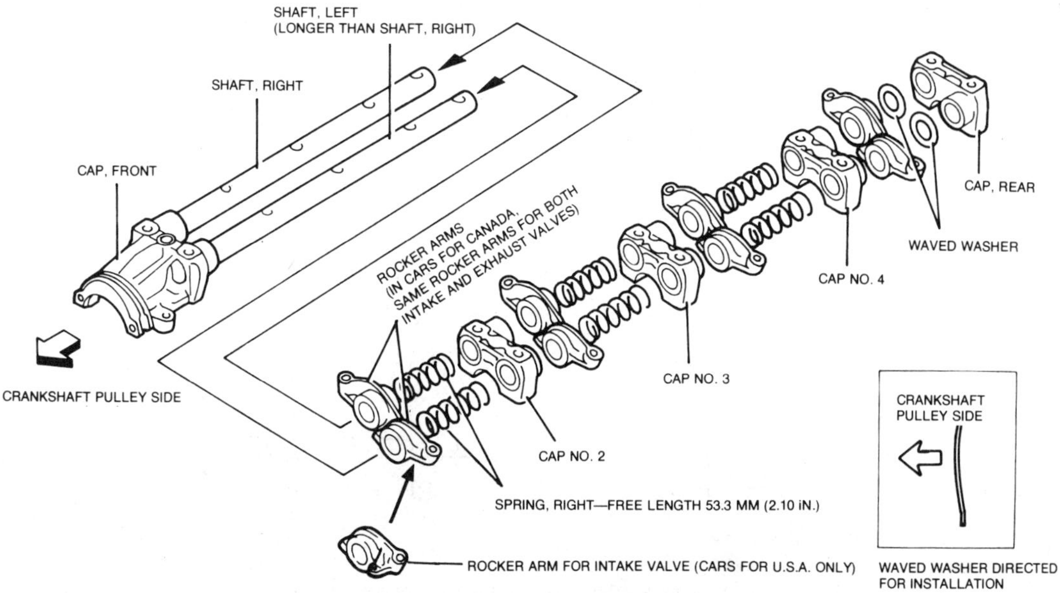

Late model rocker arm shaft assembly (typical)

car and remove the cam sprocket, timing chain/belt and rocker arm cover.

REMOVAL AND INSTALLATION

If the cylinder head has been removed from the car or the proceeding steps have been followed:

1. Match-mark the camshaft/rocker arm bearing caps to their cylinder head location. (Except 1400cc engine).
2. Loosen the bearing cap bolts, or the rocker shaft bolts (1400cc engine) from the cylinder head but *do not* remove them from the caps or shafts. Lift the rocker assembly from the cylinder head as a unit.
3. The rocker arm assembly can be disassembled by the removal of the mounting bolts (and dowel pins on some models) from the bearing caps and or shafts.

NOTE: *a. Keep the rocker arms and springs in the same order as dissembly. The left and right springs have different tension ratings and free length.*

b. Observe the location of the rocker arms as they are removed. Exhaust and intake, right and left are different. Do not get them mixed up.

4. Observe the mating marks and reassemble the units, in the reverse order of removal, after all necessary service has been done.

CAMSHAFT REMOVAL

On all engines except the 1400cc, the camshaft may be lifted from the head after the rocker arm assembly has been removed. Before removal note location of front end drive key or pin for ease of reinstallation.

NOTE: *On some engines, a distributor drive gear and spacer are used on the front of the camshaft.*

The 1400cc engine has three cam bearing bosses cast into the cylnder head. To remove

1. Cylinder head
2. Intake valve seat
3. Exhaust valve seat
4. Intake valve guide
5. Exhaust valve guide
6. Front camshaft bearing cap
7. Center camshaft bearing caps
8. Rear camshaft bearing cap
9. Stud
10. Stud
11. Dowel bushing
12. Joint
13. Washer
14. Valve cover bracket
15. Baffle plate
16. Nut
17. Stud
18. Stud
19. Stud
20. Plug
21. Plug
22. Expansion plug
23. Hose fitting
24. Cylinder head gasket
25. Bolt
26. Washer
27. Valve cover
28. Stud
29. Label
30. Fitting/bolt
31. Bolt
32. Washer
33. Oil seal
34. Oil filler cap
35. Valve cover gasket
36. Breather
37. Seal
38. Breather hose
39. Hose
40. Spark plug wire bracket
41. Spark plug wire bracket
42. Air cleaner bracket
43. Bolt
44. Nut
45. Washer
46. Water hose
47. Clamp

Identification mark	Installation position
1-3	No.1 and 3 cylinders (positions A and C in illustration shown below)
2-4	No.2 and 4 cylinders (positions B and D in illustration shown below)

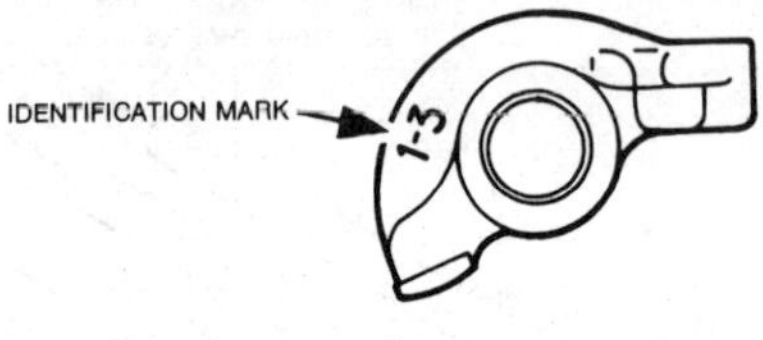

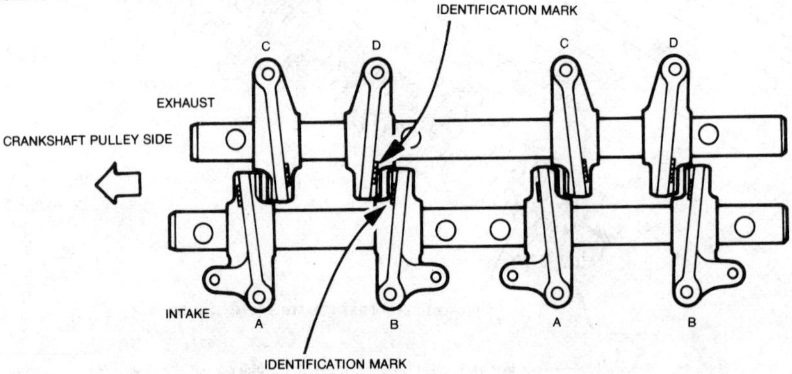

NOTE: ROCKER ARM FOR INTAKE VALVES ON ENGINE FOR U.S.A. IS SHOWN.
ON ENGINE FOR CANADA, ROCKER ARM FOR INTAKE VALVES IS THE SAME AS THAT FOR EXHAUST VALVES.

1400cc rocker arm shaft assembly

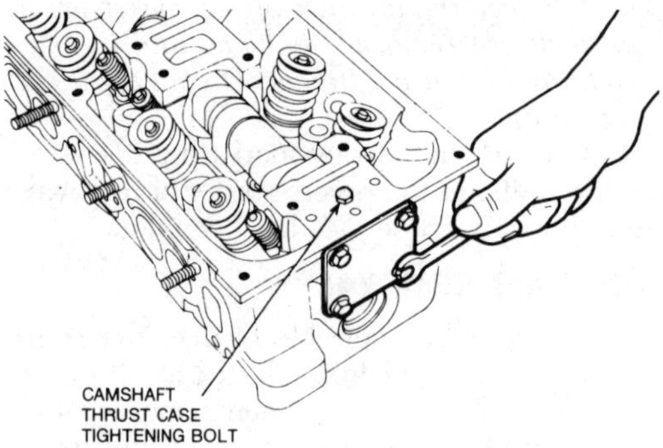

Rear cam cover 1400cc engine

the camshaft (rocker shaft assemblies are already removed) from the 1400cc engine;

1. Remove the cylinder head rear cover (see illustration).
2. Remove the camshaft thrust case tightening bolt located on top of the rear mounting boss.
3. Carefully slide the camshaft and thrust case (attached to rear of cam) out the rear of the cylinder head (transaxle side).

CAMSHAFT INSPECTION—ALL ENGINES

Check the camshaft journals for wear and the lobes for damage. Replace the cam if wear is apparent. If the machined camshaft support surfaces in the cylinder head or rocker shaft mounts are excessively scored or damaged the cylinder head will have to be replaced.

NOTE: *Install a new camshaft oil seal when you have disturbed the camshaft.*

Intake Manifold

REMOVAL AND INSTALLATION

CAUTION: *The intake manifold is made from cast aluminum and should not be removed until the engine is cold.*

1. Remove the air cleaner assembly.
2. Disconnect the fuel line and the EGR lines (models equipped with EGR).
3. Disconnect the throttle positioner and fuel cut off solenoid wires.
4. Disconnect the throttle linkage. On automatic transmission cars disconnect the shift cable linkage.
5. Drain the engine coolant and remove the water hose from the carburetor.
6. Remove the heater and water outlet hoses, disconnect the water temperature sending unit.
7. Loosen and remove the mounting nuts that hold the manifold to the cylinder head. Remove the intake manifold and carburetor as a unit.
8. Clean all mounting surfaces. Before reinstalling the manifold, coat both sides with a gasket sealer.

CAUTION: *If the engine is equipped with the jet air system, take care not to get any sealer into the jet air intake passage.*

9. The rest of the installation is the reverse of the removal.

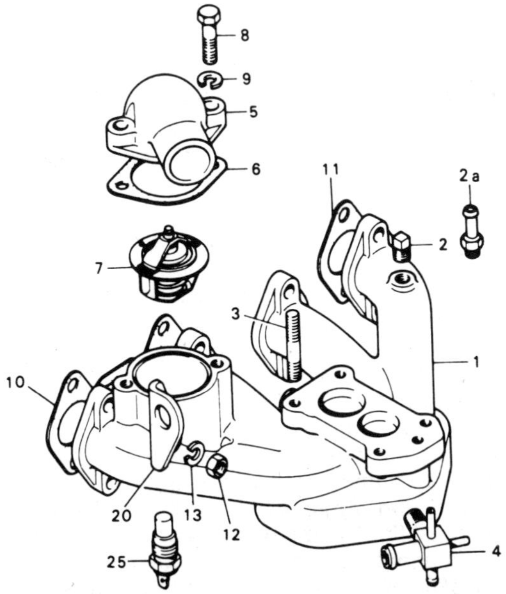

1. Intake manifold
2. Plug
2A. Fitting
3. Stud
4. Union fitting
5. Outlet neck
6. Gasket
7. Thermostat
8. Bolt
9. Lock washer
10. Gasket
11. Gasket
12. Nut
13. Lock washer
20. Engine lift bracket
25. Temperature gauge sending unit

Typical 1600cc engine intake manifold

Exhaust Manifold

REMOVAL AND INSTALLATION

1. Remove the air cleaner assembly.
2. Remove the air duct/heat stove and shroud. Disconnect any EGR or heat lines. Disconnect the reed valve (if equipped).
3. Remove the exhaust pipe support bracket from the engine block (if equipped).
4. Remove the exhaust pipe from exhaust manifold by removing the exhaust pipe flange nuts. It may be necessary to remove one nut or bolt from underneath the car. If you jack up the car, remember to support it on jackstands.
5. On models with a catalytic converter mounted between the exhaust manifold and exhaust pipe; first remove the exhaust pipe, then the secondary air supply pipe.
6. Remove the nuts mounting the exhaust manifold to the cylinder head. On cars without a converter, remove the exhaust manifold. On cars with a converter, slide the manifold from the cylinder head so you have enough room to remove the converter mounting bolts. When the converter is disconnected, remove the exhaust manifold.
7. Installation is the reverse of removal. New gaskets should be used and on some engines, port liner gaskets are used.

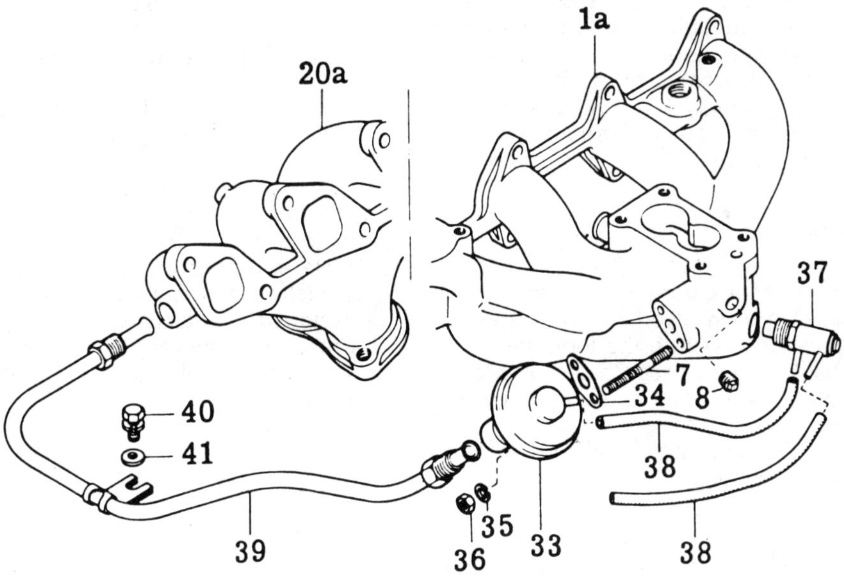

1a. Intake manifold
7. Stud
8. Plug
20a. Exhaust manifold
33. EGR valve
34. Gasket
35. Lockwasher
36. Nut
37. Thermo valve
38. Hose
39. EGR pipe
40. Bolt
41. Washer

Typical 2000cc engine manifolds

ENGINE OVERHAUL

Most engine overhaul procedures are fairly standard. In addition to specific parts replacement procedures and complete specifications for your individual engine, this chapter also is a guide to accepted rebuilding procedures. Examples of standard rebuilding practice are shown and should be used along with specific details concerning your particular engine.

Competent and accurate machine shop services will ensure maximum performance, reliability and engine life. Procedures marked with the symbol shown above should be performed by a competent machine shop, and are provided so that you will be familiar with the procedures necessary to a successful overhaul.

In most instances it is more profitable for the do-it-yourself mechanic to remove, clean and inspect the component, buy the necessary parts and deliver these to a shop for actual machine work.

On the other hand, much of the rebuilding work (crankshaft, block, bearings, pistons, rods, and other components) is well within the scope of the do-it-yourself mechanic.

Tools

The tools required for an engine overhaul or parts replacement will depend on the depth of your involvement. With a few exceptions, they will be the tools found in a mechanic's tool kit (see Chapter 1). More in-depth work will require any or all of the following:

- a dial indicator (reading in thousandths) mounted on a universal base
- micrometers and telescope gauges
- jaw and screw-type pullers
- scraper
- valve spring compressor
- ring groove cleaner
- piston ring expander and compressor
- ridge reamer
- cylinder hone or glaze breaker
- Plastigage®
- engine stand

Use of most of these tools is illustrated in this chapter. Many can be rented for a one-time use from a local parts jobber or tool supply house specializing in automotive work.

Occasionally, the use of special tools is called for. See the information on Special Tools and the Safety Notice in the front of this book before substituting another tool.

Inspection Techniques

Procedures and specifications are given in this chapter for inspecting, cleaning and assessing the wear limits of most major components. Other procedures such as Magnaflux and Zyglo can be used to locate material flaws and stress cracks. Magnaflux is a magnetic process applicable only to ferrous materials. The Zyglo process coats the material with a flourescent dye penetrant and can be used on any material. Check for suspected surface cracks can be more readily made using spot check dye. The dye is sprayed onto the suspected area, wiped off and the area sprayed with a developer. Cracks will show up brightly.

Overhaul Tips

Aluminum has become extremely popular for use in engines, due to its low weight. Observe the following precautions when handling aluminum parts:

- Never hot tank aluminum parts (the caustic hot-tank solution will eat the aluminum)
- Remove all aluminum parts (identification tag, etc.) from engine parts prior to hot-tanking.
- Always coat threads lightly with engine oil or anti-seize compounds before installation, to prevent seizure.
- Never over-torque bolts or spark plugs, especially in aluminum threads.

Stripped threads in any component can be repaired using any of several commercial repair kits (Heli-Coil, Microdot, Keenserts, etc.)

When assembling the engine, any parts that will be in frictional contact must be prelubed to provide lubrication at initial start-up. Any product specifically formulated for this purpose can be used, but engine oil is not recommended as a pre-lube.

When semi-permanent (locked, but removable) installation of bolts or nuts is desired, threads should be cleaned and coated with Loctite® or other similar, commercial non-hardening sealant.

Repairing Damaged Threads

Several methods of repairing damaged threads are available. Heli-Coil® (shown here), Keenserts® and Microdot® are among the most widely used. All involve basically the same principle—drilling out stripped threads, tapping the hole and installing a prewound insert—making welding, plugging and oversize fasteners unnecessary.

Two types of thread repair inserts are usually supplied—a standard type for most Inch Coarse, Inch Fine, Metric Coarse and Metric Fine thread sizes and a spark plug type to fit most spark plug port sizes. Consult the individual manufacturer's catalog to determine exact applications. Typical thread repair kits will contain a selection of prewound threaded inserts, a tap (corresponding to the outside diameter threads of the insert) and an installation tool. Spark plug inserts usually differ because they require a tap equipped with pilot threads and a combined reamer/tap section. Most manufacturers also supply blister-packed thread repair inserts separately in addition to a master kit containing a variety of taps and inserts plus installation tools.

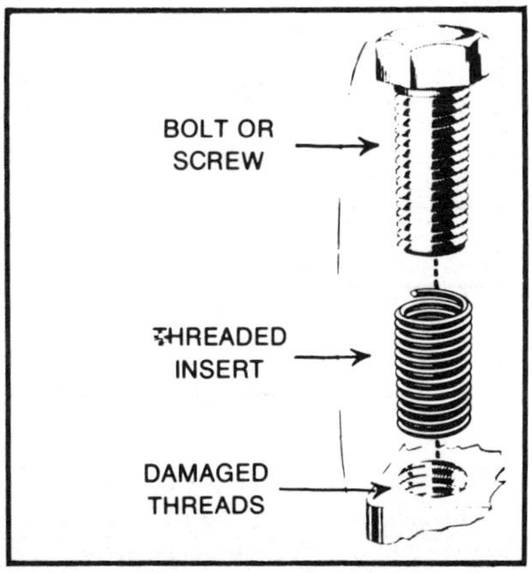

Damaged bolt holes can be repaired with thread repair inserts

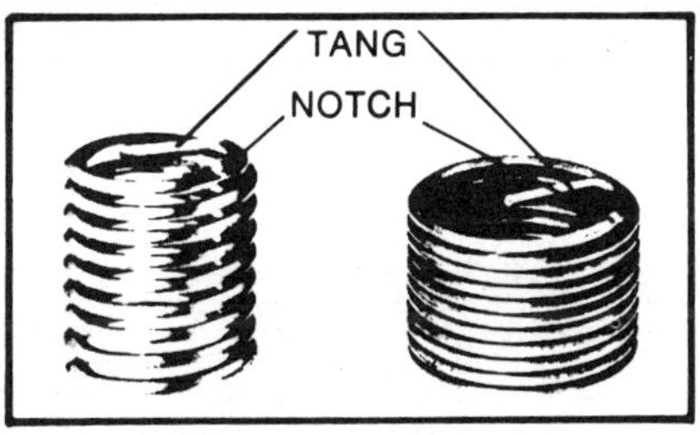

Standard thread repair insert (left) and spark plug thread insert (right)

Before effecting a repair to a threaded hole, remove any snapped, broken or damaged bolts or studs. Penetrating oil can be used to free frozen threads; the offending item can be removed with locking pliers or with a screw or stud extractor. After the hole is clear, the thread can be repaired, as follows:

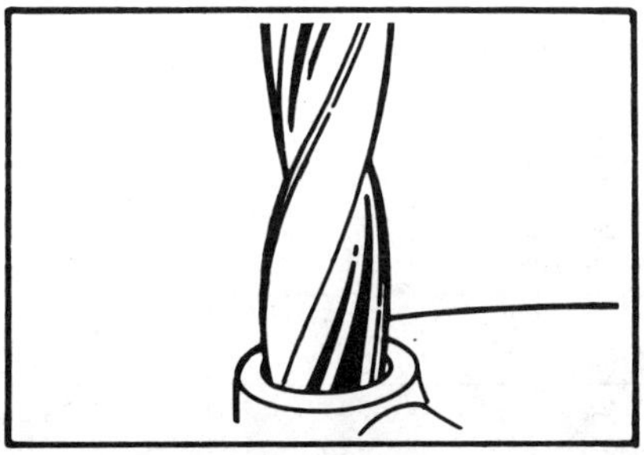

Drill out the damaged threads with specified drill. Drill completely through the hole or to the bottom of a blind hole

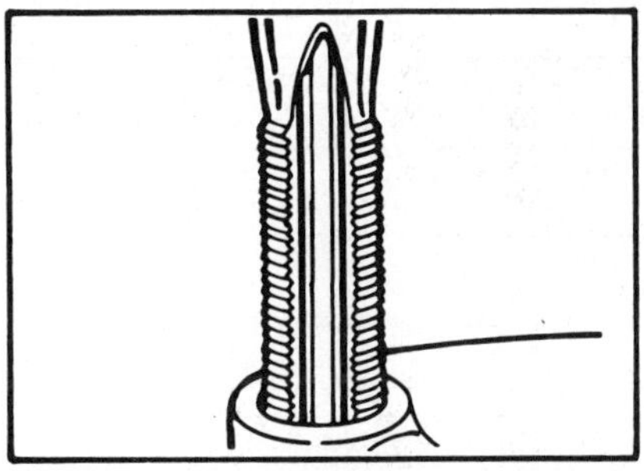

With the tap supplied, tap the hole to receive the thread insert. Keep the tap well oiled and back it out frequently to avoid clogging the threads

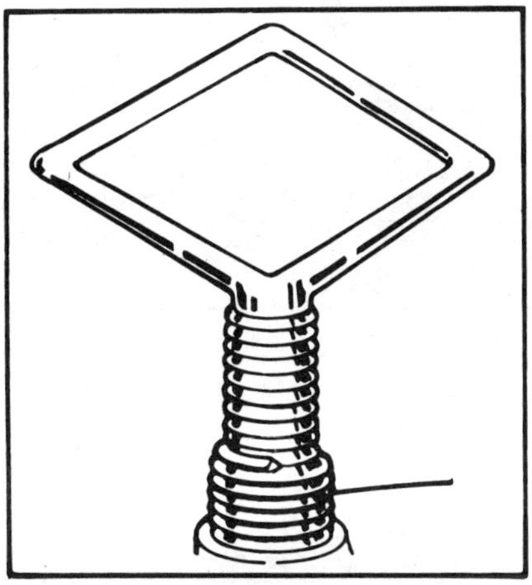

Screw the threaded insert onto the installation tool until the tang engages the slot. Screw the insert into the tapped hole until it is ¼–½ turn below the top surface, After installation break off the tang with a hammer and punch

Standard Torque Specifications and Fastener Markings

In the absence of specific torques, the following chart can be used as a guide to the maximum safe torque of a particular size/grade of fastener.

- There is no torque difference for fine or coarse threads.
- Torque values are based on clean, dry threads. Reduce the value by 10% if threads are oiled prior to assembly.
- The torque required for aluminum components or fasteners is considerably less.

U.S. Bolts

SAE Grade Number	1 or 2			5			6 or 7		
Number of lines always 2 less than the grade number.									
Bolt Size	Maximum Torque			Maximum Torque			Maximum Torque		
(Inches)—(Thread)	Ft./Lbs.	Kgm	Nm	Ft./Lbs.	Kgm	Nm	Ft./Lbs.	Kgm	Nm
¼—20	5	0.7	6.8	8	1.1	10.8	10	1.4	13.5
—28	6	0.8	8.1	10	1.4	13.6			
5/16—18	11	1.5	14.9	17	2.3	23.0	19	2.6	25.8
—24	13	1.8	17.6	19	2.6	25.7			
⅜—16	18	2.5	24.4	31	4.3	42.0	34	4.7	46.0
—24	20	2.75	27.1	35	4.8	47.5			
7/16—14	28	3.8	37.0	49	6.8	66.4	55	7.6	74.5
—20	30	4.2	40.7	55	7.6	74.5			
½—13	39	5.4	52.8	75	10.4	101.7	85	11.75	115.2
—20	41	5.7	55.6	85	11.7	115.2			
9/16—12	51	7.0	69.2	110	15.2	149.1	120	16.6	162.7
—18	55	7.6	74.5	120	16.6	162.7			
⅝—11	83	11.5	112.5	150	20.7	203.3	167	23.0	226.5
—18	95	13.1	128.8	170	23.5	230.5			
¾—10	105	14.5	142.3	270	37.3	366.0	280	38.7	379.6
—16	115	15.9	155.9	295	40.8	400.0			
⅞— 9	160	22.1	216.9	395	54.6	535.5	440	60.9	596.5
—14	175	24.2	237.2	435	60.1	589.7			
1— 8	236	32.5	318.6	590	81.6	799.9	660	91.3	894.8
—14	250	34.6	338.9	660	91.3	849.8			

Metric Bolts

Relative Strength Marking	4.6, 4.8			8.8		
Bolt Markings	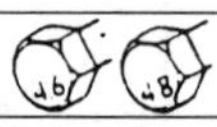			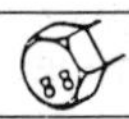		
Bolt Size	Maximum Torque			Maximum Torque		
Thread Size x Pitch (mm)	Ft./Lbs.	Kgm	Nm	Ft./Lbs.	Kgm	Nm
6 x 1.0	2–3	.2–.4	3–4	3–6	.4–.8	5–8
8 x 1.25	6–8	.8–1	8–12	9–14	1.2–1.9	13–19
10 x 1.25	12–17	1.5–2.3	16–23	20–29	2.7–4.0	27–39
12 x 1.25	21–32	2.9–4.4	29–43	35–53	4.8–7.3	47–72
14 x 1.5	35–52	4.8–7.1	48–70	57–85	7.8–11.7	77–110
16 x 1.5	51–77	7.0–10.6	67–100	90–120	12.4–16.5	130–160
18 x 1.5	74–110	10.2–15.1	100–150	130–170	17.9–23.4	180–230
20 x 1.5	110–140	15.1–19.3	150–190	190–240	26.2–46.9	160–320
22 x 1.5	150–190	22.0–26.2	200–260	250–320	34.5–44.1	340–430
24 x 1.5	190–240	26.2–46.9	260–320	310–410	42.7–56.5	420–550

Cylinder Head

The timing chain/belt and the cam gear must be removed and secured together after the engine is turned to No. 1 cylinder at the TDC position. The exception being the 1400cc engine (see following paragraphs). The cylinder head bolts on the 1400 and 1600cc engines require a 5/16 inch Allen socket to remove. On 2000 and 2600cc engines the cylinder head bolts are hex headed.

REMOVAL

CAUTION: *Never remove the cylinder head unless the engine is absolutely cold or the cylinder head will warp.*

1. Turn the crankshaft to put No. 1 piston at top dead center with timing marks aligned (see chapter two).

2. Disconnect the battery ground (negative) cable from the battery. Remove the air cleaner assembly and the attached breather hoses. Drain the radiator coolant. Remove the upper radiator hose and disconnect the heater hoses.

3. Remove the fuel line from the carburetor and fuel pump. Disconnect the accelerator linkage, distributor vacuum lines, purge valve and water temperature gauge wire.

4. Remove the spark plug wires, spark plugs and the fuel pump. If it is necessary to remove the distributor, mark the mounting flange location (see chapter two).

5. Disconnect the exhaust pipe from the exhaust manifold. Remove the exhaust manifold (see exhaust manifold removal).

6. Remove the intake manifold and the carburetor as a unit. (See intake manifold removal.)

NOTE: *During the following procedures, do not turn the crankshaft from TDC.*

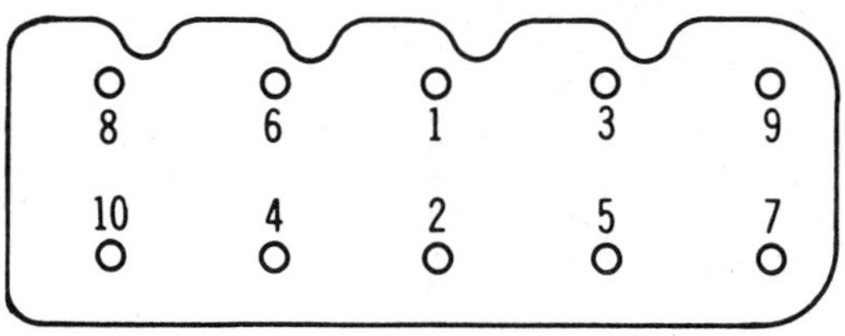

1400 and 1600cc cylinder head bolt tightening sequence

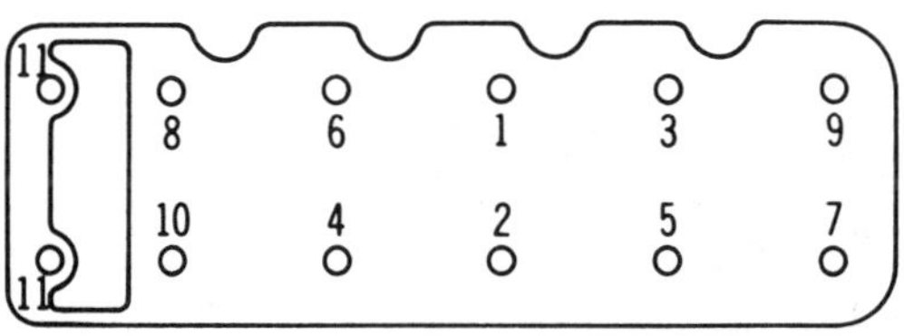

2000 and 2600cc cylinder head bolt tightening sequence

1400 cc Engine 1979–82

7a. Remove the timing belt cover. Be sure the knockout pin (cam sprocket) is at 12 o'clock and the cam sprocket mark and cylinder head pointer aligned at 3 o'clock.

7b. Loosen the timing belt tensioner mounting. Move the tensioner toward the water pump and secure it in that position. Remove the timing belt from the camshaft pulley.

NOTE: *The camshaft pulley need not be removed, and the timing belt may be left mounted on the crankshaft pulley.*

7c. Remove the rocker arm cover.

1600 cc Engine—With or Without Silent Shaft 1977–82

8a. Align the timing mark on the upper under cover of the timing belt with that of the camshaft sprocket.

8b. Match-match the timing belt and the timing mark on the camshaft sprocket with a felt tip pen.

8c. Remove the sprocket and insert a 2 inch piece of timing belt or other material between the bottom of the camshaft sprocket and the sprocket holder on the timing belt lower front cover, to hold the sprocket and belt so that the valve timing will not be changed.

8d. Remove the timing belt upper under cover and the rocker arm cover.

2000 cc and 2600 cc Engines 1977–83

9a. Remove the rocker arm cover.

9b. Position the camshaft sprocket dowel pin at the 2 o'clock position with the crankshaft pulley notch aligned with the timing mark "T" at the front of the timing chain case.

9c. Match the timing chain with the timing mark on the camshaft sprocket.

9d. Remove the camshaft sprocket bolt, distributor, gear and the sprocket from the camshaft.

10. Loosen and remove the cylinder head bolts in two or three stages to avoid cylinder head warpage.

11. Remove the cylinder head from the engine block. Lift the head from the engine, locater pins in the engine block will prevent sliding.

INSTALLATION

1. Clean the cylinder head and block mating surfaces and install a new cylinder head gasket.

2. Position the cylinder head on the engine block, engage the dowel pins and install the cylinder head bolts.

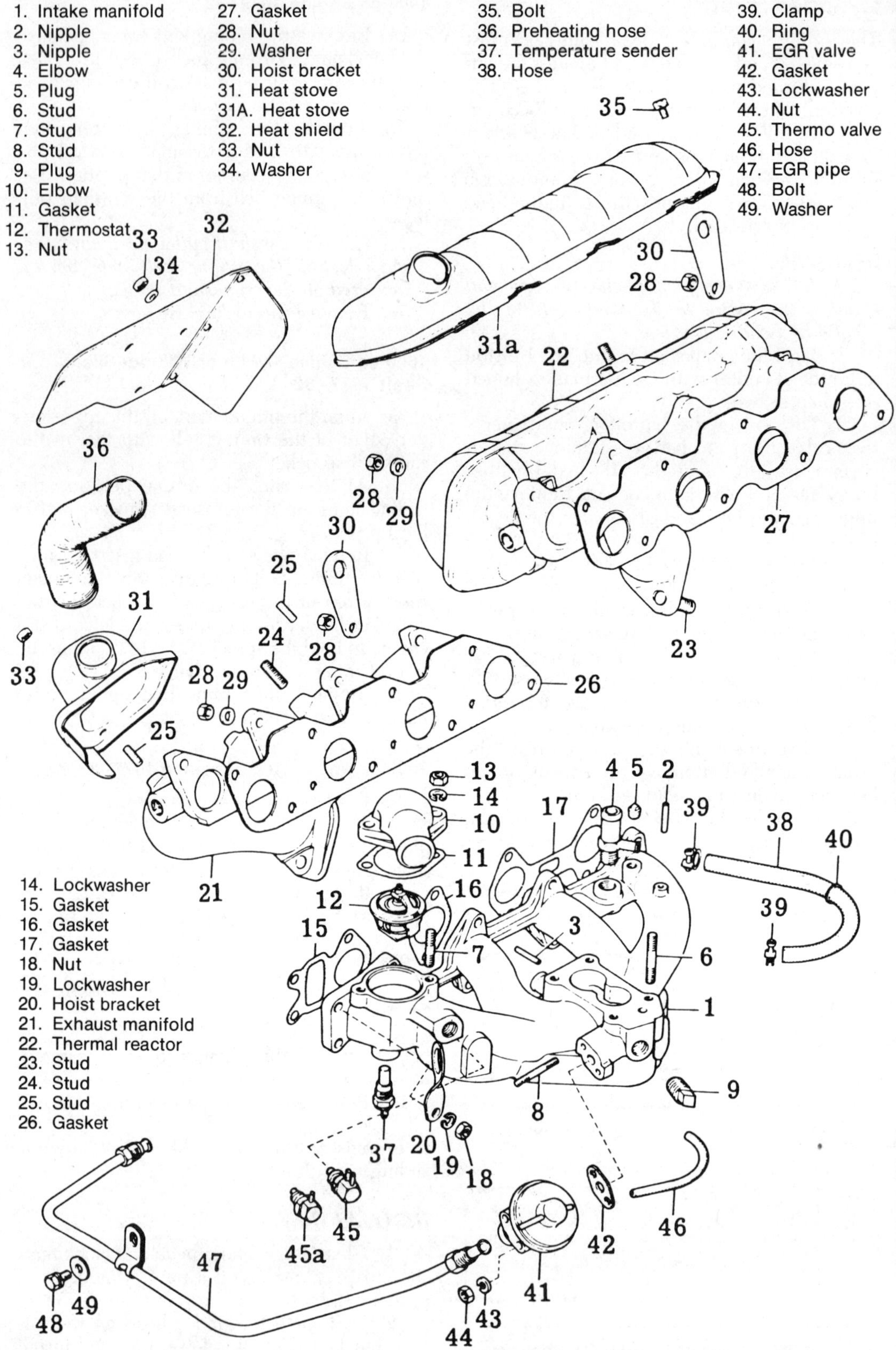

2000cc intake and exhaust manifolds with California thermal reactor shown

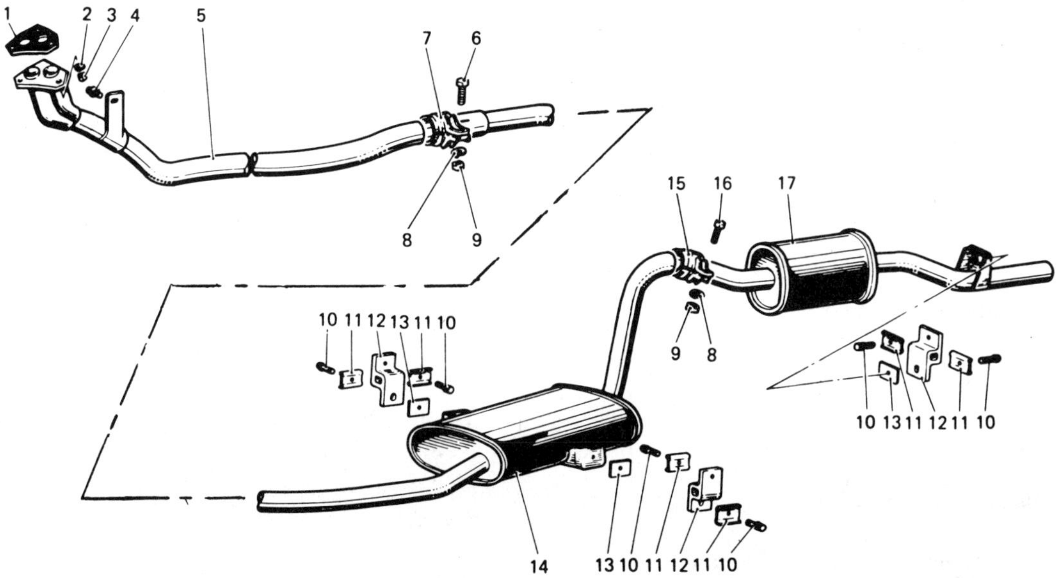

Older sedan and hardtop exhaust system

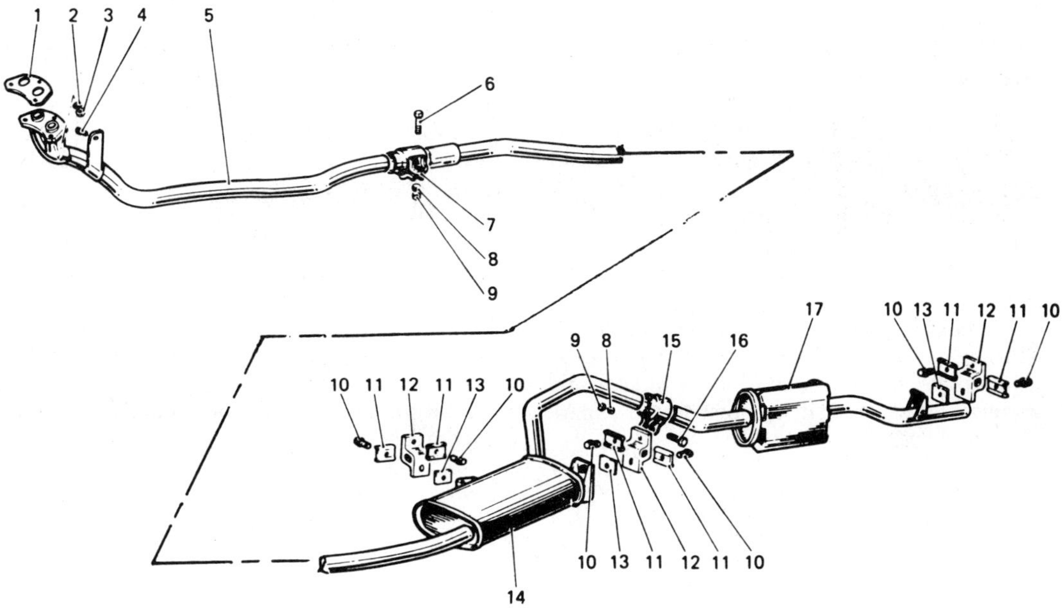

Station wagon exhaust system

1. Manifold gasket
2. Lock washer
3. Nut
4. Bolt
5. Exhaust pipe
6. Bolt
7. Clamp
8. Washer
9. Nut
10. Bolt
11. Shim
12. Hanger
13. Gasket
14. Muffler
15. Clamp
16. Bolt
17. Resonator

Typical exhaust system without a catalytic converter

3. Tighten the head bolts in three stages and then torque to specifications.

4. On 1600cc engines from 1977, install the timing belt upper under cover.

5. Locate the camshaft in the original position. Pull the camshaft sprocket, belt or chain up and install on the camshaft.

NOTE: *If you experience any difficulty while installing the timing chain, belt or sprocket; refer to the timing chain/belt installation section of this chapter.*

If the dowel pin and the dowel pin hole do not line up between the sprocket and the spacer or camshaft, move the camshaft by bumping either of the two projections (provided at the rear of number two cylinder exhaust lobe of the camshaft) with a light hammer or other tool until the hole and pin align. Be certain that the crankshaft does not turn.

6. Install the camshaft sprocket bolt and distributor drive gear and tighten. (The gear is used on 2000cc and 2600cc engines from 1977).

7. Install the timing belt upper front cover and spark plug cable support or timing belt cover, depending on which model you are working on.

8. Apply sealant to the intake manifold gasket on both sides. Position the gasket and install the intake manifold. Tighten the nuts to specification.

CAUTION: *Be sure that no sealant enters the jet air passages on models that are equipped with jet valves.*

9. Install the exhaust manifold gaskets and the exhaust manifold. Tighten the nuts to specifications.

10. Connect the exhaust pipe to the exhaust manifold assembly and tighten the nuts to specifications. Install the fuel pump and purge valve.

11. Install the water temperature gauge wire, heater hoses and the upper radiator hose. Connect the fuel lines, accelerator linkage and vacuum hoses. Install the distributor, spark plugs and spark plug wires.

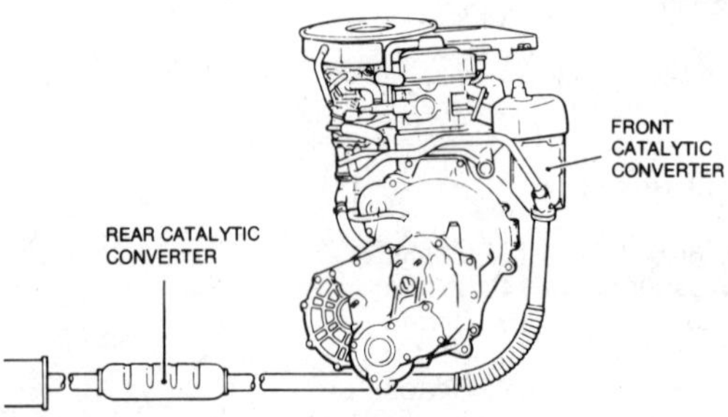

Front wheel drive model showing front and rear converters installed

12. Fill the cooling system. Connect the battery ground (negative) cable.

13. Adjust the valve clearances to the cold engine specifications. (Refer to chapter two).

14. Install the gasket on the rocker arm cover and temporarily install the cover on the engine.

15. Start the engine and allow it to reach normal operating temperature. Stop the engine and remove the rocker arm cover.

16. Adjust the valves to hot engine specifications. See Chapter Two for valve adjustment.

17. Reinstall the rocker arm cover and tighten securely.

18. Install the air cleaner, hoses, purge valve hose and any other removed unit.

OVERHAUL

NOTE: *With the cylinder head removed from the engine, the rocker arm assemblies and camshaft removed, the valves, valve springs and valve stem oil seals can now be serviced.*

Since the machining of valve seats and valves, and the insertion of new valve guides or valve seats may tax the experience and equipment resources of the car owner, it is suggested that the cylinder head be taken to an automotive machine shop for rebuilding.

1. Remove the cylinder head from the car engine (see Cylinder Head Removal). Place the head on a workbench and remove any manifolds that are still connected. Remove all rocker arm assembly parts, if still installed and the camshaft (see Camshaft Removal).

2. Turn the cylinder head over so that the mounting surface is facing up and support evenly on wooden blocks.

3. Use a scraper and remove all of the gasket material and carbon stuck to the head mounting surface. Mount a wire carbon removal brush in an electric drill and clean away the carbon on the valve heads and head combustion chambers.

CAUTION: *When scraping or decarbonizing the cylinder head, take care not to damage or nick the gasket mounting surface or combustion chamber.*

4. Number the valve heads with a permanent felt-tipped marker for cylinder location.

RESURFACING

If the cylinder head is warped resurfacing, by an automotive machine shop, will be required. After cleaning the gasket surface, place a straight-edge across the mounting surface of the head. Using feeler gauges, determine the clearance at the center and along the length between the head and straight-edge. Measure clearance at the center and along the lengths of both diagonals. If warpage exceeds .003 inches in a six inch span, or .006 inches over the total length the cylinder head must be resurfaced.

Jet Valves

REMOVAL AND INSTALLATION

The jet valve can be removed from the cylinder head with the rocker arm either in place or removed. Care must be taken not to twist the socket while removing the valve, it can be easily broken. When installing the valve, the torque is 13.5 to 15.5 ft. lbs.

Valves and Springs

REMOVAL AND INSTALLATION

1. Block the head on its side, or install a pair of head-holding brackets made especially for valve removal.
2. Use a socket slightly larger than the valve stem and keepers, place the socket over the valve stem and gently hit the socket with a plastic hammer to break loose any varnish build-up.
3. Remove the valve keepers, retainer, spring shield (if equipped) and valve spring using a valve spring compressor (the locking C-clamp type is the easiest to use).
4. Do not mix removed parts. Place the parts from each valve in a separate container, numbered and identified for the valve and cylinder.
5. Remove and discard the valve stem oil seal, a new seal will be used at assembly time.
6. Remove the valve from the cylinder head and place, in order, through holes punched in a stiff piece of cardboard or wooden valve holding stick. Number the cardboard or stick in case the numbers marked on the valve head gets rubbed off.
7. Use an electric drill and rotary wire brush to clean the intake and exhaust valve ports, combustion chamber and valve seats. In some cases, the carbon build-up will have to be chipped away. Use a blunt pointed drift for carbon chipping, be careful around valve seat areas.

   NOTE: *When using a wire brush to clean carbon on the valve ports, valves etc., be sure the deposits are actually removed, rather than burnished.*
8. Use a valve guide cleaning brush and safe solvent to clean the valve guides.
9. Clean the valves with a revolving wire brush. Heavy carbon deposits may be removed with a blunt drift.
10. Wash and clean all valve springs, keepers, retaining caps etc., in safe solvent. Remember to keep parts from each valve separate.
11. Clean the head with safe solvent and wipe dry.
12. Check the cylinder head for cracks. Cracks usually start around the exhaust valve seat because it is the hottest part of the combustion chamber. If a crack is suspected but cannot be detected visually, have the area checked with dye penetrant or other method by the machine shop.
13. After all cylinder head parts are reasonably clean check the valve stem-to-guide clearance. If a dial indicator is not on hand, a visual inspection can give you a fairly good idea if the guide, valve stem or both are worn.
14. Insert the valve into the guide until slightly away from the valve seat. Wiggle the valve sideways. A small amount of wobble is normal, excessive wobble means a worn guide and/or valve stem. If a dial indicator is on hand, mount the indicator so that gauge stem is 90° to the valve stem, as close to the top of the valve guide as possible. Move the valve from the seat, and measure the valve guide-to-stem clearance by rocking the stem back and forth to actuate the dial indicator. Measure the valve stem using a micrometer and compare to specifications to determine whether stem or guide is causing excessive clearance.
15. The valve guide, if worn, must be repaired before the valve seats can be resurfaced. A new valve guide should be installed or, in some cases, knurled. Consult the automotive machine shop.
16. Valve faces and valve seats should be machined to specifications; the machine shop can handle the job for you. Only enough material to clean up any pits or grooves should be removed. The valve seat should not be too wide or too narrow. The valve face should contact the seat on their respective centers. The valve seat can be narrowed or widened as required.

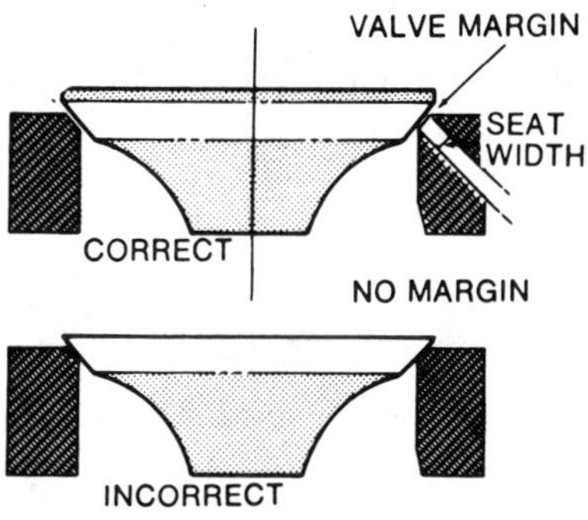

Valve seat width and centering

17. After the valves and valve seats have been machined they should be hand lapped. Use valve grinding compound and a small suction cupped valve stick. Place a small amount of compound on the valve face. Install the valve and rotate the valve face against the seat with the valve stick. Remove the valve and clean the compound from the valve face and seat. If the contact ring is too close to the outer edge of the valve face, narrow the seat; if to close to the inner edge widen the seat. If the edge of a valve head, after machining, is $^1/_{32}$ inch or less replace the valve. The tip of the valve stem should also be dressed on the valve grinding machine, however do not remove too much material.

18. After all valve and valve seats have been machined, check the remaining valve train parts (springs, retainers, keepers, etc.) for wear. Check the valve springs for straightness and tension.

19. Reassemble the head in the reverse order of disassembly using new valve stem guide seals. Lubricate the valve stems before installation. Check the valve spring installed height, shim or replace as necessary.

CHECKING VALVE SPRINGS

Place the valve spring on a flat surface next to a carpenters square. Measure the height of the spring, and rotate the spring against the edge of the square to measure distortion. If the spring height varies (by comparison) by more than $^1/_{16}$ inch or if the distortion exceeds $^1/_{16}$ inch, replace the spring.

Have the valve springs tested for spring pressure at the installed and compressed (installed height minus valve lift) height using a valve spring tester. Springs should be within one pound, plus or minus each other. Replace springs as necessary.

VALVE SPRING INSTALLED HEIGHT

After installing the valve spring, measure the distance between the spring mounting pad and the lower edge of the spring retainer. Compare the measurement to specifications. If the installed height is incorrect, add shim washers between the mounting pad and the base of the spring. Use only washers designed for spring shimming; available at parts houses.

Valve Stem Oil Seals

Positive valves seals are used. The seal fits over the top of the valve guide. Always install new valve stem seals when reassembling the cylinder head.

Valve Seats

If a valve seat is damaged, burnt or loose, the seat may be resurfaced or replace as necessary. The automotive machine shop can handle the job for you.

Camshaft Drive Chain or Belt

The correct installation and adjustment of the camshaft drive chain or belt is mandatory if the engine is to run properly. The camshaft controls the opening of the engine valves through coordination of the movement of the crankshaft and camshaft. When any given piston is on the intake stroke the corresponding intake valve must open to admit air/fuel mixture into the cylinder. When the same piston is on the compression and power strokes, both valves in that cylinder must be closed. When the piston is on the exhaust stroke, the exhaust valve for that cylinder must be open. If the opening and closing of the valves is not coordinated with the movements of the pistons, the engine will run very poorly, if at all.

Timing Gear Cover, Chain, Counterbalance Shafts, and Tensioner

REMOVAL AND INSTALLATION

The following outlines are the recommended removal and installation procedures for the timing chain or belt. Some modifications to the procedures may be necessary due to added accessories, sheetmetal parts, or emission control units and connecting hoses.

NOTE: *The timing chain case is cast aluminum, so exercise caution when handling this part.*

Chain Equipped 1600 cc Engine-Standard (1977)

1. Disconnect the battery ground (negative) cable. Drain the coolant. Disconnect and remove the radiator hoses. Remove the radiator.

2. Remove the alternator and accessory belts.

3. Rotate the crankshaft to bring No. 1 piston to TDC on the compression stroke, by aligning the notch on the crankshaft pulley with the "T" mark on the timing indicator scale.

4. Remove the crankshaft pulley and bolt.

NOTE: *Do not move the crankshaft when removing the pulley. If the crankshaft is turned, return the shaft to the original position as in step 3.*

5. Remove the crankshaft pulley and bolt.

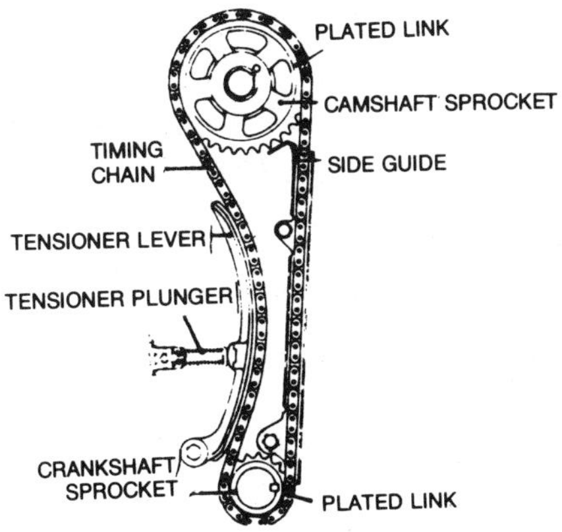

1600cc timing chain and tensioner

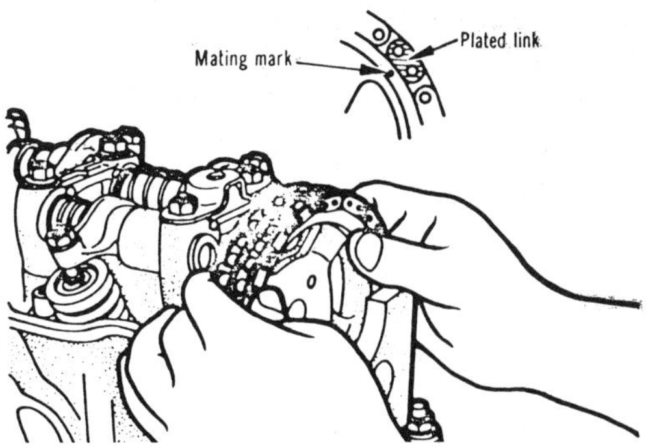

1600cc camshaft sprocket alignment

6. Remove the fan blades and the water pump assembly.

7. Remove the cylinder head assembly. (See cylinder head removal section).

8. Raise the car and support it safely on jackstands.

9. Drain the engine oil and remove the oil pan, oil pressure switch, oil filter, and oil pump.

NOTE: *Undercar splash pans may have to be removed to gain access to the oil pan.*

10. Remove the chain tension holder, spring, and plunger, on the right side of the chain cover.

11. Remove the timing chain cover from the engine block.

12. Remove the oil slinger and crankshaft gear from the crankshaft. Do not loose the woodruff key from the crankshaft.

13. Remove the crankshaft and camshaft sprockets with the chain attached, from the engine block.

14. If needed, remove the chain tension lever and side guide.

15. If removed, install the chain tensioner lever and the side guide, with the jet of the guide toward the chain and sprocket meshing point.

16. Be sure the No. 1 piston is at TDC. Using a new gasket, install the cylinder head assembly.

17. Rotate the camshaft until the dowel pin is between the 1 and 2 O'clock position on the 1600 cc engines.

18. Position the crankshaft sprocket and the camshaft sprocket so that the punch marks on the sprockets align with the chrome or buff plated links of the timing chain.

19. Install the woodruff key on the crankshaft and while holding the timing chain and sprockets in position, install the sprockets onto the camshaft and the crankshaft.

20. If the dowel pin does not align with the hole in the camshaft sprocket, bump the camshaft on the projections provided to align the two. Install the camshaft sprocket bolt and torque to 36 to 43 ft. lbs.

NOTE: *The chain must be fitted in the guide groove and against the tensioner lever.*

21. Install the woodruff key, crankshaft gear with the "F" mark toward the front on 1600 cc engines. The oil slinger must be installed with its concave side facing the front of the engine.

22. Install a new gasket and seal on the front timing cover case and install the case on the engine block. Torque the bolts to 11 to 13 ft. lbs.

23. Install the tensioner lever plunger and spring into the case and torque to 29 to 36 ft. lbs.

CAUTION: *Because the timing chain is supported and stretched by the tensioner lever, it is important to align the marks on the sprockets and chain.*

24. Install the oil screen and oil pump.

25. Install the oil pan, oil filter, and the oil pressure gauge sender. Fill the oil pan.

26. Reinstall any splash pans and lower the car to the floor.

27. Align the oil pump shaft in a vertical position on the 1600 cc engine. Align the distributor marks to fire No. 1 cylinder, and install the distributor.

28. Install the crankshaft pulley and torque the bolt to 43 to 59 ft lbs.

29. Install the water pump, fan blades, alternator and belt. Adjust the belt.

30. Install the radiator and radiator hoses, add coolant to the system, and connect the battery ground cable.

31. Refer to the Cylinder Head Installation Section and adjust the valves as for a cold engine. Temporarily install the rocker arm cover, start the engine, and warm it up.

32. Stop the engine and remove the rocker arm cover. Adjust the valves to the hot specifications.

2000 cc Engine-W/Silent Shaft (1977–80)
2600 cc Engine-W/Silent Shaft (1978–83)

1. Disconnect the battery ground (negative) cable. Drain the coolant. Disconnect and remove the radiator hoses. Remove the radiator.
2. Remove the alternator and accessory belts.
3. Rotate the crankshaft to bring No. 1 piston to TDC, on the compression stroke.
4. Mark and remove the distributor.
5. Remove the crankshaft pulley.
6. Remove the water pump assembly.
7. Remove the cylinder head (See cylinder head removal section).

NOTE: *It may be possible to replace the timing chain without removing the cylinder head, however removing the "head" will make the job easier.*

8. Raise the front of the car and support it safely on jackstands.
9. Drain the engine oil and remove the oil pan and screen.
10. Remove the timing case cover.
11. Remove the chain guides, Side (A), Top (B), Bottom (C), from the "B" chain (outer). See illustration.
12. Remove the locking bolts from the "B" chain sprockets.
13. Remove the crankshaft sprocket, counterbalance shaft sprocket and the outer chain.
14. Remove the crankshaft and camshaft sprockets and the inner chain.
15. Remove the camshaft sprocket holder and the chain guides, both left and right. Remove the tensioner spring and sleeve from the oil pump.

NOTE: *For further service to shafts and oil pump follow Steps 16 and 17.*

16. Remove the oil pump by first removing the bolt locking the oil pump driven gear and the right counterbalance shaft, and then remove the oil pump mounting bolts. Remove the counterbalance shaft from the engine block.

NOTE: *If the bolt locking the oil pump driven gear and the counterbalance shaft is hard to loosen, remove the oil pump and the shaft as a unit.*

17. Remove the left counterbalance shaft thrust washer and take the shaft from the engine block.

NOTE: *If the tensioner rubber hose, or chain guide show wear, they should be replaced.*

18. Install the right counterbalance shaft into the engine block if removed.
19. Install the oil pump assembly if removed. Do not lose the woodruff key from the end of the counterbalance shaft. Torque the oil pump mounting bolts to 6 to 7 ft. lbs.
20. If they have been removed tighten the counterbalance shaft and the oil pump driven gear mounting bolt.

NOTE: *The counterbalance shaft and the oil pump can be installed as a unit, if necessary.*

21. Install the left counterbalance shaft into the engine block if removed.
22. Install a new "O" ring on the thrust plate and install the unit into the engine block, using a pair of bolts without heads, as alignment guides.

CAUTION: *If the thrust plate is turned to align the bolt holes, the "O" ring may be damaged.*

23. Remove the guide bolts and install the regular bolts into the thrust plate and tighten securely.
24. Rotate the crankshaft to bring No. 1 Piston to TDC.
25. Using a new head gasket install the cylinder head.
26. Install the sprocket holder and the right and left chain guides.
27. Install the tensioner spring and sleeve on the oil pump body.
28. Install the camshaft and crankshaft sprockets on the timing chain, aligning the sprocket punch marks to the plated chain links.
29. While holding the sprocket and chain as a unit, install the crankshaft sprocket over the crankshaft and align it with the keyway.
30. Keeping the dowel pin hole on the camshaft in a vertical position, install the camshaft sprocket and chain on the camshaft.

NOTE: *The sprocket timing mark and the plated chain link should be at the 2 to 3 o'clock position when correctly installed.*

CAUTION: *The chain must be aligned in the right and left chain guides with the tensioner pushing against the chain. The tension for the inner chain is predetermined by spring tension.*

31. Install the crankshaft sprocket for the outer or "B" chain.
32. Install the two counterbalance shaft sprockets and align the punched mating marks with the plated links of the chain.
33. Holding the two shaft sprockets and chain, install the outer chain in alignment with the mark on the crankshaft sprocket. Install the shaft sprockets on the counterbalance shaft and the oil pump driver gear. Install the lock bolts and recheck the alignment of the punch marks and the plated links.
34. Temporarily install the chain guides, *Side* (A), *Top* (B), and *Bottom* (C).
35. Tighten *Side* (A) chain guide securely.
36. Tighten *Bottom* (B) chain guide securely.

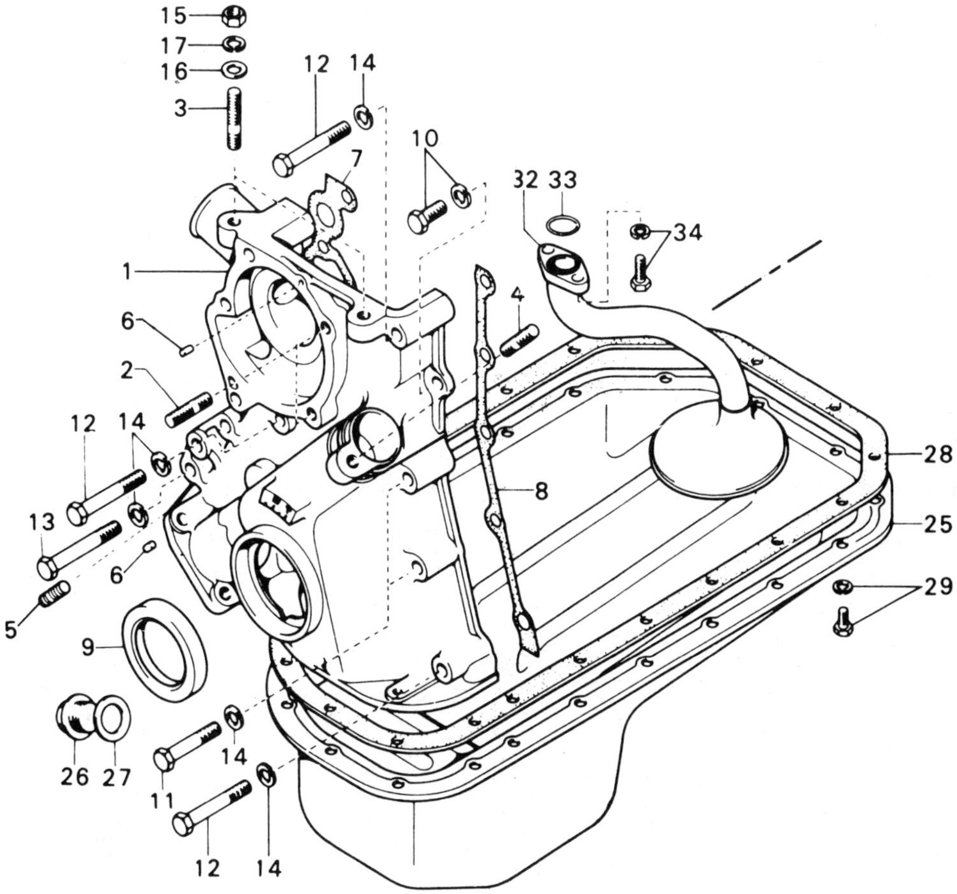

1. Timing gear cover
2. Stud
3. Stud
4. Stud
5. Stud
6. Dowel pin
7. Right gasket
8. Left gasket
9. Front oil seal
10. Bolt
11. Bolt
12. Bolt
13. Bolt
14. Washer
15. Nut
16. Washer
17. Washer
25. Oil pan
26. Drain plug
27. Gasket
28. Gasket
29. Bolt
30. Bellhousing cover
31. Bolt
32. Oil screen assembly
33. O-ring
34. Bolt

1600cc timing cover and oil pan assembly

37. Adjust the position of the *Top* (B) chain guide, after shaking the right and left sprockets to collect any chain slack, so that when the chain is moved toward the center, the clearance between the chain guide and the chain links will be approximately 9/64 inch. Tighten the *Top* (B) chain guide bolts.

38. Install the timing chain cover using a new gasket, being careful not to damage the front seal.

39. Install the oil screen and the oil pan, using a new gasket. Torque the bolts to 4.5 to 5.5 ft. lbs.

40. Install the crankshaft pulley, alternator and accessory belts, and the distributor.

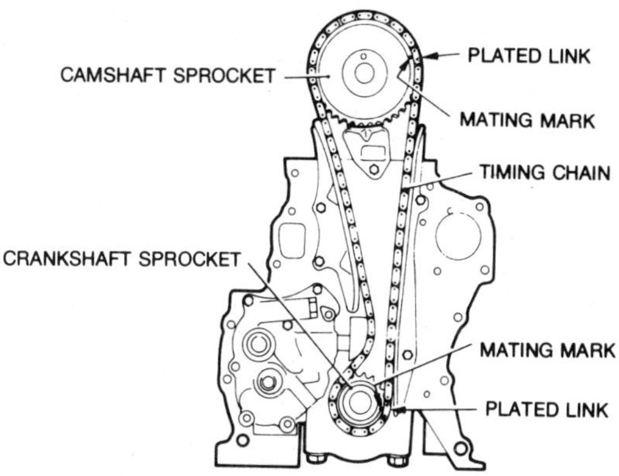

Timing chain installation, engine with silent shaft

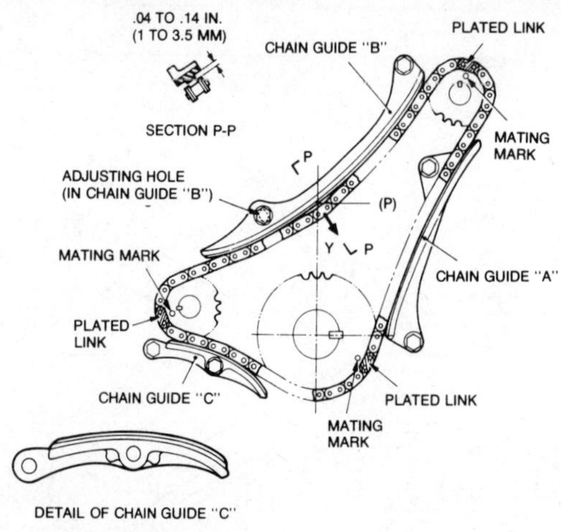

Balance shaft, timing chain installation

41. Install the oil pressure switch, if removed, and install the battery ground cable.

42. Install the fan blades, radiator, fill the system with coolant and start the engine.

Belt Equipped 1600 cc engine-Standard (1978–82) 1600 cc engine-W/Silent Shaft (1977–80)

1. Disconnect the battery ground (negative) cable. Drain the coolant. Disconnect the radiator hoses. Remove the radiator.

2. Remove the alternator and accessory belts.

3. Rotate the crankshaft to bring No. 1 piston to TDC on the compression stroke. Align the notch on the crankshaft pulley with the "T" mark on the timing indicator scale and the timing mark on the upper under cover of

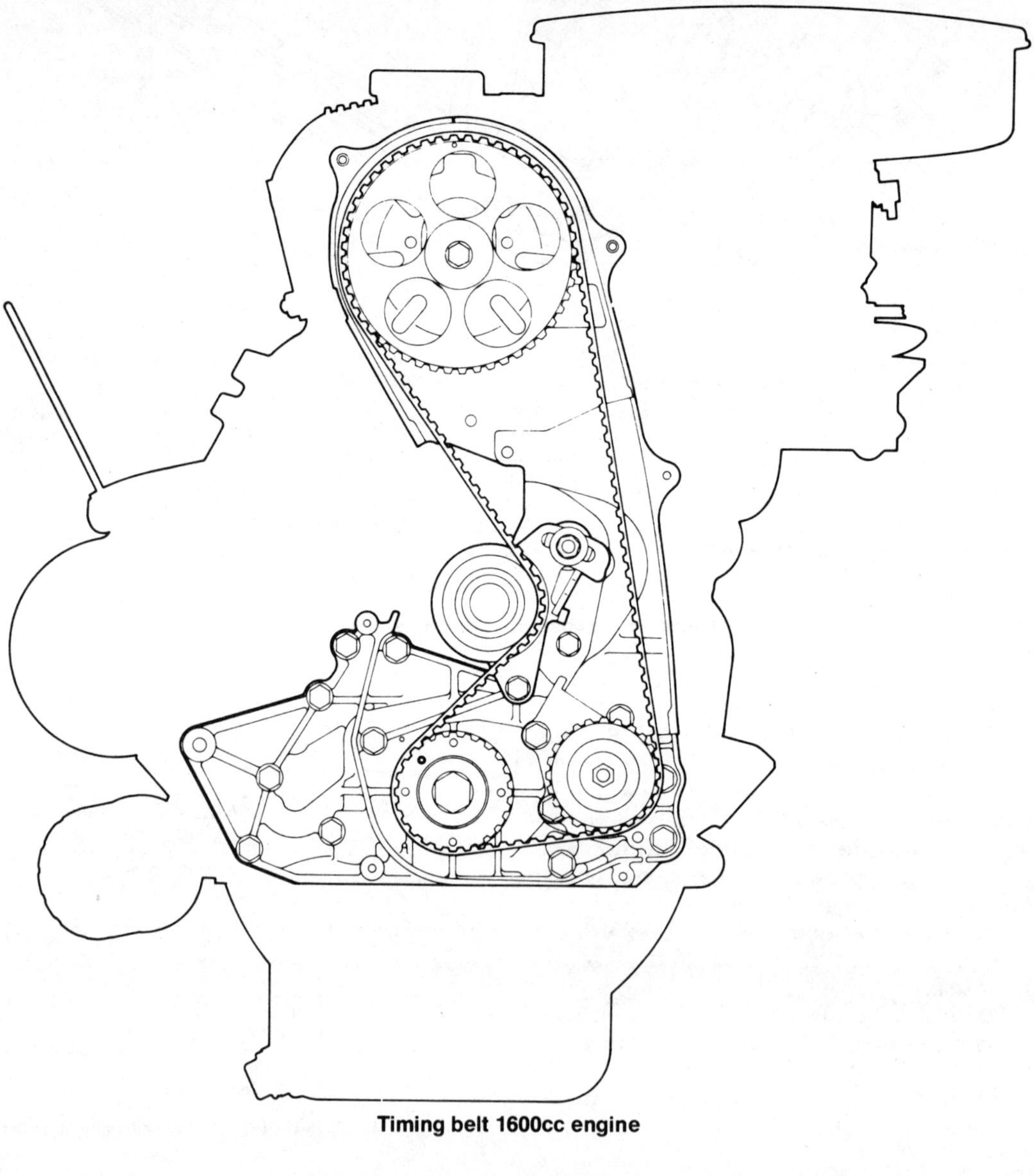

Timing belt 1600cc engine

the timing belt with the mark on the camshaft sprocket. Mark and remove the distributor.

4. Remove the crankshaft pulley and bolt.

5. Remove the fan blades.

6. Remove the timing belt covers, upper front and lower front.

7. Remove the crankshaft sprocket bolt.

8. Loosen the tensioner mounting nut and bolt. Move the tensioner away from the belt and retighten the nut to keep the tensioner in the off position. Remove the belt.

NOTE: *If the belt is all that needs servicing, proceed to the Installation section.*

9. Remove the camshaft sprocket, crankshaft sprocket, flange, and tensioner.

10. Silent shaft engines:

a. Loosen the counterbalance shaft sprocket mounting bolt.

b. Remove the belt tensioner and remove the timing belt.

NOTE: *If the belt is all that needs servicing, proceed to the Installation section.*

c. Remove the crankshaft sprocket (inner) and counterbalance shaft sprocket.

d. Remove the upper and lower under timing belt covers.

11. The water pump or cylinder head may be removed at this point, depending upon the type of repairs needed.

12. Raise the front of the car and support it safely. Remove any interfering splash pans.

13. Drain the oil pan and remove the pan from the block.

14. Remove the oil pump sprocket and cover.

NOTE: *On the silent shaft engines, remove the plug at the bottom of the left side of the cylinder block and insert a screwdriver to keep the left counter balance shaft in position while removing the sprocket nut.*

15. Remove the front cover and oil pump as a unit, with the left counter shaft attached, if equipped.

16. Remove the oil pump gear and left counterbalance shaft.

NOTE: *To aid in removal of the front cover, a driver groove is provided on the cover, above the oil pump housing. Avoid prying on the thinner parts of the housing flange or hammering on it to remove the case.*

17. Remove the right counterbalance shaft from the engine block.

INSTALLATION—STANDARD ENGINE

1. Install a new front seal in the cover. Install a new gasket on the front of the cylinder block, and using a seal protector on the front of the crankshaft, install the front cover on the engine block.

2. Tighten the front case mounting bolts to 11 to 13 ft. lbs.

3. Install the oil screen, and using a new gasket, install the oil pan. Tighten bolts to 4.5 to 5.5 ft. lbs.

4. If the cylinder head and/or water pump had been removed, reinstall them, using new gaskets.

5. Install the upper and lower under covers.

6. Install the spacer, flange and crankshaft sprocket and tighten the bolt to 43.5 to 50 ft. lbs.

7. Align the timing mark on the crankshaft sprocket with the timing mark on the front case.

8. Align the camshaft sprocket timing mark with the upper under cover timing mark.

9. Install the tensioner spring and tensioner. Temporarily tighten the nut. Install the front end of the tensioner spring (bent at right angles) on the projection of the tensioner and the other end (straight) on the water pump body.

10. Loosen the nut and move the tensioner in the direction of the water pump. Lock it by tightening the nut.

11. Ensure that the sprocket timing marks are aligned, and install the timing belt. The belt should be installed on the crankshaft sprocket, the oil pump sprocket, and then the camshaft sprocket, in that order, while keeping the belt tight.

12. Loosen the tensioner mounting bolt and nut and allow the spring tension to move the tensioner against the belt.

NOTE: *Make sure the belt comes in complete mesh with the sprocket by lightly pushing the tensioner up by hand toward the mounting nut.*

13. Tighten the tensioner mounting nut and bolt.

NOTE: *Be sure to tighten the nut before tightening the bolt. Too much tension could result from tightening the bolt first.*

14. Recheck all sprocket alignments.

15. Turn the crankshaft through a complete rotation in the normal direction.

CAUTION: *Do not turn in a reverse direction or shake or push the belt.*

16. Loosen the tensioner bolt and nut. Retighten the nut and then the bolt.

17. Install the lower and upper front outer covers.

18. Install the crankshaft pulley and tighten the bolts to 7.5 to 8.5 ft. lbs.

19. Install the alternator and belt and adjust. Install the distributor.

20. Install the radiator, fill the cooling system, and inspect for leaks.

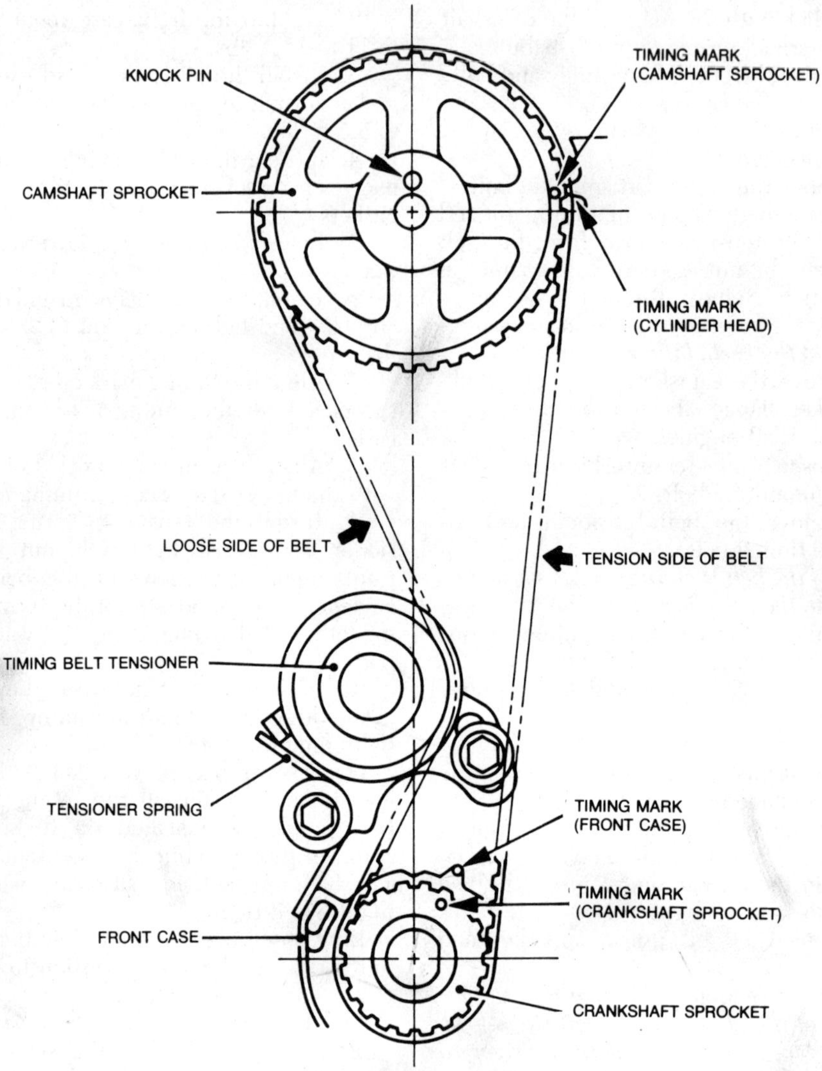

Timing belt 1400cc engine

INSTALLATION—W/SILENT SHAFT

1. Install a new front seal in the cover. Install the oil pump drive and driven gears in the front case, aligning the timing marks on the pump gears.
2. Install the left counterbalance shaft in the driven gear and temporarily tighten the bolt.
3. Install the right counterbalance shaft into the cylinder block.
4. Install an oil seal guide on the end of the crankshaft, and install a new gasket on the front of the engine block for the front cover.
5. Install a new front case packing, if equipped.
6. Insert the left counterbalance shaft into the engine block and at the same time, guide the front cover into place on the front of the engine block.
7. Insert a screwdriver at the bottom of the left side of the block and hold the left counterbalance shaft and tighten the bolt. Install the hole plug.
8. Install an "O" ring on the oil pump cover.
9. Install the oil pump on the front cover. Tighten the oil pump cover bolts and the front cover bolts to 11 to 13 ft. lbs.
10. Install the oil screen, and using a new gasket, install the oil pan.
11. Install the water pump and/or the cylinder head, if removed previously.
12. Install the upper and lower under covers.
13. Install the spacer on the end of the right

Description	Flaw conditions
1. Hardened back surface rubber	Back surface glossy. Non-elastic and so hard that even if a finger nail is forced into it, no mark is produced.

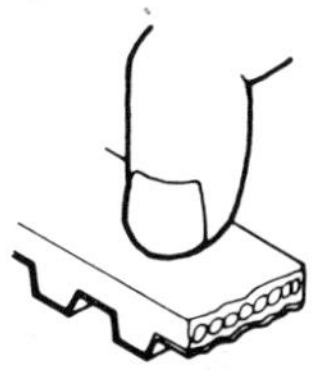

Description	Flaw conditions
2. Cracked back surface rubber	

Description	Flaw conditions
3. Cracked or exfoliated canvas	

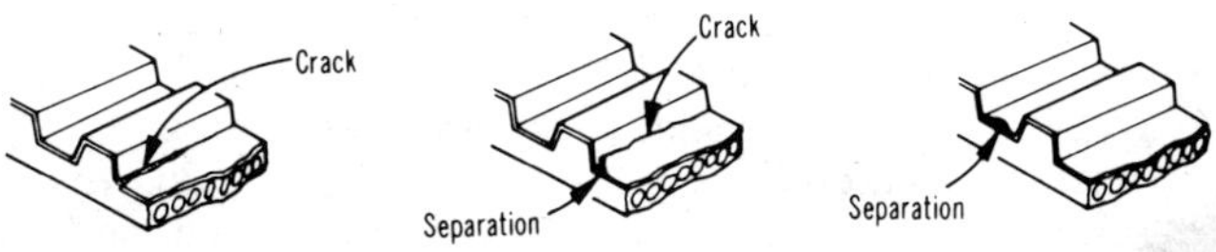

Description	Flaw conditions
4. Badly worn teeth (initial stage)	Canvas on load side tooth flank worn (Fluffy canvas fibers, rubber gone and color changed to white, and unclear canvas texture)

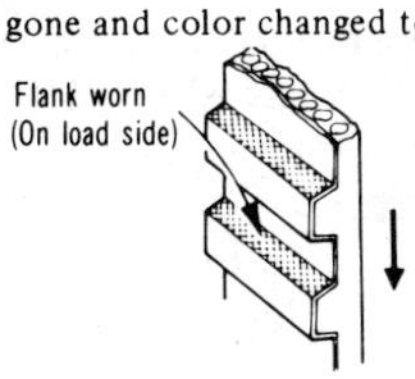

Description	Flaw conditions
5. Badly worn teeth (last stage)	Canvas on load side tooth flank worn down and rubber exposed (tooth width reduced)

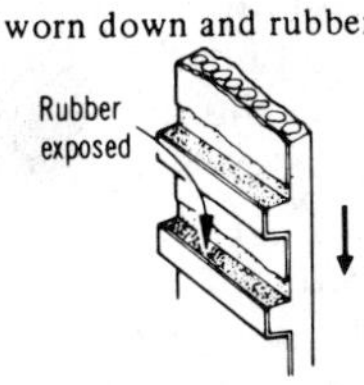

Description	Flaw conditions
6. Cracked tooth bottom	

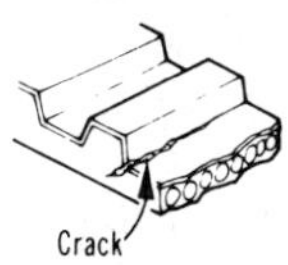

Description	Flaw conditions
7. Missing tooth	

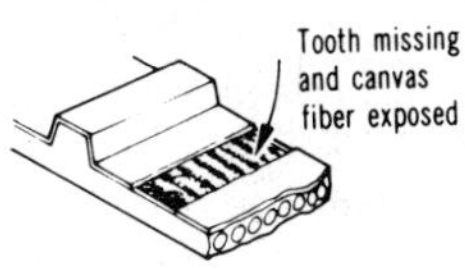

Description	Flaw conditions
8. Side of belt badly worn	

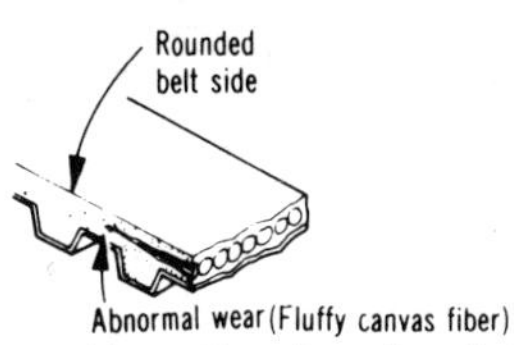

Note: Normal belt should have clear-cut sides as if cut by a sharp knife.

Description	Flaw conditions
9. Side of belt cracked	

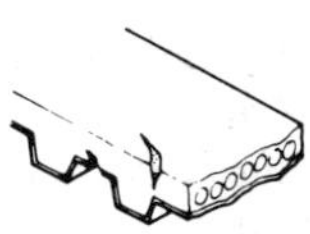

Checking timing belt wear

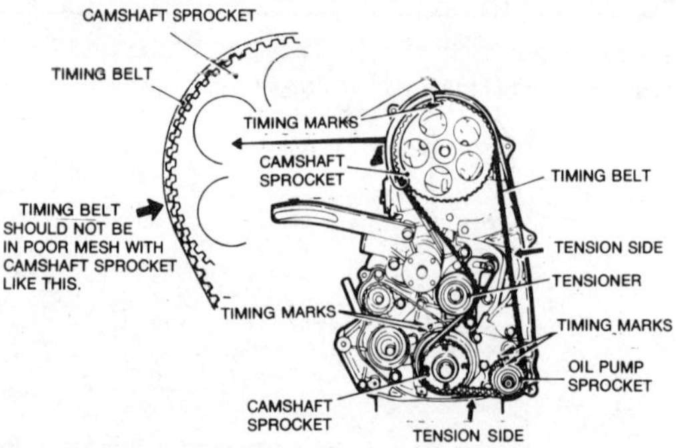

Silent shaft engines—timing belt installation

counterbalance shaft, with the chamfered edge toward the rear of the engine.

14. Install the counterbalance shaft sprocket and temporarily tighten the bolt.

15. Install the inner crankshaft sprocket and align the timing marks on the sprockets with those on the front case.

16. Install the inner tensioner (B) with the center of the pulley on the left side of the mounting bolt and with the pulley flange toward the front of the engine.

17. Lift the tensioner by hand, clockwise, to apply tension to the belt. Tighten the bolt to secure the tensioner.

18. Check that all alignment marks are in their proper places and the belt deflection is approximately ¼ to ½ inch on the tension side.

NOTE: *When the tensioner bolt is tightened, make sure the shaft of the tensioner does not turn with the bolt. If the belt is too tight there will be noise, and if the belt is too loose, the belt and sprocket may come out of mesh.*

19. Tighten the counterbalance shaft sprocket bolt to 22 to 28.5 ft. lbs.

20. Install the flange and crankshaft sprocket. Tighten the bolt to 43.5 to 50.5 ft. lbs.

21. Install the camshaft spacer and sprocket. Tighten the bolt to 44 to 57 ft. lbs.

22. Align the camshaft sprocket timing mark with the timing mark on the upper inner cover.

23. Install the oil pump sprocket, tightening the nut to 25 to 28.5 ft. lbs. Align the timing mark on the sprocket with the mark on the case.

CAUTION: *To be assured that the phasing of the oil pump sprocket and the left counterbalance shaft is correct, a screwdriver or a metal rod should be inserted in the plugged hole on the left side of the cylinder block. If it can be inserted more than 2⅝ inches, the phasing is correct. If the tool can only be inserted approximately one inch, turn the oil pump sprocket through one turn and realign the timing marks. Keep the screwdriver or metal rod inserted until the installation of the timing belt is completed. Remove the tool from the hole and install the plug, before starting the engine.*

24. Refer to step 9 of the belt installation for the standard engine.

25. If the timing belt is correctly tensioned, there should be about 0.5 in. clearance between the outside of the belt and the edge of the belt cover. This is measured about halfway down the side of the belt opposite the tensioner.

26. Complete the assembly by installing the upper and lower front covers.

27. Install the crankshaft pulley, alternator, and accessory belts, and adjust to specifications.

28. Install the radiator, fill the cooling system, and start the engine.

1400 cc Engine (1979–82)

1. Turn the engine until No. 1 piston is on TDC with the timing marks aligned.

2. Disconnect the ground (negative) battery cable.

3. Remove the fan drive belt, the fan blades, spacer and water pump pulley.

4. Remove the timing belt cover.

5. Loosen the timing belt tensioner mounting bolt and move the tensioner toward the water pump. Temporarily secure the tensioner.

6. Remove the crankshaft pulley and slide the belt off of the camshaft and crankshaft drive sprockets.

7. Inspect the drive sprockets for abnormal wear, cracks or damage and replace as necessary. Remove and inspect the tensioner. Check for smooth pulley rotation, excessive play or noise. Replace tensioner if necessary.

8. Reinstall the tensioner, if it was removed, and temporarily secure it close to the water pump.

9. Make sure that the timing mark on the

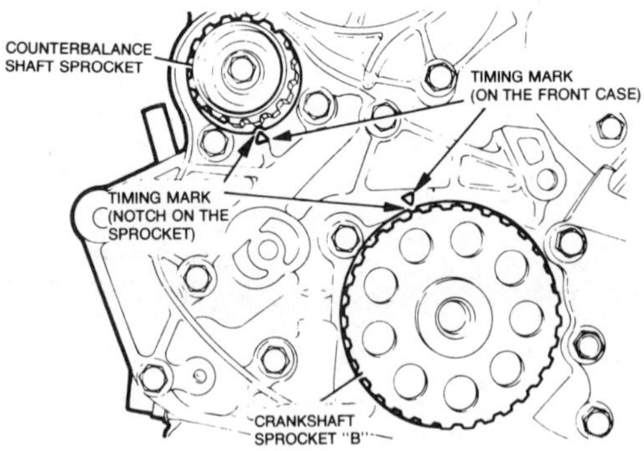

Timing marks—belt drive silent shaft engines

camshaft sprocket is aligned with the pointer on the cylinder head and that the crankshaft sprocket mark is aligned with the mark on the engine case. (See illustration on page 70).

10. Install the timing belt on the crankshaft sprocket.

11. Install the belt counter-clockwise over the camshaft sprocket making sure there is no play on the tension side of the belt. Adjust the belt fore and aft so that it is centered on the sprockets.

12. Loosen the tensioner from it's temporary position so that the spring pressure will allow it to contact the timing belt.

13. Rotate the crankshaft two complete turns in the normal rotation direction to remove any belt slack. Turn the crankshaft until the timing marks are lined up. If the timing has slipped, remove the belt and repeat the procedure.

14. Tighten the tensioner mounting bolts, slotted side (right) first then the spring side.

15. Once again rotate the engine two complete revolutions until the timing marks line up. Recheck the belt tension.

NOTE: *When the tension side of the timing belt and the tensioner are pushed in horizontally with a moderate force (about 11 lbs.) and the cogged side of the belt covers about a quarter of an inch of the tensioner right side mounting bolt head, (across flats) the tension is correct.*

16. Reinstall the timing belt cover, the water pump pulley, spacer, fan blades and drive belt.

17. Connect the battery ground cable.

Pistons and Connecting Rods

REMOVAL AND INSTALLATION

NOTE: *Although, in most cases, the pistons and connecting rods can be removed from the engine (after the cylinder head and oil pan are removed) while the engine is still in the car; it is far easier to work on the engine when removed from the car.*

NOTE: *If removing pistons with the engine still installed, disconnect the radiator hoses, automatic transmission cooler lines and radiator shroud. Unbolt frontmounts before jacking up the engine. Block the engine in position with wooden blocks between the mounts.*

1. Remove the engine from the car. Remove cylinder head, oil pan and front cover.

2. Because the top piston ring does not travel to the very top of the cylinder bore, a ridge is built up between the end of the travel and the top of the cylinder. Pushing the piston and connecting rod assembly past the ridge is difficult and may cause damage to the piston. If new rings are installed and the ridge has not been removed, ring breakage and piston damage can occur when the ridge is encountered at engine speed.

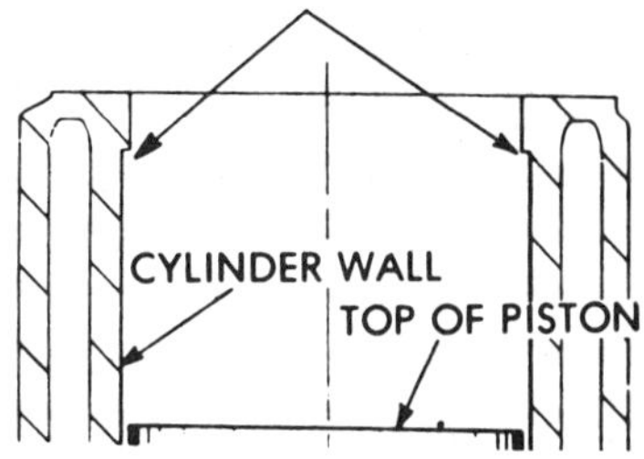

Cylinder bore ridge

3. Turn the crankshaft to position the piston at the bottom of the cylinder bore. Cover the top of the piston with a rag. Install a ridge reamer in the bore and follow the manufacturer's instructions to remove the ridge. Use caution, avoid cutting too deeply. Remove the rag and cuttings from the top of the piston. Remove the ridge from all cylinders.

4. Check the edges of the connecting rod and cap numerically and in sequence from front to back of engine. The numbers or marks not only tell from which cylinder the piston came from but also helps ensure that the rod caps are installed in the correct matching position.

5. Turn the crankshaft until the connecting rod is at the bottom of travel. Remove the two attaching nuts and the bearing cap. Take two pieces of rubber tubing and cover the rod bolts to prevent crank or cylinder scoring. Use a wooden hammer handle to help push the piston and rod up and out of the cylinder. Rein-

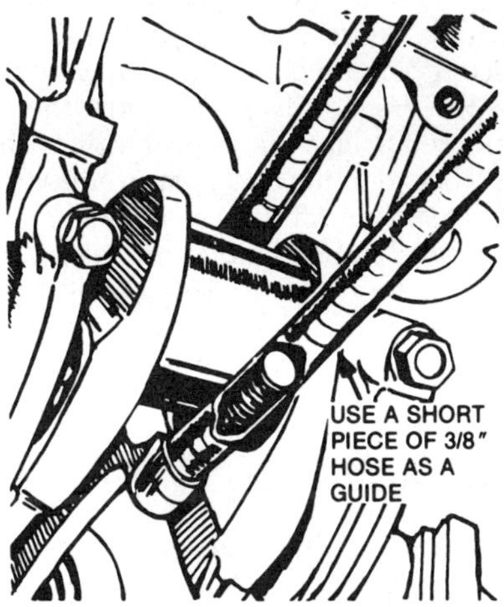

Use lengths of vacuum hose or rubber tubing to protect the crankshaft journal and cylinder walls during piston and rod removal and installation

stall the rod cap in proper position. Remove all pistons and connecting rods. Inspect cylinder walls and deglaze or hone as necessary.

6. Installation is in the reverse order of removal. Lubricate each piston, rod bearing and cylinder wall. Install a ring compressor over the piston, position piston with mark toward front of engine and carefully install into engine. Position connecting rod with bearing insert installed over the crank journal. Install the rod cap with bearing in proper position. Secure with rod nuts and torque to proper specifications. Install all rod and piston assemblies.

CLEANING AND INSPECTION

1. Use a piston ring expander and remove the rings from the piston.
2. Clean the ring grooves using an appropriate cleaning tool, exercise care to avoid cutting too deeply.
3. Clean all varnish and carbon from the piston with a safe solvent. Do not use a wire brush or caustic solution on the pistons.
4. Inspect the pistons for scuffing, scoring, cracks, pitting or excessive ring groove wear. If wear is evident, the piston must be replaced.
5. Have the piston and connecting rod assembly checked by a machine shop for correct alignment, piston pin wear and piston diameter. If the piston has "collapsed" it will have to be replaced or knurled to restore original diameter. Connecting rod bushing replacement, piston pin fitting and piston changing can be handled by the machine shop.

Cylinder Bore

Check the cylinder bore for wearing using a telescope gauge and a micrometer, measure the cylinder bore diameter perpendicular to the piston pin at a point 2½ inches below the top of the engine block. Measure the piston skirt perpendicular to the piston pin. The difference between the two measurements is the piston clearance. If the clearance is within specifications, finish honing or glaze breaking is all that is required. If clearance is excessive a slightly oversize piston may be required. If greatly oversize, the engine will have to be bored and .010 inch or larger oversized pistons installed.

PISTON PINS

The pin connecting the piston and connecting rod is press fitted. If too much free play develops take the piston assemblies to the machine shop and have oversize pins installed. Installing new rods or pistons requires the use of a press—have the machine shop handle the job for you.

Fitting and Positioning Piston Rings

1. Take the new piston rings and compress them, one at a time into the cylinder that they will be used in. Press the ring about one inch below the top of the cylinder block using an inverted piston.
2. Use a feeler gauge and measure the distance between the ends of the ring, this is called, measuring the ring end-gap. Compare the reading to the one called for in the specifications table. File the ends of the ring with a fine file to obtain necessary clearance.

   NOTE: *If inadequate ring end-gap is utilized ring breakage will result.*
3. Inspect the ring grooves on the piston for excessive wear or taper. If necessary have the grooves recut for use with a standard ring and spacer. The machine shop can handle the job for you.
4. Check the ring groove by rolling the new piston ring around the groove to check for burrs or carbon deposits. If any are found, remove with a fine file. Hold the ring in the groove and measure side clearance with a feeler gauge. If clearance is excessive, spacer(s) will have to be added.

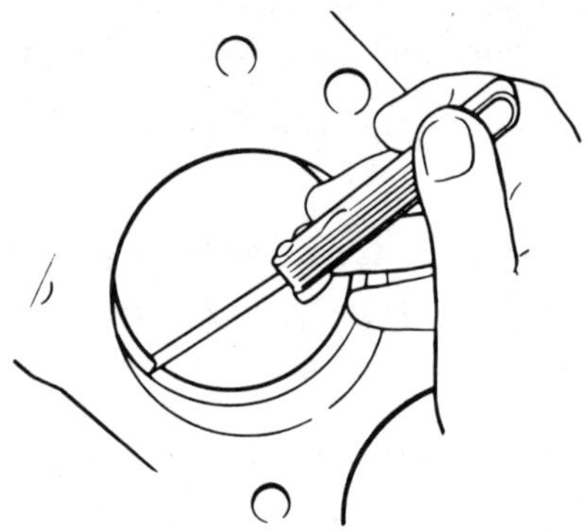

Check the piston ring and cap

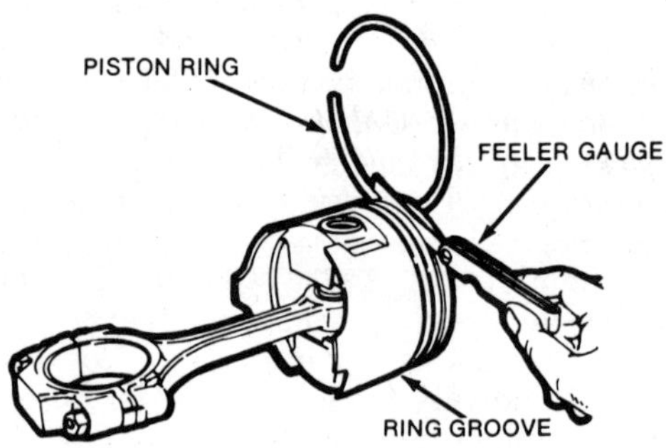

Check the piston ring side clearance

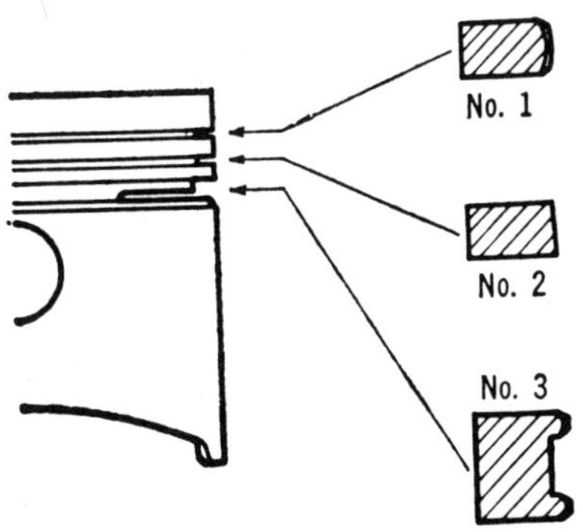

Piston ring installation

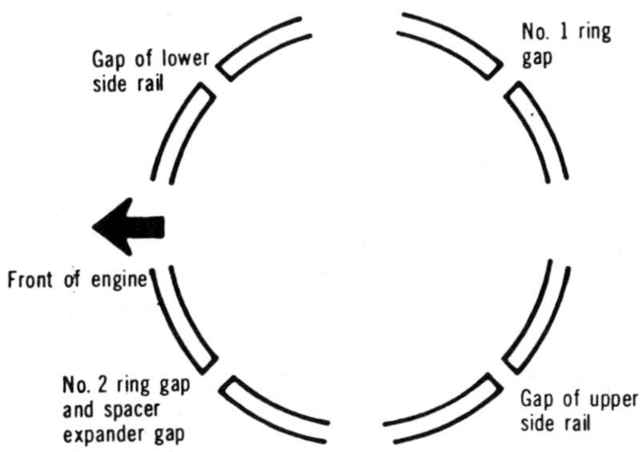

Piston ring positioning

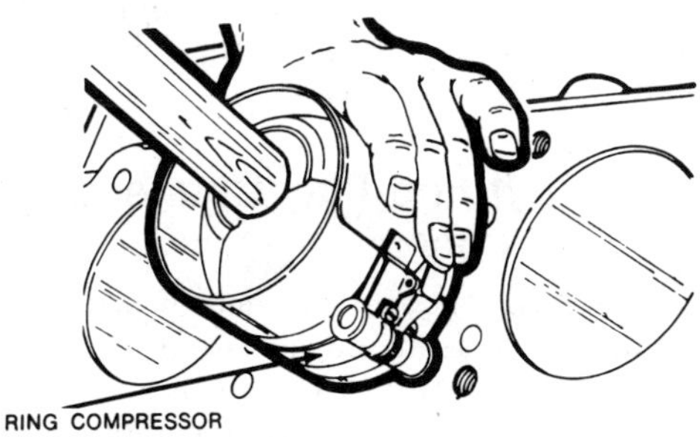

Piston installation

NOTE: *Always add spacers above the piston ring.*

5. Install the rings on the piston, lower ring first using a ring installing tool. Consult the instruction sheet that comes with the rings to be sure they are installed with the correct side up. A mark on the ring usually faces upward.

6. When installing oil rings; first, install the ring in the groove. Hold the ends of the ring butted together (they must not overlap) and install the bottom rail (scraper) with the end about one inch away from the butted end of the control ring. Install the top rail about an inch away from the butted end of the control but on the opposite side from the lower rail.

7. Install the two compression rings.

8. Consult the illustration with piston ring set instruction sheet for ring positioning, arrange the rings as shown, install a ring compressor and insert the piston and rod assembly into the engine.

Crankshaft and Bearings

1. Rod bearings can be installed when the pistons have been removed for servicing (rings etc) or, in most cases, while the engine is still in the car. Rearing replacement, however, is far easier with the engine out of the car and disassembled.

2. For in car service, remove the oil pan, spark plugs and front cover if necessary. Turn the engine until the connecting rod to be serviced is at the bottom of it's travel. Remove the bearing cap, place two pieces of rubber hose over the rod cap bolts and push the piston and rod assembly up the cylinder bore until enough room is gained for bearing insert removal. Take care not to push the rod assembly up too far or the top ring will engage the cylinder ridge or come out of the cylinder and require head removal for reinstallation.

3. Clean the rod journal, the connecting rod end and the bearing cap after removing the old bearing inserts. Install the new inserts in the rod and bearing cap, lubricate them with oil. Position the rod over the crankshaft journal and install the rod caps. Make sure the cap and rod numbers match, torque the rod nuts to specifications.

4. Main bearings may be replaced while the engine is still in the car by "rolling" them out and in.

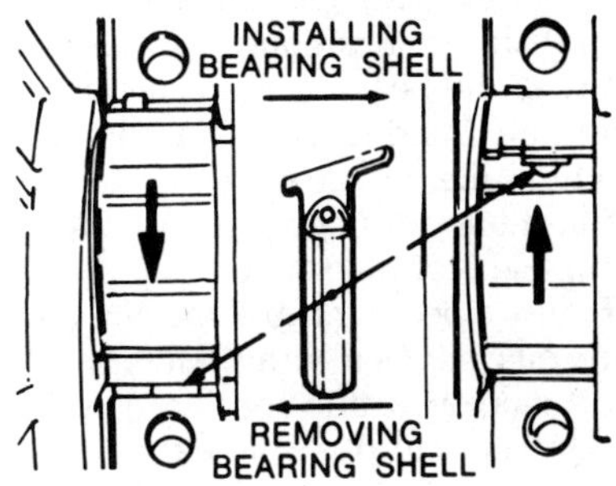

Remove the upper main bearing insert using a roll-out pin

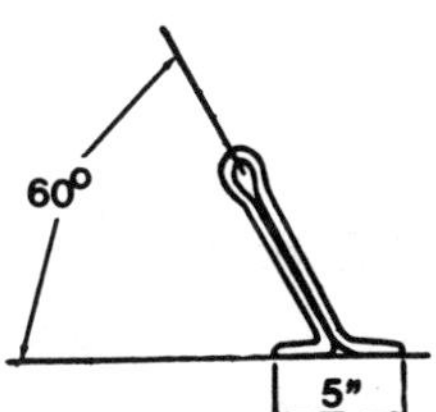

Home made roll-out pin

5. Special roll-out pins are available from automotive parts houses or can be fabricated from a cotter pin. The roll out pin fits in the oil hole of the main bearing journal. When the crankshaft is rotated opposite the direction of the bearing lock tab, the pin engages the end of the bearing and "rolls" out the insert.

6. Remove main bearing cap and roll out upper bearing insert. Remove insert from main bearing cap. Clean the inside of the bearing cap and crankshaft journal.

7. Lubricate and roll upper insert into position, make sure the lock tab is anchored and the insert is not "cocked." Install the lower bearing insert into the cap; lubricate and install on the engine. Make sure the main bearing cap is installed facing in the correct direction and torque to specifications.

8. With the engine out of the car. Remove the intake manifold, cylinder head, front cover, timing gears and/or chain, oil pan, oil pump and flywheel.

9. Remove the piston and rod assemblies. Remove the main bearing caps after marking them for position and direction.

10. Remove the crankshaft bearing inserts and rear main oil seal. Clean the engine block and cap bearing saddles. Clean the crankshaft and inspect for wear. Check the bearing journals with a micrometer for out-of-round condition and to determine what size rod and main bearing inserts to install.

11. Install the main bearing upper inserts and rear main oil seal half into the engine block.

12. Lubricate the bearing inserts and the crankshaft journals. Slowly and carefully lower the crankshaft into position.

13. Install the bearing inserts and rear main seal into the bearing caps, install the caps working from the middle out. Torque cap bolts to specifications in stages, rotate the crankshaft after each torque stage.

14. Remove bearing caps, one at a time and check the oil clearance with Plastigage.® Reinstall if clearance is within specifications. Check the crankshaft end-play, if within specifications install connecting rod and piston assemblies with new rod bearing inserts. Check connecting rod bearing oil clearance and rod side play, if correct and assemble the rest of the engine.

Bearing Oil Clearance

Remove cap from the bearing to be checked. Using a clean, dry rag, thoroughly clean all oil from crankshaft journal and bearing insert.

NOTE: *Plastigage® is soluble in oil; therefore, oil on the journal or bearing could result in erroneous readings.*

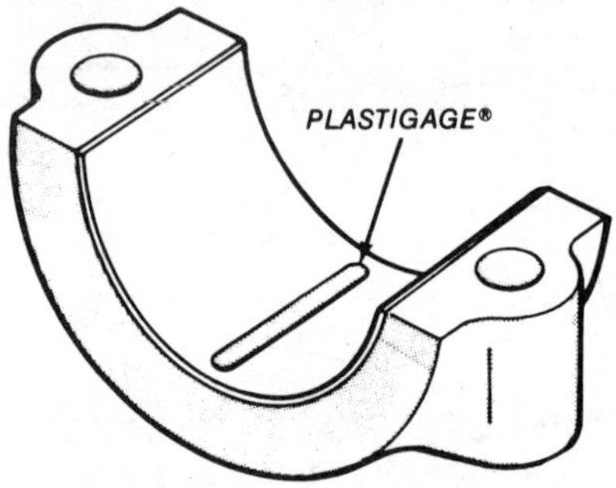

Plastigage® installed on lower bearing shell

Place a piece of Plastigage® along the full width of the insert, reinstall cap, and torque to specifications.

NOTE: *Specifications are given in the engine specifications earlier in this chapter.*

Remove bearing cap, and determine clearance by comparing width of Plastigage® to the scale on Plastigage envelope. Journal taper is determined by comparing width of the Plastigage® strip near its ends. Rotate crankshaft 90° and retest, to determine journal eccentricity.

NOTE: *Do not rotate crankshaft with Plastigage® installed. If bearing insert and journal appear intact, and are within tolerances, no further main bearing service is required. If bearing or journal appear defective, cause of failure should be determined before replacement.*

Crankshaft End-Play/Connecting Rod Side Play

Place a pry bar between a main bearing cap and crankshaft casting taking care not to damage any journals. Pry backward and forward measure the distance between the thrust bearing (center main 3) and crankshaft with a feeler gauge. Compare reading with specifications. If too great a clearance is determined, a larger thrust bearing or crank machining may be required. Check with an automotive machine shop for their advice.

Connecting rod clearance between the rod and crankthrow casting can be checked with a feeler gauge. Pry the rod carefully to one side as far as possible and measure the distance on the other side of the rod.

Crankshaft Repairs

If a journal is damaged on the crankshaft, repair is possible by having the crankshaft machined, after removal from engine to a standard undersize. Consult the machine shop for their advice.

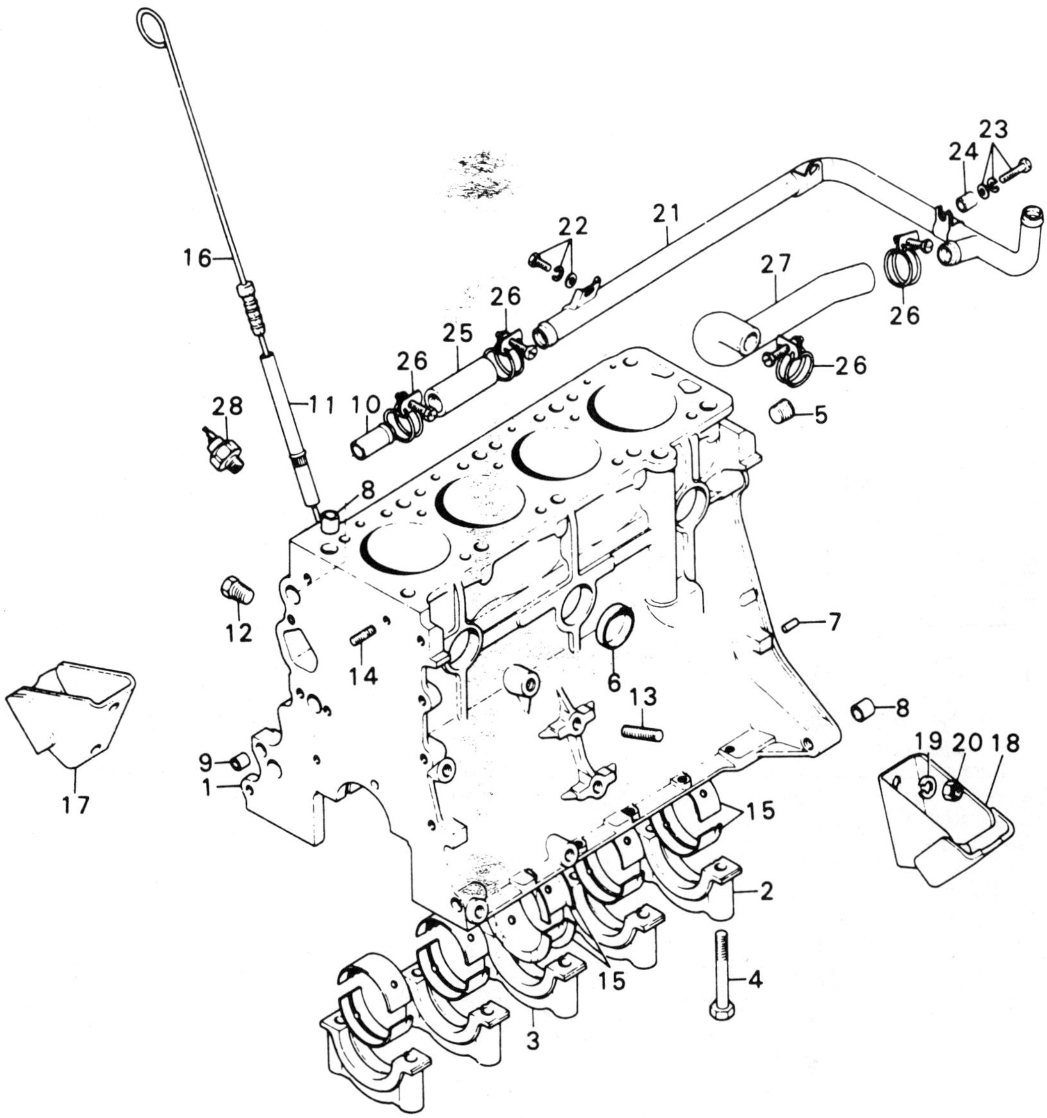

1. Cylinder block
2. Bearing cap
3. Center bearing cap
4. Bearing cap bolt
5. Taper plug
6. Expansion plug
7. Dowel pin
8. Dowel bushing
9. Dowel bushing
10. Fitting
11. Dipstick tube
12. Taper plug
13. Stud
14. Stud
15. Crankshaft bearings
16. Dipstick
17. Engine mount
18. Engine mount
19. Washer
20. Nut
21. Heater pipe assembly
22. Bolt
23. Bolt
24. Spacer
25. Heater hose
26. Clip
27. Heater hose
28. Oil pressure switch

Typical cylinder block assembly

ENGINE LUBRICATION

Oil Pan

REMOVAL AND INSTALLATION

The engine must be raised off its mounts to provide for the pan to clear the suspension crossmember. However, most of the front wheel drive models have enough clearance to provide for pan removal without raising the engine.

1. Jack up the front of the car and support it on stands.
2. Drain the oil.
3. Remove the underbody splash shield.

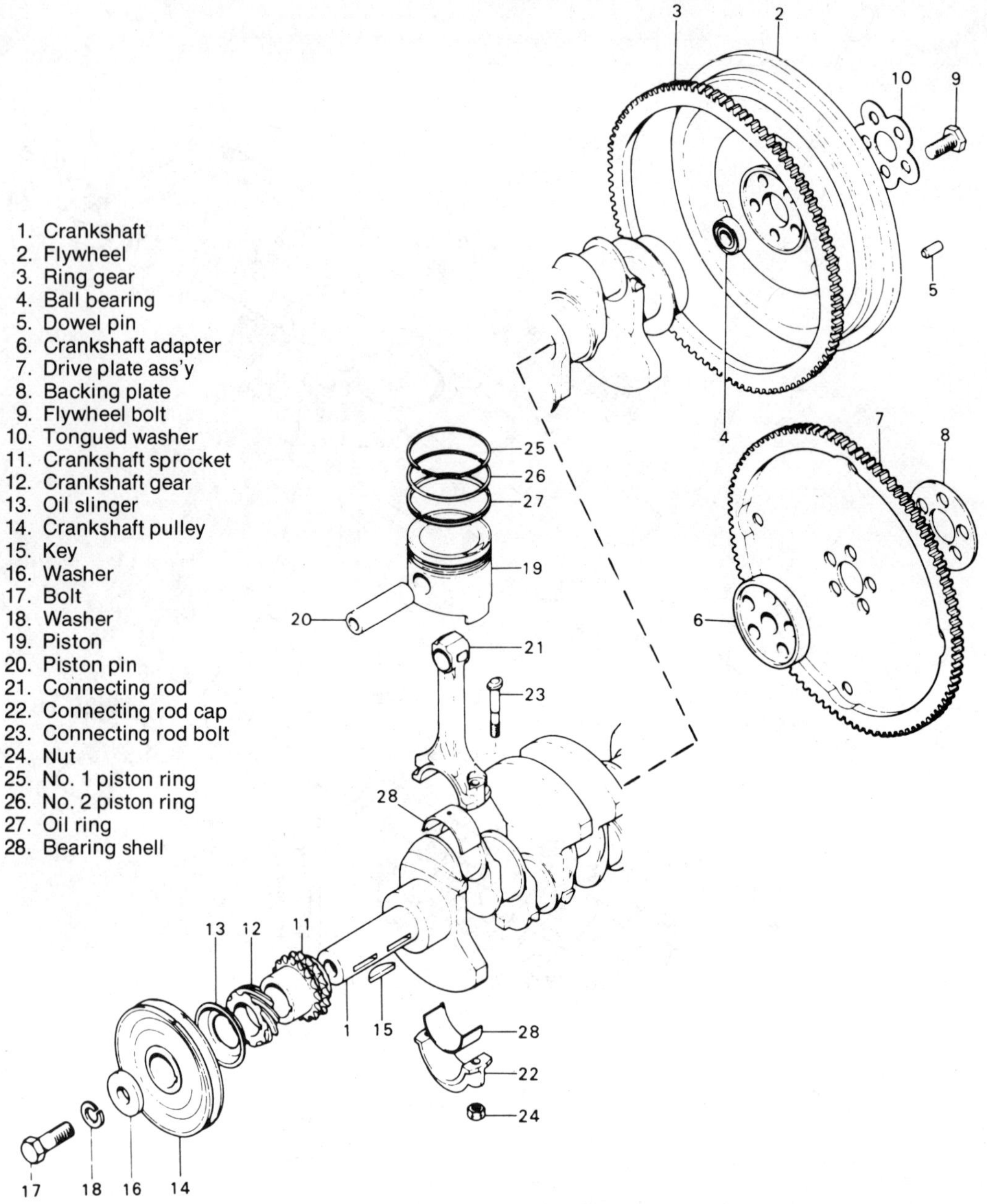

Typical engine crankshaft, connecting rod and piston assembly

4. Remove the retaining nuts from the left and right engine mounts.

5. Place a jack under the bell housing. Use a board to evenly distribute the pressure and then raise the engine.

6. Remove the oil pan bolts, drop the pan, and slide it out from under the car.

7. Clean the mating surfaces of the oil pan and the engine block.

8. Apply sealer to the engine block at the block-to-chain case and block-to-rear oil seal case joint faces.

9. Using non-hardening sealer, glue a new gasket to the oil pan.

10. Install the oil pan. Hand-tighten the retaining bolts.

11. Starting at one end of the pan, gradually tighten the retaining bolts to 4–6 ft. lbs. in a criss-cross pattern.

12. Lower the engine and tighten the mount retaining nuts.

13. Install the oil pan drain plug.

14. Install the splash shield and lower the car.

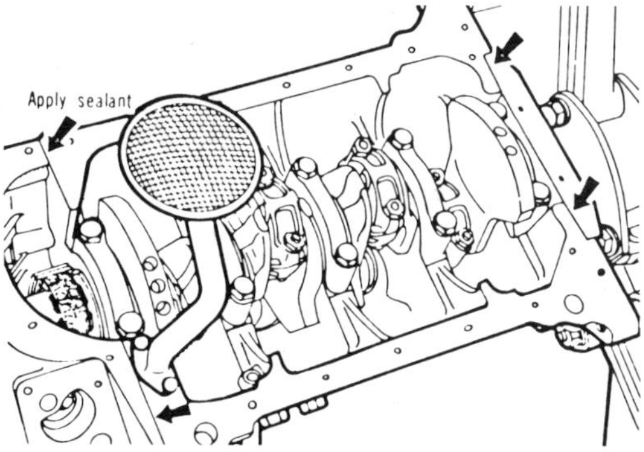

Apply a good sealer at these four points

15. Refill the crankcase with oil. Start the engine and check for leaks.

Rear Main Oil Seal

REPLACEMENT

The rear main oil seal is located in a housing on the rear of the block. To replace the seal, it is necessary to remove the transmission and perform the work from underneath the car or remove the engine and perform the work on an engine stand or work bench. See Chapter 6 for "Transmission Removal and Installation."

NOTE: *Front wheel drive models require the engine be removed from the car.*

1. Unscrew the retaining bolts and remove the housing from the block.
2. Remove the separator from the housing.
3. Using a screwdriver, pry out the old seal.
4. Clean the housing and the separator.
5. Lightly oil the replacement seal. Tap the seal into the housing using a canister top or other circular piece of metal. The oil seal should be installed so that the seal plate fits into the inner contact surface of the seal case.
6. Install the separator into the housing so that the oil hole faces down.
7. Oil the lips of the seal and install the housing on the rear of the engine block.

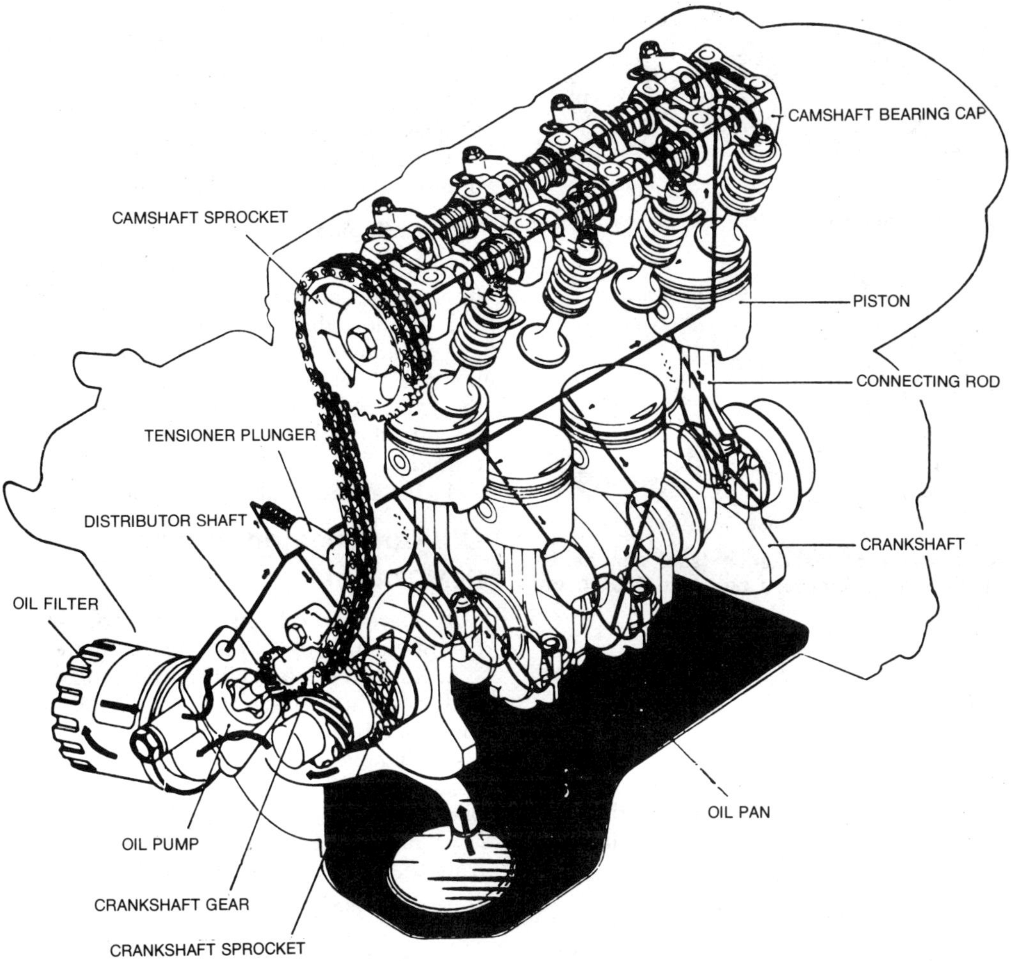

Engine lubrication system (typical)

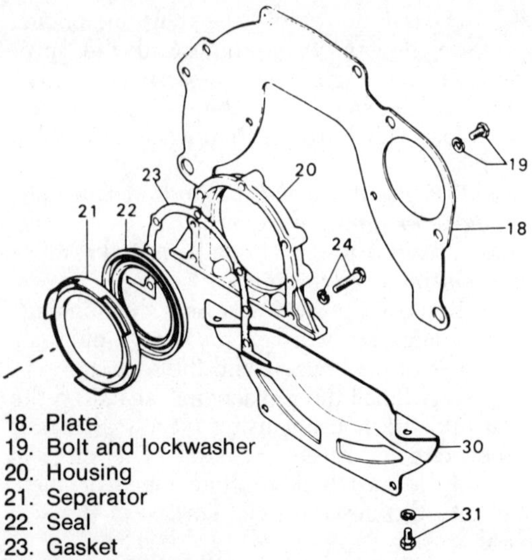

18. Plate
19. Bolt and lockwasher
20. Housing
21. Separator
22. Seal
23. Gasket
24. Bolt and lockwasher
30. Cover
31. Bolt and lockwasher

Typical rear main seal and components

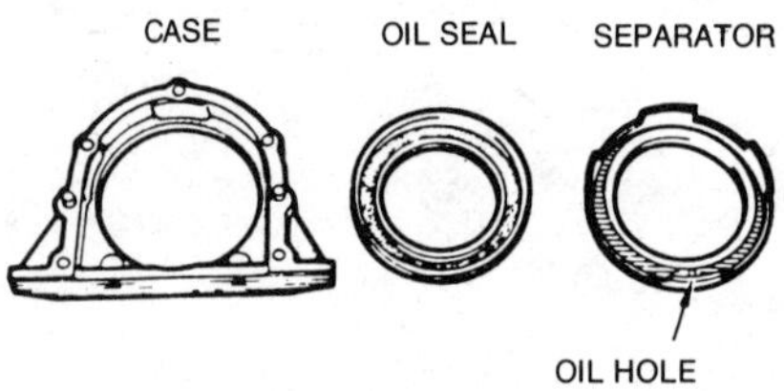

Rear main seal components

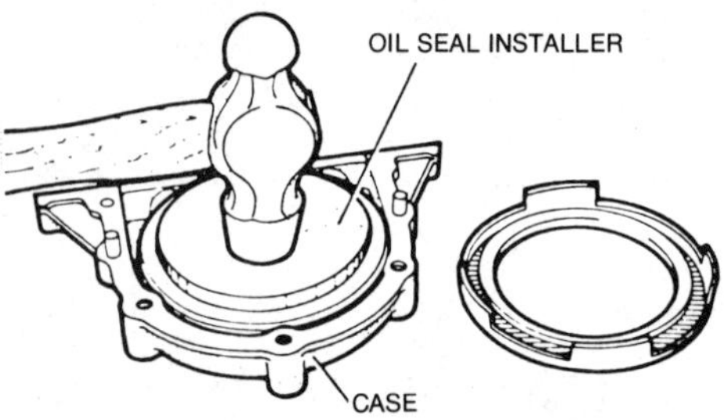

Typical rear seal installation (seal can be installed by hand pressure on some 2000cc engines)

Oil Pump

LOCATIONS

1400 cc Engine

A gear driven oil pump mounted in the front case and driven directly by the crankshaft.

1600 cc Engine

WITH TIMING CHAIN

A rotor type oil pump located in the timing chain case and driven by a crankshaft gear.

WITH TIMING BELT

A rotor type oil pump located on the lower left side of the front case and driven by the timing belt.

SILENT SHAFT ENGINES

A gear type oil pump located on the front of the left counterbalance shaft and driven by the timing belt.

2000 cc Engine

SILENT SHAFT ENGINE

A gear type oil pump located on the front of the right counterbalance shaft and driven by the timing chain.

2600 cc Engine

SILENT SHAFT ENGINE

A gear type oil pump located on the front of the right counterbalance shaft and driven by the timing chain.

OIL PUMP REMOVAL AND INSTALLATION

To remove the rotor type pumps that are located behind the front cover (except 1400 cc), refer to the Timing Gear Cover, Chain, Counterbalance Shaft and Tensioner section of this chapter and follow the procedures listed there to remove the pump. The 1400 cc engine oil pump and oil pan located oil pumps follow.

1400 cc Engine

1. Remove the timing belt. See timing belt removal section in this chapter.
2. Remove the engine oil pan and oil screen.
3. Remove the front case assembly (seven bolts). The oil pump is mounted in the rear of the front case. Turn the front case over and remove the oil pump cover. Service as required.
4. Installation is the reverse of removal.

Oil Pan Located Pumps

REMOVAL

1. Place No. 1 piston at TDC on the compression stroke (timing marks aligned).
2. Loosen the left and right engine mounts and raise and block the engine off of the mounting brackets.
3. Remove the front splash shields, if necessary. Drain the oil and remove the engine oil pan.
4. Remove the screen and the oil pump from the engine block.

INSTALLATION

1. Be sure that No. 1 piston is still on TDC.
2. Remove the distributor cap and make

sure that the rotor is pointing to the No. 1 position.

NOTE: *This should align the distributor pawl parallel with the crankshaft center line.*

3. Align the mating marks of the distributor gear and body (if necessary). Insert the oil pump assembly with a new gasket into the engine block until the oil pump shaft gear is in mesh with the crankshaft gear and engaged with the distributor pawl.

4. Using a new gasket, install the oil pan, connect the engine mounts and install the splash shields.

5. Fill the engine with fresh oil, start the engine and check the ignition timing.

ENGINE COOLING

Your car is equipped with a conventional, liquid cooling system consisting of a radiator, possibly an expansion tank, a belt-driven water pump and a thermostat. Automatic transmission cars are equipped with an additional oil cooler located in the bottom of the radiator.

CAUTION: *Disconnect the negative battery cable when working on front wheel drive models. The fan may come on even though the switch is off.*

Radiator

REMOVAL AND INSTALLATION

1. Remove the splash panel from the bottom of the car. Drain the radiator by opening the petcock. Remove the shroud on models so equipped. On front wheel drive models disconnect the fan motor wiring harness.

2. Disconnect the radiator hoses at the engine. On automatic transmission cars, disconnect and plug the transmission lines to the bottom of the radiator. On models that have an expansion tank be sure to disconnect the feed hose.

3. Remove the two retaining bolts from either side of the radiator. Lift out the radiator. On front wheel drive models the fan and motor may be left attached to the radiator and be removed with the radiator as one unit.

4. Install the radiator in the reverse order of removal. Tighten the retaining bolts gradually in a criss-cross pattern.

Water Pump

REMOVAL AND INSTALLATION

1. Open the radiator petcock and the engine drain plug on the passenger's side. Drain the cooling system. Disconnect the battery ground (negative) cable.

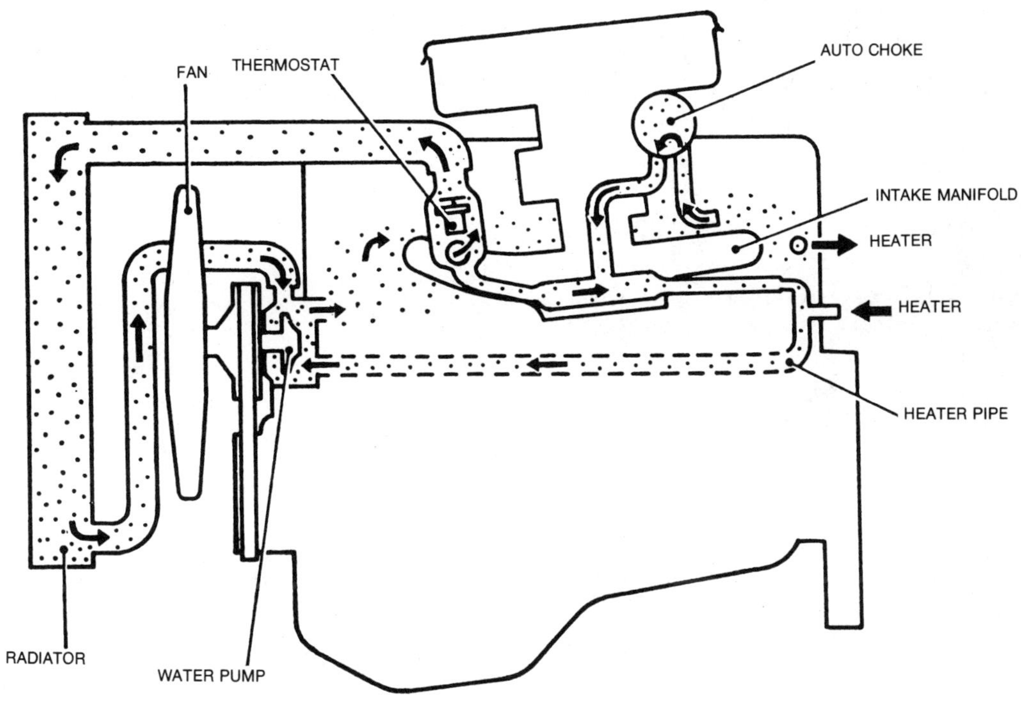

Typical cooling system (1600cc shown)

2. Remove the fan belt, fan, and the generator brace.

3. Unscrew the retaining nuts and bolts. Remove the water pump.

4. Install a new gasket on the timing gear cover with sealer.

5. Apply sealer to the mating surface of the water pump. Install the pump. Tighten the nuts and bolts gradually in a criss-cross pattern.

CAUTION: *Don't overtighten the fasteners, as the pump is aluminum.*

6. Spin the pump to make sure that it doesn't interfere with the case.

7. Install the fan.

8. Install and tension the fan belt as described in Chapter 3.

9. Refill the cooling system with a 50/50 mixture of antifreeze and water.

Thermostat

REMOVAL AND INSTALLATION

The Thermostat is located in the intake manifold under the upper radiator hose.

1. Drain the coolant below the level of the thermostat.

2. Remove the two retaining bolts and lift

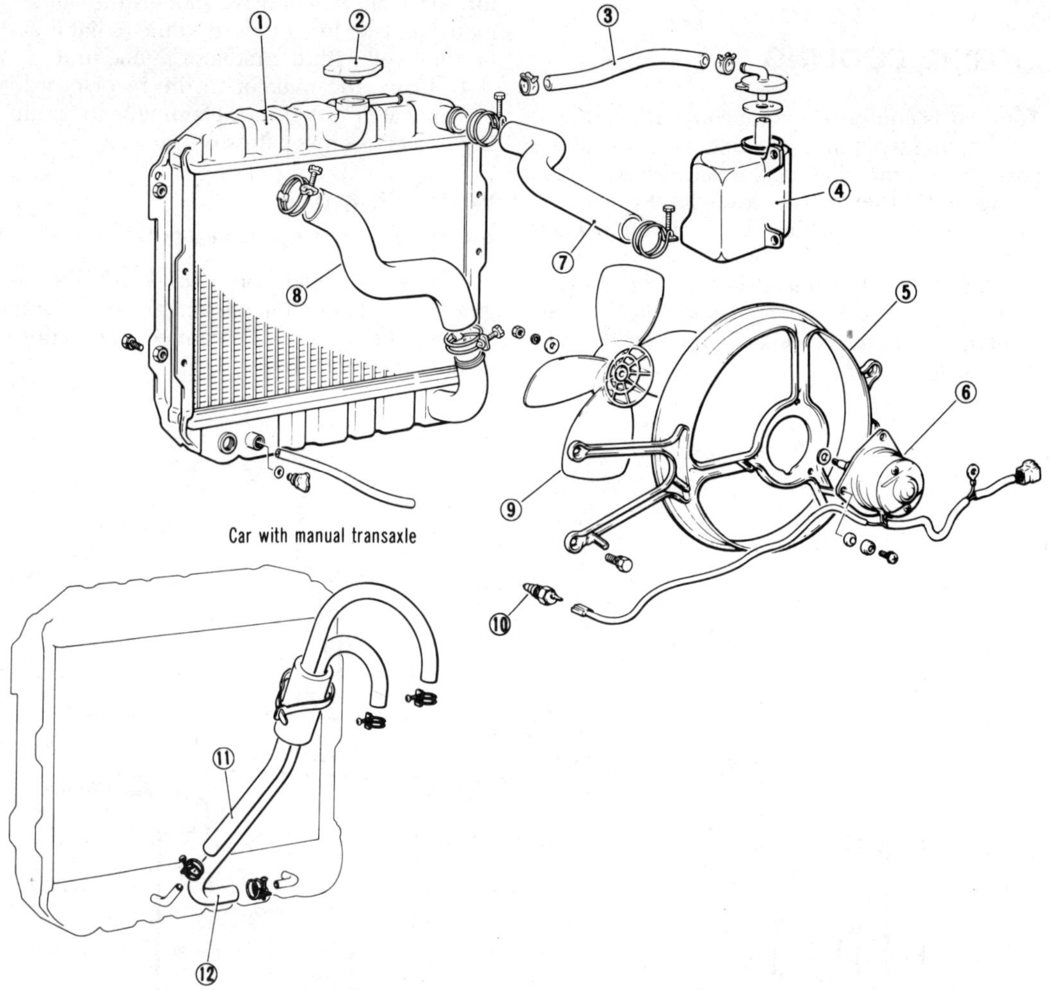

1. Radiator
2. Radiator cap
3. Rubber hose
4. Reserve tank
5. Radiator shroud
6. Motor assembly
7. Radiator upper hose
8. Radiator lower hose
9. Fan
10. Thermo sensor
11. Fluid cooler hose
12. Fluid return hose

Radiator and fan assembly—front wheel drive models (typical)

the thermostat housing off the intake manifold with the hose still attached.

NOTE: *If you are careful, it is not necessary to remove the upper radiator hose.*

3. Lift the thermostat out of the manifold.

4. Install the thermostate in the reverse order of removal. Use a new gasket and coat the mating surfaces with sealer.

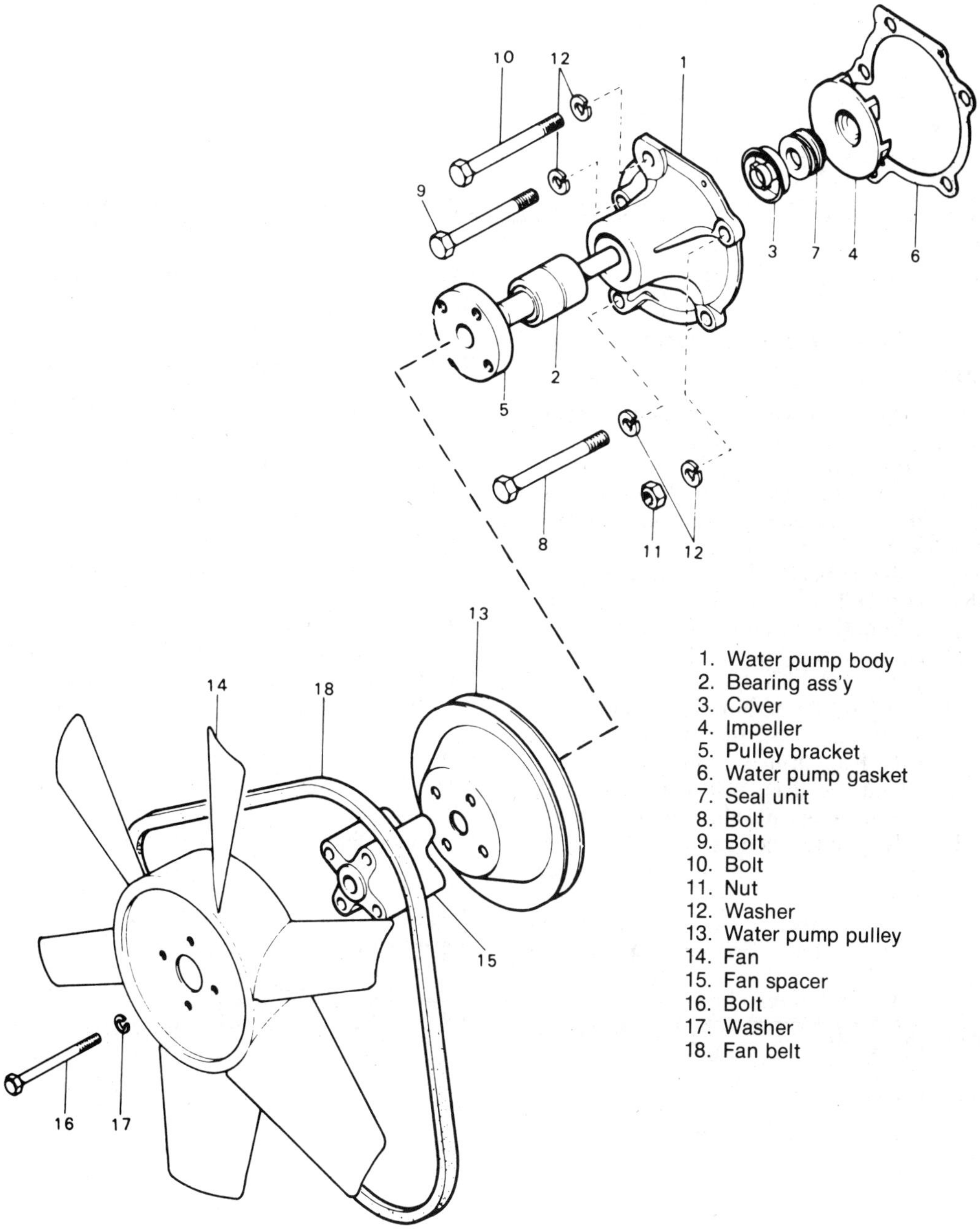

Water pump and fan assembly (1600cc shown)

Emission Controls and Fuel System

4

EMISSION CONTROLS

Crankcase Emission Control System

A closed-type crankcase ventilation system is used to prevent engine blow-by gases from escaping into the atmosphere.

A small fixed orifice, located in the intake manifold, is connected to the rear section of the rocker arm cover by a hose. Some later models have replaced the orifice with a PCV valve. The PCV valve is generally located in the hose from the rocker cover.

A larger hose is connected from the front of the rocker arm cover to the air cleaner assembly. Under light to medium carburetor throttle opening, the blow-by gases are drawn through the fixed orifice. Under heavy acceleration, both the fixed orifice and the large hose route the gases into the engine.

The only maintenance required is to regularly check the breather hose condition, clean the orifice in the intake manifold, and clean the steel wool filter, in the air cleaner. Replace the PCV valve (if equipped) when it becomes clogged or at the recommended service intervals.

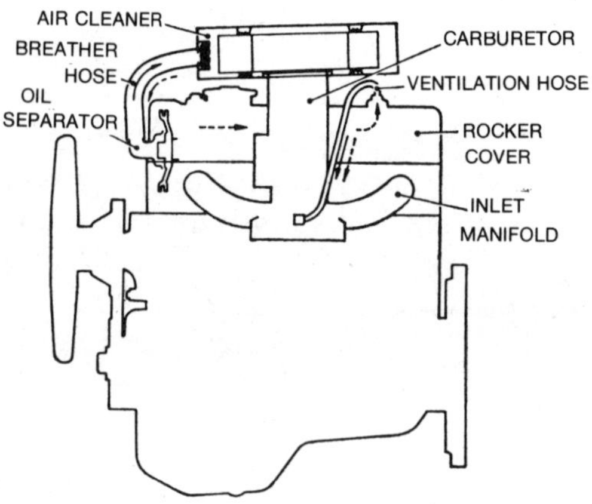

Typical crankcase ventilation system

Fuel Evaporation Control System

This system is designed to prevent hydrocarbons from escaping into the atmosphere from the fuel tank, due to normal evaporation.

The parts of the system are as follow:

Separator tank—Located near the gasoline tank, used to accomodate expansion, and to allow maximum condensation of the fuel vapors.

Canister—Located in the engine compartment to trap and retain gasoline vapors while the engine is not operating. When the engine is started, fresh air is drawn into the canister or canisters, removing the stored vapors, and is directed to the air cleaner.

Two-way Valve (1977–83)—Because of different methods of tank venting and the use of a sealed gasoline tank cap, the two-way valve is used in the vapor lines. The valve relieves either pressure or vacuum in the tank.

Purge Control Valve (1977–83)—The purge control valve replaces the check valve used in

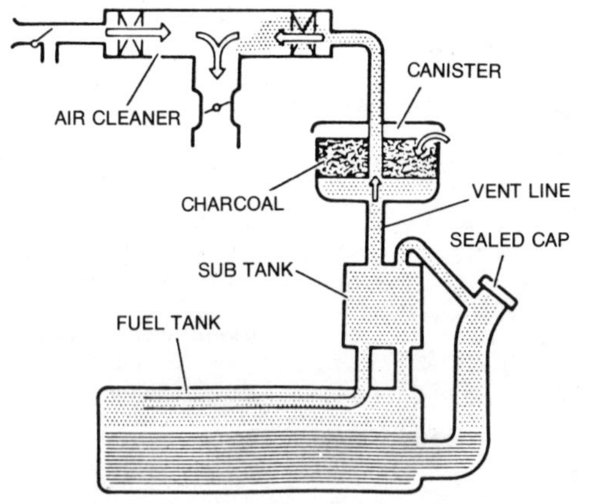

Typical later model evaporative emissions system

previous years. During idle, the valve closes off the vapor passage to the air cleaner.

Fuel Check Valve (1977–83)—This valve is used to prevent fuel leakage in case of roll over. It is installed in the vapor line between the two-way valve and the canister on the coupe, sedan, and hatchback, and between the separator and the two-way valve on the station wagon.

Bowl Vent Valve (1980–83)—Controls carburetor bowl vapors between canister and carburetor.

Carbon Element (1980–83)—Element is located in the air cleaner to store vapors generated in the carburetor. Replace if clogged or dirty.

MAINTENANCE

Be sure that all hoses are clamped and not dry-rotted or broken. Check the valves for cracks, signs of gasoline leakage, and proper operating condition.

The canister air filter (models equipped) should be inspected and changed at least every 24,000 miles.

COMPONENT REMOVAL AND INSTALLATION

Charcoal Canister

The canister or canisters used on these models is replaced periodically. No other maintenance is necessary except for an occasional check of connecting hose condition.

To replace the canister:

1. Remove the two connecting hoses from the canister.
2. Loosen and remove the canister retaining band bolt.
3. Remove the canister.
4. Installation is the reverse of removal. Replace any brittle hoses.

Thermostatically Controlled Air Cleaner

Your car is equipped with a thermostically controlled air cleaner which maintains the intake air admitted to the carburetor between 95°F and 105°F. To do this, the air cleaner snorkel has a movable door which allows intake air to be drawn from either a manifold heat stove (cold operation) or from under the hood (normal operation). The door is operated by a vacuum motor which is regulated by a bimetallic sensor located within the air cleaner. The sensor is connected by hoses to the intake manifold and the vacuum motor. At low temperatures, the sensor supplies manifold vacuum to the motor which then maintains the air door in a closed position. This allows only preheated air drawn from around the exhaust manifold to reach the carburetor. As the engine warms, the sensor allows less and less manifold vacuum to reach the motor. The vacuum motor begins to open the door and permits cooler air to be drawn through the snorkel. When the engine reaches normal operating temperature, no vacuum reaches the motor and it closes off the exhaust manifold

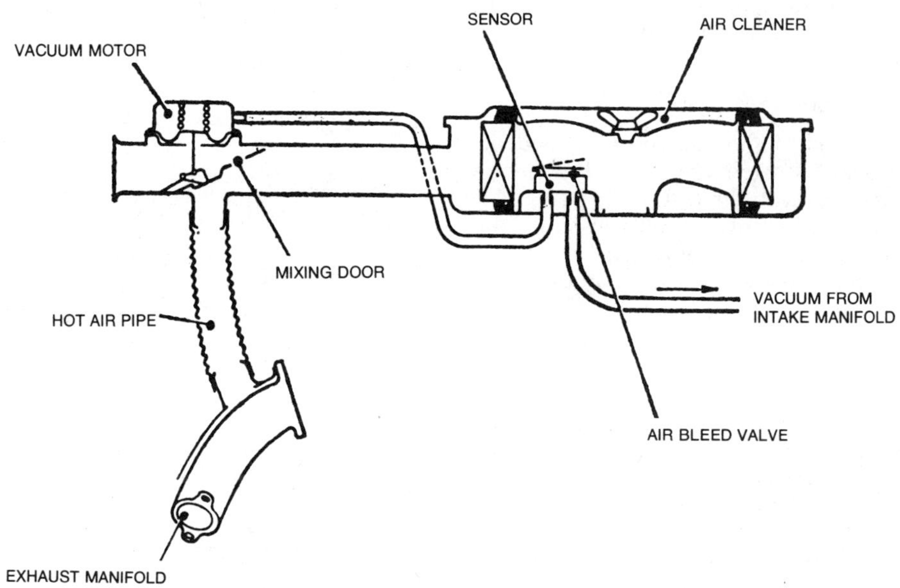

Cross section of a thermostatically controlled air intake system

heat stove duct. A vacuum override provides cold air intake during periods of hard acceleration when exhaust manifold heated air is normally being supplied.

TESTING

Air Door

1. Either start with a cold engine or remove the air cleaner from the engine for at least half an hour. While cooling the air cleaner, leave the engine compartment hood open.
2. Tape a thermometer of known accuracy to the inside of the air cleaner so that it is near the temperature sensor unit. Install the air cleaner on the engine but do not fasten its wing nut.
3. Start the engine. With the engine cold and the outside temperature less than 90°F, the door should be in the "heat on" position (closed to outside air).
4. Operate the throttle lever rapidly to ½–¾ of its opening and release it. The air door should open to allow outside air to enter and then it should close again.
5. Allow the engine to warm up to normal operating temperature. Watch the door. When it opens to the outside air, remove the top from the air cleaner. The temperature should be over 90°F and no more than 130°F; 115°F is about normal. If the door does not work within these temperature ranges or fails to work at all, check for linkage or door binding.

If binding is not present and the air door is not working, proceed with the vacuum tests given below. If these indicate no faults in the vacuum motor and the door is not working, the temperature sensor is defective and must be replaced.

Vacuum Motor

1. Check all of the vacuum lines and fittings for leaks. Correct any leaks. If none are found, proceed with the test.
2. Remove the hose which runs from the sensor to the vacuum motor. Run a hose directly from the manifold vacuum source to the vacuum motor.
3. If the motor closes the air door, it is functioning properly and the temperature sensor is defective.
4. If the motor does not close the door and no binding is present in its operation, the vacuum motor is defective and must be replaced.

NOTE: *If an alternate vacuum source is applied to the motor, insert a vacuum gauge in the line by using a T-fitting. Apply at least 9 in. Hg. of vacuum in order to operate the motor.*

Secondary Air Supply System

This system supplies air for the further combustion of unburned gases in the thermal reactor (California only) or exhaust manifold and consists of a reed valve, air hoses, and air passages built into the cylinder head.

The reed valve is operated by exhaust pulsations in the exhaust manifold. It draws fresh air through the air cleaner and supplies it to the exhaust ports.

MAINTENANCE

Check for damage to the air hoses and air pipes. Make sure the air passages are open in the head.

Pulse Air Feeder System (1981–83)

The Pulse Air Feeder System supplies "secondary air" into the exhaust system between the front and rear catalytic converters to promote oxidation of exhaust emissions in the rear converter. The system consists of a main reed valve, a subreed valve, air hoses and crankcase passages.

The main reed valve is actuated by pressure created by No. 3 piston. The subreed valve is actuated by exhaust pulsations. Fresh air is drawn through the air cleaner.

Exhaust Gas Recirculation System

The EGR system recirculates part of the exhaust gases into the combustion chambers. This dilutes the air/fuel mixture, reducing formation of oxides of nitrogen in the exhaust gases by lowering the peak combustion temperatures.

The parts of the EGR system are:

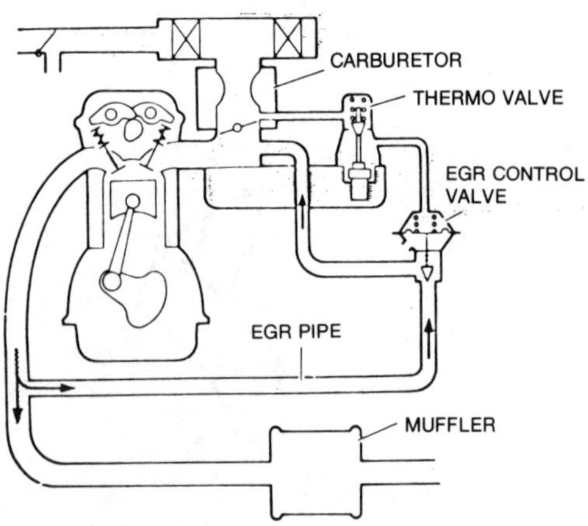

Typical EGR system

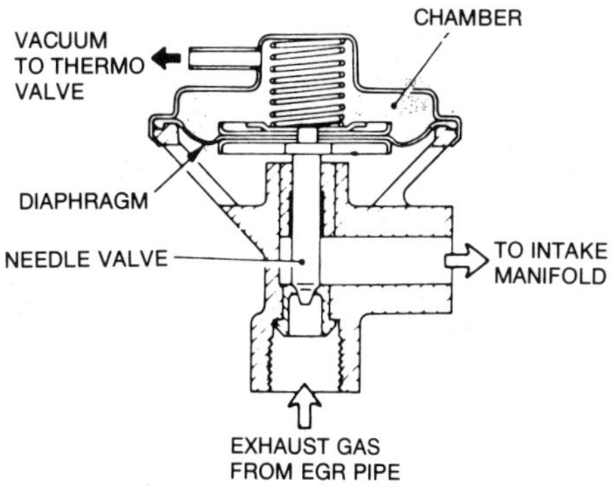

Cutaway of an EGR valve

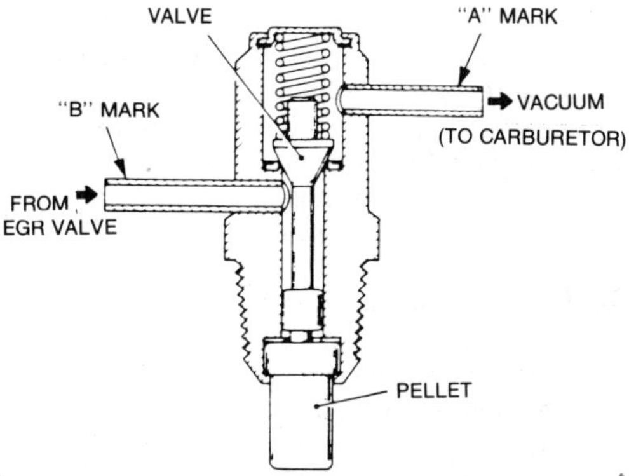

Cutaway of a thermo valve

EGR valve—Operated by vacuum drawn from a point above the carburetor throttle plate. The vacuum controls the raising and lowering of the valve pintle to allow exhaust gases to pass from the exhaust system to the intake manifold.

Thermo Valve—Used to stop EGR valve operation below approximately 131 degrees, in order to improve cold driveability and starting.

Dual EGR Control Valve (1978–83)

The EGR vacuum flow is suspended during idle and wide open throttle operation.

The primary valve controls EGR flow when the throttle valve opening is relatively narrow, while the secondary control valve operates at wider openings.

Sub EGR Control Valve— Linked to the throttle valve to closely modulate the EGR gas flow.

EGR Maintenance Warning Light (1977–78)

A light in the speedometer assembly to alert the driver to the need for EGR system maintenance.

This device has a mileage sensor to light the visual signal at 15,000 mile intervals.

Upon completion of the required EGR system maintenance, the warning light can be turned off by resetting the switch. It is in the speedometer cable, under the instrument panel.

MAINTENANCE

1. Check all vacuum hoses for cracks, breakage and correct installation.
2. Check EGR valve operation by applying vacuum to the EGR valve vacuum nipple with the engine idling. The idle should become rough.
3. Check the passages in the cylinder head and intake manifold for clogging. Clean as necessary.
4. Cold start the engine. The EGR port nipple should be open. When the coolant is warmed to over 131 degrees, the port should be closed.

COMPONENT REMOVAL AND INSTALLATION

EGR Valve

1. Remove the vacuum hose.
2. Disconnect the exhaust line from the EGR valve.
3. Remove the EGR valve.
4. Installation is the reverse of removal. Be sure to tighten the nut on the EGR line to 22–25 ft. lbs.

Thermo Valve

The thermo valve is located on the left side of the intake manifold. It is threaded into the manifold and can be removed with an open-end wrench.

1. Disconnect the vacuum lines.
2. Using an open-end wrench, carefully turn the thermo valve out of the intake manifold.
3. Apply a good sealer to the valve threads before installation.
4. Connect the vacuum lines. The "A" nipple should be connected to the vacuum hose from the carburoetor and the "B" nipple to the EGR valve.

Thermal Reactor (1977) California and High Altitude

This unit is used to further the combustion of the exhaust gases. It consists of a shell and a core with heat insulation material between, mounted at the exhaust manifold.

MAINTENANCE

1. Listen for any abnormal sound from the reactor.
2. Check for cracks and damage.
3. Check the thermal reactor flange on the cylinder head for warpage.

NOTE: *The thermal reactor must be replaced when defective. It cannot be disassembled.*

Catalytic Converter (1978–83)

This unit or units (two used in 1981–83) replaces the thermal rector. It is filled with catalyst to oxidize hydrocarbons and carbon monoxide in the exhaust gases. Two units are used on some late models.

MAINTENANCE

1. Check the core for cracks and damages.
2. If the idle carbon monoxide and hydrocarbon content exceeds specifications and the ignition timing and idle mixture are correct, the converter must be replaced.

Jet Air System (1978–83)

A jet air passage is provided in the carburetor, intake manifold, and cylinder head to direct air to a jet valve, operated simultaneously with the intake valve.

On the intake stroke, jet air is forced into the combustion chamber because of the pressure difference between the ends of the air jet passage.

This jet of air produces a strong swirl in the combustion chamber scavenging the residual gases around the spark plug.

The jet air volume lessens with increased throttle opening. It is at a maximum at idle.

MAINTENANCE

No maintenance is required, other than clearance adjustment during valve adjustment. The valve can be removed from the cylinder head for service or replacement.

NOTE: *Refer to Valve Lash Adjustment for adjusting jet valve clearance.*

Ignition Timing Control System (1977–83)

When the engine is idling or operating at low speeds under light load or deceleration, the exhaust gas temperature is low, resulting in incomplete combustion of the air/fuel mixture. To prevent this, ignition timing is retarded under these conditions to maintain high exhaust gas temperature.

The units in the Ignition Timing Control system are as follows:

Dual-diaphragm distributor—This distributor has both retard and advance mechanisms operated by vacuum.

Thermo Valve—This valve is used to protect the engine from overheating. When coolant temperature reaches 203 degrees, the advance unit is allowed to operate, causing an increase in engine speed and a decrease in coolant temperature.

Single diaphragm distributor—This distributor has a single diaphragm vacuum advance unit, which advances the ignition timing as engine vacuum dictates. The single diaphragm distributor must not be interchanged with the dual diaphragm distributor. The dis-

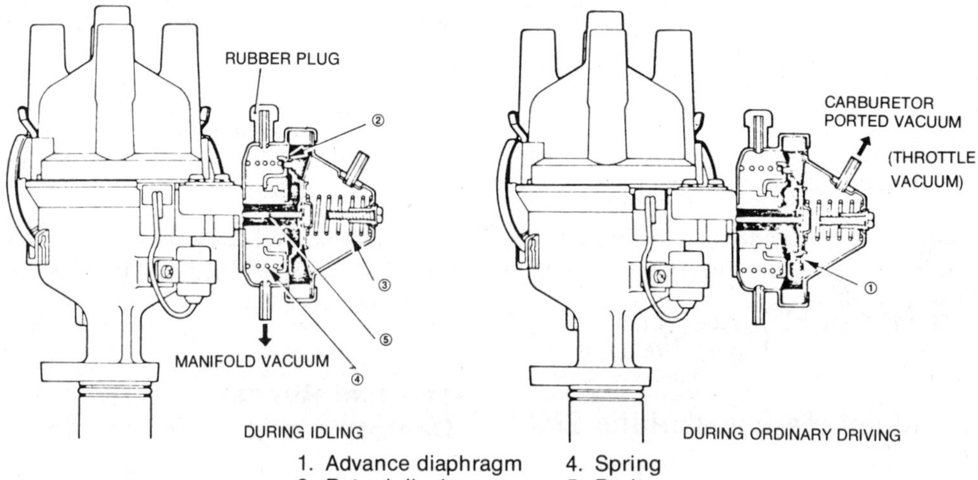

1. Advance diaphragm
2. Retard diaphragm
3. Spring
4. Spring
5. Rod

Dual diaphragm distributor operation

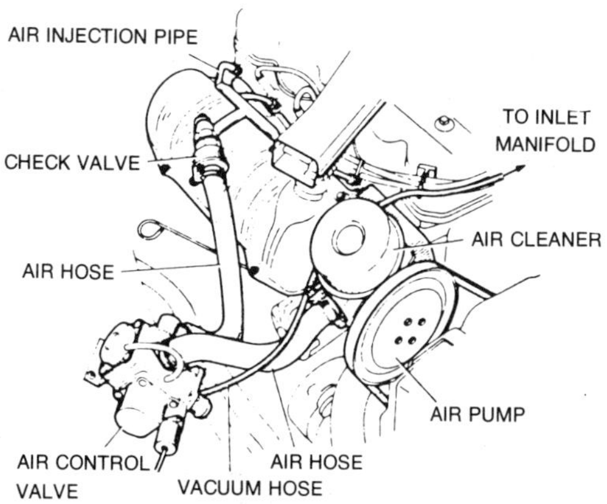

Typical air injection system

tributor operating curves are different and would cause increased emissions. A thermo valve is *not* used with this type of distributor.

MAINTENANCE

Distributor maintenance is at tune-up intervals.

Orifice Spark Advance Control (1977)

The OSAC valve is located in the vacuum line between the distributor and the carburetor. Its function is to delay vacuum advance during medium to high speed operation, when high vacuum would be present. It is used only with the single diaphragm distributor.

MAINTENANCE

No maintenance is required.

Deceleration Device (1977–83)

Closing of the throttle valve on deceleration is delayed in order to burn the air/fuel mixture more thoroughly. A vacuum controlled dashpot, attached to the carburetor linkage is used.

A servo valve detects intake manifold vacuum and closes if vacuum exceeds a preset value. Since the air in the dash pot diaphragm chamber can not escape, the throttle linkage opening is temporarily retained. If the vacuum is below the preset value, the servo valve opens and the dashpot works normally.

MAINTENANCE

Inspect the hoses for breaks and damage, and the valve body for cracks.

ADJUSTMENT

1. Have the engine running, brakes locked, and a tachometer attached.
2. Push the dashpot rod, connected to the carburetor arm, upward and into the dashpot until it stops.
3. Note the rpm at the dash pot stop and adjust to the following specifications. Note the time required between suddenly releasing the dashpot rod and the return to normal curb idle.
4. The specifications are as follow:
   a. 1600 cc engine—Calif. and H/Alt.
   Set Speed—1900± 100 RPM
   Required Time—3 to 6 Sec.
   b. 2000 cc engine—Calif.
   Set Speed—1500± 100 RPM
   Required time—3 to 6 sec.
   c. 1400 and 1600 cc engine—49 States, 2000 cc engine—49 States
   Set speed—2000± 100 RPM
   Required time—3 to 6 sec.
   d. All engines: 1981–83
   Set Speed—2000± 100 rpm

Mixture Control Valve (1977–83)

This control valve is used to supply additional air into the intake manifold to decrease manifold vacuum during deceleration, and is activated by the intake manifold vacuum level.

Manual Altitude Compensation System (1977–83)

An off-on valve is used to increase the air supply to the carburetor to lean the mixture and decrease the EGR flow for high altitude operation.

MAINTENANCE

The required maintenance is to inspect any vacuum hoses and routing for kinks, breakage and cracks. The off-on valve should be on for high altitude and off for driving under 4000 ft.

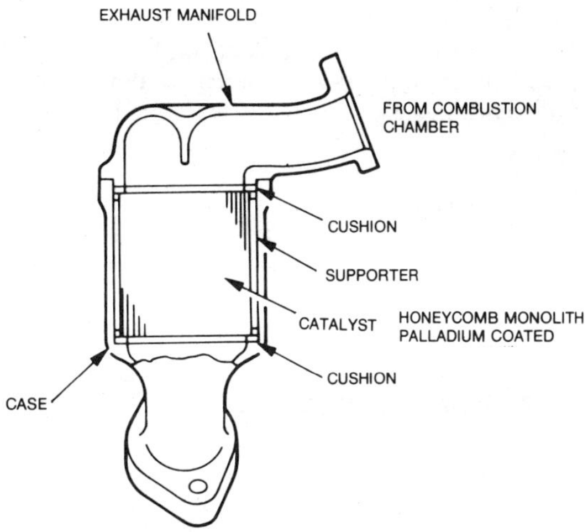

Cutaway view of the manifold mounted catalytic converter

FUEL SYSTEM

Fuel Filter

REPLACEMENT

All models use an in-line filter which should be replaced every 12,000 miles.

Mechanical Fuel Pump

The mechanical fuel pump operates directly off of a camshaft eccentric. A fuel return valve is located in the upper body of the pump. If the fuel temperature rises above 122°F, the valve opens and routes fuel back to the tank, preventing percolation.

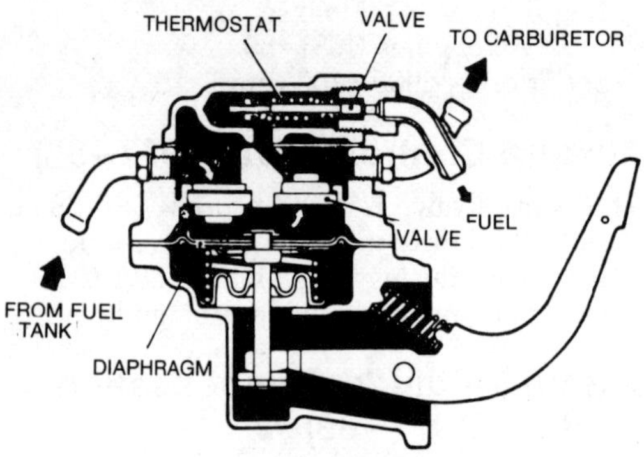

Section view of a mechanical fuel pump

REMOVAL AND INSTALLATION

1. Undo the two screws and remove the plastic heat shield.
2. Disconnect the three fuel pump lines.
3. Unscrew the two retaining nuts and remove the fuel pump. Remove the gasket and insulator.
4. Clean the fuel pump mounting surface on the cylinder head.
5. Position two new gaskets on the cylinder head studs. Apply non-hardening sealer to both sides of the gaskets.

TESTING

Disconnect the fuel line from the carburetor and attach a pressure tester to the end of the line. Crank the engine. The tester should show psi as listed on the tune up charts.

Carburetor

REMOVAL AND INSTALLATION

1. Remove the air cleaner. Pull the large crankcase ventilation hose off the front of the air cleaner. Disconnect the two smaller hoses, one goes to the rear of the rocker arm cover and one to the intake manifold.
2. Loosen and remove the two nuts and one bracket which attach the air cleaner to the rocker arm cover.
3. Lift the bottom housing of the air cleaner off of the carburetor and, with it, the hose coming up from the exhaust manifold heat stove.
4. Disconnect the wiring to the throttle positioner solenoid and the fuel cut-off solenoid.
5. Disconnect the accelerator rod and, on cars equipped with automatic transmissions, the shift rod.
6. Remove the fuel line and vacuum lines.
7. Remove the plug on the passenger's side of the cylinder block and drain the coolant.

   CAUTION: *Not draining the cooling system will allow the anti-freeze/water mixture to leak down into the intake manifold and enter the combusion chambers where it can do all sorts of damage.*
8. Disconnect the water hose which runs between the carburetor and the cylinder head.
9. Unscrew the four retaining nuts and remove the carburetor.
10. Install the carburetor in the reverse order of removal. Use a new mounting gasket and sealer.

OVERHAUL

NOTE: *Specific procedures for rebuilding your carburetor are provided with the rebuilding kit.*

Efficient carburetion depends greatly on careful cleaning and inspection during overhaul, since dirt, gum, water, or varnish in or on the carburetor parts are often responsible for poor performance.

Overhaul your carburetor in a clean, dust-free area. Carefully disassemble the carburetor, referring often to the exploded views. Keep all similar and lookalike parts segregated during disassembly and cleaning to avoid accidental interchange during assembly. Make a note of all jet sizes.

When the carburetor is disassembled, wash all parts (except diaphragms, electric choke units, pump plunger, and any other plastic, leather, fiber, or rubber parts) in clean carburetor solvent. Do not leave parts in the solvent any longer than is necessary to sufficiently loosen the deposits. Excessive cleaning may remove the special finish from the float bowl and choke valve bodies, leaving these parts unfit for service. Rinse all parts in clean solvent and blow them dry with compressed air or allow them to air dry. Wipe clean all cork, plastic, leather, and fiber parts with a clean, lint-free cloth.

1. Stud
2. Choke
3. Water hose
4. Return spring
5. Depression chamber
6. Float chamber cover
7. Float chamber gasket
8. Fuel inlet nipple
9. Filter
10. Needle valve
11. Float
12. Secondary pilot jet
13. Secondary main jet
14. Primary main jet
15. Valve weight
16. Check valve

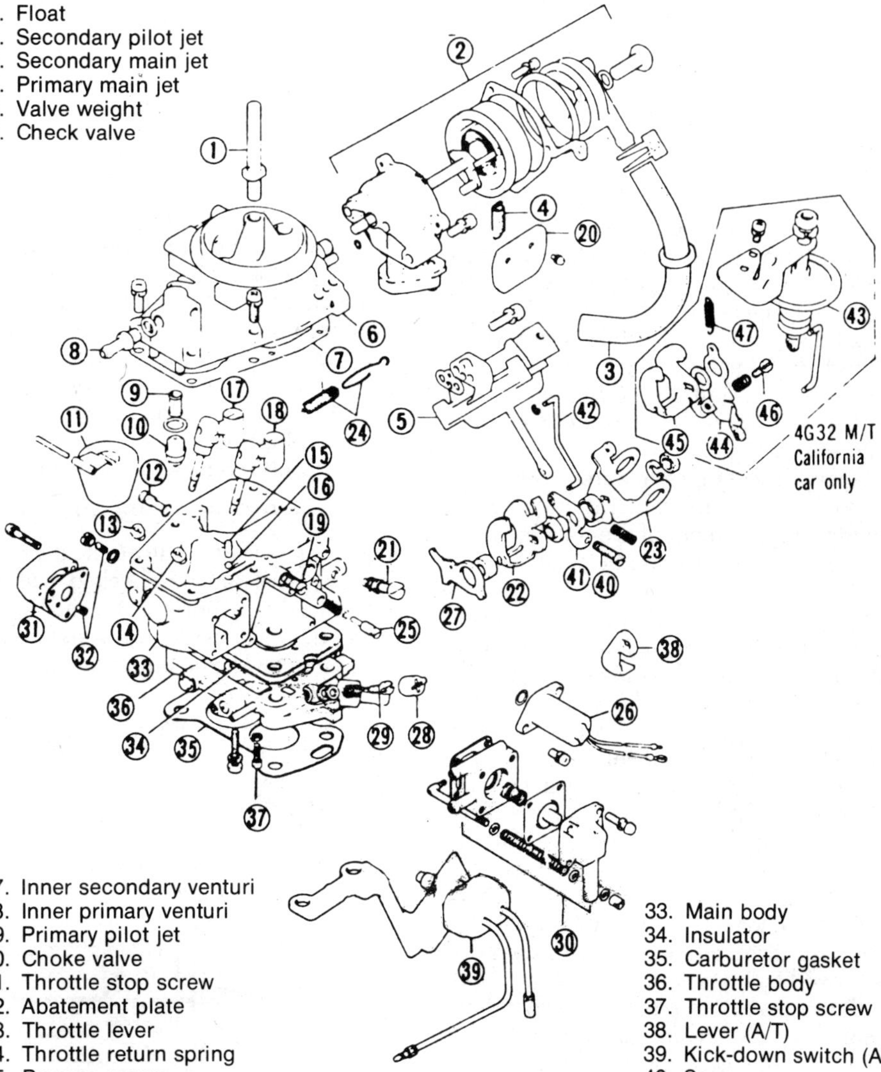

17. Inner secondary venturi
18. Inner primary venturi
19. Primary pilot jet
20. Choke valve
21. Throttle stop screw
22. Abatement plate
23. Throttle lever
24. Throttle return spring
25. By-pass screw
26. Fuel cut solenoid
27. Intermediate lever
28. Idle limiter
29. Pilot screw
30. Accelerator pump
31. Enrichment body assembly
32. Enrichment jet
33. Main body
34. Insulator
35. Carburetor gasket
36. Throttle body
37. Throttle stop screw
38. Lever (A/T)
39. Kick-down switch (A/T)
40. Screw
41. Lever
42. Choke rod
43. Dashpot
44. Lever
45. Abatement plate
46. Adjusting screw
47. Lever spring

Exploded view of a typical carburetor

Blow out all passages and jets with compressed air and be sure that there are no restrictions or blockages. Never use wire or similar tools to clean jets, fuel passages, or air bleeds. Clean all jets and valves separately to avoid accidental interchange.

Check all parts for wear or damage. If wear or damage is found, replace the defective parts. Especially check the following:

1. Check the float needle and seat for wear. If wear is found; replace the complete assembly.
2. Check the float hinge pin for wear and the float(s) for dents or distortion. Replace the float if fuel has leaked into it.
3. Check the throttle and choke shaft bores for wear or an out-of-round condition. Damage or wear to the throttle arm, shaft, or shaft bore will often require replacement of the throttle body. These parts require a close tolerance of fit; wear may allow air leakage, which could affect starting and idling.

NOTE: *Throttle shafts and bushings are not included in overhaul kits. They can be purchased separately.*

4. Inspect the idle mixture adjusting needles for burrs or grooves. Any such condition requires replacement of the needle, since you will not be able to obtain a satisfactory idle.
5. Test the accelerator pump check valves. They should pass air one way but not the other. Test for proper seating by blowing and sucking on the valve. Replace the valve if necessary. If the valve is satisfactory, wash the valve again to remove breath moisture.
6. Check the bowl cover for warped surfaces with a straight edge.
7. Closely inspect the valves and seats for wear and damage, replacing as necessary.
8. After the carburetor is assembled, check the choke valve for freedom of operation.

Carburetor overhaul kits are recommended for each overhaul. These kits contain all gaskets and new parts to replace those that deteriorate most rapidly. Failure to replace all parts supplied with the kit (especially gaskets) can result in poor performance later.

After cleaning and checking all components, reassemble the carburetor, using new parts and referring to the exploded view. When reassembling, make sure that all screws and jets are tight in their seats, but do not overtighten as the tips will be distorted. Tighten all screws gradually, in rotation. Do not tighten needle valves into their seats; uneven jetting will result. Always use new gaskets. Be sure to adjust the float level when reassembling.

THROTTLE LINKAGE ADJUSTMENT

1977

Throttle linkage is adjusted at the clamp which joins the accelerator pedal rod to the carburetor rod. With the carburetor throttle valves closed, (engine at normal operating temperature), the distance between the top of the clamp and the toe-board should be about 1.4 inches. The distance between the end of the connecting rod to the toe-board should be a minimum of 0.4 inch, and the clearance between the stopper bolt and the pedal lever should be 0 to 0.8 inch.

1978–83

Adjust the stopper bolt, at the firewall, to a distance of .75±0 to 0.4 inch from the inside of the bolt holding bracket, to the contact point of the pedal lever, while holding the carburetor throttle plates closed. The yoke at the carburetor end of the accelerator rod is serrated to allow the yoke to be loosened and moved so that a minimal readjustment of the stopper adjusting bolt is needed to give the proper throttle release and opening.

FLOAT AND FUEL LEVEL ADJUSTMENT

A sight glass is fitted at the float chamber and the fuel level can be checked without disassembling the carburetor. Normal fuel level is within the level mark on the sight glass.

The fuel level adjustment is corrected by increasing or decreasing the number of needle valve packings between the valve and top cover. The float level may be off 0.160 inch. above or below the level mark and the operation of the engine would not be affected.

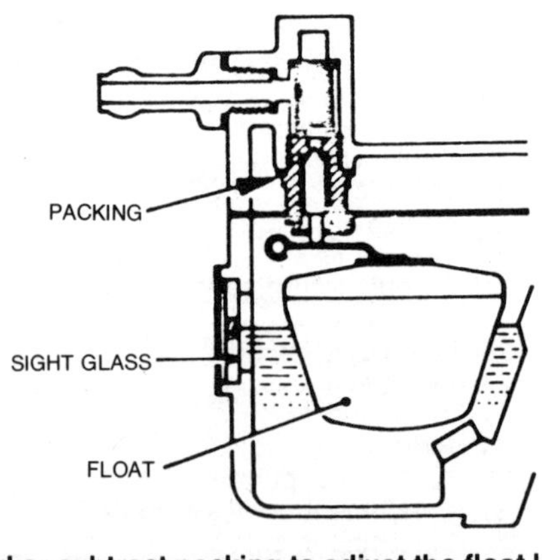

Add or subtract packing to adjust the float level

FAST IDLE ADJUSTMENT

1. Start the engine and open the throttle valve about 45 degrees. Manually close the

55 WAYS TO IMPROVE FUEL ECONOMY

CHILTON'S FUEL ECONOMY & TUNE-UP TIPS

Tune-up • Spark Plug Diagnosis • Emission Controls

Fuel System • Cooling System • Tires and Wheels

General Maintenance

CHILTON'S FUEL ECONOMY & TUNE-UP TIPS

Fuel economy is important to everyone, no matter what kind of vehicle you drive. The maintenance-minded motorist can save both money and fuel using these tips and the periodic maintenance and tune-up procedures in this Repair and Tune-Up Guide.

There are more than 130,000,000 cars and trucks registered for private use in the United States. Each travels an average of 10-12,000 miles per year, and, and in total they consume close to 70 billion gallons of fuel each year. This represents nearly ⅔ of the oil imported by the United States each year. The Federal government's goal is to reduce consumption 10% by 1985. A variety of methods are either already in use or under serious consideration, and they all affect you driving and the cars you will drive. In addition to "down-sizing", the auto industry is using or investigating the use of electronic fuel delivery, electronic engine controls and alternative engines for use in smaller and lighter vehicles, among other alternatives to meet the federally mandated Corporate Average Fuel Economy (CAFE) of 27.5 mpg by 1985. The government, for its part, is considering rationing, mandatory driving curtailments and tax increases on motor vehicle fuel in an effort to reduce consumption. The government's goal of a 10% reduction could be realized — and further government regulation avoided — if every private vehicle could use just 1 less gallon of fuel per week.

How Much Can You Save?

Tests have proven that almost anyone can make at least a 10% reduction in fuel consumption through regular maintenance and tune-ups. When a major manufacturer of spark plugs sur-

TUNE-UP

1. Check the cylinder compression to be sure the engine will really benefit from a tune-up and that it is capable of producing good fuel economy. A tune-up will be wasted on an engine in poor mechanical condition.
2. Replace spark plugs regularly. New spark plugs alone can increase fuel economy 3%.
3. Be sure the spark plugs are the correct type (heat range) for your vehicle. See the Tune-Up Specifications.

Heat range refers to the spark plug's ability to conduct heat away from the firing end. It must conduct the heat away in an even pattern to avoid becoming a source of pre-ignition, yet it must also operate hot enough to burn off conductive deposits that could cause misfiring.

The heat range is usually indicated by a number on the spark plug, part of the manufacturer's designation for each individual spark plug. The numbers in bold-face indicate the heat range in each manufacturer's identification system.

Manufacturer	**Typical Designation**
AC	R **45** TS
Bosch (old)	WA **145** T30
Bosch (new)	HR **8** Y
Champion	RBL **15** Y
Fram/Autolite	41**5**
Mopar	P-**62** PR
Motorcraft	BRF-**42**
NGK	BP **5** ES-15
Nippondenso	W **16** EP
Prestolite	14GR **5** 2A

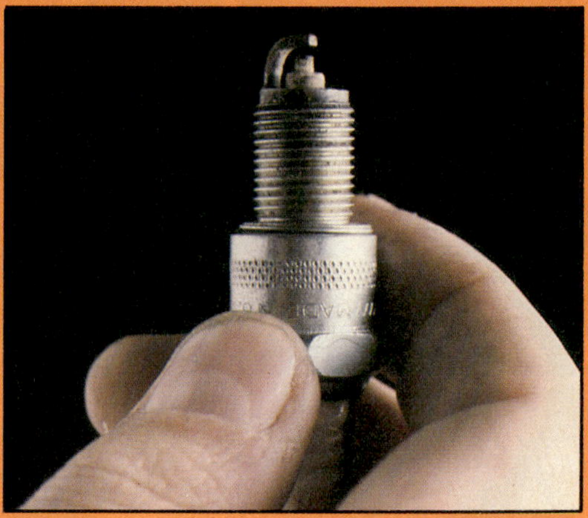

Periodically, check the spark plugs to be sure they are firing efficiently. They are excellent indicators of the internal condition of your engine.

On AC, Bosch (new), Champion, Fram/Autolite, Mopar, Motorcraft and Prestolite, a higher number indicates a hotter plug. On Bosch (old), NGK and Nippondenso, a higher number indicates a colder plug.

4. Make sure the spark plugs are properly gapped. See the Tune-Up Specifications in this book.
5. Be sure the spark plugs are firing efficiently. The illustrations on the next 2 pages show you how to "read" the firing end of the spark plug.
6. Check the ignition timing and set it to specifications. Tests show that almost all cars have incorrect ignition timing by more than 2°.

veyed over 6,000 cars nationwide, they found that a tune-up, on cars that needed one, increased fuel economy over 11%. Replacing worn plugs alone, accounted for a 3% increase. The same test also revealed that 8 out of every 10 vehicles will have some maintenance deficiency that will directly affect fuel economy, emissions or performance. Most of this mileage-robbing neglect could be prevented with regular maintenance.

Modern engines require that all of the functioning systems operate properly for maximum efficiency. A malfunction anywhere wastes fuel. You can keep your vehicle running as efficiently and economically as possible, by being aware of your vehicle's operating and performance characteristics. If your vehicle suddenly develops performance or fuel economy problems it could be due to one or more of the following:

PROBLEM	POSSIBLE CAUSE
Engine Idles Rough	Ignition timing, idle mixture, vacuum leak or something amiss in the emission control system.
Hesitates on Acceleration	Dirty carburetor or fuel filter, improper accelerator pump setting, ignition timing or fouled spark plugs.
Starts Hard or Fails to Start	Worn spark plugs, improperly set automatic choke, ice (or water) in fuel system.
Stalls Frequently	Automatic choke improperly adjusted and possible dirty air filter or fuel filter.
Performs Sluggishly	Worn spark plugs, dirty fuel or air filter, ignition timing or automatic choke out of adjustment.

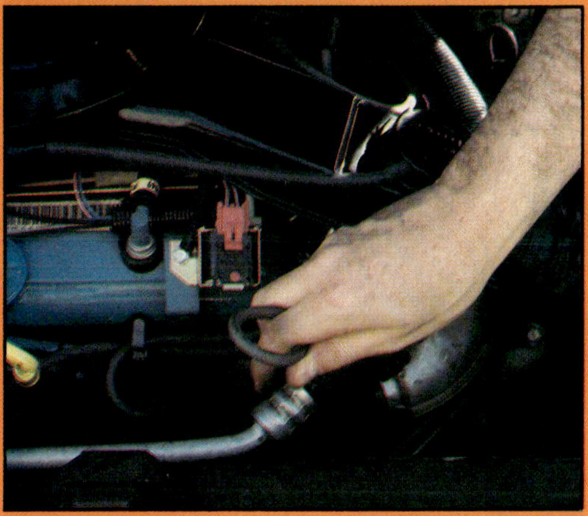

Check spark plug wires on conventional point type ignition for cracks by bending them in a loop around your finger.

Be sure that spark plug wires leading to adjacent cylinders do not run too close together. (Photo courtesy Champion Spark Plug Co.)

7. If your vehicle does not have electronic ignition, check the points, rotor and cap as specified.

8. Check the spark plug wires (used with conventional point-type ignitions) for cracks and burned or broken insulation by bending them in a loop around your finger. Cracked wires decrease fuel efficiency by failing to deliver full voltage to the spark plugs. One misfiring spark plug can cost you as much as 2 mpg.

9. Check the routing of the plug wires. Misfiring can be the result of spark plug leads to adjacent cylinders running parallel to each other and too close together. One wire tends to pick up voltage from the other causing it to fire "out of time".

10. Check all electrical and ignition circuits for voltage drop and resistance.

11. Check the distributor mechanical and/or vacuum advance mechanisms for proper functioning. The vacuum advance can be checked by twisting the distributor plate in the opposite direction of rotation. It should spring back when released.

12. Check and adjust the valve clearance on engines with mechanical lifters. The clearance should be slightly loose rather than too tight.

SPARK PLUG DIAGNOSIS

Normal

APPEARANCE: This plug is typical of one operating normally. The insulator nose varies from a light tan to grayish color with slight electrode wear. The presence of slight deposits is normal on used plugs and will have no adverse effect on engine performance. The spark plug heat range is correct for the engine and the engine is running normally.
CAUSE: Properly running engine.
RECOMMENDATION: Before reinstalling this plug, the electrodes should be cleaned and filed square. Set the gap to specifications. If the plug has been in service for more than 10-12,000 miles, the entire set should probably be replaced with a fresh set of the same heat range.

Incorrect Heat Range

APPEARANCE: The effects of high temperature on a spark plug are indicated by clean white, often blistered insulator. This can also be accompanied by excessive wear of the electrode, and the absence of deposits.
CAUSE: Check for the correct spark plug heat range. A plug which is too hot for the engine can result in overheating. A car operated mostly at high speeds can require a colder plug. Also check ignition timing, cooling system level, fuel mixture and leaking intake manifold.
RECOMMENDATION: If all ignition and engine adjustments are known to be correct, and no other malfunction exists, install spark plugs one heat range colder.

Photos Courtesy Fram Corporation

Oil Deposits

APPEARANCE: The firing end of the plug is covered with a wet, oily coating.
CAUSE: The problem is poor oil control. On high mileage engines, oil is leaking past the rings or valve guides into the combustion chamber. A common cause is also a plugged PCV valve, and a ruptured fuel pump diaphragm can also cause this condition. Oil fouled plugs such as these are often found in new or recently overhauled engines, before normal oil control is achieved, and can be cleaned and reinstalled.
RECOMMENDATION: A hotter spark plug may temporarily relieve the problem, but the engine is probably in need of work.

Carbon Deposits

APPEARANCE: Carbon fouling is easily identified by the presence of dry, soft, black, sooty deposits.
CAUSE: Changing the heat range can often lead to carbon fouling, as can prolonged slow, stop-and-start driving. If the heat range is correct, carbon fouling can be attributed to a rich fuel mixture, sticking choke, clogged air cleaner, worn breaker points, retarded timing or low compression. If only one or two plugs are carbon fouled, check for corroded or cracked wires on the affected plugs. Also look for cracks in the distributor cap between the towers of affected cylinders.
RECOMMENDATION: After the problem is corrected, these plugs can be cleaned and reinstalled if not worn severely.

MMT Fouled

APPEARANCE: Spark plugs fouled by MMT (Methycyclopentadienyl Maganese Tricarbonyl) have reddish, rusty appearance on the insulator and side electrode.
CAUSE: MMT is an anti-knock additive in gasoline used to replace lead. During the combustion process, the MMT leaves a reddish deposit on the insulator and side electrode.
RECOMMENDATION: No engine malfunction is indicated and the deposits will not affect plug performance any more than lead deposits (see Ash Deposits). MMT fouled plugs can be cleaned, regapped and reinstalled.

Ash (Lead) Deposits

APPEARANCE: Ash deposits are characterized by light brown or white colored deposits crusted on the side or center electrodes. In some cases it may give the plug a rusty appearance.
CAUSE: Ash deposits are normally derived from oil or fuel additives burned during normal combustion. Normally they are harmless, though excessive amounts can cause misfiring. If deposits are excessive in short mileage, the valve guides may be worn.
RECOMMENDATION: Ash-fouled plugs can be cleaned, gapped and reinstalled.

High Speed Glazing

APPEARANCE: Glazing appears as shiny coating on the plug, either yellow or tan in color.
CAUSE: During hard, fast acceleration, plug temperatures rise suddenly. Deposits from normal combustion have no chance to fluff-off; instead, they melt on the insulator forming an electrically conductive coating which causes misfiring.
RECOMMENDATION: Glazed plugs are not easily cleaned. They should be replaced with a fresh set of plugs of the correct heat range. If the condition recurs, using plugs with a heat range one step colder may cure the problem.

Detonation

APPEARANCE: Detonation is usually characterized by a broken plug insulator.
CAUSE: A portion of the fuel charge will begin to burn spontaneously, from the increased heat following ignition. The explosion that results applies extreme pressure to engine components, frequently damaging spark plugs and pistons.

Detonation can result by over-advanced ignition timing, inferior gasoline (low octane) lean air/fuel mixture, poor carburetion, engine lugging or an increase in compression ratio due to combustion chamber deposits or engine modification.
RECOMMENDATION: Replace the plugs after correcting the problem.

Photos Courtesy Champion Spark Plug Co.

EMISSION CONTROLS

13. Be aware of the general condition of the emission control system. It contributes to reduced pollution and should be serviced regularly to maintain efficient engine operation.

14. Check all vacuum lines for dried, cracked or brittle conditions. Something as simple as a leaking vacuum hose can cause poor performance and loss of economy.

15. Avoid tampering with the emission control system. Attempting to improve fuel econ-

FUEL SYSTEM

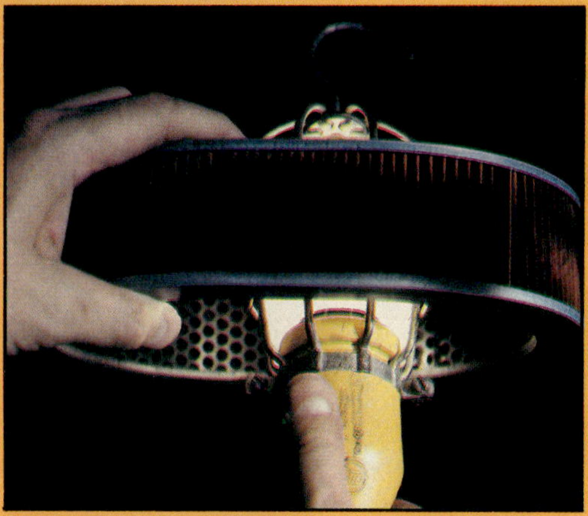

Check the air filter with a light behind it. If you can see light through the filter it can be reused.

Extremely clogged filters should be discarded and replaced with a new one.

18. Replace the air filter regularly. A dirty air filter richens the air/fuel mixture and can increase fuel consumption as much as 10%. Tests show that ⅓ of all vehicles have air filters in need of replacement.

19. Replace the fuel filter at least as often as recommended.

20. Set the idle speed and carburetor mixture to specifications.

21. Check the automatic choke. A sticking or malfunctioning choke wastes gas.

22. During the summer months, adjust the automatic choke for a leaner mixture which will produce faster engine warm-ups.

COOLING SYSTEM

29. Be sure all accessory drive belts are in good condition. Check for cracks or wear.

30. Adjust all accessory drive belts to proper tension.

31. Check all hoses for swollen areas, worn spots, or loose clamps.

32. Check coolant level in the radiator or expansion tank.

33. Be sure the thermostat is operating properly. A stuck thermostat delays engine warm-up and a cold engine uses nearly twice as much fuel as a warm engine.

34. Drain and replace the engine coolant at least as often as recommended. Rust and scale

TIRES & WHEELS

38. Check the tire pressure often with a pencil type gauge. Tests by a major tire manufacturer show that 90% of all vehicles have at least 1 tire improperly inflated. Better mileage can be achieved by over-inflating tires, but never exceed the maximum inflation pressure on the side of the tire.

39. If possible, install radial tires. Radial tires deliver as much as ½ mpg more than bias belted tires.

40. Avoid installing super-wide tires. They only create extra rolling resistance and decrease fuel mileage. Stick to the manufacturer's recommendations.

41. Have the wheels properly balanced.

omy by tampering with emission controls is more likely to worsen fuel economy than improve it. Emission control changes on modern engines are not readily reversible.

16. Clean (or replace) the EGR valve and lines as recommended.

17. Be sure that all vacuum lines and hoses are reconnected properly after working under the hood. An unconnected or misrouted vacuum line can wreak havoc with engine performance.

23. Check for fuel leaks at the carburetor, fuel pump, fuel lines and fuel tank. Be sure all lines and connections are tight.

24. Periodically check the tightness of the carburetor and intake manifold attaching nuts and bolts. These are a common place for vacuum leaks to occur.

25. Clean the carburetor periodically and lubricate the linkage.

26. The condition of the tailpipe can be an excellent indicator of proper engine combustion. After a long drive at highway speeds, the inside of the tailpipe should be a light grey in color. Black or soot on the insides indicates an overly rich mixture.

27. Check the fuel pump pressure. The fuel pump may be supplying more fuel than the engine needs.

28. Use the proper grade of gasoline for your engine. Don't try to compensate for knocking or "pinging" by advancing the ignition timing. This practice will only increase plug temperature and the chances of detonation or pre-ignition with relatively little performance gain.

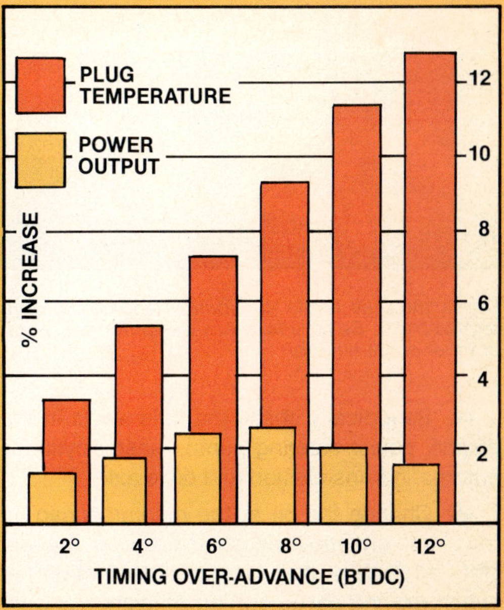

Increasing ignition timing past the specified setting results in a drastic increase in spark plug temperature with increased chance of detonation or preignition. Performance increase is considerably less. (Photo courtesy Champion Spark Plug Co.)

that form in the engine should be flushed out to allow the engine to operate at peak efficiency.

35. Clean the radiator of debris that can decrease cooling efficiency.

36. Install a flex-type or electric cooling fan, if you don't have a clutch type fan. Flex fans use curved plastic blades to push more air at low speeds when more cooling is needed; at high speeds the blades flatten out for less resistance. Electric fans only run when the engine temperature reaches a predetermined level.

37. Check the radiator cap for a worn or cracked gasket. If the cap does not seal properly, the cooling system will not function properly.

42. Be sure the front end is correctly aligned. A misaligned front end actually has wheels going in differed directions. The increased drag can reduce fuel economy by .3 mpg.

43. Correctly adjust the wheel bearings. Wheel bearings that are adjusted too tight increase rolling resistance.

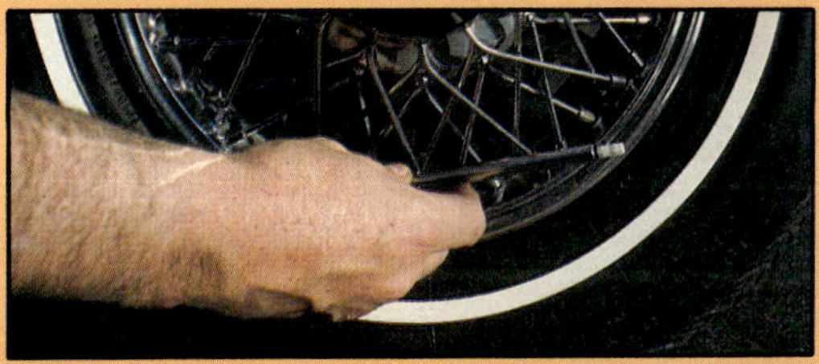

Check tire pressures regularly with a reliable pocket type gauge. Be sure to check the pressure on a cold tire.

GENERAL MAINTENANCE

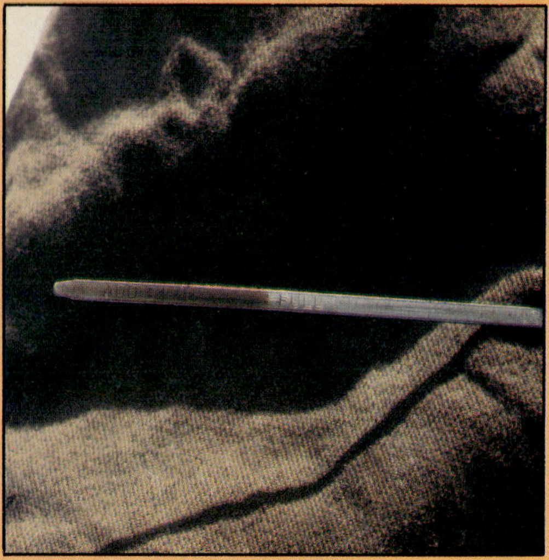

Check the fluid levels (particularly engine oil) on a regular basis. Be sure to check the oil for grit, water or other contamination.

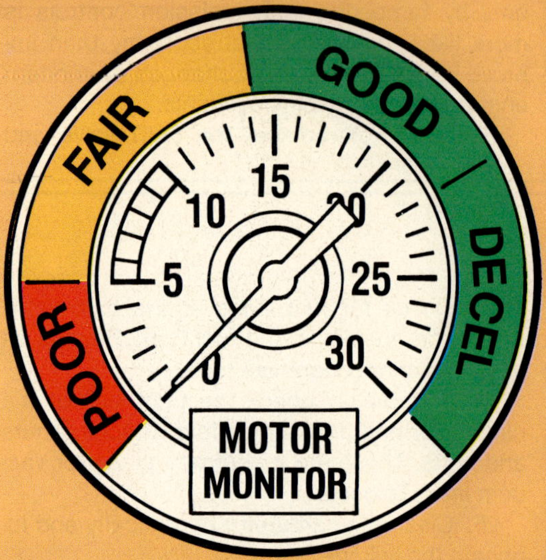

A vacuum gauge is another excellent indicator of internal engine condition and can also be installed in the dash as a mileage indicator.

44. Periodically check the fluid levels in the engine, power steering pump, master cylinder, automatic transmission and drive axle.

45. Change the oil at the recommended interval and change the filter at every oil change. Dirty oil is thick and causes extra friction between moving parts, cutting efficiency and increasing wear. A worn engine requires more frequent tune-ups and gets progressively worse fuel economy. In general, use the lightest viscosity oil for the driving conditions you will encounter.

46. Use the recommended viscosity fluids in the transmission and axle.

47. Be sure the battery is fully charged for fast starts. A slow starting engine wastes fuel.

48. Be sure battery terminals are clean and tight.

49. Check the battery electrolyte level and add distilled water if necessary.

50. Check the exhaust system for crushed pipes, blockages and leaks.

51. Adjust the brakes. Dragging brakes or brakes that are not releasing create increased drag on the engine.

52. Install a vacuum gauge or miles-per-gallon gauge. These gauges visually indicate engine vacuum in the intake manifold. High vacuum = good mileage and low vacuum = poorer mileage. The gauge can also be an excellent indicator of internal engine conditions.

53. Be sure the clutch is properly adjusted. A slipping clutch wastes fuel.

54. Check and periodically lubricate the heat control valve in the exhaust manifold. A sticking or inoperative valve prevents engine warm-up and wastes gas.

55. Keep accurate records to check fuel economy over a period of time. A sudden drop in fuel economy may signal a need for tune-up or other maintenance.

choke valve and slowly return the throttle valve to the stop position.

2. With a tachometer connected, check that the fast idle speed is 2000 rpm or lower. (Not less than 1700 rpm). Adjust the speed as necessary with the fast idle speed screw. On earlier models, bend the cam operating link rod to alter the fast idle.

3. Cold start the engine and check the automatic choke and fast idle operation.

IDLE MIXTURE ADJUSTMENT

See chapter two.

SECONDARY THROTTLE BLADE ADJUSTMENT

The secondary throttle blade stop screw is adjusted to keep the throttle blade from closing too tightly. This adjustment is only made with the carburetor off of the engine. The screw is set at the factory and doesn't normally need adjustment.

AUTOMATIC CHOKE ADJUSTMENT

The choke case has five projections. Align the center projection with the punch mark of the bimetal case.

On 1980 and later models the choke is adjusted by turning the screw located on the choke spring bracket. The latest model years could have a tamper resistant cover on the screw. If choke adjustment is absolutely necessary the cover must be removed. A new cover should be installed on the screw after adjustment.

THROTTLE OPENER ADJUSTMENT

Champ-4 Speed Manual Transmission-From 1982

The system is not available on California models. The throttle opener increases engine rpm if it drops below a specified amount. The system can be adjusted if necessary by;

1. Attach a tachometer, check and adjust the curb idle if needed.

2. Turn off all accessories and disconnect the electric radiator fan.

3. Warm the engine to normal operating temperature.

4. Remove pressure on the throttle opener by lifting the unit with a finger. Do not push on the throttle opener lever or rod.

5. Adjust the throttle opener screw to obtain 800 to 900 rpm.

Fuel Tank

REMOVAL AND INSTALLATION

CAUTION: *When working on fuel tanks, be sure to disconnect the battery ground (negative) cable.*

1. Remove the drain plug (if equipped) or disconnect the fuel line to drain the fuel in the tank.

CAUTION: *No smoking!*

2. Loosen the fuel hose (main and return) clamps and disconnect the fuel lines.

3. Disconnect the filler hose and breather hose from the filler neck.

4. Remove the fuel tank mounting band while supporting the tank. Lower the fuel tank slightly and disconnect the fuel gauge wiring connector.

5. Remove the fuel tank.

6. Installation is the reverse of removal.

Chassis Electrical

5

NOTE: *A guide to basic electrical troubleshooting may be found in Chapter Ten.*

HEATER

Blower

REMOVAL AND INSTALLATION

1977–81 Coupe, Sedan, and Hatchback

1. Disconnect the battery ground cable. Remove the instrument cluster (coupe and sedan). Remove the instrument cluster and the glove box (hatchback).
2. Remove the heater control bracket assembly.
3. Remove the motor assembly and disconnect the wire connection.
4. (Coupe and sedan) Remove the motor in a horizontal position while holding the control bracket down.
5. (Hatchback) Remove the motor through the glove box opening if necessary.
6. Installation is the reverse of removal.

1979–82 Front Wheel Drive Models

1. Disconnect the battery ground cable. Remove the center console and parcel tray, if equipped.

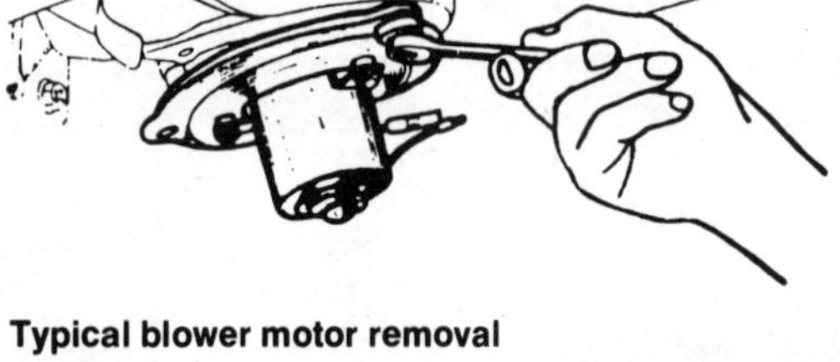

Typical blower motor removal

2. Remove the center vent duct and defroster duct. Remove the instrument panel trim. Remove the` two heater unit top bolts and loosen the bottom attaching bolt.
3. Disconnect the wiring to the motor.
4. Tilt the heater unit toward yourself, remove the three motor attaching bolts and remove the motor.
5. The blower fan may be removed from the shaft if necessary.
6. Installation is the reverse of the removal procedure.

1981 and Later Sapporo

1. Remove the lower instrument pad cover assembly from under the glove box.
2. Remove the passenger side console cover.
3. Remove the glove box to center support attaching screw.
4. Loosen the stops at either side of the glove box so that the glove box swings free.
5. Disconnect the glove box light.
6. Remove the glove compartment assembly from the instrument pad.
7. Remove the ducts, heater fan switch connector and control cables.
8. Remove three attaching bolts and lift out the blower assembly.
9. Remove the wiring bracket and the motor connector. Remove the vent tube and three motor attaching screws. Lift out the motor and remove the fan from the motor assembly.
10. Installation is the reverse of removal.

Heater Core

NOTE: *This procedure doesn't apply to air conditioned cars. The heater core is contained within the heater unit and is not serviced separately.*

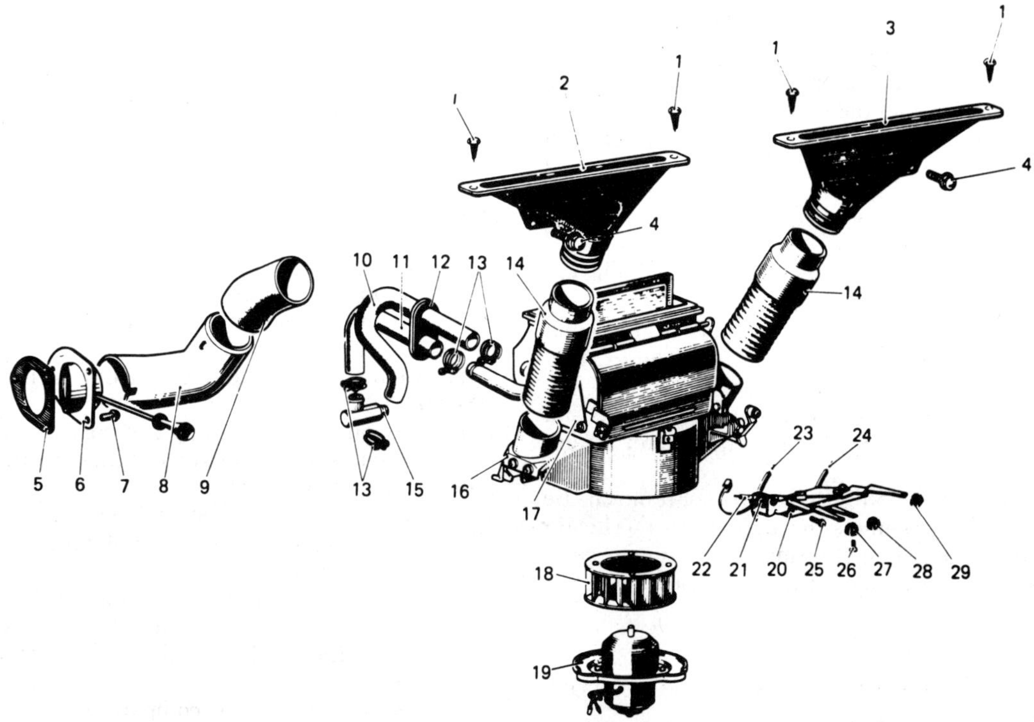

1. Screw
2. L.H. defroster nozzle
3. R.H. defroster nozzle
4. Washer assembled machine screw
5. Ventilator duct packing
6. Ventilator duct ass'y
7. Washer assembled machine screw
8. L.H. and R.H. air ducts
9. Rubber joint
10. (A) water hose
11. (B) water hose
12. Grommet
13. Clip
14. Air hose
15. Joint
16. Heater ass'y
17. Heater water valve ass'y
18. Heater fan ass'y
19. Heater motor ass'y
20. Heater control ass'y
21. Heater switch
22. Bowden (temperature control) wire
23. Bowden (heater-defroster change) wire
24. Bowden (air control) wire
25. Washer assembled machine screw
26. Machine screw
27. Fan knob
28. Air knob
29. Temp. knob

Exploded view of a typical heater assembly

REMOVAL AND INSTALLATION

1977–81 Coupe, Sedan and Hatchback

1. Disconnect the battery ground cable. Drain the cooling system.
2. Disconnect the battery ground cable.
3. Place the water valve in the OFF position.
4. Remove the under tray, defroster nozzle and console box.
5. Disconnect each heater control wire and connectors at the heater assembly.
6. Disconnect the water hoses, heater duct and wiring harness.
7. Remove the heater assembly.
8. Installation is the reverse of removal.

1977–81 Hardtop

1. Disconnect the battery ground cable. Drain the cooling system.
2. Remove the glove box, instrument cluster and console assembly.
3. Disconnect the heater control wires at the heater box.
4. Remove the heater control assembly.
5. Disconnect all heater hoses and air ducts.
6. Remove the heater assembly.
7. The installation is in the reverse of the removal procedure.

NOTE: *Upon removal of the heater control box, the heater core is removable. Replace all gaskets and insulation in its proper place.*

1979–83 Front Wheel Drive Models

1. Disconnect the battery ground cable.
2. Place the water valve lever in the HOT position. Drain the coolant.
3. Remove the center console and parcel tray, if equipped.
4. Remove the center ventilation duct and the defroster duct. Disconnect the instrument trim panel and cluster hood.
5. Disconnect all control wires at the heater unit.
6. Disconnect the heater hose from the engine. Remove the clamps from the hoses. Disconnect the heater wiring harness.
7. Remove the two top mounting bolts and the one lower nut. Remove the heater assembly.
8. Installation is the reverse of removal. Be sure the grommets through which the heater hoses pass when entering the passenger compartment are secured when reinstalling.

1981 and Later Sapporo

1. Disconnect the negative battery terminal.
2. Remove the steering wheel horn pad attaching screws, from the back of the steering wheel. Remove the horn pad.
3. Remove the steering wheel lock nut and remove the steering wheel using a steering wheel puller tool.

CAUTION: *Do not apply impact to the column or wheel with a hammer to loosen the wheel from the column. Use the steering wheel puller tool.*

4. Loosen the tilt lock lever and lower the steering column fully.
5. Remove the meter (instrument cluster) hood. Remove the meter (instrument cluster) assembly and disconnect the electrical and cable connectors.
6. Remove the inner box from the console accessory box. Press on the spring catch, to remove the remote control mirror switch from the accessory box.
7. Remove the accessory box assembly and disconnect the electrical connector.
8. Pull off the heater control knob, pull out the control panel and take out the illumination harness.
9. Pull off the radio knobs and remove the radio to panel attaching nuts. Remove the radio panel.
10. Remove the cover assembly attaching screws from below the glove box and remove the cover assembly.
11. Remove the console side covers (both sides).
12. Remove the shift knob on manual transmission vehicles and remove the center console.
13. Remove the instrument pad bolt covers at both ends of the instrument pad and remove the attaching nuts.
14. Take off the hood lock release knob and remove the release cable attaching screws. Remove the hood lock release assembly from the instrument pad.
15. Remove the defroster garnish.
16. Remove the screws attaching the glove compartment to the center dash reinforcement.
17. Remove all remaining instrument pad attaching bolts.
18. Disconnect the clock, glove box, chime and dimmer control and remove the instrument pad.
19. Disconnect the defogger switch, radio, chime driver, defogger relay connectors and the antenna feeder end.
20. Remove the center reinforcement.
21. Set the heater temperature control to "WARM" position and drain the coolant from the radiator.
22. From the engine compartment, remove the heater hoses from the heater assembly.
22. From under the dash, remove the heater ducts from the heater assembly. To remove the rear seat heater duct, move the outlet control link to the "VENT" side, insert a finger into the outlet and remove the duct from inside heater.
23. Disconnect the power relay connector, remove three attaching bolts and remove the heater assembly. Remove the heater core.
24. The installation is the reverse of removal.
25. Connect the heater hoses in a fully seated position on the inlet and outlet fittings of the heater core assembly, so they will not leak.
26. Adjust the heater control cable by setting the control panel to "COOL" and heater unit lever on "COOL" and tighten the cable at that position.

NOTE: *In order to fill the engine cooling and heating system completely it may be necessary to open the water valve fully, run the engine to circulate the coolant and then stop the engine and add more coolant.*

RADIO

REMOVAL AND INSTALLATION

1977–83

1. Disconnect the battery ground cable. Remove glove box, then loosen the knobs and attaching nuts on the front of the radio.

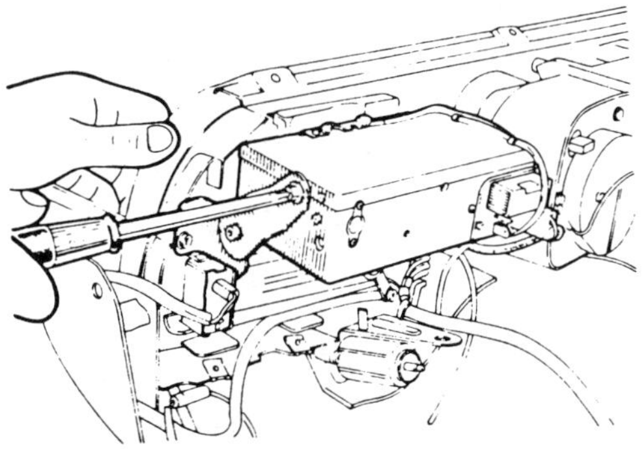

Typical radio removal

2. Remove speaker, antenna, and power wires from the back of the radio. Remove the radio attaching bracket and take out the radio.
3. Installation is the reverse of removal.

1979–82 Front Wheel Drive

1. Remove the instrument cluster or instrument panel trim.
2. Remove the radio knobs from the radio panel.
3. Disconnect the wiring harness. Remove the nuts from behind the knobs, the screw from the bracket and remove the radio (AM radio). Remove the bolts from under the brackets and remove the radio (AM/FM radio).

CAUTION: *Be careful not to reverse the ground and power leads. This will cause serious damage to the radio. The power lead is the one with an in-line fuse. Never operate the radio without a speaker connected or with the speaker leads shorted. This will result in transistor failure.*

NOTE: *To remove the speaker, remove the radio as described above. Unscrew the four speaker retaining nuts. Remove the speaker from the bottom. When replacing a speaker, it should be replaced with one of the same impedance, measured in ohms. Mismatched impedance can cause rapid transistor failure as well as poor radio performance. This should also be taken into consideration when adding a second speaker.*

INSTRUMENT CLUSTER

REMOVAL AND INSTALLATION

1977–82 Except Arrow/Sapporo

NOTE: *Disconnect the battery ground cable before cluster removal.*

1. Loosen screws at the upper and lower part of the instrument cluster. Loosen the screws holding the heater control knobs, ash tray, and cigarette lighter from their respective brackets; if necessary. Remove blind cover (if equipped) on the right side of the glove box and remove the attaching screws on the right side of the cluster.
2. Remove the harness cover at the bottom of the instrument panel and disconnect lighting switch and the instrument panel harness.
3. Pull the instrument panel cluster a little toward you, disconnect multiple connector, antenna feeder, speaker connector, heater fan connector and meter cables and then remove instrument cluster assembly.
4. Installation is the reverse of removal.

After the instrument cluster has been installed, draw out the meter cables as long as the marking tape can be seen from the engine compartment.

Arrow

1. Remove the air intake control knob, the ash tray and heater control knobs and the radio knobs and retaining nuts.
2. Remove the three upper screws and a lower screw, a screw located behind the blind cover above the air intake control panel, and the three screws behind and in the upper inside part of the ash tray.
3. Pull the ash tray out a little and disconnect the heater, meter and speedometer connectors.
4. Remove the ground cable which is attached to the body by a screw and remove the cluster.
5. To install reverse the removal procedure.

Sapporo

1. Remove the battery ground cable.
2. Remove three screws from the top and three screws from the bottom of the cluster assembly.

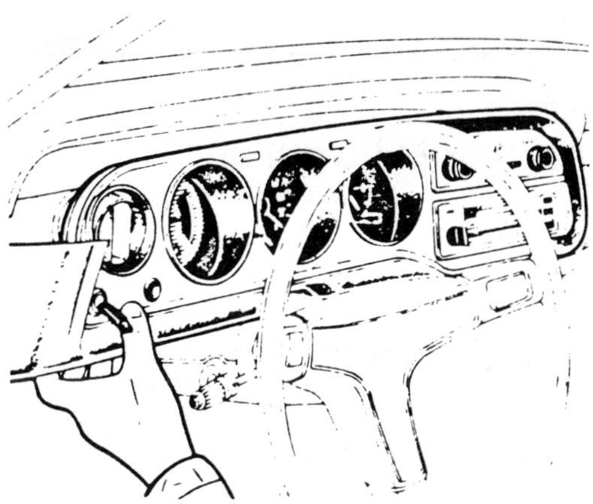

Typical late model instrument cluster removal

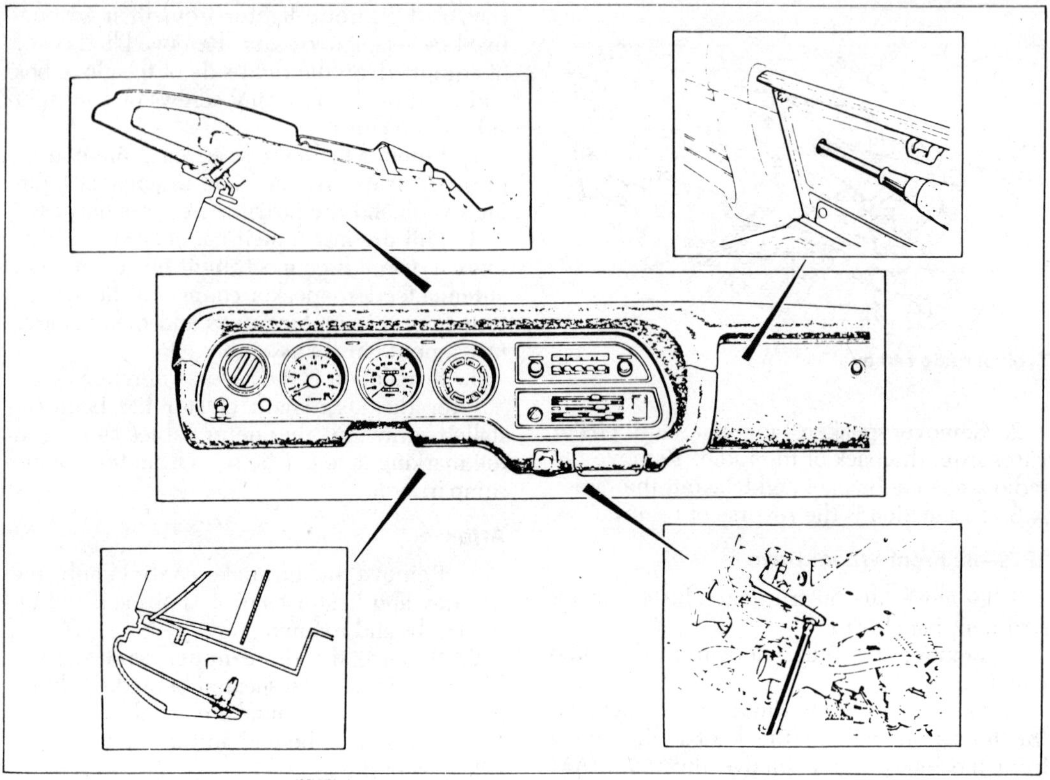

Instrument cluster mounting points (typical)

NOTE: *Two of the bottom screws are located behind the "brake warning" and "fasten seat belt" lens and the third bottom screw is located at the ash tray opening. A thin tipped screwdriver or a wire hook is required to remove the lenses to gain access to the screws.*

3. Move the instrument cluster away from the dash and disconnect the meter connections, heater fan connections, speedometer cable and any other connector or ground cables.
4. Remove the cluster assembly from the dash.
5. Installation is the reverse of removal.

WINDSHIELD WIPERS

Motor

NOTE: *The wiper motor may be located on either the right or left side of the front deck, depending upon the year and model. A wiper removing hole is provided to gain access to the linkage for removal purposes.*

REMOVAL AND INSTALLATION

1. Remove the motor bracket and body retaining bolts.
2. Remove the wiper arm shaft nut on the driver's side of the car and pull the motor assembly out toward yourself.
3. Remove the bushing and disconnect the motor crank arm and linkage.
4. Install the motor in the reverse order of removal.

Linkage

REMOVAL AND INSTALLATION

1. Remove the wiper arm.
2. Remove the wiper arm retaining nuts and push the shaft in toward the body.
3. Remove the wiper motor and bracket assembly.
4. Pull the wiper linkage out through the access hole. To disconnect the wiper linkage, press the bushing out by hand while holding the crank arm and linkage parallel.

When installing the linkage:

5. When installing the wiper arm shaft on the body, insert the shaft bracket positioning boss into the matching hole in the body.
6. Before installing the center shaft bracket, remove the canister and make sure that the shaft bracket boss is inserted in the hole.
7. Adjust the wiper blade position in the stopped position approximately ½ to ¾ inch above the windshield moulding or rubber seal

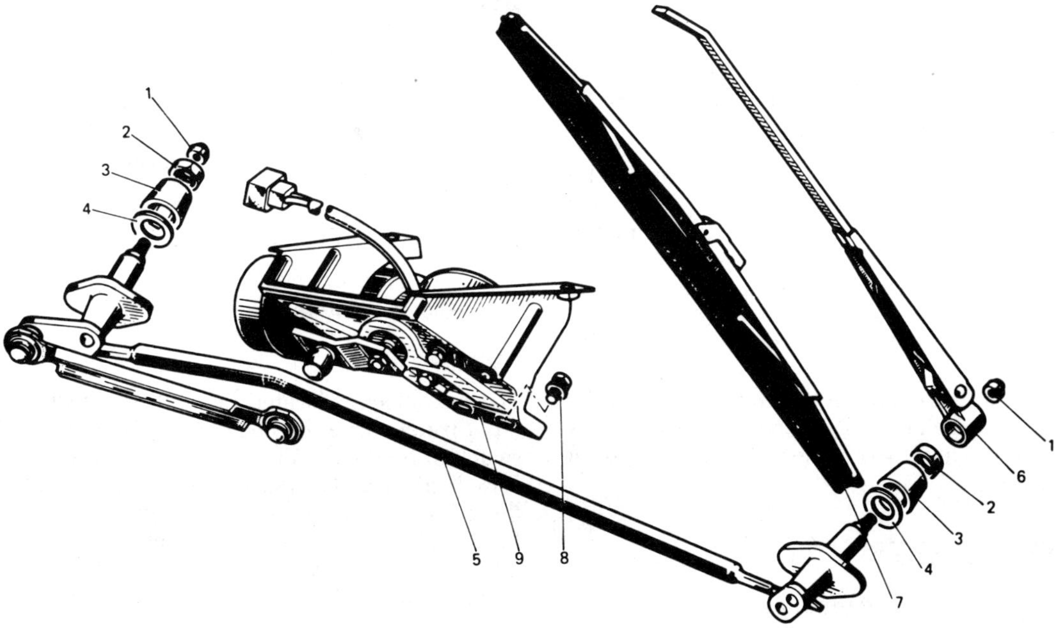

1. Nut
2. Nut
3. Collar
4. Washer
5. Wiper link
6. Wiper arm
7. Wiper blade
8. Washer assembled bolt
9. Wiper motor and bracket ass'y

Typical windshield wiper linkage

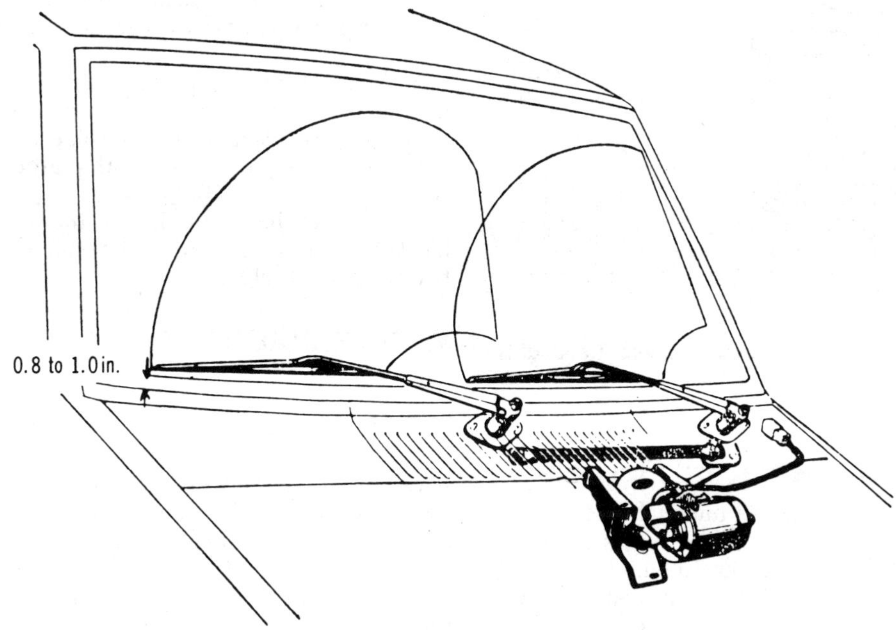

Positioning the wiper blades

and then tighten the wiper arm nuts to 8–12 ft. lbs.

Rear Window Windshield Wipers

REMOVAL AND INSTALLATION

1. Remove the wiper blade and arm. The arm is retained by a lock nut; lift up the cover and remove the nut; pull the arm from the shaft.
2. Remove the lift gate panel, disconnect the wiring harness connector. Remove the motor mounting nuts (inside and outside). Remove the motor.

If you must remove the crank arm from the motor, match mark its location. The arm is installed so the wiper blades will stop at a preset position.

HEADLIGHTS

REMOVAL AND INSTALLATION

1. Remove the grill or grilles covering the headlights.
2. Unscrew the retaining screws and pull the bulb out from its mounting.

   NOTE: *Refer to the illustration; do not unscrew the adjustment screws or a headlight adjustment will be required.*
3. Unplug the electrical connectors and remove the bulb.
4. Install the replacement bulb in the reverse order of removal.

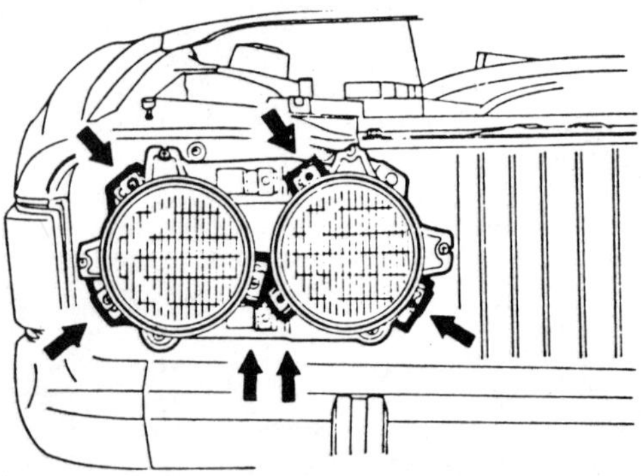

Headlight retaining screws (single headlights similar)

Turn Signal & Hazard Flashers

The flashers are located under the left side of the instrument panel. If the turn signals operate in only one direction, a bulb is probably burned out. If they operate in neither direction, a bulb on each side may be burned out, or the flasher may be defective.

REMOVAL AND INSTALLATION

1. Pull the flasher from its spring clip mounting.
2. Unplug and discard the flasher. Plug in the new flasher.
3. Replace the flasher in the spring clip and check operation.

CIRCUIT PROTECTION

NOTE: *Trouble shooting of electrical components is found in Chapter Ten.*

Fuses

The fuse block is located beneath the instrument panel above the headlight dimmer floor switch or on the driver's side front pillar post. Fuse holders are labeled as to their service and the correct amperage. Always replace blown fuses with new ones of the correct amperage. Otherwise electrical overloads and possible wiring damage will result.

Fusible Links

Fusible links are sections of wire, with special insulation, designed to melt under electrical overload. Replacements are simply spliced into the wire. There may be as many as five of these in the engine compartment wiring harnesses.

REPLACEMENT

1. Disconnect the battery ground cable.
2. Disconnect the fusible link from the junction block or starter solenoid.
3. Cut the harness directly behind the connector to remove the damaged fusible link.
4. Strip the harness wire approximately ½ in.
5. Connect the new fusible link to the harness wire using a crimp on connector. Solder the connection using rosin core solder.
6. Tape all exposed wires with plastic electrical tape.
7. Connect the fusible link to the junction block or starter solenoid and reconnect the battery ground cable.

WIRING DIAGRAMS

Wiring diagrams have been left out of this book. As cars have become more complex, and available with longer and longer option lists, wiring diagrams have grown in size and complexity also. It has become virtually impossible to provide a readable reproduction in a reasonable number of pages. Information on ordering wiring diagrams from the vehicle manufacturer can be found in the owners manual.

Clutch and Transmission

6

MANUAL TRANSMISSION

REMOVAL AND INSTALLATION

NOTE: *The clutch housing and transmission are removed as a unit.*

From inside the engine compartment.

1. Disconnect the battery cables negative (ground) cable first.
2. Remove the battery cable from the starter and fasten it away from the transmission.
3. Remove the starter.
4. Remove the top two clutch housing bolts.

From inside the passenger compartment:

5. Untie the leather or rubber shift boot and pull the rug back over the shift lever. If the car is equipped with a console it is necessary to remove same for access to the shift lever retaining plate etc.
6. Place the four speed transmission in second gear and the five speed transmission in first gear. Unscrew the four retaining bolts and remove the gear shift lever from the tailshaft housing.

From underneath the car:

7. Jack up the front of the car and support it on stands.
8. Drain the transmission oil.
9. Disconnect the transmission backup light switch and the speedometer cable.
10. Remove the drive shaft as outlined in the next chapter.
11. Disconnect the exhaust pipe at the manifold (three bolts), the engine side bracket (one bolt), and drop the pipe down and out of the way.
12. Disconnect the clutch cable.
13. Position a jack under the transmission cover to support it when the cross-member is removed. Use a board between the cover and the jack.
14. Remove the two attaching bolts from the transmission-to-crossmember mount.
15. Unscrew the two bolts at each side of the crossmember and remove the crossmember.
16. Remove the remaining bolts from the clutch housing.
17. Pull the transmission rearward and lower it to the floor.

CAUTION: *When removing the transmission, pull it straight back so as not to damage the pilot bearing, clutch disc, or pressure plate.*

18. Installation of the transmission is basically the reverse of the removal procedure, noting the following points:
    a. When installing the gearshift assembly, position the lever in First gear so that the nylon bushing is vertical. Make sure that no dirt enters the transmission housing during the installation of the shifter.
    b. Refill the transmission with gear oil.
    c. Adjust the clutch as described in the following "Clutch" section.

TRANSAXLE REMOVAL—MANUAL

1. Disconnect the battery ground (negative) cable.
2. Disconnect from the transaxle; the clutch cable, speedometer cable, back-up light harness, starter motor and the four upper bolts connecting the engine to the transaxle.
3. Jackup the car and support on jackstands.
4. Remove the front wheels. Remove the splash shield.
5. Remove the shift rod and extension. It may be necessary to remove any heat shields that can interfere with your progress.
6. Drain the transaxle fluid.
7. Remove the right and left drive shafts from the transaxle case. See drive axle removal in this chapter.

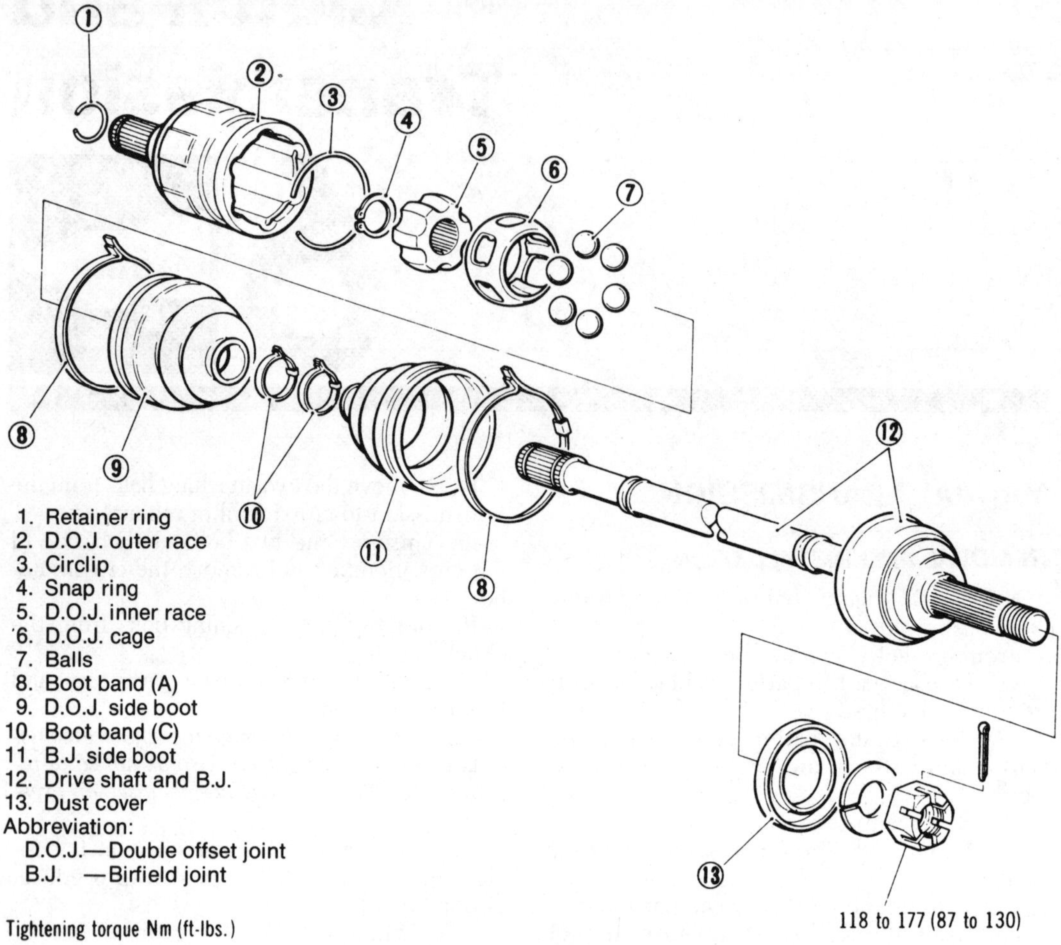

Front wheel drive cars—drive shaft

8. Disconnect the range selector cable (if equipped). Remove the engine rear cover.

9. Support the weight of the engine from above (chain hoist). Support the transaxle and remove the remaining lower mounting bolts.

10. Remove the transaxle mount insulator bolt.

11. Remove (slide back and away from the engine) and lower the transaxle.

12. To install reverse the removal procedure. Be sure to connect all controls and wiring. Use new retaining rings when installing the drive shafts.

Drive Axle

REMOVAL

1. Remove the hub center cap and loosen the driveshaft (axle) nut. Loosen the wheel lug nuts.

2. Lift the car and support on jackstands. Remove the front wheels. Remove the engine splash shield.

3. Remove the lower ball joint and strut bar from the lower control arm.

4. Drain the transaxle fluid.

5. Insert a pry bar between the transaxle case (on the raised rib) and the drive shaft inner joint case.

CAUTION: *Do not insert the pry bar too deeply or you will damage the oil seal.*

Move the bar to the right to withdraw the left driveshaft; to the left to remove the right driveshaft.

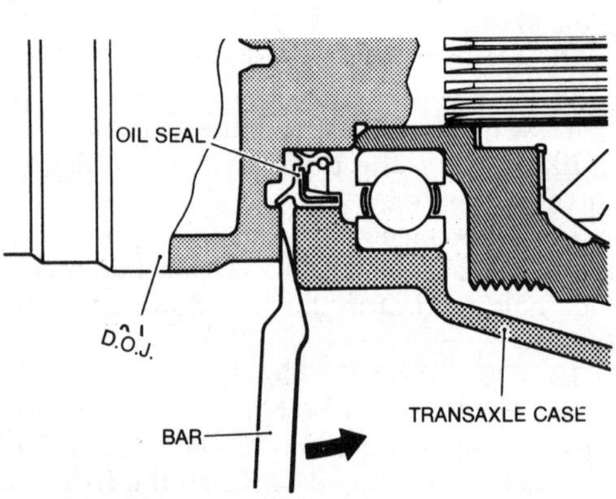

Removing the drive shaft (step one)

6. Plug the transaxle case with a clean rag to prevent dirt from entering the case.

7. Use a puller-driver mounted on the wheel studs to push the driveshaft from the front hub. Take care to prevent the spacer-shims from falling out of place.

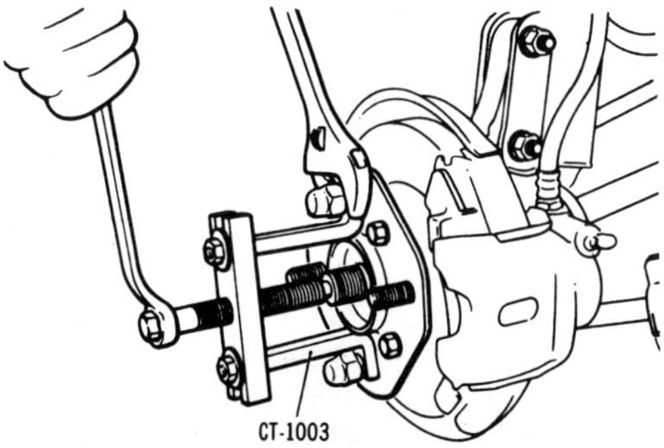

Removing the drive shaft (step two)

8. Assembly is the reverse of removal. Insert the driveshaft into the hub first, then install the transaxle end.

NOTE: *Always use a new inner joint retaining ring every time you remove the driveshaft.*

OVERHAUL

Two types of drive axles are used on front wheel drive models. 1979 through 1981 use a shaft equipped with a double offset joint (DOJ) at the transaxle end and a Birfield joint (BJ) at the wheel end. In 1981 a drive axle using a Tripod joint (TJ) at the transaxle end and a Rzeppa joint (RJ) at the wheel end was introduced. 1981 and later cars are equipped with either the DOJ-BJ or the TJ-RJ axle.

The drive axles are equipped with different style rubber boots for quick identification. The TJ boot has three folds as opposed to two on the DOJ boot. The RJ boot is equipped with two annular projections on the small end while the BJ boot is smooth.

NOTE: *Boot kits containing grease, clamps, snap ring or circlip and necessary boot are available for all joints. If joint replacement is necessary, all drive axles are serviced with a DOJ or BJ kit which replaces the TJ or RJ joint.*

CAUTION: *Do not disassemble a Birfield or Rzeppa joint (wheelend). Service with new joint or clean and repack using a new boot kit. The driveshaft joints use special grease, do not add any other type grease other than supplied with kit.*

Double Offset Joint Service

1. Remove the boot band from double offset joint (DOJ) and slide the boot away from the joint.

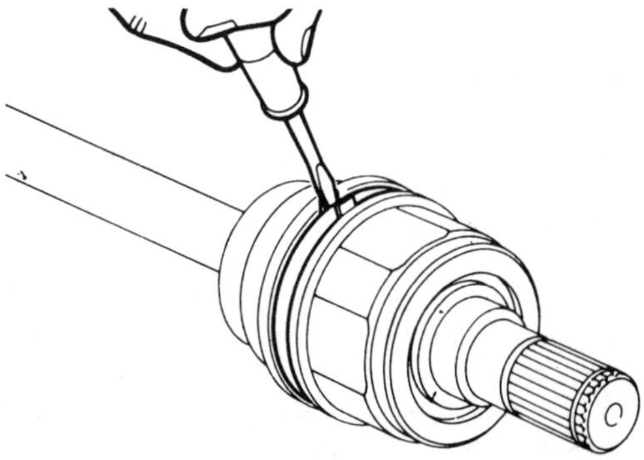

Removing the boot band

2. Remove the circlip from the DOJ with a flat-blade screwdriver. Remove the drive shaft from the DOJ and wipe off the grease.

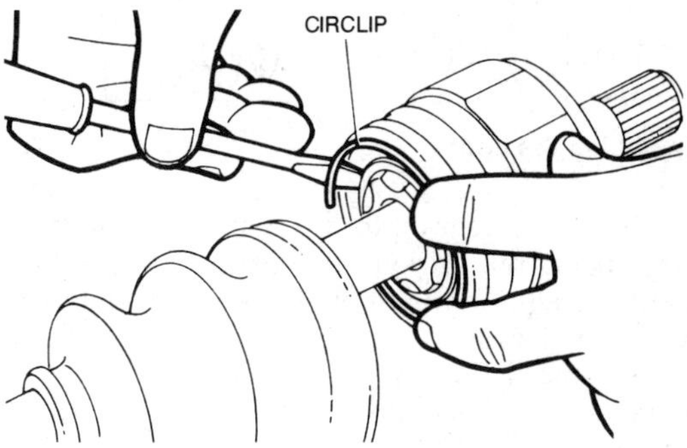

Removing the clip

3. Remove the snap ring that retains the inner race. Remove the inner race, cage and balls as an assembly.

4. Clean the inner race, cage and balls without disassembly.

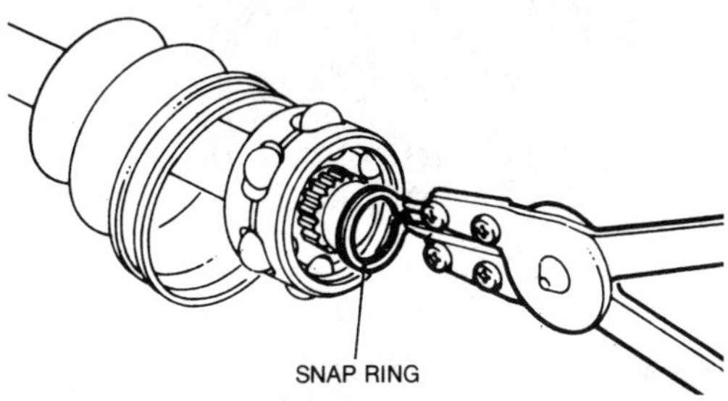

Removing the inner race, cage and balls

5. Remove the Birfield joint boot, clean grease away and inspect the joint for wear; check the splines on both ends of the shaft for wear.

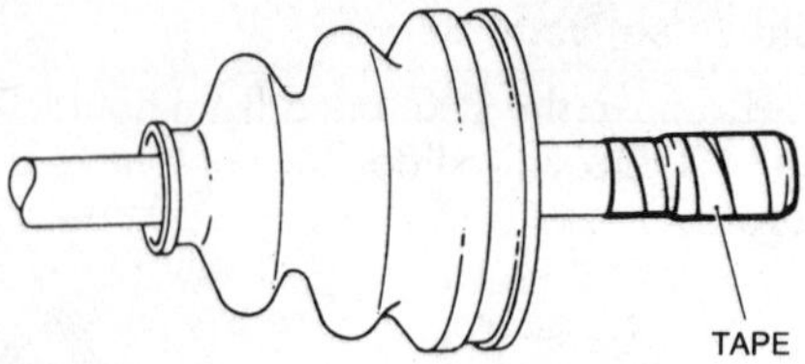

Removing the boot

6. Check the DOJ for rust, damage or wear to the outer race, inner race, cage and balls. If any parts show wear, replace with the necessary kit. It is a good idea to at least replace the boots. Kits available are; Drive shaft and Birfield joint, Double offset joint, Birfield boot kit and DOJ boot kit.

7. To reassemble; Tape the ends of the splines to prevent damage to the boots when they are installed.

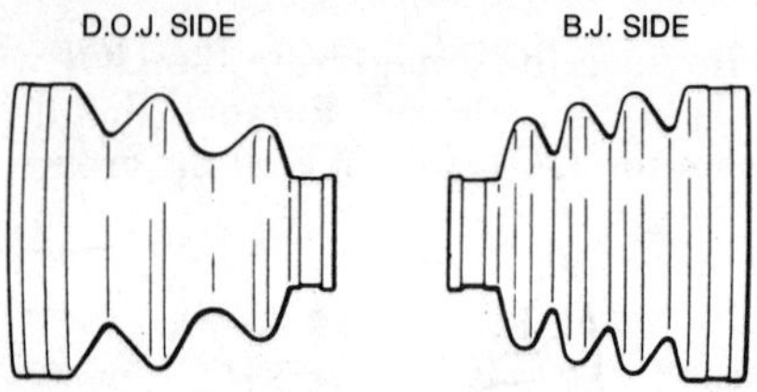

Installing the boot

8. Apply gear oil to the shaft and slide the new boots on. If you are not installing a kit apply an equal amount of grease as the amount you wiped away.

9. Installation of the old parts is the reverse of removal after you have regreased them. To install the DOJ kit. Use the grease supplied with the kit and apply an amount to the inner race and cage. Install the inner race and cock slightly.

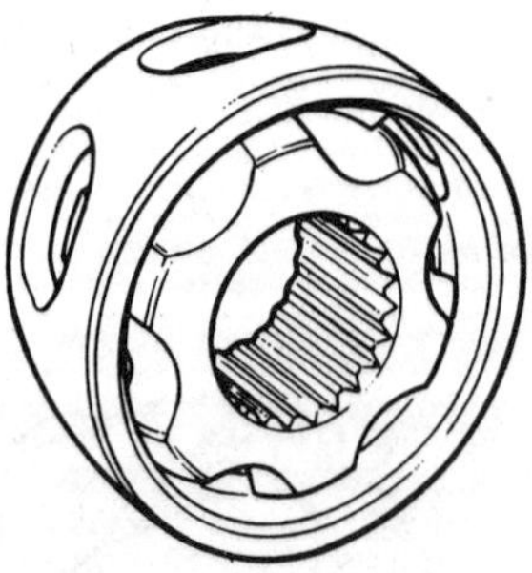

Installing inner race and cage

10. Apply to the balls and install them in the cage. Place the inner race on the driveshaft and install the snap ring. Apply grease to the outer race and install. Install the boots and bands.

11. Install the drive shaft using a new retainer ring on the DOJ side.

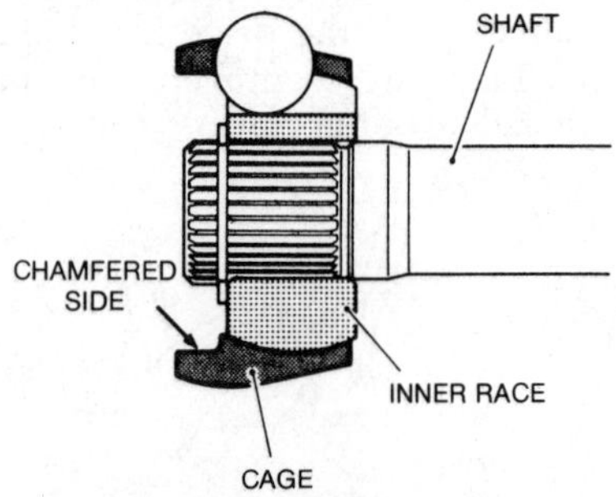

Cage installation direction

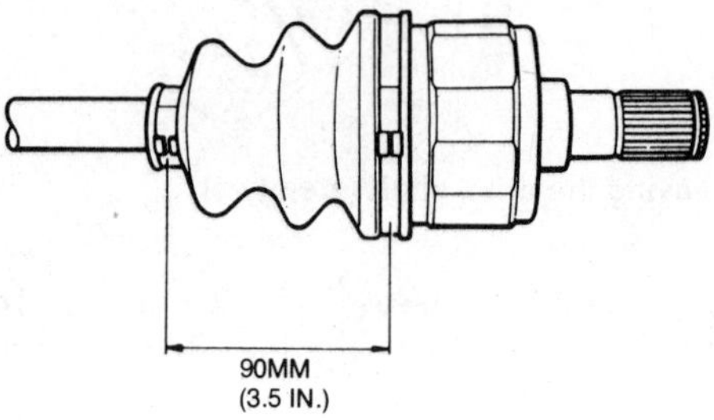

Installing the DOJ side boots

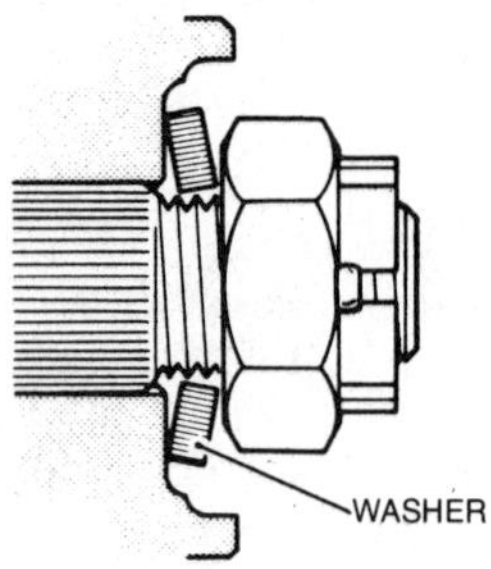

Installing hub nut washer

Tripod Joint Service

1. Remove the boot retaining bands and slide the boot away from the joint.

2. Pull the axle shaft out of the TJ case. Remove the snap ring that retains the spider assembly.

3. Remove the spider assembly, boot and boot bands. Discard old boot and bands. Clean all parts.

4. Inspect the spider rollers for smooth rotation. Check for rusted or damaged TJ case and spider assembly.

5. If TJ parts are damaged a DOJ repair kit is required for repair.

6. To reassemble the old TJ, first wrap tape around the shaft splines to protect the new boot from getting cut.

7. Apply grease to the shaft and slide on the boot.

8. Install the spider assembly onto the shaft and install the retaining snap ring.

9. Apply 2½ to 3 ozs. of the supplied grease into the TJ case and install the axle shaft. Apply the rest of the grease and secure the boot.

10. Install the drive axle using a new retaining ring on the transaxle side.

CLUTCH

The clutch assembly consists of a single dry disc and a diaphragm spring pressure plate. The throwout bearing is controlled by a shaft mounted horizontally in the clutch housing. Clutch actuation is controlled by a cable from the pedal.

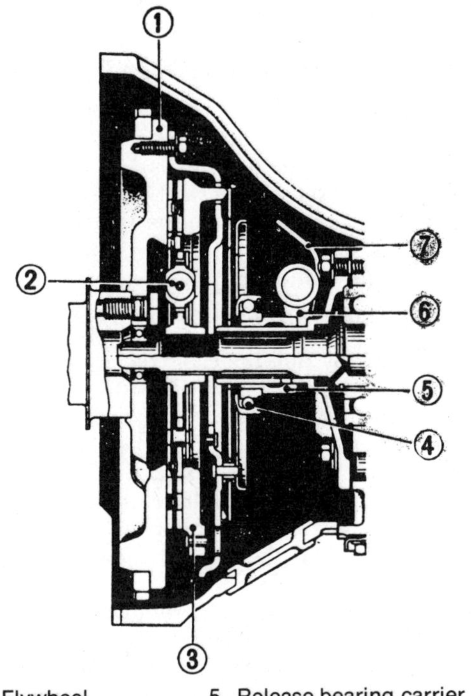

1. Flywheel
2. Clutch disc
3. Pressure plate
4. Release bearing
5. Release bearing carrier
6. Clutch shift arm
7. Return spring

Cross section of the clutch assembly

REMOVAL AND INSTALLATION

1. Remove the transmission or transaxle as outlined.

2. Insert a pilot shaft or an old input shaft into the center of the clutch disc, pressure plate, and the pilot bearing in the crankshaft.

3. With the pilot tool supporting the clutch disc, loosen the pressure plate bolts gradually and in a criss-cross pattern.

4. Remove the pressure plate and clutch disc.

5. Clean the transmission and clutch housing. Clean the flywheel surface with a non-oil based solvent. Wash your hands before installing or handling the clutch assembly parts. Hold the clutch disc by the center hob only.

NOTE: *Before assembly, slide the clutch disc up and down on the transmission input shaft to check for any binding. Remove any rough spots with crocus cloth and then lightly coat the shaft with Lubriplate®.*

To remove the throwout bearing assembly:

6. Remove the return clip and take out the throwout bearing carrier and the bearing.

7. To remove the throwout arm use a $^{3}/_{16}$ in. punch, knock out the throwout shaft spring pin and remove the shaft, springs, and the center lever.

8. Do not immerse the throwout bearing in solvent, it is permanently lubricated. Blow and wipe it clean. Check the bearing for wear, deterioration, or burning. Replace the bearing if there is any question about its condition.

9. Check the shafts, lever, and springs for wear and defects. Replace them if necessary.

10. If you hadn't planned on replacing the clutch disc, examine it for the following before reusing it:

- Loose rivets
- Burned facing

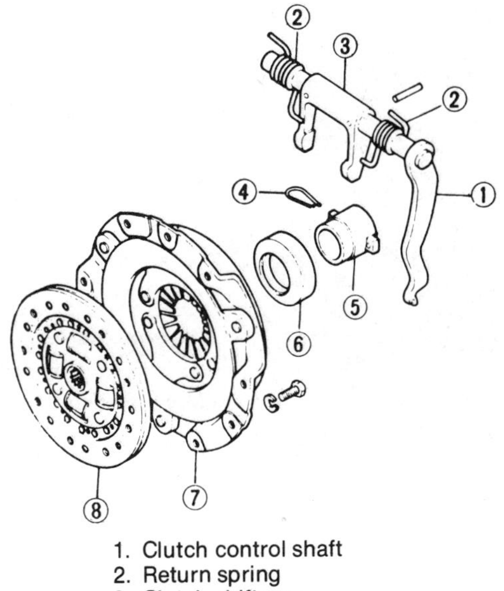

1. Clutch control shaft
2. Return spring
3. Clutch shift arm
4. Return clip
5. Release bearing carrier
6. Release bearing
7. Pressure plate assembly
8. Clutch disc

Clutch and throwout bearing components (typical)

- Oil or grease on the facing
- Less than 0.012 in. left between the rivet head and the top of the facing.

NOTE: *On early 1600 cc models, when replacing a clutch disc, use the later model which is identified by a number and letter on one of the rivet heads. This disc is effective in dampening rumbling or growling sounds from the transmission when decelerating or coasting between 25 and 65 mph.*

11. Check the pressure plate and replace it if any of the following conditions exist:
    - Scored or excessively worn
    - Bent or distorted diaphragm spring
    - Loose rivets
12. Insert the control lever into the clutch housing. Install the two return springs and the throwout shaft.
13. Lock the shift lever to the shaft with the spring pin.
14. Fill the shaft oil seal with multipurpose grease.
15. Install the throwout bearing carrier and the bearing. Install the return clip.
16. Grease the carrier groove and inner surface.
17. Lightly grease the clutch disc splines.

NOTE: *The clutch is installed with the larger boss facing the transmission.*

18. Support the clutch disc and pressure plate with the pilot tool.

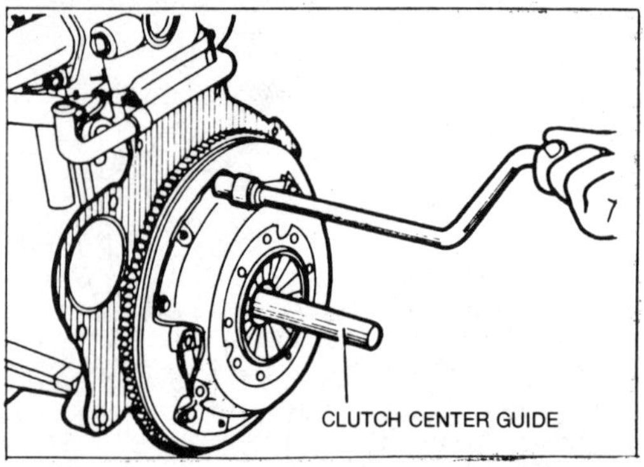

A pilot tool is used during clutch removal and installation

19. Turn the pressure plate so that its balance mark aligns with the notch in the flywheel.
20. Install the pressure plate-to-flywheel bolts hand-tight. Using a torque wrench and, working in a criss-cross pattern, tighten the bolts to 11–15 ft. lbs.
21. Install the transmission as outlined.
22. Adjust the clutch as described in the following section.

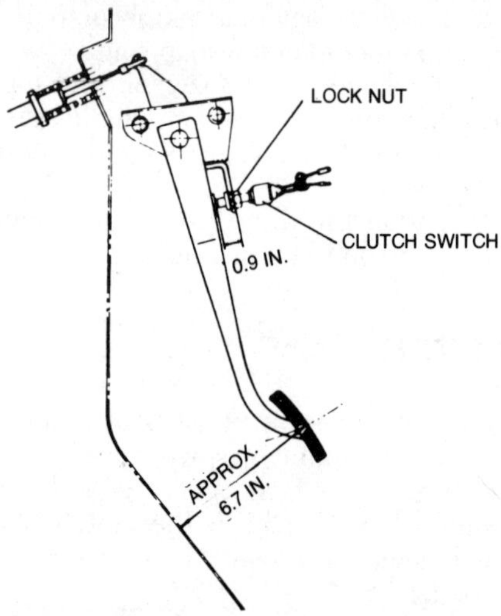

Clutch pedal adjustment (typical)

PEDAL HEIGHT ADJUSTMENT

1. Measure the distance between the floor and the top of the clutch pedal.
2. Refer to the height chart in this chapter for proper distance, if it's not, loosen the clutch switch locknut and move the switch in or out as necessary.
3. Tighten the locknut.

CABLE AND FREE-PLAY ADJUSTMENTS

1. Slightly pull the cable out from the firewall.
2. Turn the adjusting wheel on the cable until the play between the wheel and the cable retainer is between 0.20 and 0.24 in. (.020–.030 in. for front wheel drive models).
3. Check the clutch free-play:
    a. Jack up the front of the car and support it on stands.
    b. Slide under and remove the rubber cover from the clutch housing.
    c. Using a 0.03 in. feeler gauge, check the clearance between the pressure plate

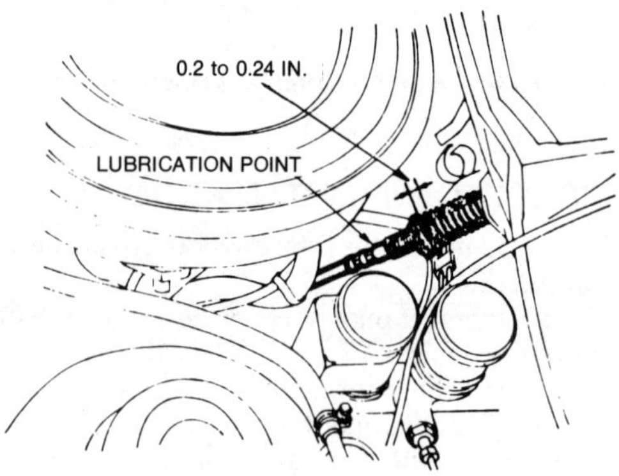

Clutch free play adjustment

diaphragm spring and the throwout bearing.

4. If the free travel is not correct, make further adjustments at the cable adjusting wheel.

NOTE: *Each turn of the adjusting wheel equals 0.06 in. of adjustment to the wheel and retainer clearance.*

5. Lower the car and check the clutch operation.

Clutch Adjustment Specifications—Front Wheel Drive Cars

	1979–82
Pedal upper face from toe board	7.1 to 7.3
Pedal stroke	5.7
Clearance between adjusting nut & cable	0.20–0.24

Removal and Installation

1. Loosen the cable adjusting wheel inside the engine compartment.
2. Loosen the clutch pedal adjusting bolt locknut and loosen the adjusting bolt.
3. Remove the cable end from the clutch throwout lever.
4. Remove the cable end from the clutch pedal.
5. Installation is the reverse of removal.

NOTE: *Lubricate the cable with engine oil and after installation, install pads isolating the cable from the intake manifold and from the rear side of the engine mount insulator on coupe, sedan, and hatchbacks only.*

AUTOMATIC TRANSMISSION/ TRANSAXLE

The Torqueflite is used on all except front wheel drive models. The transmission combines a torque converter and a fully automatic 3-speed gear system. The converter housing and transmission case are an integral aluminum casting. The transmission consists of two multiple disc clutches, an overrunning clutch, two servos and bands, and two planetary gear sets to provide three forward and a reverse ratio.

The KM 170 automatic transaxle appeared in 1980 models. It uses a torque converter in a fully automatic 3-speed transmission, including transfer gearing and differential into a compart front wheel drive unit. There are four centers of rotation in the KM170. They are; main center line plus valve body, idler gear center line, transfer shaft center line and differential center line. An aluminum die-cast converter housing and transmission case are used and the transmission and differential oil sump is common to both. The torque converter is attached to the crankshaft through a flexible driving plate. Converter cooling is through an oil-to-water cooler, located in the radiator lower tank. The torque converter is a sealed unit and cannot be disassembled.

REMOVAL AND INSTALLATION

Torqueflite

1. The transmission and converter must be removed as an assembly; otherwise, the converter drive plate, pump bushing, or oil seal may be damaged. The drive plate will not support a load; therefore, none of the weight of the transmission should be allowed to rest on the plate during removal.
2. Disconnect negative cable from the battery for safety.
3. Remove cooler lines at transmission.
4. Remove starter motor and cooler line bracket.
5. Loosen pan to drain transmission.
6. Rotate engine clockwise with socket wrench on crankshaft pulley bolt to position the bolts attaching torque converter to drive plate, and remove them.
7. Mark parts for reassembly then disconnect driveshaft at rear universal joint. Carefully pull shaft assembly out of the extension housing.
8. Disconnect gearshift rod and torque shaft assembly from transmission.
9. Disconnect throttle rod from lever at the left-side of transmission. Remove linkage bellcrank from transmission if so equipped.
10. Remove the oil filler tube and speedometer cable.
11. Support the rear of the engine with jack or similar device.
12. Raise transmission slightly with service jack to relieve load on the supports.
13. Remove bolts securing transmission mount to crossmember and crossmember to frame, then remove crossmember.
14. Remove all bellhousing bolts.
15. Carefully work transmission converter assembly rearward off engine block dowels and disengage converter hub from end of crankshaft. Attach a small C-clamp to edge of bellhousing to hold converter in place during transmission removal.
16. Lower transmission and remove assembly from under the vehicle.
17. To remove converter assembly, remove C-clamp from edge of bellhousing, then carefully slide assembly out of the transmission.

Clutch and Pedal Adjustment Specifications—Rear Wheel Drive Cars

	Dimension	1977	1978	1979	1980	1981	1982–83
Pedal height from toe board	A	6.5 to 6.7 inch	6.8 inch	6.8 ⑤	6.8 ⑤	7.1	7.5
Pedal stroke	B	5.1 inch ①	5.5 inch ②	5.5 ②	5.9	5.8	6
Clutch pedal free-play	C	0.8 to 1.4 inch	0.8 to 1.2 inch ③	0.6–0.8 ⑥	0.6–0.8 ⑥	0.6–0.8	0.6–0.8
Adjusting nut to cable holder clearance	D	0.2 to 0.24 inch	0.2 to 0.24 inch ④	.12 to .16	0.12–0.16	0.12–0.16	0.12–0.16
Clearance between release bearing face and pressure plate	E	0.080 inch	0.080 inch	—	—	—	—

① 1977 Coupe, Sedan and Hatchback 5.9 inch
② 2600 cc engine 5.9 inch
③ Station wagon 0.4 to 0.6 inch
④ Station wagon w/2000 cc engine 0.14 to 0.18 inch
⑤ 2600 cc engine 7.2
⑥ Arrow: 0.8–1.2

18. Follow the removal procedure in reverse order to install Torqueflite transmission.

TRANSAXLE REMOVAL—AUTOMATIC

NOTE: *The transaxle and converter must be removed and installed as an assembly.*

1. Disconnect the battery ground (negative) cable.
2. Disconnect the throttle control cable at the carburetor and the manual control cable at the transaxle.
3. Disconnect from the transaxle; the inhibitor switch (neutral safety) connector, fluid cooler hoses and the four upper bolts connecting the engine to the transaxle.
4. Jack up the car and support on jackstands.
5. Remove the front wheels. Remove the engine splash shield.
6. Drain the transaxle fluid.
7. Remove the right and left drive shafts from the transaxle case. See drive axle removal in this chapter.
8. Disconnect the speedometer cable. Remove the starter motor.
9. Remove the lower cover from the converter housing. Remove the three bolts connecting the converter to the engine drive plate.

NOTE: *Never support the full weight of the transaxle on the engine drive plate.*

10. Turn and force the converter back and away from the engine drive plate.
11. Support the weight of the engine from above (chain hoist). Support the transaxle and remove the remaining mounting bolts.
12. Remove the transaxle mount insulator bolt.
13. Remove (slide away from the engine) and lower the transaxle and converter as an assembly.
14. To install reverse the removal, procedure. Be sure to connect all controls, wiring and hoses. Use new retaining rings when installing the drive axles.

PAN REMOVAL

Torqueflite

1. Jack up the front of the car and support it safely on jackstands. Place a drain container with a large opening, under transmission and pan.
2. Loosen pan bolts and tap the pan at one corner to break it loose allowing fluid to drain, then remove the oil pan.
3. If necessary, adjust the reverse band.
4. Install a new filter on bottom of the valve body, and tighten retaining screws to 35 in. lbs.
5. Clean the oil pan, and reinstall using a new gasket. Tighten oil pan bolts to 150 in. lbs. in a criss-cross pattern. Lower car.
6. Pour four quarts of DEXRON II automatic transmission fluid through the filler tube.
7. Start engine and allow to idle for at least two minutes. Then, with parking brake on, move selector lever momentarily to each position, ending in the neutral position.
8. Add sufficient fluid to bring level to the "ADD 1 PINT" mark.

Recheck fluid level after transmission is at normal operating temperature. The level should be between the "FULL" and "ADD 1 PINT" mark.

Transaxle

1. Jack up the front of the car and support it safely on jackstands. Remove splashshield.
2. Slide a drain pan under the differential drain plug. Loosen and remove the plug and drain the fluid. Move the drain pan under the transaxle oil pan, remove the plug and drain the fluid. The transmission fluid cannot all be drained by just draining the oil pan.
3. Remove the pan retaining bolts and remove the pan.
4. The filter may be serviced at this time.
5. Use a new oil pan gasket and reinstall the pan in the reverse order of removal.
6. Replace both drain plugs. Lower car. Refill the transmission with 4.2 qts. of Dexron II fluid. Start the engine and allow to idle for at least two minutes. With the parking brake applied, move the selector to each position ending in neutral.
7. Add sufficient fluid to bring the level to the lower mark. Recheck the fluid level after the transmission is up to normal operating temperature.

KICKDOWN BAND ADJUSTMENT

Torqueflite

The kickdown band adjusting screw is located on the left-side of the transmission case.

1. Loosen the locknut and back off approximately 5 turns. Test the adjustment screw for free turning in the transmission case.
2. *On models through 1980;* Use an inch pound torque wrench and tighten the adjusting screw to 72 inch pounds. *1981 and later;* tighten the adjusting screw to 69 inch pounds. (The torque specifications shown are true torque with no adapter on the wrench).
3. *On models through 1980;* back off the adjusting screw 3 full turns. *1981 and later models;* back off the adjusting screw 3½ turns.
4. Hold the adjusting screw to prevent turning and secure the locknut to 30–41 foot pounds.

Transaxle

1. Wipe all dirt and other contamination from the kickdown servo cover and surrounding area. The cover is located to the right of the dipstick hole.
2. Remove the snap ring and then the cover.
3. Loosen the locknut.
4. Holding the kickdown servo piston from turning, tighten the adjusting screw to 7 ft. lbs. (84 in. lbs.) and then back it off. Repeat the tightening and backing off two times in order to ensure seating of the band on the drum.
5. Tighten the adjusting screw to 3.5 ft. lbs. (42 in. lbs.) and back off 3.5 turns (counterclockwise).
6. Holding the adjusting screw against rotation, tighten the locknut nut to 11–15 ft. lbs.
7. Install a new seal ring (D-shaped) in the groove in the outside surface of the cover. Use care not to distort the seal ring.
8. Install the cover and then the snap ring.

LOW AND REVERSE BAND ADJUSTMENT

Torqueflite

1. Raise and safely support the front of the car. Drain the transmission fluid and remove the oil pan.
2. The allen socket headed adjusting screw is located at the servo end of the strut. *On models through 1980;* Loosen and remove the locknut from the adjusting screw. Tighten the adjusting screw to 41 inch pounds of true torque (no adapter on wrench). Back off adjusting screw 7½ turns. *On 1981 and later models;* Loosen and remove the locknut from the adjusting screw. Tighten the adjusting screw to 43 inch pounds of true torque. Back off the adjusting screw 7 turns.
3. Install the locknut on the adjusting screw. Hold the adjusting screw in position and tighten the locknut to 25–35 ft. lbs.
4. Reinstall the oil pan using a new gasket. Refill the transmission with the proper amount of transmission fluid.

THROTTLE ROD ADJUSTMENT

Torqueflite

Warm the engine until it reaches the normal operating temperature. With the carburetor automatic choke off the fast idle cam, adjust the engine idle speed by using a tachometer. Then make the throttle rod adjustment.

1. Install each linkage. Loosen its bolts so that the rods B and C can slide properly.
2. Lightly push the rod A or the transmission throttle lever and the rods to idle position. In this case the carburetor automatic choke must be fully released. Tighten the bolt securely to connect the rods B and C.
3. Make sure that when the carburetor throttle valve is wide-open, the transmission throttle lever smoothly moves from idle to wide-open position (operating angle: 45°–54°) and that there exists some room in the lever stroke.

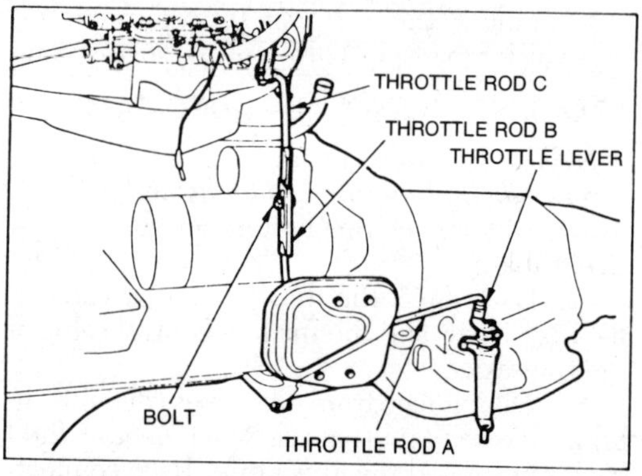

Torqueflite throttle rod and linkage

TRANSAXLE—MANUAL LINKAGE

The transaxle manual control linkage, removal, inspection, installation and adjustment are covered in this section.

Removal

1. Using the proper size Allen wrench remove the selector handle assembly from the selector lever.
2. Remove the console box.
3. Remove the position indicator cover and indicator light.
4. Disconnect the control cable at the console and at the transmission.
5. Working under the car (on lift) remove the selector lever bolts and detach the manual control cable.

Inspection

Check the cable for:

1. Brake, excessive bend or damage.
2. Inner cable stuck in outer cable.
3. Excessive sliding resistance.

Check the bushings for wear and damage.

Installation

1. Apply grease to all sliding parts.
2. When installing the rod adjusting cam, place the selector lever in Neutral position.
3. Depress the selector lever knob and turn it to adjust clearance between detent plate and at the end of the selector lever. Detent plate to selector lever end pin clearance should be .008 to .035 in.

4. Place the selector lever and neutral safety switch in neutral position and install the manual control cable.

5. Turn the adjusting nut to remove slack from the manual control cable.

6. Confirm that the selector lever operates smoothly and is set properly in every selector position. Be sure that the respective position indicator turns red.

TRANSAXLE—THROTTLE CONTROL CABLE

1980 and Later

1. Place carburetor throttle lever in wide open position.

2. Loosen the lower cable bracket mounting bolt.

3. Move the lower cable bracket until there is 1.02–.06 in. between the nipple at the bracket and the center of the nipple at the other end. Fasten the lower bracket in position.

4. Check the cable for freedom of movement. If it is binding it may need replacement.

NEUTRAL SWITCH ADJUSTMENT

Torqueflite

1. The inhibitor (Neutral) switch is located at the base of the shift control under the console cover.

2. Loosen the set screw that retains the shift lever handle to the shift lever. Remove the handle.

3. Remove the screws at the top and rear of the console, place the shift lever in "L" and remove the console. Put lever in "P" position.

4. Remove the top and side shift indicator panel mounting screws and pull the panel up. The inhibitor switch can now be disconnected and removed if necessary.

5. Adjust the switch by moving the selector lever to the "N" position. Loosen the mounting screws and adjust the inhibitor switch so that the pin in the forward end of the rod assembly will be in the position near the lobe of the detent plate and that this position will be at the front end of the range of the N connection of the switch. Temporarily tighten the switch mounting screws. After adjusting the selector lever clearance to .059 inches tighten the mounting screws.

6. To test the switch; disconnect the wiring connector and set the selector lever in each of its positions. With a continuity tester connected current should be available in the P.N. and R positions only. Replace switch if necessary. Install console and shift handle.

Transaxle

1. Place manual control lever in the Neutral position.

2. Loosen the two switch attaching bolts. Switch is located on side of transmission.

3. Turn the switch body until the flat end of the manual lever overlaps the square end of the switch body flange.

4. While keeping the switch body flange and manual lever aligned torque the two attaching bolts to 7.5–8.5 ft. lbs.

Drive Train 7

DRIVELINE

Driveshaft and Universal Joints

The driveshaft is the means by which the power from the engine and transmission (in the front of the car) is transferred to the differential and rear axles, and finally to the rear wheels.

The driveshaft assembly through 1980, incorporates two universal joints—one at each end—and a slip yoke at the front end of the assembly, which fits into the back of the transmission. Beginning with 1981 models, a two piece driveshaft with a center bearing support and universal joint is installed.

All driveshafts are balanced when installed in a car. It is, therefore, imperative that before applying undercoating to the chassis, the driveshaft and universal joint asembly be completely covered to prevent the accidental application of undercoating to their surfaces, and the subsequent loss of balance.

DRIVESHAFT REMOVAL

1. Mark the relationship of the rear driveshaft yoke and the drive pinion flange of the axle. The purpose of this marking is to facilitate installation of the assembly in its exact original position, thereby maintaining proper balance of the driveshaft assembly.

2. Remove the four bolts which hold the rear universal joint to the pinion flange. Re-

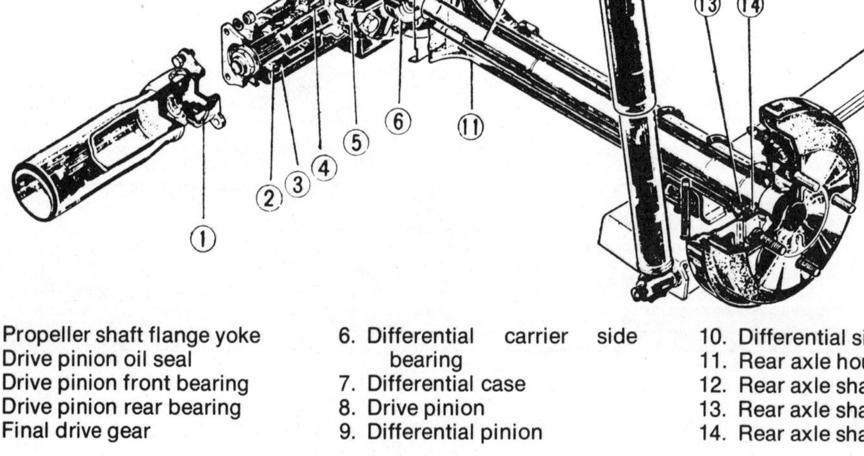

1. Propeller shaft flange yoke
2. Drive pinion oil seal
3. Drive pinion front bearing
4. Drive pinion rear bearing
5. Final drive gear
6. Differential carrier side bearing
7. Differential case
8. Drive pinion
9. Differential pinion
10. Differential side pinion
11. Rear axle housing
12. Rear axle shaft
13. Rear axle shaft oil seal
14. Rear axle shaft bearing

Typical rear axle and differential

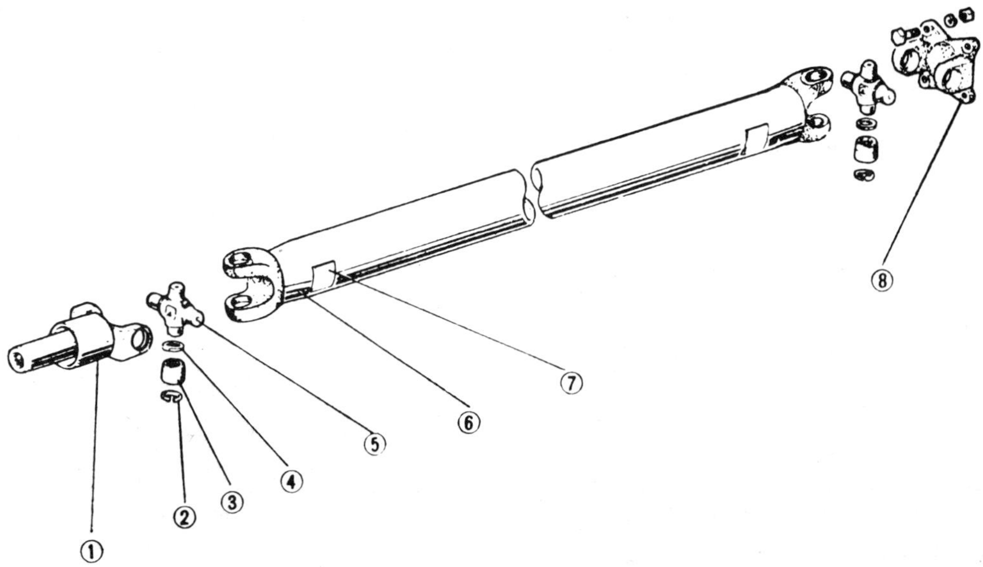

1. Sleeve yoke
2. Snap ring
3. Needle bearing
4. Dust seal
5. Universal joint journal
6. Propeller shaft
7. Balance weight
8. Propeller shaft flange yoke

Driveshaft and universal joints

move center support mounting bolts if equipped.

3. Pull the driveshaft toward the rear of the vehicle until the slip yoke clears the transmission housing and the seal. Plug the hole at the rear of the transmission housing or place a container under the opening to catch any fluid which might leak out.

UNIVERSAL JOINT OVERHAUL

NOTE: *Match mark rear yoke to shaft and/or center yoke to yoke for proper reinstallation.*

1. Position the driveshaft assembly in a sturdy vise.

2. Remove the snap-rings which retain the bearing caps in the slip yoke and in the driveshaft.

3. Using a large punch or an arbor press, drive one of the bearing caps in toward the center of the universal joint, which will force the opposite bearing cap out.

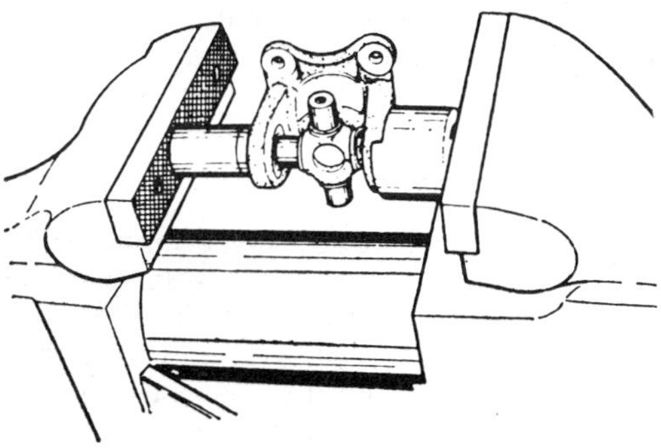

Universal joint disassembly

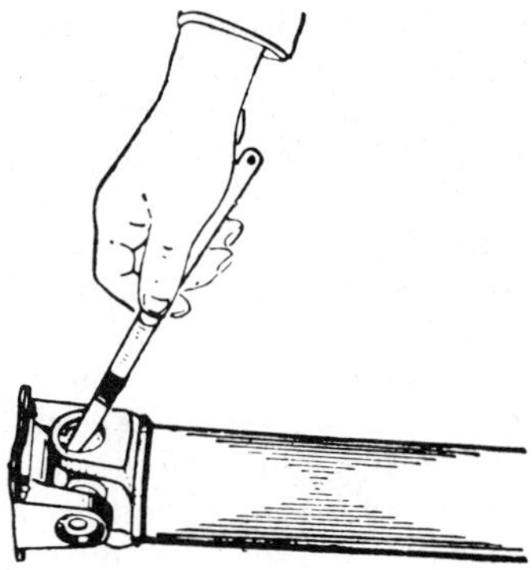

Checking the snap-ring clearance

4. As each bearing cap is pressed or punched far enough out of the universal joint assembly so that it is accessible, grip it with a pair of pliers, and pull it from the driveshaft yoke. Then drive or press the spider in the opposite direction in order to make the opposite bearing cap accessible and pull it free with a pair of pliers. Use this procedure to remove all bearings from both universal joints.

5. After removing the bearings, lift the spider from the yoke.

6. Thoroughly clean all dirt and foreign matter from the yoke area on both ends of the driveshaft.

NOTE: *When installing new bearings within*

the yokes, it is advisable to use an arbor press. However, if this tool is not available, the bearings should be driven into position with exreme care, as a heavy jolt on the needle bearings can easily damage or misalign them, greatly shortening their life and hampering their efficiency.

7. Start a new bearing into the yoke at the rear of the driveshaft.

8. Position a new spider in the rear yoke and press (or drive) the new bearing cap ¼ in. below the outer surface of the yoke.

9. With the bearing cap in position, install a new snap-ring.

10. Start a new bearing cap into the opposite side of the yoke.

11. Press (or drive) the bearing cap until the opposite bearing—which you have just installed—contacts the inner surface of the snap-ring.

12. Install a new snap-ring on the second bearing cap. Measure the clearance between the bearing cap face and the snap-ring. If it exceeds 0.001 in., insert a thicker snap-ring. Four sizes of snap-rings are available.

13. Reposition the driveshaft in the vise to facilitate work on the front universal joint.

14. Install the new bearing caps, new spider, and new snap-rings in the same manner as you did for the rear universal joint.

15. Position the slip yoke on the spider. Install new bearings and snap-rings.

16. Check both reassembled joints for freedom of movement. If misalignment of any part is causing a blind, a sharp rap on the side of the yoke with a brass hammer should seat the bearing needles, and provide the desired freedom of movement. Care should be exercised to firmly support the shaft end during this operation, as well as to prevent blows to the bearings themselves. Under no circumstances should a driveshaft be installed in a car if there is any bind in the universal joints.

CENTER BEARING AND SUPPORT REMOVAL AND INSTALLATION

1. After removing the driveshaft from the car, put mating marks on the front shaft flange, center yoke and rear shaft flange for reinstallation alignment.

2. Disconnect the front and rear shaft sections by disassembling the universal joint.

3. Remove the center yoke from the front shaft by removing the center retaining nut. Remove center support bracket, the support will slide off of the bearing by applying alternate side pressure.

4. Remove the center bearing, if necessary, with a two legged puller.

5. Inspect the center support: the bracket for damage, the rubber for deterioration and the bearing for noise, looseness or rough rotation. Replace as necessary.

6. Fill the groove on the inside center of the bearing with a multi-purpose grease (NLGI Grade 2). Partially install the bearing onto the driveshaft and install the center bearing bracket over the bearing. Make sure the bearing is securely fitted in the rubber mount. Slide assembly into place on the driveshaft. Install yoke and rear driveshaft.

NOTE: *Always use a new self locking nut to secure the center yoke.*

DRIVESHAFT INSTALLATION

1. Carefully inspect the rubber seal in the end of the transmission extension housing. Replace it if it is damaged.

2. Examine the lugs on the axle pinion flange and replace the flange if the lugs are shaved or distorted.

3. Coat the yoke spline with lubricant.

4. Remove the plug which you inserted into the rear of the transmission housing.

5. Insert the yoke into the transmission housing and onto the transmission output shaft. Make sure that the yoke assembly does not bottom on the output shaft with excessive force.

6. Locate the marks which you made on the rear driveshaft yoke and the pinion flange prior to removal of the driveshaft assembly. Install the driveshaft assembly with the marks properly aligned. Secure center support if equipped.

7. Install the bolts that attach the universal joint to the pinion flange. Torque the bolts to 25–30 ft. lbs. Center support bolts are torqued to 22–29 ft. lbs.

Drive Axle

UNDERSTANDING REAR AXLES

The rear axle is a special type of transmission that reduces the speed of the drive from the engine and transmission and divides the power to the rear wheels. Power enters the rear axle from the driveshaft via the companion flange. The flange is mounted on the drive pinion shaft. The drive pinion shaft and gear which carry the power into the differential turn at engine speed. The gear on the end of the pinion shaft drives a large ring gear the axis of rotation of which is 90° away from that of the pinion. The pinion and gear reduce the speed and multiply the power by the gear ratio of the axle, and change the direction of rotation to turn the axle shafts which drive both wheels. The rear axle gear ratio is found by dividing

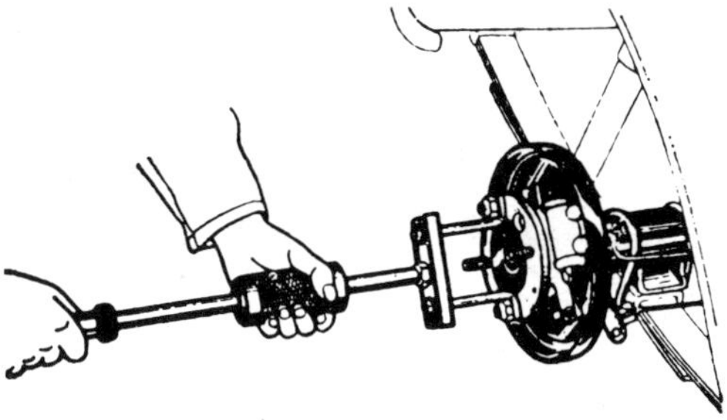

Axle shaft removal

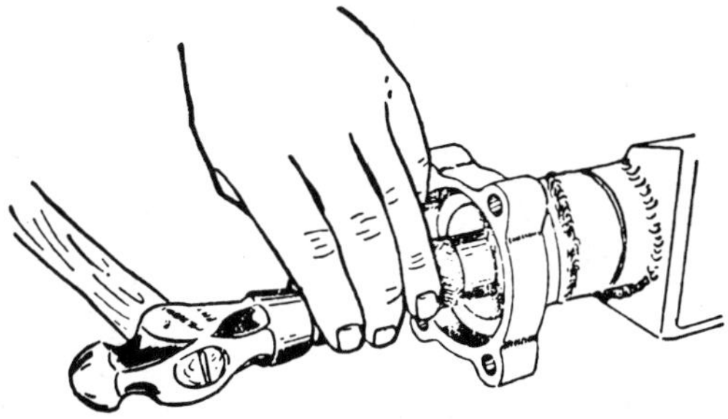

Oil seal installation

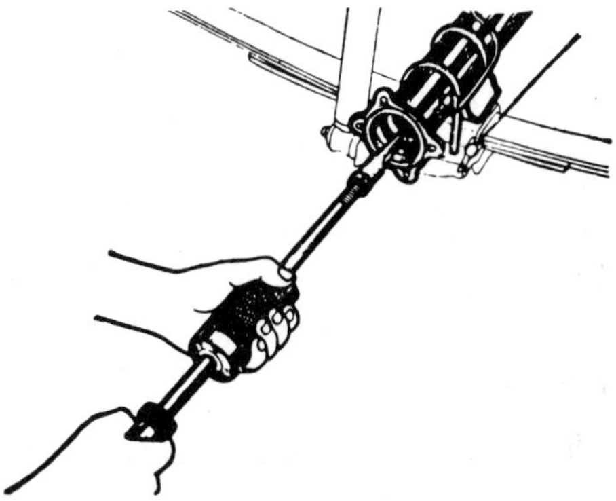

Oil seal removal

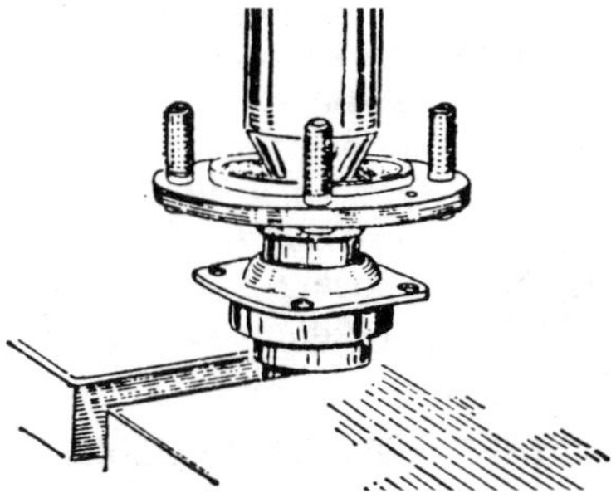

Bearing and retainer installation

the number of pinion gear teeth into the number of ring gear teeth.

The ring gear drives the differential case. The case provides the two mounting points for the ends of a pinion shaft on which are mounted two pinion gears. The pinion gears drive the two side gears, one of which is located on the inner end of each axle shaft.

By driving the axle shafts through this arrangement, the differential allows the outer drive wheel to turn faster than the inner drive wheel in a turn.

The main drive pinion and the side bearings, which bear the weight of the differential case, are shimmed to provide proper bearing preload, and to position the pinion and ring gears properly.

NOTE: *The proper adjustment of a relationship of the ring and pinion gears is critical. It should be attempted only by those with extensive equipment and/or experience.*

The rear wheels are connected to the differential assembly by axle shafts. The axle shafts are supported in the rear axle housing by bearings and are retained in the housing by bearing retainer plates which bolt to the rear brake mounting plates.

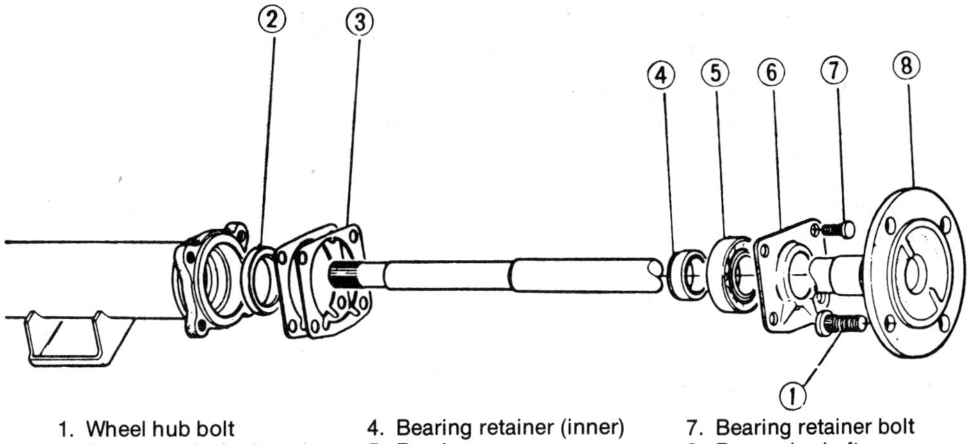

1. Wheel hub bolt
2. Rear axle shaft oil seal
3. Packing
4. Bearing retainer (inner)
5. Bearing
6. Bearing retainer (outer)
7. Bearing retainer bolt
8. Rear axle shaft

Exploded view of axle shaft assembly

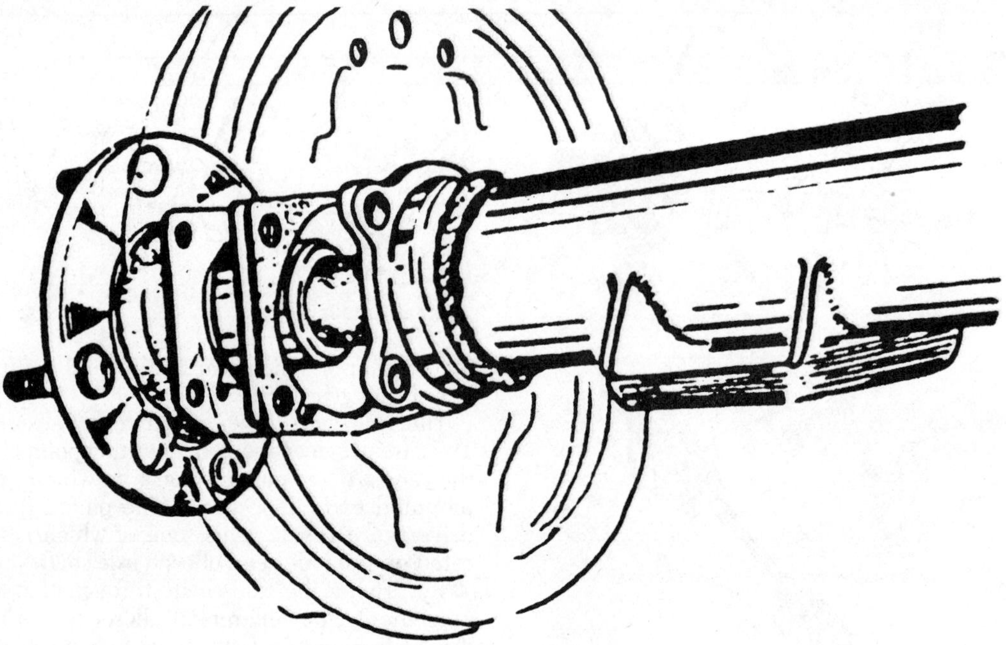

Insert the axle shaft into the housing

The differential assembly is mounted on two tapered bearings. These bearings are retained in the axle housing by removable bearing caps.

The drive pinion is mounted in the axle on two roller bearings.

An identification tag is attached to one of the inspection plate attaching bolts. The information on this tag must be used when ordering replacement parts.

AXLE SHAFT AND/OR BEARING REPLACEMENT

NOTE: *Bearings should be pressed on and off the shaft with an arbor press. An automotive machine shop can handle the job for you.*

1. Remove the wheel, tire, and brake drum.
2. Remove the nuts holding the axle retainer plate to the backing plate.
3. Remove the retainer and install the nuts, fingertight, to prevent the brake backing plate from being dislodged.
4. Pull out the axle shaft and bearing assembly, using a slide hammer.

NOTE: *If a slide hammer is not available, the axle can sometimes be pried out using pry bars on opposing sides of the hub.*

If end-play is found to be excessive, the bearing should be replaced. Shimming the bearing is not recommended as this ignores end-play of the bearing itself and could result in improper seating of the bearing.

5. Using a chisel, nick the bearing retainer in three or four places. The retainer does not have to be cut, merely collapsed sufficiently, to allow the bearing retainer to be slid from the shaft.
6. Press off the bearing and install the new one by pressing it into position.
7. Press on the new retainer.

NOTE: *Do not attempt to press the bearing and the retainer on at the same time.*

8. Assemble the shaft and bearing in the housing, being sure that the bearing is seated properly in the housing.
9. Install the retainer, drum, wheel, and tire.

AXLE SHAFT SEAL REPLACEMENT

1. Remove the axle shaft from the rear axle. See the previous procedure for details.
2. Using a two-fingered seal puller (slide hammer), remove the seal from the axle housing.
3. Clean the recess in the rear axle housing from which the seal was removed.
4. Position a new seal on the housing and drive it into the housing with a seal installation tool.
5. Install the axle shaft.

Rear Axle-Front Wheel Drive Models

The rear wheel, on front wheel drive models, rides on bearings contained in the hub of the rear brake drum. The axle is similar to a conventional front wheel spindle. Refer to the brake section in this book, for bearing removal and service.

Suspension and Steering 8

FRONT SUSPENSION

The front suspension consists of MacPherson struts, lower control arms and a stabilizer bar. The strut assembly performs several suspension functions: it provides the steering knuckle mounting, the concentric coil acts the springing medium, the integral shock absorber provides dampening and the strut assembly locates the wheel. The stabilizer bar minimizes body roll when cornering. The lower control arm acts to longitudinally locate the suspension/wheel.

Strut

REMOVAL AND INSTALLATION

1. Loosen the lug nuts, jack up the front of the car (after blocking the rear wheels) and support safely on jackstands.
2. On models without front wheel drive; remove the brake caliper, hub and brake disc rotors as outlined in the next chapter. Disconnect the stabilizer link from the lower arm, remove the three steering knuckle-to-strut assembly bolts. Carefully force the lower control arm down and separate the strut assembly and the steering knuckle. Unscrew the three retaining nuts at the top and remove the strut assembly.

   NOTE: *On some models the lower splash shield may interfere with the strut removal. If so, remove the splash shield.*

3. On front wheel drive models; remove the two strut mounting bolts at the steering knuckle, disconnect the brake hose and remove the upper mounting nuts at the top insulator. Remove the strut.
4. To install the strut; position the strut assembly in the fender. Install the upper retaining nuts hand tight.
5. Apply sealer on the mounting flange and fasten the strut assembly to the steering knuckle. Connect the brake hose if removed.
6. Tighten the upper retaining nuts to 7–11 ft. lbs. Torque the knuckle bolts on models except front wheel drive to 30–36 ft. lbs. On front wheel drive models the torque is 54–66 ft. lbs.
7. Assemble the stabilizer link and fasten to the lower control arm if removed.
8. Assemble the remaining parts in the opposite order of removal. If the brake line was disconnected during the strut removal, the brake system will have to be bled. Refer to chapter nine for the brake bleeding procedure.

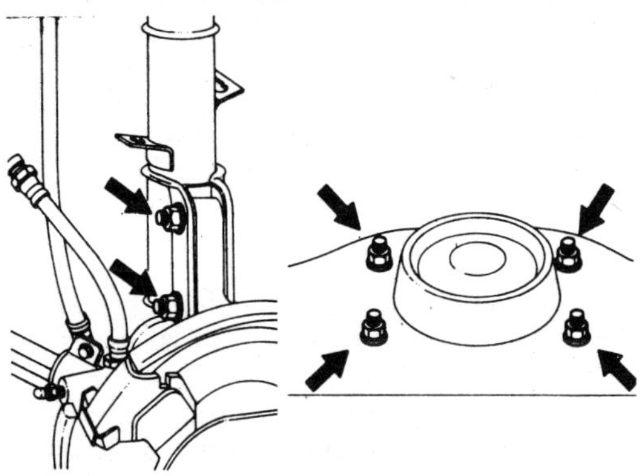

Removing the strut assembly, front wheel drive models

Spring

REMOVAL AND INSTALLATION

Remove the strut assembly as previously outlined.

1. Clamp the strut assembly in a soft-jawed vise or wrap heavy rags around the strut.
2. Install a coil spring compressor on the spring to retain it while the cover and spring-seat are removed.

   CAUTION: *A compressed coil spring can release tremendous energy. Be very careful when compressing or releasing the spring.*

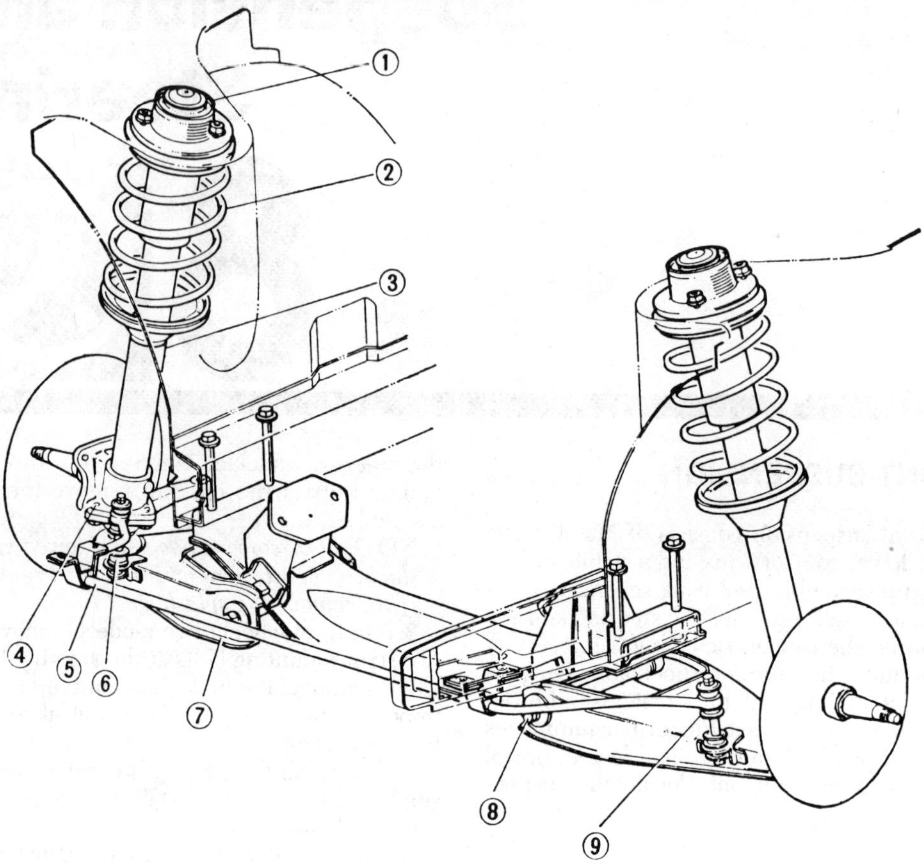

1. Strut insulator assembly
2. Front spring
3. Strut assembly
4. Knuckle arm
5. Stabilizer
6. Ball joint
7. Lower arm assembly
8. Lower arm shaft
9. Stabilizer link kit

Typical front suspension

3. Remove the dust cover.
4. Remove the nuts which couple the insulator to the strut. Remove the insulator.
5. Remove the spring.
6. Compress the spring with the compressor.
7. Install the spring on the strut.
8. Fully extend the shock absorber piston rod.
9. Align the spring seat upper assembly with the indentation on the piston rod and the D-shaped hole.

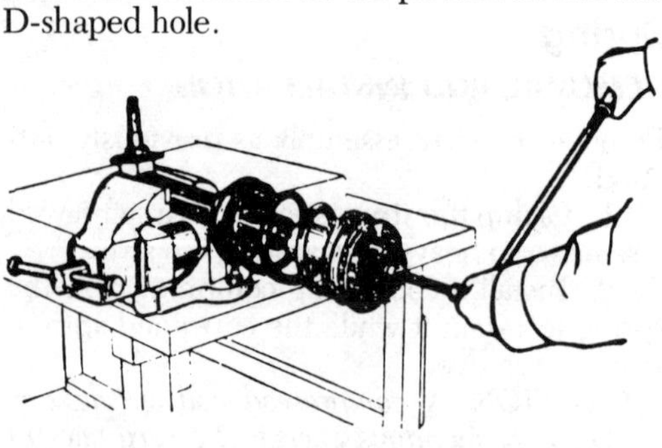

Spring removal

10. Install the insulator assembly, and then install and temporarily tighten the self-locking nut.
11. After correctly seating the upper and lower ends of the coil spring on the grooves of the upper and lower seats, release the spring compressor.
12. While holding the upper spring seat stationary, tighten the retaining nut to 30–36 ft. lbs.

STRUT OVERHAUL

1. Remove the strut from the car. Remove the coil spring (see preceding procedures).

NOTE: *Matchmark the upper end of the coil spring and bearing plate to avoid confusion during reassembly.*

2. Keep the upper mounting parts in order of their removal again to avoid confusion during reassembly.
3. Clean the outside of the strut body, especially around the top. Use the proper size wrench or a pipe wrench to loosen the top strut body nut.

4. Remove the body nut and discard if a new body nut came with the replacement cartridge. If not, save the nut.
5. Use a suitable tool and remove the O-ring from the top of the housing.
6. Grasp the piston rod and slowly pull the cartridge out of the housing. Remove the cartridge slowly to prevent the oil between the housing and the cartridge from splashing.
7. Pour all of the strut oil into a suitable container, clean the inside of the housing and inspect the cylinder for dents and to insure that all loose parts have been removed from the inside of the strut body.
8. Replenish the strut cylinder with one ounce of the original or fresh oil. The oil helps dissipate internal heat during operation and results in a cooler running, longer lasting unit. Do not put too much oil in—otherwise the oil may leak at the body nut after expansion when heated.
9. Insert the replacement cartridge into the strut body. Push the piston rod all of the way down to avoid damage if the wrench slips when installing the top nut. Install top body nut, take care not to cross-thread. Tighten the body nut securely.
10. Install the coil spring and top parts, pay attention to the indexing marks you made when disassembling the strut.
11. Install the strut on the car.

Lower Control Arm

REMOVAL AND INSTALLATION—EXCEPT FRONT WHEEL DRIVE MODELS

1. Loosen the lug nuts and then raise the front end of the car.
2. Remove the caliper, hub, and disc as outlined in Chapter 9.
3. Disconnect the stabilizer link and strut bar from the lower control arm. Depending on year, remove the idler arm support from the chassis and move the steering linkage to gain clearance.
4. Remove the steering knuckle-to-strut assembly bolts.
5. Carefully force the lower control arm down and separate the strut assembly and the steering knuckle.
6. Unscrew the three retaining nuts at the top and withdraw the strut assembly if necessary.
7. Using a puller, disconnect the steering knuckle arm and the tie-rod ball joint.
8. Again using a puller, disconnect the knuckle arm and the lower arm ball joint.
9. Remove the control arm-to-crossmember bolts and remove the control arm.
10. Install the lower arm on the crossmember. Tighten the bolts to 51–57 ft. lbs. (through 1980) and 58–69 ft. lb. (from 1981). The chamfered end of the nut should be facing the round surface of the bracket.

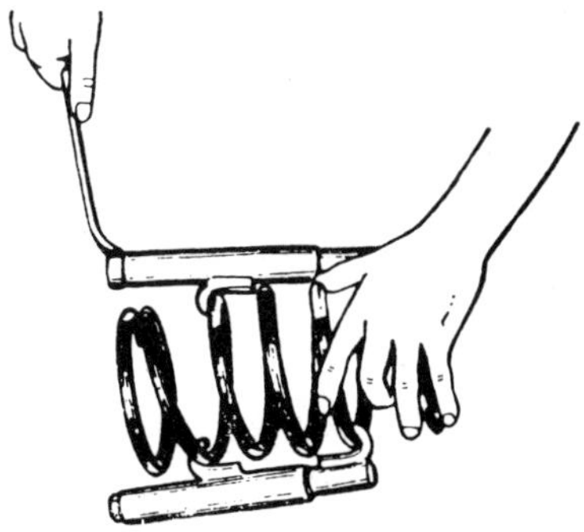

Spring compression

11. Tighten the steering knuckle arm-to-control arm ball joint nut to 30–40 ft. lbs. (through 1980) and 58–69 ft. lbs. (from 1981).
12. Install the strut assembly into the fender. Tighten the top mounting nuts to 7–10 ft. lbs. (through 1980) and 18–25 ft. lbs. (from 1981).
13. Apply sealer to the lower end of the strut. Install and tighten the strut-to-steering knuckle arm bolts to 30–36 ft. lbs. (through 1980) and 58–72 ft. lbs. (from 1981).
14. Assemble the stabilizer link and fasten it and strut bar to the lower control arm.
15. Install the backing plate, brake disc, hub, and caliper. Tighten strut bar to 18–25 ft. lbs.
16. Install the wheel and lower the car.
17. Jounce the car up and down a few times and then tighten the stabilizer bolt to 7–10 ft. lbs.

REMOVAL AND INSTALLATION—FRONT WHEEL DRIVE MODELS

1. Loosen front wheel lugs, block rear wheels, jack up the front of the car and support on jackstands.
2. Remove the front wheels. Remove the lower splash shield.
3. Disconnect the lower ball joint by unfastening the nuts and bolts mounting it to the control arm. It is not necessary to remove the ball joint from the knuckle.
4. Remove the strut bar and the control arm inner mounting nut and bolt. Remove the control arm.
5. Assembly is the reverse of removal.

Torque Specifications are;

- Inner mounting bolt—69–87 ft. lbs.
- Ball joint mounting—69–87 ft. lbs.
- Ball joint nut—40–51 ft. lbs.

1. Dust cover
2. Self locking nut
3. Washer
4. Hexagon nut
5. Spring washer
6. Strut insulator
7. Ball bearing
8. Upper spring seat ass'y
9. Rubber bumper
10. Front suspension spring
11. Oil seal ass'y
12. Oil seal
13. Front shock absorber
14. Strut
15. L.H. and R.H. knuckle arms
16. Spring washer
17. Bolt
18. Cross member ass'y
19. Nut
20. Bolt
21. Plain washer
22. Self locking nut
23. Lower arm bushing
24. Washer
25. Spring washer
26. Bolt
27. Spacer
28. Bolt
29. Spring washer
30. Lower arm shaft
31. Stopper
32. L.H. and R.H. lower arms
33. Suspension joint

33A. Packing

33B. Plain washer

34. Hexagon bolt
35. Joint cover
36. Self locking nut
37. Snap-ring

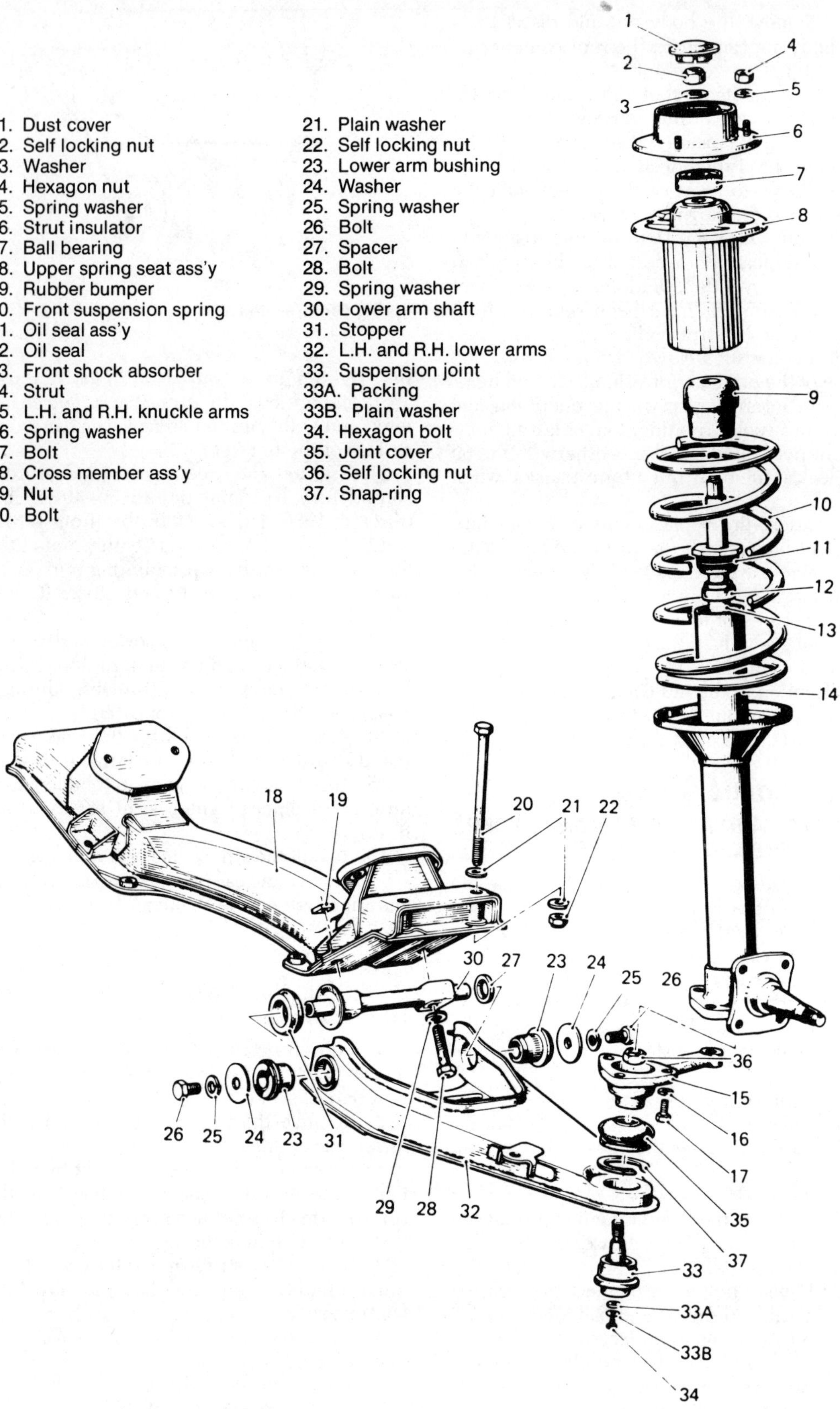

Exploded view of lower control arm and strut assembly (typical)

Ball Joints

INSPECTION

1. Jack up the front and support on jackstands. There must be no weight on the front wheels.

2. Apply downward and upward pressure to the wheel avoiding any compression to the spring. If excessive play is encountered between the control arm and the steering knuckle the ball joint probably needs replacing.

REMOVAL AND INSTALLATION

1. *On models except front wheel drive and 1981 and later rear wheel drive;* remove the lower control arm as previously outlined. Remove the snap-ring retaining the ball joint to the control arm. Press out the ball joint using a ball joint remover or have your local automotive machine shop do the job for you. Press a new ball joint into the control arm. Make sure the ball joint does not cock when install-

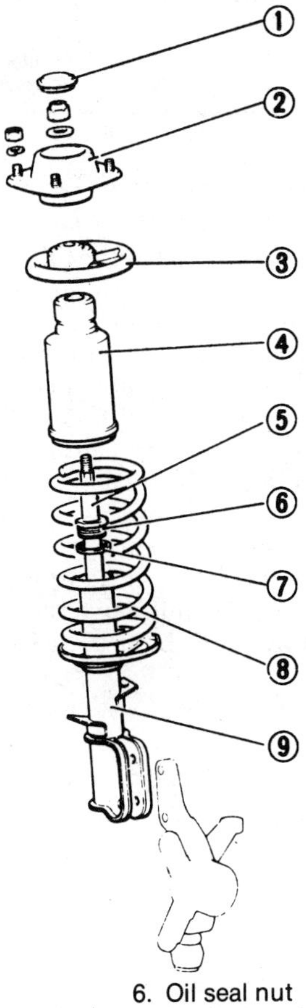

1. Cap
2. Insulator
3. Spring seat
4. Bump rubber
5. Piston
6. Oil seal nut
7. Square section O-ring
8. Spring
9. Outer shell

Exploded view of the strut assembly, front wheel drive models

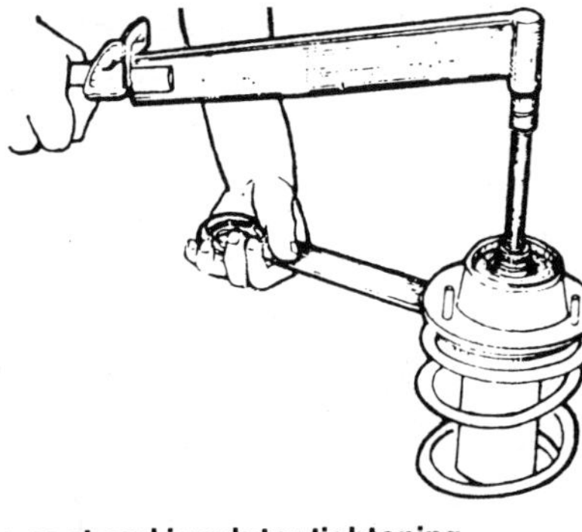

Spring seat and insulator tightening

ing in control arm seat. Installation is in reverse order. Refer to control arm section for torque specifications.

2. *On front wheel drive models;* Unbolt the ball joint from the control arm. Use a ball joint removing tool and separate the ball joint from the steering knuckle after removing the stud retaining nut. Install in the reverse order. Torque specifications are; Ball joint to control arm; 69–87 ft. lbs. Ball joint stud nut; 40–51 ft. lbs.

3. *On rear wheel drive cars from 1981;* remove the tire and wheel assembly. Refer to Chapter 9 and remove the brake caliper and support from the mounting adapter. Anchor assembly out of the way with wire to the strut spring. Remove the tie rod end nut and separate the tie rod end from the steering knuckle using a removing tool. Remove the bolts securing the strut assembly to the steering knuckle. Tap the connection with a plastic hammer to separate. Remove the ball joint to control arm mounting bolts and remove the ball joint with the knuckle arm attached. Remove the ball joint stud nut and separate the ball joint and knuckle arm. Installation is the reverse of removal. *Torque specifications are;* Ball joint stud nut; 43–52 ft. lbs. Strut to knuckle bolts; 58–78 ft. lbs. Ball joint to control arm bolts; 43–51 ft. lbs.

CAUTION: *When self-locking nuts are removed, always replace with new self-locking nuts.*

Front End Alignment

CASTER AND CAMBER

Caster and camber are preset at the factory. They require service only if the suspension and steering linkage components are damaged, in which case, repair is accomplished by replacing the damaged part. Caster, however, can be adjusted slightly by moving the strut bar nut.

Wheel Alignment—Rear Wheel Drive Cars

Year	Model	Caster (degrees)	Camber (degrees)	Toe-in (in.)	Steering Angle Inner Wheel (degrees)	Steering Angle Outer Wheel (degrees)	King Pin Angle (degrees)
1977	Coupe Sedan Hatchback	2°05′ ± ½°	1° ± 45′	0.08–0.23	35	30	8°53′
	Hardtop	1°9′ ± ½°	51′ ± ½°	0.08–0.23	39	30½	9°
1978	All	2°05′ ± ½°	1° ± ½°	0.08–0.24	35	36	9°
1979	Arrow	2°05′ ± 30′	1° ± 30′	0.08 to 0.24	35	30	9°01′
	Sapporo	2°38′ ± 30′	1°28′ ± 30′	0.08 to 0.35	37	32	8°52′
1980	Arrow	2°05′ ± 30′	1° ± 30′	0.08 to 0.24	35	30	9°01′
	Sapporo	2°38′ ± 30′	1°14′ ± 30′	0.08 to 0.35	37	32	8°52′
1981–83	Sapporo	2°40′	1°10′	0 to 0.28	37	32	9°30′

Wheel Alignment—Front Wheel Drive Cars

Year	Model	Caster (degrees)	Camber (degrees)	Toe-in (in.)	Steering Angle Inner (degrees)	Steering Angle Outer (degrees)	King Pin Angle (degrees)
1979–82	All	50° ± 20′	30′ ± 30′	0.16 in to 0.08 out	35°40′	29°17′	12°42′

TOE ADJUSTMENT

Toe-in is the difference in the distance between the front wheels, as measured at both the front and rear of the front tires.

1. Raise the front of the car so that its front wheels are just clear of the ground.
2. Use a scribing block to hold a piece of chalk at the center of each tire tread while rotating the wheels by hand.
3. Measure the distance between the marked lines at both the front and rear.

NOTE: *Take both measurements at equal distances from the ground.*

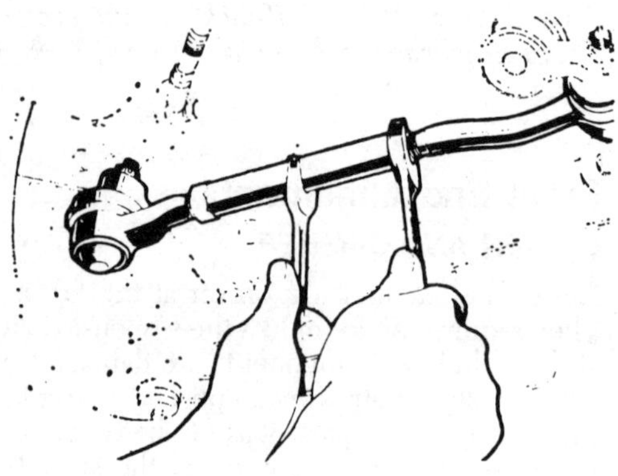

Toe adjustment

4. Toe-in is equal to the difference between the front and rear measurements. This difference should be between 5/64 in. and 15/64 in.
5. Toe-in is adjusted by screwing the tie-rod turnbuckle in or out as necessary. Leftside toe-in may be reduced by turning the tie-rod turnbuckle toward the front of the car and right-side toe-in by turning the turnbuckle toward the rear of the car. The turnbuckles should always be tightened or loosened the same amount for both tie-rods; the difference in length between the two tie-rods should not exceed 0.2 in. Tighten the locknuts to 36–40 ft. lbs.

REAR SUSPENSION

Depending on the year and model of your car, the rear suspension could either be leaf springs, 4-link coil spring or on front wheel drive models, a trailing arm mounting two coil springs.

Leaf Springs

REMOVAL AND INSTALLATION

1. Remove the hub cap or wheel cover. Loosen the lug nuts.

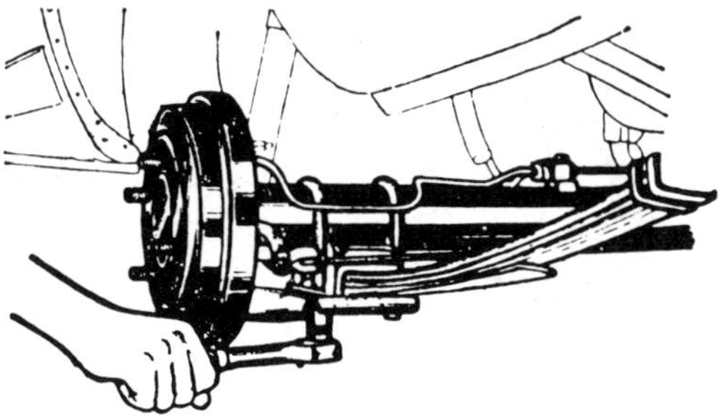

U-bolt removal

2. Block the front wheels and raise the rear of the car. Install jackstand under the sill. Two dimples on the sill indicate the exact point for location of the jackstands.

CAUTION: *Damage to the unit body can result from installing a stand at any other location.*

3. Disconnect the lower mounting nut of the shock absorber.
4. Remove the four U-bolt fastening nuts from the spring seat.

NOTE: *It's not necessary to remove the shock absorber, leave the top connected.*

5. Place a floor jack under the rear axle and raise it just enough to remove the load from the springs. Remove the spring pad and seat.
6. Remove the two rear shackle attaching nuts and remove the rear shackle.
7. Remove the front pin retaining nut. Remove the two pin retaining bolts and take off the pin.
8. Remove the spring.

NOTE: *It is a good safety practice to replace used suspension fasteners with new parts.*

9. Install the front spring eye bushings from both sides of the eye with the bushing flanges facing out.
10. Insert the spring pin assembly from the body side and fasten it with the bolts. Temporarily tighten the spring pin nut.
11. Install the rear eye bushings in the same manner as the front, insert the shackle pins from the outside of the car, and temporarily tighten the nut after installing the shackle plate.
12. Install the pads on both sides of the spring, aligning the pad center holes with the spring center bolt collar, and then install the spring seat with its center hole through the spring center collar.
13. Attach the assembled spring and spring seat to the axle housing with the axle housing spring center hole meeting the spring center bolt and install the U-bolt nuts. Tighten the nuts to 33–36 ft. lbs.
14. Tighten the lower shock absorber nut to 12–15 ft. lbs. on all models.
15. Lower the car to the floor, jounce it a few times, and then tighten the spring pin and shackle pin nuts to 36–43 ft. lbs.

Coil Springs

REMOVAL AND INSTALLATION

1. Raise and support the car safely allowing the rear axle to hang unsupported.
2. Place a jack under the rear axle or under the side trailing arm. Remove the bottom bolts or nuts mounting the shock absorbers.
3. Lower the rear axle or trailing arm and remove the coil spring.
4. To install reverse the removal procedure.

Shock Absorbers

REMOVAL AND INSTALLATION

1. Remove the hub cap or wheel cover. Loosen the lug nuts.
2. Raise the rear of the car. Support the car with jackstands.
3. Remove the upper mounting bolt/nut or nut.
4. While holding the bottom stud mount nut with one wrench, remove the locknut with

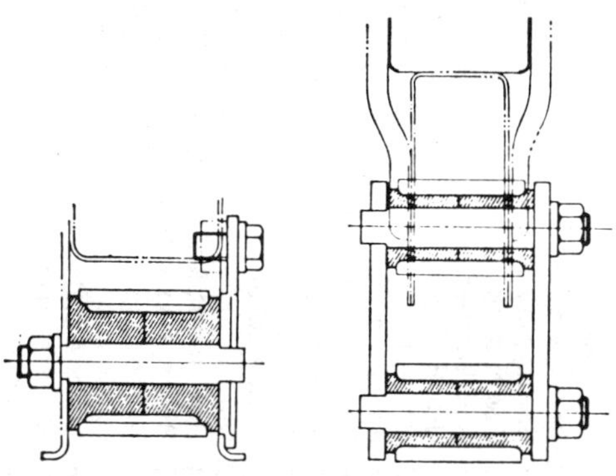

Front and rear bushing positioning

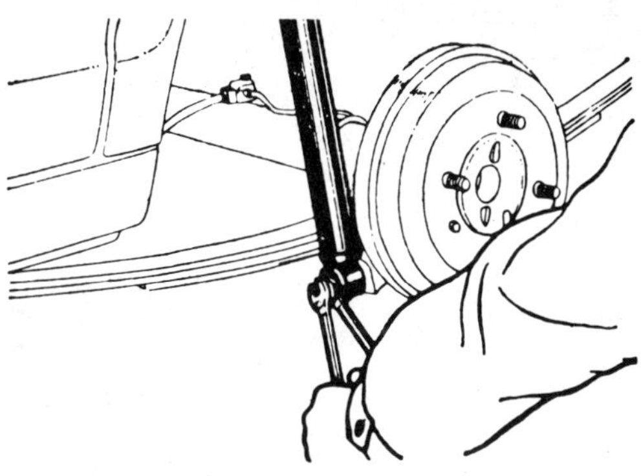

Lower shock absorber mounting

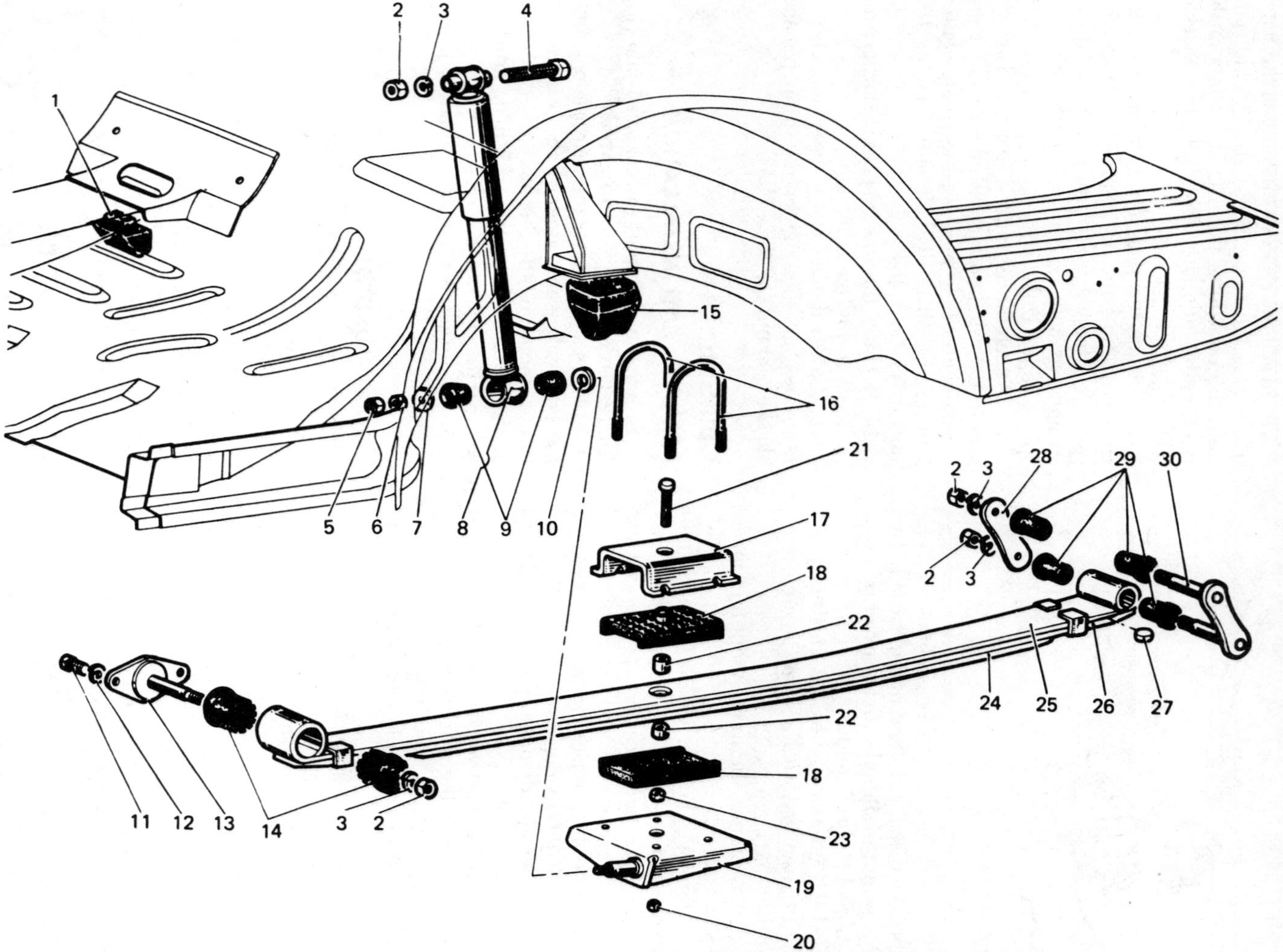

1. Carrier bumper
2. Hexagon nut
3. Spring washer
4. Hexagon bolt
5. Hexagon nut
6. Jam nut
7. Eye washer
8. Rear shock absorber ass'y
9. Rubber bushing
10. Eye washer
11. Hexagon bolt
12. Spring washer
13. Spring pin ass'y
14. Eye bushing
15. Axle bumper
16. U-bolt
17. Bracket
18. Spring pad
19. L.H. and R.H. U-bolt seats
20. Self locking nut
21. Center bolt
22. Center collar
23. Nut
24. Rear spring leaf No. 3
25. Rear spring leaf No. 1
26. Rear spring leaf No. 2
27. Silencer
28. Shackle plate
29. Shackle bushing
30. Rear spring shackle

Typical rear suspension (except station wagon and front wheel drive models)

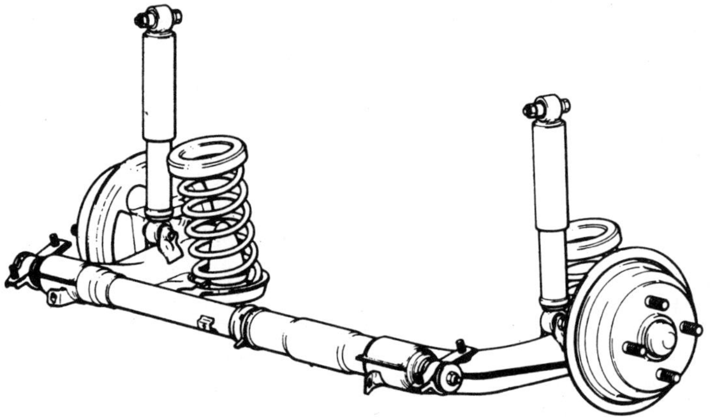

1. Shock absorber
2. Spring upper seat
3. Coil spring
4. Spring lower seat
5. Bump stopper
6. Suspension arm, right
7. Dust cover
8. Clamp
9. Bushing A
10. Bushing B
11. Stopper
12. Suspension arm, left
13. Fixture
14. Rubber bushing
15. Washer
16. Stabilizer bar

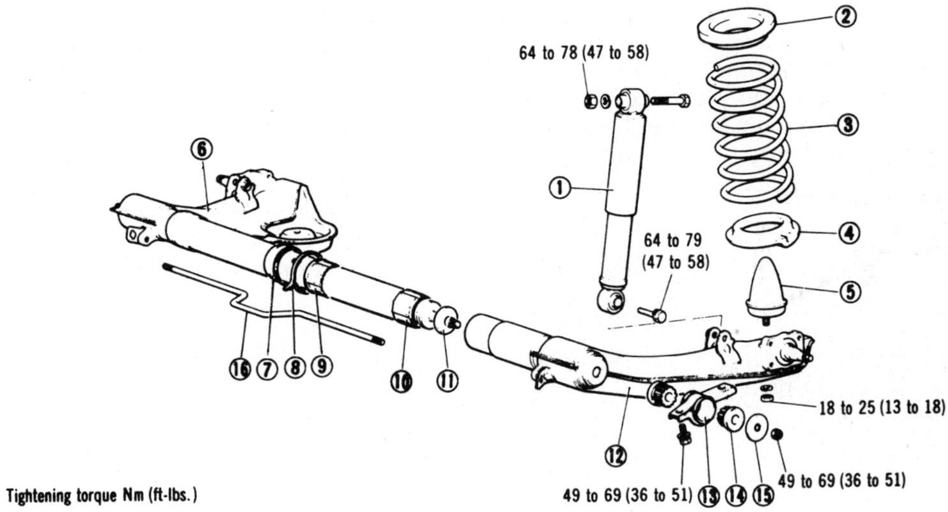

Rear suspension, front wheel drive models

another wrench. Or, on some models remove the nut and bolt from the mounting bracket.

5. Remove the shock absorber.
6. Check the shock for:

   a. Excessive oil leakage, some minor weeping is permissible;

   b. Bent center rod, damaged outer case, or other defects;

   c. Pump the shock absorber several times, if it offers even resistance on full strokes it may be considered serviceable.

7. Install the upper shock mounting nut and bolt. Hand-tighten the nut.
8. Install the bottom eye of the shock over the spring stud or into the mounting bracket and insert the bolt and nut. Tighten the nut to 12–15 ft. lbs.
9. Finally, tighten the upper nut to 47–58 ft. lbs. on all models except station wagons, which are tightened to 12–15 ft. lbs.

Lower Control Arm—Rear Drive

REMOVAL

1. Support the vehicle body on safety stands. Use a jack under the rear axle to raise the rear axle assembly slightly.
2. Remove the wheel and the upper control arm rod.
3. Detach the parking brake rear cable from the lower arm.
4. Remove the lower arm from the rear axle housing and from the bracket attached to the body.

INSTALLATION

1. Temporarily install the lower arm (check for marking on left side arm) and torque the bolts to 94.0–108.0 ft. lbs. (127.0–147.0 Nm). Torque the assist link bushing bolt to 47.0–58.0 ft. lbs. (64.0–78.0 Nm).

2. With the special nut assembly placed securely against the rear axle housing bracket, install the upper control arm rod to the bracket. Torque the bolt to 94.0 ft. lbs. (127.0–147.0 Nm).

CAUTION: *Always use new bolts.*

Lower Control Arm—Front Drive

REMOVAL

1. Support the side frame on jack stands and remove the rear wheels. Remove the rear brake assembly.
2. Remove the muffler and jack the control arm just enough to raise it slightly.
3. Remove the shock absorber and lower the jack. Remove the coil spring and temporarily install the shock absorber to the control arm.
4. Disconnect the brake hoses at the rear suspension arms and remove the rear suspension from the body as an assembly.

INSTALLATION

1. Install the fixture to body bolts and torque to 36.0–51.0 ft. lbs. (49.0–69.0 Nm).
2. Install the coil springs and loosely install the shock absorbers. Tighten the shock absorber bolts to specification after the vehicle is lowered to the floor.
3. Install the rear brake assembly.
4. Lower the vehicle and tighten the suspension arm end nuts to 36.0–51.0 ft. lbs. (49.0–69.0 Nm). and the shock bolts to 47.0–58.0 ft. lbs. (64.0–78.0 Nm).
5. Install the brake drums and wheels.
6. Bleed the brake system and adjust the rear brake shoe clearance.

STEERING

Steering Wheel

1. Disconnect the battery ground cable. Remove the center pad retaining screws located on the back of the wheel on some models, or pull off the worn pad using steady pressure. Disconnect the horn wiring on some models and remove the center pad.
2. Paint or chalk matchmarks on the steering shaft and the steering wheel so that they can be correctly reinstalled.

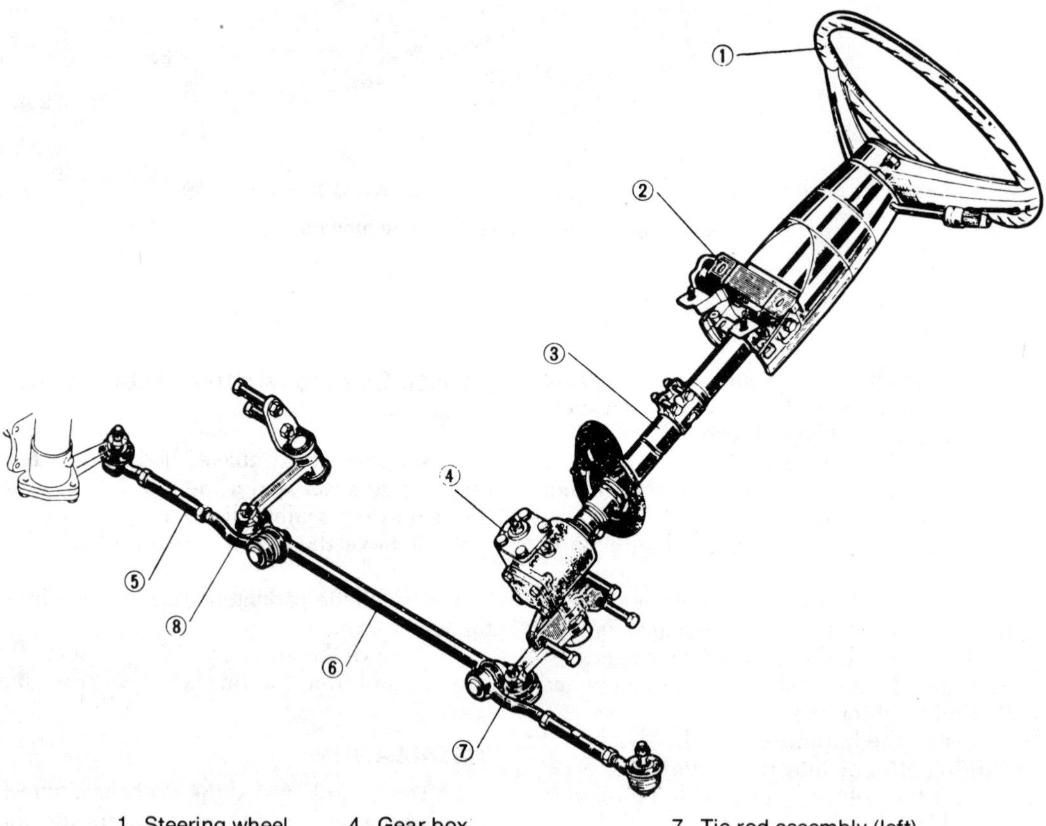

1. Steering wheel
2. Tilt bracket
3. Steering shaft
4. Gear box
5. Tie rod assembly (right)
6. Relay rod
7. Tie rod assembly (left)
8. Idler arm

Steering system (typical) except cars with rack and pinion steering

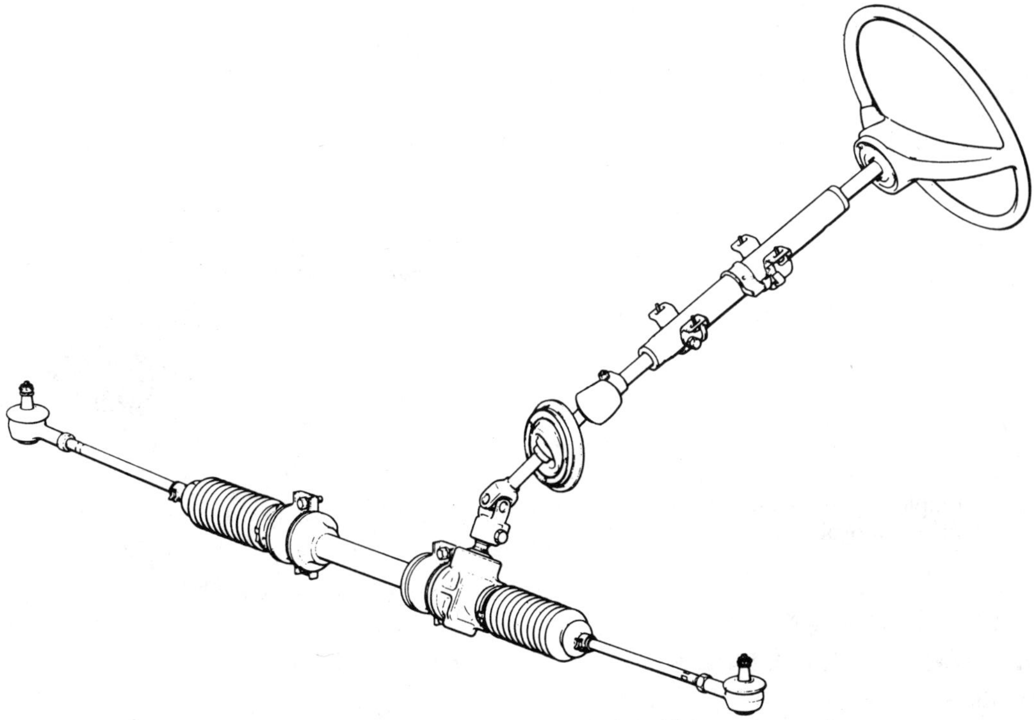

Rack and pinion steering assembly

Typical steering wheel removal

3. Unscrew the hub nut and, using a puller, remove the steering wheel.

CAUTION: *Don't hammer or otherwise pound on the steering column, as it is collapsible.*

4. Installation of the steering wheel is performed in the reverse order of removal. Tighten the steering wheel hub nut to 15–18 ft. lbs.

Turn Signal and Flasher Switch

REMOVAL AND INSTALLATION

1. Remove the steering wheel as previously outlined.
2. Remove the instrument cluster using the procedure in Chapter 5.
3. Undo the retaining screws and remove the top and bottom steering column covers.
4. Disconnect each column switch connector and then remove the column switch from the column tube.
5. Remove the switch assembly retaining screws from the back of the column switch.
6. Remove the turn signal and flasher switch contact points.
7. Examine the switch contact points for corrosion. Clean or replace them as necessary.
8. Switch installation is the reverse of the removal procedure. Be sure that the switch is centered in the column or the self-cancelling will be affected. The switch wiring harness should be securely retained with clips.

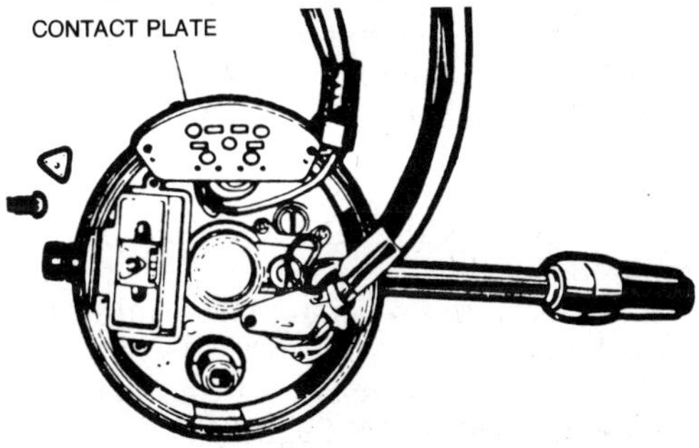

Typical turn signal switch assembly removal

Ignition Switch/Steering Lock

1. Perform Steps 1–6 above.
2. Disconnect the electrical wiring to the switch.
3. Drill out the shear bolts or cut a slot in the mounting screw heads and bracket with a hacksaw and remove with a flat blade screwdriver.

NOTE: *Use new screws and bracket when installing switch.*

4. Remove the switch.
5. Align the column tube hole with wheel lock guide dowel for initial assembly.
6. Insert the ignition key to make sure that the lock functions correctly.
7. Install the shear bolts. Tighten them evenly until the heads break off.
8. Complete the assembly using the reverse of the removal steps.

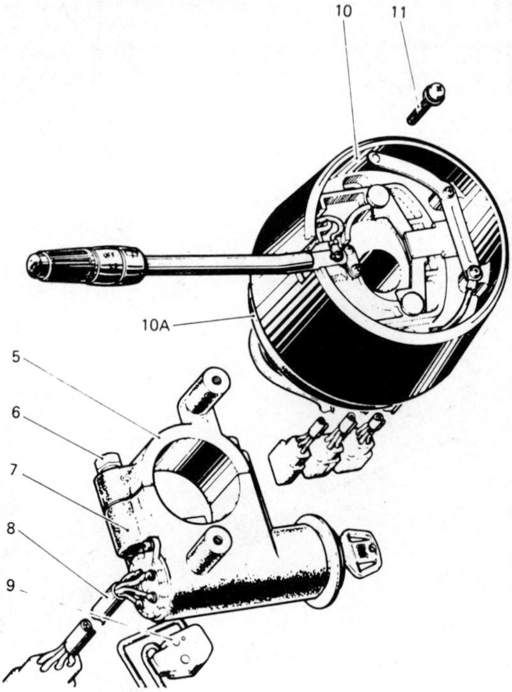

5. Bracket
6. Bolt
7. Body and cylinder
8. Ignition and starter switch
9. Door warning switch
10. Column switch
10A. Column switch rubber ring
11. Washer assembled machine screw

Exploded view of ignition switch/steering lock/turn signal

Steering Linkage

REMOVAL AND INSTALLATION

Tie-Rods

1. Using a puller, disconnect the tie-rod ends from the steering knuckle.
2. Loosen the jam nut and remove the tie-rod ends from the tie-rod. The outer end is left-hand threaded and the inner is right-hand threaded.
3. Grease the tie-rod threads and install the ends. Turn each end in an equal amount.
4. Install the tie-rod assembly on the steering knuckle and relay rod. Tighten the castellated nuts to 29–36 ft. lbs. Use new cotter pins.
5. Adjust the toe-in as described under "Wheel Alignment."

Relay Rod

1. Disconnect the tie-rod ends from the steering knuckles with a puller.
2. Again using the puller, disconnect the relay rod from the idler arm and the pitman arm.
3. Remove the relay rod.
4. Install the rod in the reverse order of removal. Tighten the tie-rod end nuts to 29–36 ft. lbs. Tighten the relay rod-to-idler arm nut to 29–43 ft. lbs. Always use new cotter pins.

Idler Arm

1. Disconnect the idler arm from the relay rod using a puller.
2. Remove the retaining bolts and remove the idler arm.
3. Mount the idler arm on the frame and tighten the bolts to 25–29 ft. lbs.
4. Attach the relay rod to the idler arm and tighten the stud nut to 29–43 ft. lbs. Use a new cotter pin.

Manual Steering Gear

REMOVAL AND INSTALLATION

1. Remove the clamp bolt connecting the steering shaft with the steering gear.
2. Disconnect the tie rod and pitman arm from the relay rod using a linkage puller.
3. Remove the gear box from the frame by loosening the side mounting bolts. To install reverse the removal procedures.

ADJUSTMENT

1. Measure the mainshaft preload with an inch pound torque wrench. The allowable torque is 3 to 4.8 in. lbs.
2. The preload torque is corrected by reducing or increasing the number of shims under the end plate.
3. Seat the cross shaft and bearings by turning the steering mainshaft and the adjusting bolt two or three times.
4. Tighten the adjusting bolt to obtain zero

freeplay with the cross shaft in the center position. Tighten the lock nut on the adjusting bolt.

Power Steering Pump

REMOVAL

1. Remove the drive belt. If the pulley is to be removed, do so now.
2. Disconnect the pressure and return lines. Catch any leaking fluid.
3. Remove the pump attaching bolts and lift the pump from the brackets.

INSTALLATION

1. Make sure the bracket bolts are tight and install the pump to the brackets.
2. If pulley had been removed, install it and tighten the nut securely. Bend the lock tab over the nut.
3. Install the drive belt and adjust to a tension of 22 lbs. at a deflection of .28 to housing mainshaft.
4. Fill the reservoir with Dexron fluid and air bleed the system. (Refer to the bleeding procedure.)
5. Start the engine and inspect for leakage.

CAUTION: *When installing the pressure and return hoses, be careful not to twist or strip the fittings and pipes. Route the lines so as not to interfere with adjacent parts.*

Power Steering Gear

Beginning 1978, power steering became available with the 2600 cc engine.

The power steering consists of a belt driven pump, a separate fluid reservoir, pressure and return lines, and a steering gear assembly with an integral control valve.

REMOVAL

1. Match mark and disconnect the steering shaft from the gearbox main shaft.
2. Disconnect the tie rod end and pitman arm from the relay rod.
3. Remove the air cleaner and disconnect the pressure and return lines from the steering gear assembly.
4. Remove any interfering splash pans from underneath the vehicle.
5. If necessary, remove the kickdown linkage, splash pan shield and bolts. Move the fuel line aside to avoid damage during removal.
6. Remove the frame bolts from the gearbox and lower the unit from the vehicle .39 inches at the top center of the belt. Tighten the pump bolts securely to hold the tension.
7. Connect the pressure and return lines and fill the reservoir with approved fluid. (DEXRON).
8. Bleed the system. (Refer to the bleeding procedure).

ADJUSTMENT

NOTE: *The steering gear must be disconnected from the steering shaft.*

1. Measure the mainshaft preload with an inch pound torque wrench. The preload should be 3.5 to 6.9 in. lbs., with the cross-shaft adjusting bolt backed off.
2. Adjust the valve housing top cover to obtain the proper preload. When correct, lock the top cover with the locking nut.
3. Tighten the cross-shaft adjusting bolt until zero lash is present. Check the total starting torque to rotate the main shaft. The torque should be 5.2 to 8.7 in. lbs.
4. Adjust the cross-shaft until the required starting torque is obtained and lock the adjusting bolt nut securely.

BLEEDING THE SYSTEM

1. The reservoir should be full of Dexron fluid.
2. Jack up the front wheels and support the vehicle safely.
3. Turn the steering wheel fully to the right and left until no air bubbles appear in the fluid. Maintain the reservoir level.
4. Lower the vehicle and with the engine idling, turn the wheels fully to the right and left. Stop the engine.
5. Install a tube from the bleeder screw on the steering gear box to the reservoir.
6. Start the engine, turn the steering wheel fully to the left and loosen the bleeder screw.
7. Repeat the procedure until no air bubbles pass through the tube.
8. Tighten the bleeder screw and remove the tube. Refill the reservoir as needed, and check that no further bubbles are present in the fluid.

CAUTION: *An abrupt rise in the fluid level after stopping the engine is a sign of incomplete bleeding. This will cause noise from the pump or control valve.*

Rack and Pinion Steering

Rack and pinion steering is found on front wheel drive cars. The gear output shaft is connected to the steering shaft by means of a universal joint attached by bolt and clamp pressure. A pinion gear on the input shaft engages the rack and rotation of the shaft pinion causes the rack to move laterally.

The tie rod is attached at each end of the rack joint. This allows the tie-rods to move with the front suspension. The gear is sealed at each end with rubber bellows. The steering gear is filled with grease and checking or refilling is not required unless leakage is evident or repairs become necessary.

Couplings attaching the tie-rods on the rack are pinned and cannot be disassembled in service. Replacement of inner tie-rods, rack, housing or upper pinion bearing usually requires the installation of a new rack and pinion assembly.

Outer tie-rod ends are replaceable and toe adjustment can be made. Refer to previous sections of this chapter for more details.

REMOVAL AND INSTALLATION

1. Jack up the front of the car after blocking the rear wheels and loosening the wheel lug nuts on the front. Support the car safely on jackstands.
2. Remove the front wheels and the lower splash shield.
3. Remove the tie-rod end retaining nut. Use a puller and remove the tie-rod end from the steering knuckle.
4. Remove the bolt coupling the universal joint and the steering shaft. Remove the clamps mounting the rack and pinion to the crossmember. Remove the assembly from the car.
5. Installation is the reverse of removal. *Torque Specifications are:*
   - Mounting bolts; 22–29 ft. lbs.
   - Clamp bolt; 11–14 ft. lbs.

NOTE: *Inspect rubber mounting bushings. Replace as necessary. The bushings are installed with the slit towards the ground.*

Brakes

9

BRAKE SYSTEM

Your car is equipped with front disc brakes and either self-adjusting rear drum brakes or sliding caliper rear disc brakes.

HYDRAULIC SYSTEM

The hydraulic system is composed of the master cylinder, the brake lines, the brake pressure distributing valve, and the wheel cylinder, the brake lines, the brake pressure distributing valve, and the wheel cylinders (drum brakes) and/or calipers (disc brakes).

The master cylinder serves as a brake fluid reservoir and as a hydraulic pump. Brake fluid is stored in the two sections of the master cylinder. The front half of the master cylinder holds the fluid that is used to activate the rear brakes. The rear half of the master cylinder holds the fluid that activates the front brakes. This tandem master cylinder is required by federal law as a safety device. Since the front hydraulic system is independent of the rear system, a fluid leak is one system would only cause that system to fail, allowing the other system to stop the car.

When the brake pedal is depressed, it moves a piston mounted in the bottom of the master cylinder. The movement of this piston creates hydraulic pressure in the master cylinder. This pressure is carried to the wheel cylinders or calipers by the brake lines.

On the way to the wheels, the brake fluid passes through the combination (pressure differential) valve. The valve is connected between the front and rear brake lines. Each of the brake lines is connected to one of the upright sides of the valve. The brake fluid passes through each of the upright sides inside the valve and leaves at the bottom of the sides where the outgoing brake lines pick up the fluid and carry it on to the wheels. A piston is mounted in the crossbar section. It is held centered in the valve by the brake fluid in each of the upright sides. If a leak should develop in either the front or rear brake system, fluid pressure in the portion of the pressure differential valve which corresponds to that system

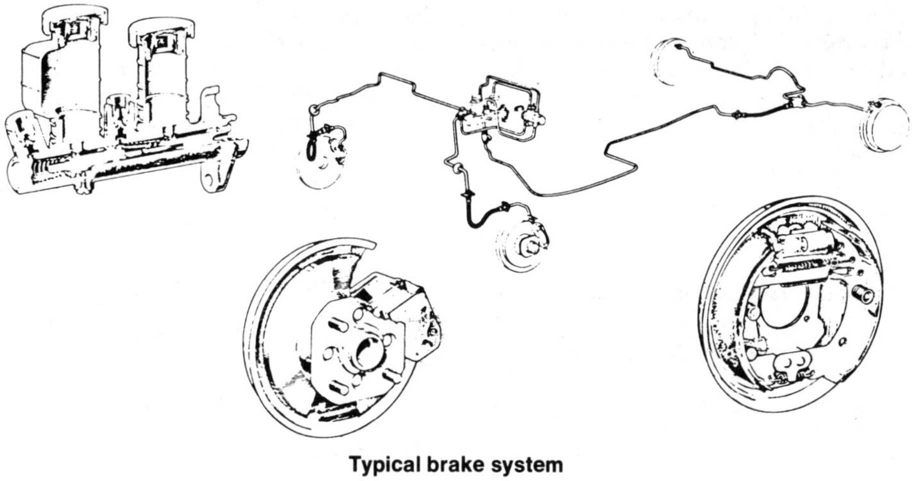

Typical brake system

would drop. This would cause the piston in the crossbar of the valve to move toward that section of the valve, since the normal fluid pressure in the other side of the valve would now be dominant.

When the hydraulic pressure reaches the wheels, after the pedal has been depressed, it enters the wheel cylinders or calipers. Here it comes into contact with a piston or pistons. The hydraulic pressure causes the piston(s) to move, which moves the brake shoes or pads (disc brakes), causing them to come into contact with the drums or rotors (disc brakes). Friction between the brake shoes and the drums causes the car to slow down. There is a relationship between the amount of pressure that is applied to the brake pedal and the amount of force which moves the brake shoes against the drums. Therefore, the harder the brake pedal is depressed, the quicker the car should stop.

Since a hydraulic system operates on fluids, air is a natural enemy. Air in the system retards the passage of hydraulic pressure from the master cylinder to the wheels. Anytime a hydraulic component below the master cylinder is opened or removed, the system must be held (of air) to ensure proper operation.

The wheel cylinders used with drum brakes are composed of a cylinder with a polished inside bore, which is mounted on the brake shoe backing plate, two boots, two pistons, two cups, a spring, and a bleeder screw. When hydraulic pressure enters the wheel cylinder, it contacts the two cylinder cups. The cups seal the cylinder and prevent fluid from leaking out. The hydraulic pressure forces the cups outward. The cups in turn force the pistons outward. The pistons contact the brake shoes and the hydraulic pressure in the wheel cylinders overcomes the pressure of the brake springs, causing the shoes to contact the brake drum. When the brake pedal is released, the brake shoe return springs pull the brake shoes away from the drum. This forces the pistons back toward the center of the wheel cylinder. Wheel cylinders can fail in two ways; they can leak or lock up. Leaking wheel cylinders are caused either by defective cups or irregularities in the wheel cylinder bore. Frozen wheel cylinders are caused by foreign matters getting into the cylinders and preventing the pistons from sliding freely.

The calipers used with disc brakes contain a piston, piston seal, piston dust boot, and bleeder screw. When hydraulic pressure enters the caliper, the piston is forced outward causing the disc brake pad to come into contact with the rotor. When the brakes are applied, the piston seal, mounted on the caliper housing, becomes slightly distorted in the direction of the rotor. When the brakes are released, the piston seal moves back to its normal position and, at the same time, pulls the piston back away from the brake pad. This allows the brake pads to move away from the rotor. Calipers can fail in three ways, two of these being caused by defective piston seals. When a piston seal becomes worn, it can allow brake fluid to leak out to contaminate the pad and rotor. If a piston seal becomes weak, it can fail to pull the piston away from the brake shoe when the brakes are released, allowing the brake pad to drag on the rotor when the car is being driven. If foreign material enters the caliper housing, it can prevent the piston fron sliding freedly, causing the brakes to stick on the rotor.

Clean, high-quality brake fluid, meeting DOT 3 "specs," is essential to the proper operation of the brake system. Always buy the highest quality brake fluid available. If the brake fluid should become contaminated, it should be drained and flushed, and the master cylinder filled with new fluid. Never reuse brake fluid. Any brake fluid that is removed from the brake system should be discarded.

Since the hydraulic system is sealed, there must be a leak somewhere in the system if the master cylinder is repeatedly low on fluid.

Master Cylinder

CAUTION: *Be careful not to spill brake fluid on the painted surfaces of your car. The brake fluid will cause damage to the paint.*

REMOVAL

1. Disconnect all hydraulic lines from the master cylinder. On models with remote reservoir; remove and plug the hoses from the master cylinder caps. If the master cylinder has a fluid level warning device, disconnect the wiring harness.
2. On non-power brake cars, remove the clevis pin that connects the master cylinder push rod to the brake pedal.
3. Loosen the remove the master cylinder mounting nuts, either from the firewall (manual brakes) or from the power brake booster. Remove the master cylinder.

INSTALLATION

1. Mount the master cylinder to the firewall (manual brakes) or to the power brake booster.
2. Connect the push rod to the brake pedal (manual brakes).
3. Connect all brake lines and wiring har-

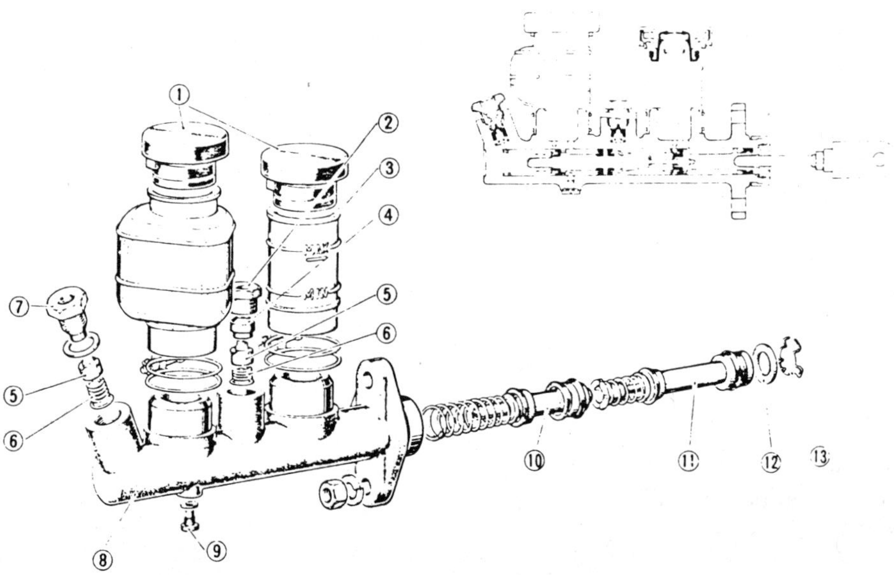

1. Reservoir cap
2. Check valve cap
3. Fluid reservoir
4. Outer pipe seat
5. Check valve
6. Check valve spring
7. Valve case
8. Master cylinder
9. Piston stopper
10. Secondary piston assembly
11. Primary piston assembly
12. Piston stopper
13. Stopper ring

Typical master cylinder

nesses and fill the master cylinder reservoir(s) with clean fluid.

4. Bleed the brake system as outlined in this chapter.

MASTER CYLINDER OVERHAUL

This is a tedious, time-consuming job. You can save yourself a lot of trouble by buying a rebuilt master cylinder from your dealer or a parts supply house. The small difference in cost between a rebuilding kit and a rebuilt part usually makes it more economical, in terms of time and work, to buy the rebuilt part.

1. Remove the master cylinder from the car.
2. Remove the reservoir caps and filters and drain the brake fluid. Discard this fluid.
3. Pry the piston stopper snap-ring from the open end of the master cylinder with a screwdriver.
4. Remove the stopper screw and washer from the bottom of the master cylinder and then remove the primary and secondary piston assemblies from the master cylinder bore.
5. Remove the caps on the underside of the master cylinder to gain access to the check valves for cleaning.

NOTE: *Do not disassemble the brake fluid level gauge, if equipped.*

6. Discard all used rubber parts and gaskets. These parts should be replaced with the new components included in the rebuilding kit.

NOTE: *Do not remove the master cylinder reservoir tanks unless they are leaking.*

7. Clean all the parts in clean brake fluid. Do *not* use mineral oil or alcohol for cleaning.
8. Check the cylinder bore and piston for wear, scoring, corrosion, or any other damage. The piston and cylinder bore can be dressed with crocus cloth soaked in brake fluid. Move the crocus cloth around the cylinder bore, not in and out. Do the same to the piston, if necessary. Wash both the cylinder bore and the piston with clean brake fluid.
9. Check the piston-to-cylinder bore clearance; it should measure .006 in. (0.15 mm). If greater clearance exists, replace the piston, the cylinder, or both.
10. Assemble the master cylinder in the reverse order of disassembly. Soak all of the components in clean brake fluid before assembling them.
11. Clamp the master cylinder in a vise by one of its flanges. Fill the reservoirs with fresh fluid, and pump the piston with a screwdriver until fluid squirts from the outlet ports. Install the master cylinder and bleed the system.

Power Brake Boosters

Power brake operate just as standard brake systems except in the actuation of the master cylinder pistons. A vacuum diaphragm is located on the front of the master cylinder and assists the driver in applying the brakes, reducing both the effort and travel he must put into moving the brake pedal.

The vacuum diaphragm housing is connected to the intake manifold by a vacuum hose. A check valve is placed at the point where the hose enters the diahragm housing, so that during periods of low manifold vacuum brake assist vacuum will not be lost.

Depressing the brake pedal closes off the vacuum souce and allows atmospheric pressure to enter on one side of the diaphragm. This causes the master cylinder pistons to move and apply the brakes. When the brake pedal is released, vacuum is applied to both sides of the diaphragm and master cylinder pistons to the released position. If the vacuum fails, the brake pedal rod will butt against the end of the master cylinder actuating rod, and direct mechanical application will occur as the pedal is depressed.

The hydraulic and mechanical problems that apply to conventional brake systems also apply to power brakes, and should be checked for if the tests below do not reveal the problem.

Test for a system vacuum leak as described below:

1. Operate the engine at idle with the transmission in Neutral without touching the brake pedal for at least one minute.
2. Turn off the engine, and wait one minute.
3. Test for the presence of assist vacuum by depressing the brake pedal and releasing it several times. Light application will produce less and less pedal travel, if vacuum was present. If there is no vacuum, air is leaking into the system somewhere.

Test for system operation as follows:

1. Pump the brake pedal (with engine off) until the supply vacuum is entirely gone.
2. Put a light, steady pressure on the pedal.
3. Start the engine, and operate it at idle with the transmission in Neutral. If the system is operating, the brake pedal should fall toward the floor if constant pressure is maintained on the pedal.

Power brake systems may be tested for hydraulic leaks just as ordinary systems are tested, except that the engine should be idling with the transmission in Neutral (manual) or Park (automatic) with the wheels blocked throughout the test.

Combination Valve or Proportioning Valve

The valve performs one or more of the following functions:

1. Controls the amount of hydraulic pressure to the rear brakes.
2. Warns of failure in the brake system. (Warning light on dash).
3. Inactivates rear pressure control in case of failure in the front service brake system.

REMOVAL AND INSTALLATION

1. Disconnect the brakes lines at the valve.

   NOTE: *Use a flare nut wrench, if possible, to avoid damage to the lines and fittings.*
2. Remove the mounting bolts and remove the valve.

   NOTE: *Do not disassemble the valve, replace with a new one if necessary.*
4. Installation is the reverse of removal. Make sure the brake lines are tight. Refill the system with fluid and bleed the brakes.

Brake Warning Light Switch

This assembly is unrepairable, and must be replaced as a unit if problems occur. The switch may be located in the combination valve, in the mastercylinder reservoir or mounted in line between the master cylinder and combination/proportioning valve. Replacement is made by disconnecting the brake lines or unscrewing the switch. If the switch is located in line, the brake system will have to be bled after replacement.

Stoplight Switch

The stoplight switch is a mechanical plunger type, activated when the brake pedal is depressed. The switch is located under the dash on the brake pedal stop.

REPLACEMENT

Disconnect the wiring, loosen the locknut and unscrew the switch. When installing, allow about .020 inch clearance between the top of the threads on the switch and the brake pedal arm.

Bleeding

The brakes should be bled whenever a brake line, caliper, wheel cylinder, or mastery cylinder has been removed or when the brake pedal is low or "soft." The bleeding sequence except from wheel drive models is, right rear wheel, left rear wheel, left front wheel, and right front wheel. The bleeding sequence for front wheel drive models is, left rear wheel, right front wheel, right rear wheel and left front wheel.

NOTE: *Some 1977 and later models don't have a bleeder fitting on the left rear brake. Both rear brakes must be bled from the right rear.*

1. Check the master cylinder fluid level. If necessary, add fluid to bring the level up.
2. Remove the bleeder cap at the wheel cylinder or caliper. Connect a rubber hose to the bleeder and immerse the other end in a glass container half filled with brake fluid.
3. Have an assistant depress the brake pedal to the floor, and then pause until the fluid flow stops and the bleeder nipple is closed.
4. Allow the pedal to return and repeat the procedure until a steady, bubble-free flow is seen.
5. Tighten the bleeder valve and replace the cap. Move on to the next wheel in sequence.

NOTE: *Frequently check the master cylinder level during this procedure. If the reservoir goes dry, air will enter the system.*

FRONT DISC BRAKES

Disc Brake Pads

REMOVAL AND INSTALLATION

Pin Type Caliper

1. Loosen the wheel lugs, raise the front of the car and support it on jackstands. Remove the wheel.
2. Pry the dust shield off the top of the caliper by lifting the clip in the center of the shield with a screwdriver.
3. Using needlenose pliers, unsnap the M-clip from the brake pad and the two retaining pins.
4. Remove the K-clip from the holes in the retaining pins.
5. Use a small punch or screwdriver to tap the retaining pins out of the caliper.

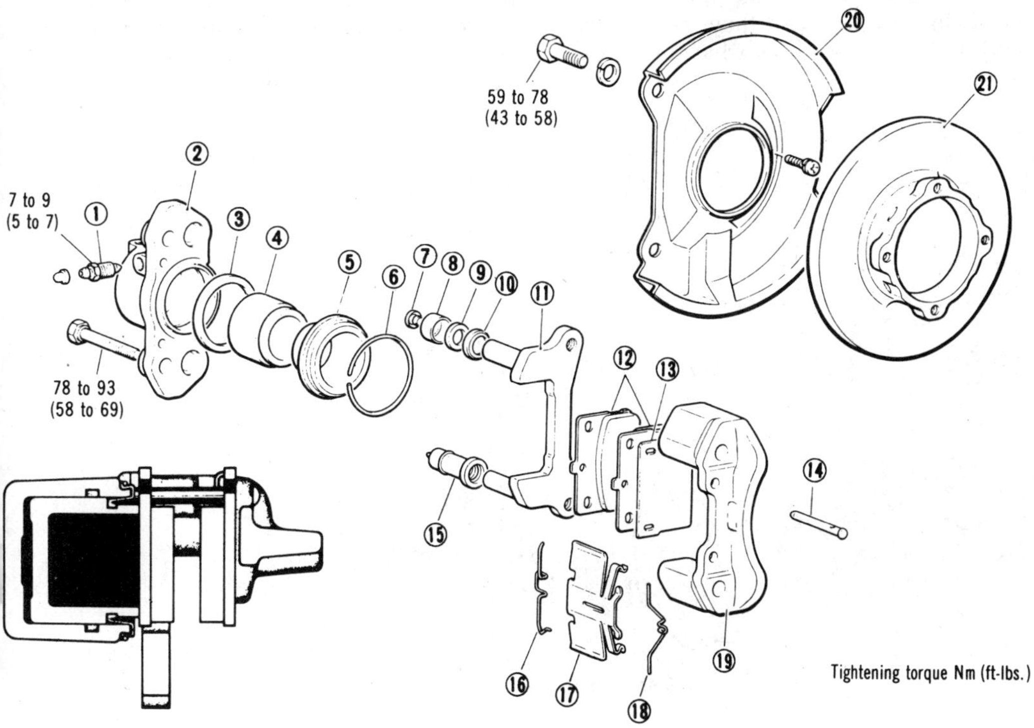

1. Bleeder screw
2. Caliper, inner
3. Piston seal
4. Piston
5. Dust seal
6. Retaining ring
7. Cap plug
8. Torque plate pin cap
9. Oil seal retainer
10. Wiper seal
11. Torque plate
12. Pad assembly
13. Anti-squeak shim
14. Pad retaining pin
15. Torque plate pin bushing
16. K-spring
17. Pad protector
18. M-clip
19. Caliper, outer
20. Dust cover
21. Brake disc

Exploded view of pin type caliper disc brake

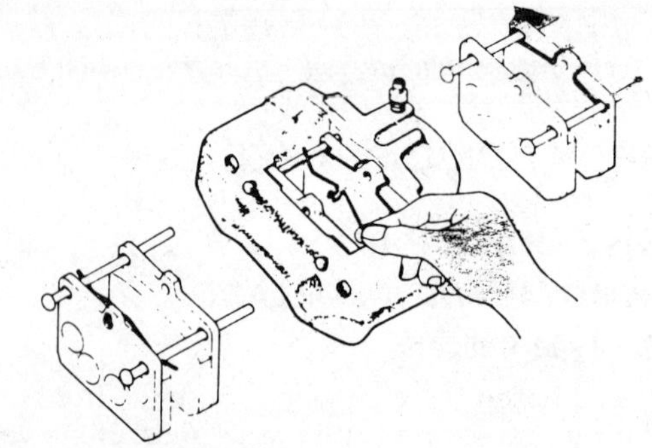

K and M clip positioning on late model pin type calipers

6. Grip the ears of each brake pad with a pliers and pull it from the caliper. Minimum serviceable thickness for the brake lining on the pad is 0.08 in. Always replace both sets at the same time.

7. Using a flat piece of hardwood and pry-bar, push the piston back into the cylinder.

8. Install the pads in the caliper.

9. Insert the retaining pins and install the K and M-clips. Be sure that they are installed properly in the positions from which they were removed.

Sliding Caliper Brake

The sliding caliper disc brake is used on station wagons and Sapporors.

1. Loosen the wheel lugs block the rear wheels raise the front of the car and support on jackstands. Remove the wheels.

2. Remove approximately half of the brake fluid from the master cylinder.

3. Remove the spring pin(s) and pull the stopper plug(s) from the upper end (and lower end) of the caliper.

4. Move the caliper back and forth to loosen, then remove the caliper from the support.

NOTE: *The hydraulic brake hose need not be removed from the caliper, but do not allow the caliper weight to hang from the hose. Secure the caliper with a piece of wire.*

5. Take the time to examine the pad holder with its related clips and springs. All parts must be returned to the same place when reinstalling the old pads or replacing with new pads.

6. Remove the anti-squeal clips then remove the brake pads from the mounting bracket. Do not remove the caliper support springs (two large wire "hair pins").

7. Under each brake pad there is a pad

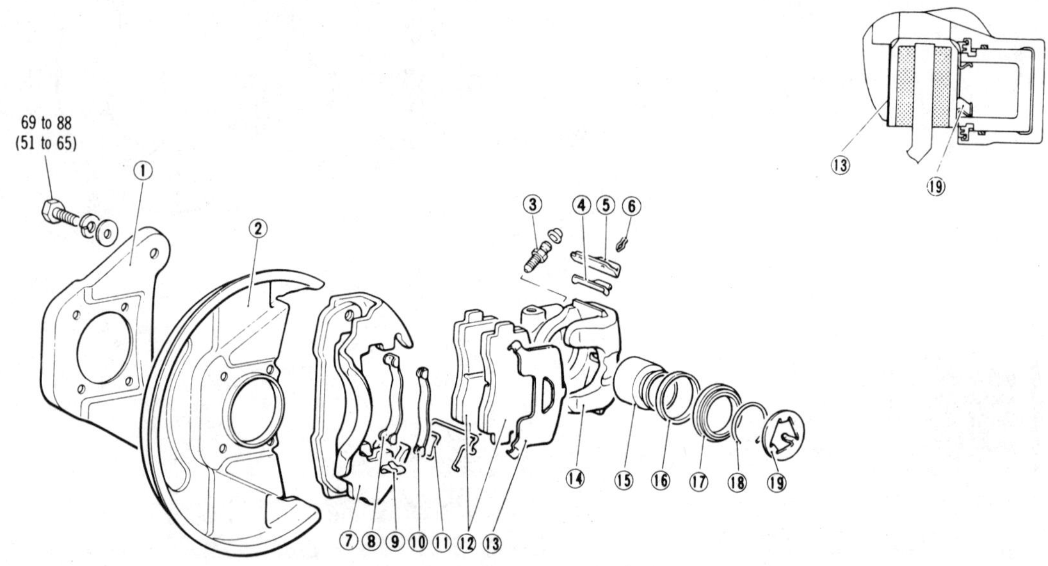

Tightening torque : Nm(ft-lbs.)

1. Disc brake adapter
2. Dust cover
3. Bleeder screw
4. Pad support plate
5. Stopper plug
6. Spigot pin
7. Caliper support
8. Pad clip (inner)
9. Pad clip B
10. Pad clip (outer)
11. Anti-rattle spring
12. Brake pad
13. Anti-squeak shim, outer
14. Caliper body
15. Piston
16. Piston seal
17. Dust boot
18. Boot ring
19. Anti-squeak shim, inner

Exploded view of sliding caliper type disc brake

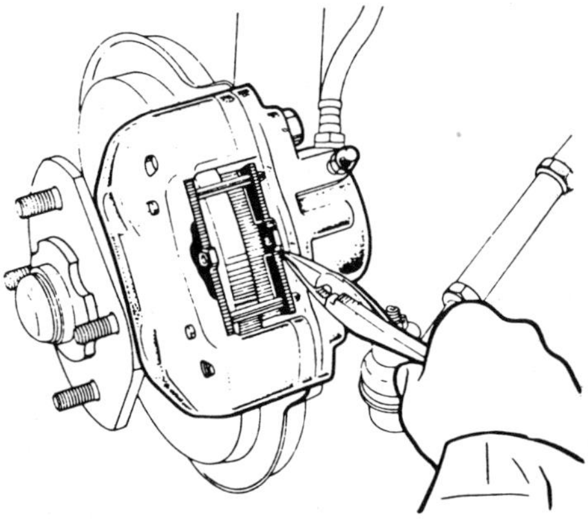

Pull the brake pads out of the caliper with a pair of pliers

support plate. These are not interchangeable and must be installed correctly.

8. Insert the new pads in the mounting bracket over the pad support plates and reinstall the anti-squeak clips.

9. Reseat the caliper piston fully into the caliper bore. Do this by opening the bleeder screw, and push the piston in with a hammer handle. If you meet too much resistance, the piston might be hanging up on a scored bore or have a gaulded piston wall, if so rebuild or replace the caliper.

10. Seat the caliper over the mounting bracket. Clean and apply No. 2 brake grease to the sliding surfaces, plug plates and stopper plug. Install the stopper plug(s) and the spring pin(s).

11. Refill the master cylinder and bleed the brake system.

12. Reinstall the tire and wheel, lower the car to the ground and road test.

Disc Brake Calipers

REMOVAL AND INSTALLATION

Pin Type Calipers

1. Remove the disc brake pads.
2. Remove the brake hose clip from the strut area, then disconnect the brake hose from the caliper.
3. Remove the caliper assembly by removing torque plate and adapter mounting bolts.

When installing the caliper assembly, observe the following instructions after referring to "Disc Brake Pads."

4. Tighten the caliper assembly (torque plate) to the adapter to 51–65 ft. lbs.
5. After tightening the brake hose to 9–12 ft. lbs., bleed the brake hydraulic system.

CAUTION: *Since the wheel cylinder uses a large piston, even the presence of a small amount of air, will have a great effect on the brake pedal stroke. Bleeding, therefore, should be performed carefully and thoroughly.*

OVERHAUL—PIN TYPE

1. Loosen and remove the caliper half retaining bolts.
2. Separate the two caliper halves.
3. Remove the dust seal, and then remove the piston by applying compressed air to the hose fitting.

CAUTION: *Be careful that the piston doesn't fly out and cause injury.*

4. Carefully remove the piston seal, so as not to damage the cylinder.
5. Clean all parts in denatured alcohol.
6. Inspect the piston and cylinder for scoring or corrosion. Replace any defective parts.
7. Reassemble the caliper using the new parts supplied in the rebuilding kit.
8. Apply brake fluid to the piston before assembly. Insert the piston seal into the piston carefully so that the seal isn't twisted.
9. Whenever the torque plate has been removed from the inner caliper half, it is necessary to clean the torque plate shaft and the shaft bore of the caliper and apply brake assembly grease to the rubber bushing, wiper seal inner surface, and torque plate shaft before assembly.
10. Tighten the caliper bridge bolts to 58–69 ft. lbs.

OVERHAUL—SLIDING CALIPER

1. Remove the caliper as previously outlined.
2. Remove the caliper piston dust boot. Cover the piston with a rag and piece of hardwood. While holding the wood, inject air pressure into the brake hose fitting and force the piston from the caliper.

CAUTION: *Do not apply the air pressure suddenly or the piston may shoot out, injuring your fingers.*

3. Remove the seal from the piston. Clean all parts with alcohol or brake fluid. Inspect the piston for scoring, replace if necessary.
4. Hone the caliper bore and clean with brake fluid or alcohol.
5. Install a new seal on the piston, lubricate the piston and caliper bore. Install the piston into the caliper bore and seat to the bottom of it's travel. Install the dust shield.
6. Be sure the brake pads are installed correctly on the support and reinstall the caliper.
7. Connect the brake line, refill the master cylinder and bleed the brake system.

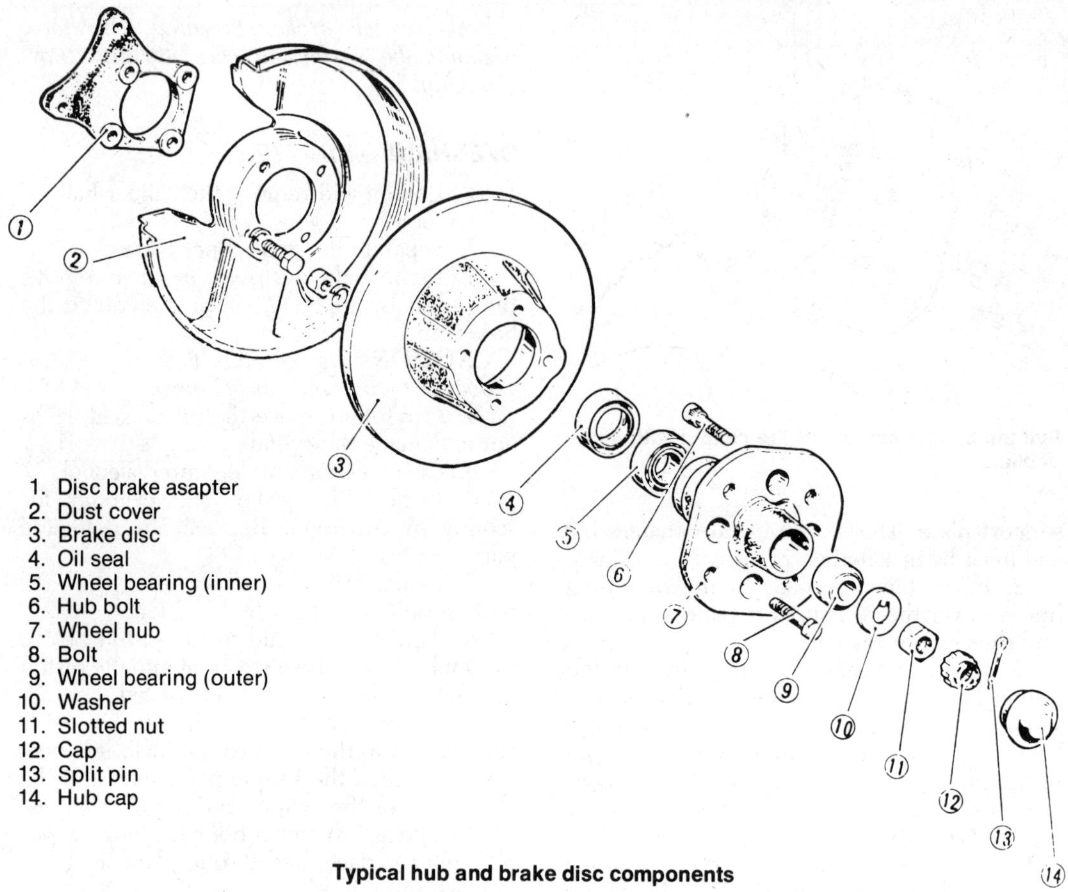

1. Disc brake asapter
2. Dust cover
3. Brake disc
4. Oil seal
5. Wheel bearing (inner)
6. Hub bolt
7. Wheel hub
8. Bolt
9. Wheel bearing (outer)
10. Washer
11. Slotted nut
12. Cap
13. Split pin
14. Hub cap

Typical hub and brake disc components

REMOVAL AND INSTALLATION—SLIDING CALIPER

The sliding caliper disc brake is used on station wagons and Sapporos.

1. Loosen the wheel lugs, block the rear wheels raise the front of the car and support on jackstands. Remove the wheels.
2. Remove approximately half of the brake fluid from the master cylinder.
3. Disconnect the brake line at the caliper. Remove the spring pin(s) and pull the stopper plug(s) from the end(s) of the caliper.
4. Move the caliper back and forth to loosen, then remove the caliper from the support.
5. To reinstall, seat the caliper over the mounting bracket (caliper piston seated in bore). Install the caliper stopper plug and the spring pin.
6. Connect the brake line, refill the master cylinder and bleed the brake system.
7. Reinstall the tire and wheel, lower the car to the ground and road test.

Wheel Bearings/Disc Rotor

REMOVAL AND INSTALLATION—EXCEPT FRONT WHEEL DRIVE MODELS

1. Remove the caliper (pin type) or the caliper and support (sliding type)

   NOTE: *On sliding type calipers, remove the caliper and support as a unit by unfastening the bolts holding it to the adapter ("backing plate"). Support the caliper with wire, do not allow the weight to be supported by the brake hose.*
2. Pry off the dust cap. Tap out and discard the cotter pin. Remove the locknut.
3. Being careful not to drop the outer bearing, pull off the brake disc and wheel hub.
4. Remove the grease inside the wheel hub.
5. Using a brass drift, carefully drive the outer bearing race out of the hub.
6. Remove the inner bearing seal and bearing.
7. Check the bearings for wear or damage and replace them if necessary.

8. Coat the inner surface of the hub with grease.

9. Grease the outer surface of the bearing race and drift it into place in the hub.

10. Pack the inner and outer wheel bearings with grease (see repacking).

NOTE: *If the brake disc has been removed and/or replaced, tighten the retaining bolts to 25–29 ft. lbs.*

11. Install the inner bearing in the hub. Being careful not to distort it, install the oil seal with its lip facing the bearing. Drive the seal on until its outer edge is even with the edge of the hub.

12. Install the hub/disc assembly on the spindle, being careful not to damage the oil seal.

13. Install the outer bearing, washer, and spindle nut. Adjust the bearing as follows.

ADJUSTMENT

1. Tighten the spindle nut to 15 ft. lbs. and then loosen it.

2. Tighten the nut to 4 ft. lbs.

3. Install the cap on the nut. Insert and bend the cotter pin. Do not back off the nut more than 15° for cotter pin hole-to-slot alignment.

4. Fill the hub cap with grease and install it.

FRONT WHEEL DRIVE MODELS

1. Remove the brake caliper assembly.

2. Remove drive axles (Refer to chapter 7 for procedure).

NOTE: *When removing the drive axle from the hub, do not lose the shims or mix them with the opposite side.*

3. Use a puller. Disconnect the ball joint and tie-rod end from the steering knuckle. Unfasten the two bolts that mount the knuckle to the strut and remove the knuckle, hub and rotor.

4. Remove the hub assembly from the knuckle. If you encounter resistance, mount the knuckle in a vise, support the rotor and hub, and drive out the hub with a soft hammer.

5. Remove the brake disc rotor from the hub.

6. Remove the oil seals and the bearings.

7. Clean and inspect the bearings and races (cups), replace if necessary.

8. If the inner and outer races (cups) need replacing, drive them from the knuckle using a brass drift.

9. Install new races (cups), if necessary, pack the bearings (see repacking) and reinstall in the reverse manner of removal.

CLEANING, INSPECTION, AND REPACKING

1. Clean the inner and outer bearings and the wheel hub with a suitable solvent. Remove all old grease.

2. Thoroughly dry and wipe clean all components.

3. Clean all old grease from the spindle or steering knuckle.

4. Carefully check the bearings for any sign of scoring or other damage. If the roller bearings or bearing cages are damaged, the bearing and the corresponding bearing cup in the rotor or knuckle must be replaced. The bearing cups must be driven out of the rotor or knuckle to be removed. The outer bearing cup is driven out of the front of the rotor or knuckle from the rear and vice versa for the inner bearing cup.

5. Whether you are reinstalling the old bearings or installing new ones, the bearings must be packed with wheel bearing grease. To do this, place a glob of grease in your left palm, then, holding one of the bearings in your right hand, drag the edge of the bearing heavily through the grease. This must be done to work as much grease as possible through the roller bearings and cage. Turn the bearing and continue to pull it through the grease until the grease is packed between the bearings and the cage all the way around the circumference of the bearing. Repeat this operation until all of the bearings are packed with grease.

6. Pack the inside of the hub with a moderate amount of grease, between the bearing cups. Do not overload the hub with grease.

7. Apply a small amount of grease to the spindle.

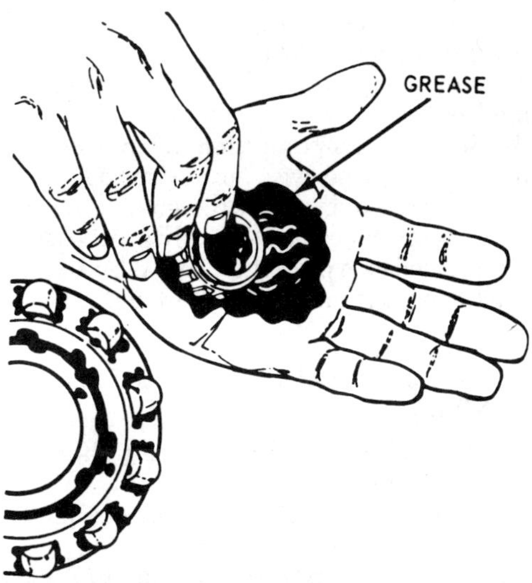

Packing the grease into the wheel bearing

8. Place the knuckle or rotor, face down, on a protected surface and install the inner bearing.

9. Coat the lip of a new grease seal with a small amount of grease and position it on the knuckle.

10. Place a block of wood on top of the grease seal and tap on the block with a hammer to install the seal. Turn the block of wood to different positions to seat it squarely in the hub.

REAR DISC BRAKES

Sliding Caliper Type

The caliper support is mounted on the rear axle housing. The support consists of an anti-rattle spring used to keep the caliper "floating" and a stopper plate installed between the caliper body and support on which the caliper body slides. The rear caliper has the parking brake mechanism, which contains an automatic adjuster to keep the parking brake stroke constant.

BRAKE PAD REPLACEMENT

1. Block the front wheels, jack up the rear of the car and support on jackstands. Remove the rear wheel and the caliper dust cover.
2. Disconnect the parking brake cable.
3. Remove the spring pin and stopper plug.
4. Move the caliper back and forth to loosen, then remove the caliper from the support,

   NOTE: *The brake hose need not be disconnected, however, do not suspend the weight of the caliper from the hose.*

5. Take time to examine the location of the various clips and springs. Remove the pads from the support. Do not mix up the inner and outer clips, they must be installed in the same location.
6. Seat the caliper piston by pushing in while turning clockwise (use a special tool). When fully seated, one of the grooves on the piston must be located vertically at 12 o'clock to accommodate a projection on the brake pad. Install new pads into the support and reinstall the caliper.

CALIPER OVERHAUL—REAR DISC BRAKES

1. Remove caliper from support after disconnecting the brake hose.
2. Remove the clevis pin connecting the parking brake lever.
3. Remove the ring that retains the lever cap and the cap. Remove the lever assembly.
4. Remove the automatic adjuster spindle by turning.
5. Remove the piston boot and the piston. The piston may be pushed from the caliper by inserting a soft round drift through the adjuster spindle hole. Remove the seal from the piston and clean all parts.
6. Hone the caliper bore.
7. Install a new piston and adjuster seal on the piston, lubricate and install into caliper. Seat the piston and install the dust shield (boot). Lubricate and install the adjuster spindle.

   NOTE: *When installing the adjuster spindle the spring washers must be in the proper direction, i.e. The first, nearest the piston, must curve toward the piston. The second, away from the piston, the third, toward and so on. It may be necessary to apply pressure while installing the lever cap and retaining ring.*

   Install the parking brake lever assembly by reversing the removal procedure.

8. Install the caliper, connect the brake hose and bleed the brakes.

REAR DISC ROTOR REPLACEMENT

1. Remove caliper, brake pads and support.
2. Remove retaining bolts.
3. Remove rotor. Installation is reverse of removal.

REAR BRAKE DRUMS

REMOVAL AND INSTALLATION

1. Remove the wheel cover and loosen the lug nuts.
2. Jack up the rear of the car and support with jackstands. Remove the lug nuts and the rear wheels.
3. On models except front wheel drive; remove the phillips head screws holding the drum to the axle flange and remove the brake drum. On front wheel drive models; remove the hub center cap, loosen and remove the axle nut, slide the drum from the spindle (take care not to drop the axle bearings).

   NOTE: *If you meet resistance while removing the drum, back off on the backing plate adjuster (lower).*

4. Inspect the drum for grooves, have machined or replace as necessary.
5. Installation is the reverse of removal. On front wheel drive models repack the wheel bearings (refer to the bearing section in this chapter).

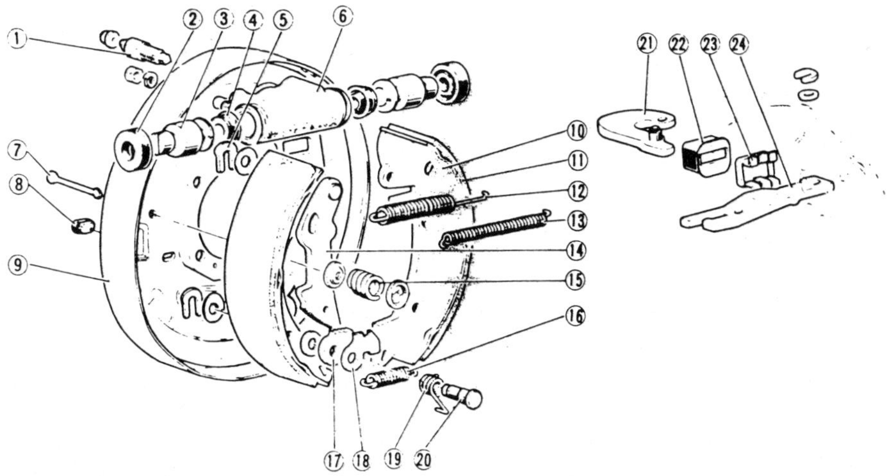

1. Bleeder screw
2. Wheel cylinder boot
3. Wheel cylinder piston
4. Wheel cylinder cup
5. Retainer
6. Wheel cylinder body
7. Shoe hold-down pin
8. Adjusting wheel cover
9. Backing plate
10. Brake shoe assembly
11. Brake lining
12. Shoe return spring (upper)
13. Automatic adjusting spring
14. Adjusting lever
15. Shoe hold-down spring
16. Shoe return spring (lower)
17. Adjusting latch
18. Stopper
19. Return spring
20. Pin
21. Parking brake extension lever
22. Parking brake extension lever cup
23. Parking brake extension lever retainer
24. Parking brake strut

Typical rear brake assembly except front wheel drive models

Brake Shoes—Except Front Wheel Drive Models

REMOVAL AND INSTALLATION

Through 1980

1. Remove wheel and brake drum.
2. Remove the brake shoe hold-down springs. Detach the strut-to-shoe spring and the upper return spring from the rear (trailing) brake shoe. Remove the brake shoes (both) as an assembly, with the lower return spring attached.
3. Pull the adjusting lever toward the center of the brake shoe while holding the adjusting latch down. Remove the adjuster from the shoe. Remove the strut and return springs.
4. The wheel cylinder can be removed at this time for service or replacement. The parking brake lever and strut may be removed, if necessary.
5. Clean the backing plate with a wire brush to remove dirt. Reinstall the parking brake lever and strut, if removed. Install the wheel cylinder, if removed.
6. Lubricate the contact surfaces on the backing plate, wheel cylinder piston ends, anchor plate shoe contact surfaces and the parking brake strut joints and contact surfaces.
7. Install the adjusting lever and latch spring assembly on the leading (front) shoe.

   NOTE: *The adjusting lever and latch spring are different for right and left.*
8. Install the brake shoes in position on the backing plate with the hold-down springs. Install the top shoe-to-shoe spring. Make sure the top web (Metal) is in the slot of the wheel cylinder piston and the bottom web is against the anchor block of the backing plate with the lower return spring installed.
9. Set the amount of engagement of the adjusting lever with the strut by pulling the adjusting lever fully toward the center of the brake. Install the strut to shoe spring.

   NOTE: *The strut to shoe springs differ in color from the side-to-side; left-white and right-neutral color.*
10. Return the adjusting lever until it touches the shoe rim.
11. Install the brake drums. The lining to drum clearance is automatically adjusted by applying the brakes several times, however, if the wheel cylinders have been serviced—the brake system will have to be bled before proper adjustment is possible.
12. Adjust the parking brake stroke. Road test the car.

From 1981

1. Raise the back of the car and support on jackstands.

2. Remove the wheel. Make sure the front wheels are blocked securely, release the parking brake and remove the brake drum.

NOTE: *The brake drum is retained by two small bolts.*

3. Disconnect the shoe-to-shoe spring and the strut-to-shoe spring. Disconnect the shoe return spring and remove the brake hold-down assemblies.

4. Disconnect the parking brake cable from the parking brake lever and remove the rear brake shoe.

5. Remove the front brake shoe. Transfer levers and adjusters to the new brake shoes using new U-shaped locks.

6. Assemble in reverse order of removal. Prior to assembly, apply #2 brake grease to the contact area of the strut and parking brake lever and strut and adjusting lever. After cleaning the backing plate apply grease to the brake shoe contact points.

CAUTION: *When cleaning brake parts, brake drums and backing plate assemblies do not use compressed air. Clean with a vacuum cleaner or solvent and a brush. Brake dust contains asbestos which when inhaled, may cause bodily harm.*

7. The lining to drum clearance is automatically adjusted by applying the brakes several times after the drums have been installed. If the wheel cylinders have been rebuilt the brake system must be bled before correct adjustment is possible.

Brake Shoes—Front Wheel Drive Models

REMOVAL AND INSTALLATION

1. Remove rear wheel and brake drum.

2. Remove the lower pressed metal spring clip, the shoe return spring (the large one piece spring between the two shoes), and the two shoe hold-down springs.

3. Remove the shoes and adjuster as an assembly. Disconnect the parking brake cable from the lever, remove the spring between the shoes and the lever from the rear (trailing shoe). Disconnect the adjuster retaining spring and remove the adjuster, turn the star wheel in to the adjuster body after cleaning and lubricating the threads.

4. The wheel cylinder may be removed for service or replacement, if necessary.

5. Clean the backing plate with a wire brush. Install the wheel cylinder if it was removed. Lubricate all contact points on the backing plate, anchor plate, wheel cylinder to shoe contact and parking brake strut joints and contacts. Installation of the brake shoes, from this point, is the reverse of removal after the lever has been transfered to the new rear (trailing) shoes.

6. Pre-adjustment of the brake shoe can be made by turning the adjuster star wheel out until the drum will just slide on over the brake shoes. Before installing the drum make sure the parking brake is not adjusted too tightly, if it is—loosen, or the adjustment of the rear brakes will not be correct.

7. If the wheel cylinders were serviced, bleed the brake system. The brake shoes are then adjusted by pumping the brake pedal and applying and releasing the parking brake. Adjust the parking brake stroke. Road test the car.

Wheel Cylinders

OVERHAUL

Since the piston travel in the wheel cylinder changes when new brake shoes are installed, it is possible for previously good wheel cylinders to start leaking after new brakes are installed. Therefore, to save yourself the expense of having to replace new brakes that become saturated with brake fluid and the aggravation of having to take everything apart again, it is strongly recommended that wheel cylinders be rebuilt every time new brake shoes are installed. This is especially true for cars with high mileage.

1. Remove the brake shoes.

2. Place a bucket or some old newspapers under the brake backing plate to catch the brake fluid that will run out of the wheel cylinder. Disconnect the brake line and remove the cylinder mounting bolts. Remove the cylinder from the backing plate.

3. Remove the boots from the ends of the wheel cylinders.

4. Push one piston toward the center of the cylinder to force the opposite piston and cup out the other end of the cylinder. Reach in the open end of the cylinder and push the spring, cup, and piston out of the cylinder.

5. Remove the bleeder screw from the rear of the cylinder.

6. Inspect the inside of the wheel cylinder. If it is scored in any way, the cylinder must be honed with a wheel cylinder hone or fine emery paper, and finished with crocus cloth if emery paper is used. If the inside of the cylinder is excessively worn, the cylinder will have to be replaced, as only 0.003 in. of material can be removed from the cylinder walls. Whenever honing or cleaning wheel

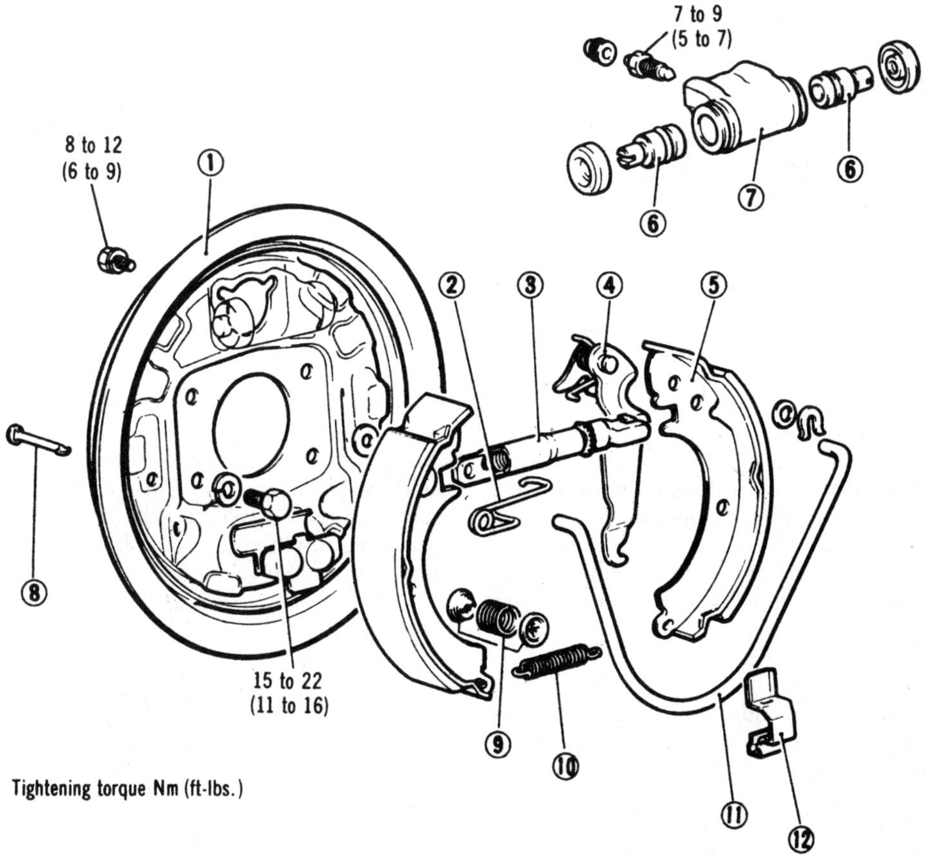

1. Backing plate
2. Spring
3. Adjuster
4. Parking lever
5. Shoe and lining assembly
6. Piston
7. Wheel cylinder body
8. Shoe hold spring pin
9. Shoe hold-down spring
10. Shoe to shoe spring
11. Shoe return spring
12. Clip spring

Exploded view of the rear brake system used on front wheel drive models

Brake Specifications—Rear Wheel Drive Cars

All measurements given are in. unless noted

Year	Lug Nut Torque ft. lbs	Master Cylinder Bore	Brake Disc Thickness Max.	Brake Disc Thickness Min.	Runout	Brake Drum Diameter	Brake Drum Maximum	Brake Drum Maximum Wear	Lining Thickness Front Max.	Lining Thickness Front Min.③	Lining Thickness Rear Max.	Lining Thickness Rear Min.③
1977	51–58	13/16	0.510	0.450	0.006	9.0	9.060	9.079	0.38	0.08	0.17	0.04
1978–80	51–58④	13/16	0.510	0.450	0.006	9.0	9.060	9.079	0.38①	0.08②	0.157	0.04
1981–83	51–58④	7/8	0.490	0.430	0.006	9.0	9.060	9.079	0.38①	0.08	0.157	0.04

① Station wagon 0.41 in.
② Station wagon 0.04 in.
③ Due to variations in state inspection regulations, the minimum allowable lining thickness may be different from that recommended by the manufacturer.
④ Aluminum wheels: 58–72

Brake Specifications—Front Wheel Drive Cars

All measurements are in. unless noted

Year	Lug Nut Torque ft. lbs.	Master Cylinder Bore	Brake Disc Thickness Max.	Brake Disc Thickness Min.	Brake Disc Runout	Brake Drum Diameter	Brake Drum Maximum	Brake Drum Maximum Wear	Lining Thickness Front Max.	Lining Thickness Front Min.②	Lining Thickness Rear Max.	Lining Thickness Rear Min.②
1979	51–58①	13/16	0.510	0.450	0.006	7.0	7.060	7.079	0.382	0.08	0.201	0.04
1980–82	51–58①	13/16	0.510	0.450	0.006	7.1	7.160	7.200	0.382	0.08	0.201	0.04

① Aluminum wheels: 58–72

② Due to variations in state inspection regulations, the minimum allowable lining thickness may be different from that recommended by the manufacturer.

cylinders, keep a small amount of brake fluid in the cylinder to serve as a lubricant.

7. Clean any foreign matter from the pistons. The sides of the pistons must be smooth for the wheel cylinders to operate properly.

8. Clean the cylinder bore with alcohol and a lint-free rag. Pull the rag through the bore several times to remove all foreign matter and dry the cylinder.

9. Install the bleeder screw and the return spring in the cylinder.

10. Coat new cylinder cups with new brake fluid and install them in the cylinder. Make sure they are square in the bore or they will leak.

11. Install the pistons in the cylinder after coating them with new brake fluid.

12. Coat the insides of the boots with new brake fluid and install them on the cylinder. Reinstall the wheel cylinder. Install and bleed the brakes.

PARKING BRAKE

Cable

ADJUSTMENT

Release the parking brake lever. Loosen the lock (rear) nuts on each side of the lever or on the frame bracket. Tighten the adjusting (front) nuts to increase tension, or loosen to reduce. Any adjustment must be made evenly on both sides. Be sure, after adjustment, that when the parking brake is released the rear wheels will turn freely with no brake shoe drag. Handbrake travel should be 6 to 8 notches.

NOTE: *Lever stroke of less than 5 notches, will cause the adjuster to malfunction i.e., not adjust.*

Handbrake Warning Switch

On most models, a dash mounted warning light indicates when the hand brake is applied. The

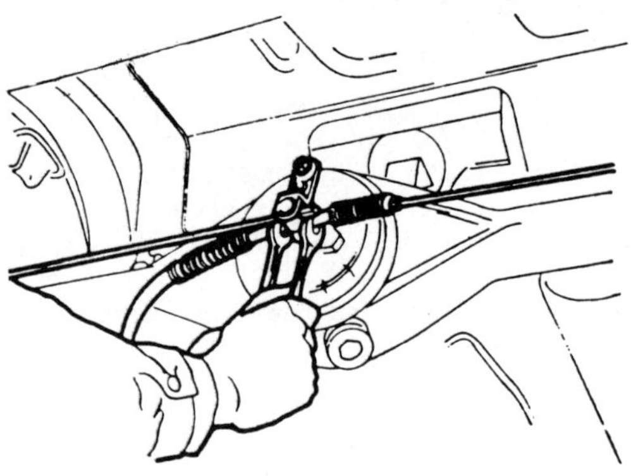

Front wheel drive models, parking brake cable

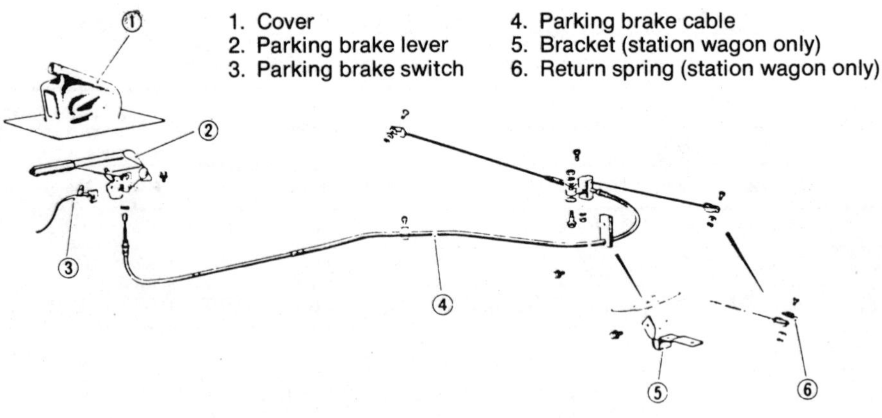

Typical parking brake cable assembly

light should go on when the parking brake lever is pulled one or more notches, and go out when the lever is fully released. Adjustment is made by loosening the mounting bolt and changing the mounted position of the switch.

REMOVAL AND INSTALLATION

Except Front Wheel Drive Models

1. Block the front wheels, jack up the rear of the car and support with jackstands.
2. Release the parking brake. Pull off the clevis pins from both sides of the rear brake. Disconnect the cable from the extension lever.
3. On drum brake (through 1980) loosen the parking brake lever mounting bolts and disconnect the front end of the rear cable from the equalizer. On 1981 and later models, remove brake drums, disconnect cable from lever, remove retaining clip and remove cable through the brake backing plate. Remove the front cable after disconnecting the parking brake lever. On rear disc brake models: Remove the rubber hanger from the center of the axle housing. Remove the parking brake lever and clevis pin linking the lever and cable. Remove the clips under the floor and remove the cable.
4. Installation is the reverse of the removal. When installing, make sure that the cable clips do not interfere with a rotating part. Adjust the extension lever to stop first. Then adjust the left cable, then the right on the Challenger/Sapporo and Wagons.

FRONT WHEEL DRIVE MODELS

1. Block front wheels, raise rear of car and support on jackstands.
2. Disconnect the brake cable at the parking brake lever (brakes released). Remove the cable clamps inside the driver's compartment (two bolts). Disconnect the clamps on the rear suspension arm.
3. Remove the rear brake drums and the brake shoe assemblies. Disconnect the parking brake cable from the lever on the trailing (rear) brake shoe. Remove the brake cables.
4. Installation is the reverse of removal.

Troubleshooting

10

This section is designed to aid in the quick, accurate diagnosis of automotive problems. While automotive repairs can be made by many people, accurate troubleshooting is a rare skill for the amateur and professional alike.

In its simplest state, troubleshooting is an exercise in logic. It is essential to realize that an automobile is really composed of a series of systems. Some of these systems are interrelated; others are not. Automobiles operate within a framework of logical rules and physical laws, and the key to troubleshooting is a good understanding of all the automotive systems.

This section breaks the car or truck down into its component systems, allowing the problem to be isolated. The charts and diagnostic road maps list the most common problems and the most probable causes of trouble. Obviously it would be impossible to list every possible problem that could happen along with every possible cause, but it will locate MOST problems and eliminate a lot of unnecessary guesswork. The systematic format will locate problems within a given system, but, because many automotive systems are interrelated, the solution to your particular problem may be found in a number of systems on the car or truck.

USING THE TROUBLESHOOTING CHARTS

This book contains all of the specific information that the average do-it-yourself mechanic needs to repair and maintain his or her car or truck. The troubleshooting charts are designed to be used in conjunction with the specific procedures and information in the text. For instance, troubleshooting a point-type ignition system is fairly standard for all models, but you may be directed to the text to find procedures for troubleshooting an individual type of electronic ignition. You will also have to refer to the specification charts throughout the book for specifications applicable to your car or truck.

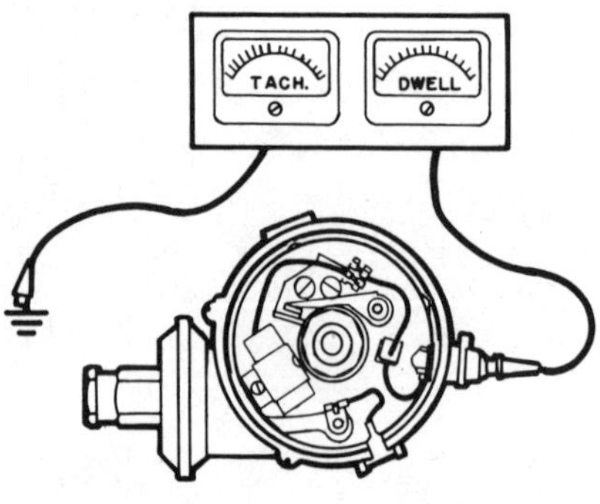

Tach-dwell hooked-up to distributor

TOOLS AND EQUIPMENT

The tools illustrated in Chapter 1 (plus two more diagnostic pieces) will be adequate to troubleshoot most problems. The two other tools needed are a voltmeter and an ohmmeter. These can be purchased separately or in combination, known as a VOM meter.

In the event that other tools are required, they will be noted in the procedures.

Troubleshooting Engine Problems

See Chapters 2, 3, 4 for more information and service procedures.

Index to Systems

System	To Test	Group
Battery	Engine need not be running	1
Starting system	Engine need not be running	2
Primary electrical system	Engine need not be running	3
Secondary electrical system	Engine need not be running	4
Fuel system	Engine need not be running	5
Engine compression	Engine need not be running	6
Engine vacuum	Engine must be running	7
Secondary electrical system	Engine must be running	8
Valve train	Engine must be running	9
Exhaust system	Engine must be running	10
Cooling system	Engine must be running	11
Engine lubrication	Engine must be running	12

Index to Problems

Problem: Symptom	Begin at Specific Diagnosis, Number ___
Engine Won't Start:	
Starter doesn't turn	1.1, 2.1
Starter turns, engine doesn't	2.1
Starter turns engine very slowly	1.1, 2.4
Starter turns engine normally	3.1, 4.1
Starter turns engine very quickly	6.1
Engine fires intermittently	4.1
Engine fires consistently	5.1, 6.1
Engine Runs Poorly:	
Hard starting	3.1, 4.1, 5.1, 8.1
Rough idle	4.1, 5.1, 8.1
Stalling	3.1, 4.1, 5.1, 8.1
Engine dies at high speeds	4.1, 5.1
Hesitation (on acceleration from standing stop)	5.1, 8.1
Poor pickup	4.1, 5.1, 8.1
Lack of power	3.1, 4.1, 5.1, 8.1
Backfire through the carburetor	4.1, 8.1, 9.1
Backfire through the exhaust	4.1, 8.1, 9.1
Blue exhaust gases	6.1, 7.1
Black exhaust gases	5.1
Running on (after the ignition is shut off)	3.1, 8.1
Susceptible to moisture	4.1
Engine misfires under load	4.1, 7.1, 8.4, 9.1
Engine misfires at speed	4.1, 8.4
Engine misfires at idle	3.1, 4.1, 5.1, 7.1, 8.4

Sample Section

Test and Procedure	Results and Indications	Proceed to
4.1—Check for spark: Hold each spark plug wire approximately ¼" from ground with gloves or a heavy, dry rag. Crank the engine and observe the spark.	→ If no spark is evident:	**4.2**
	→ If spark is good in some cases:	**4.3**
	→ If spark is good in all cases:	**4.6**

Specific Diagnosis

This section is arranged so that following each test, instructions are given to proceed to another, until a problem is diagnosed.

Section 1—Battery

Test and Procedure	Results and Indications	Proceed to
1.1—Inspect the battery visually for case condition (corrosion, cracks) and water level.	If case is cracked, replace battery:	**1.4**
	If the case is intact, remove corrosion with a solution of baking soda and water (**CAUTION:** ***do not get the solution into the battery***), and fill with water:	**1.2**

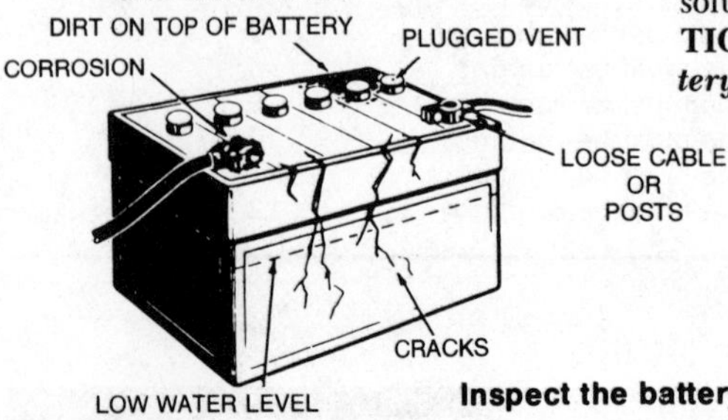

Inspect the battery case

Test and Procedure	Results and Indications	Proceed to
1.2—Check the battery cable connections: Insert a screwdriver between the battery post and the cable clamp. Turn the headlights on high beam, and observe them as the screwdriver is gently twisted to ensure good metal to metal contact.	If the lights brighten, remove and clean the clamp and post; coat the post with petroleum jelly, install and tighten the clamp:	**1.4**
	If no improvement is noted:	**1.3**

TESTING BATTERY CABLE CONNECTIONS USING A SCREWDRIVER

Test and Procedure	Results and Indications	Proceed to
1.3—Test the state of charge of the battery using an individual cell tester or hydrometer.	If indicated, charge the battery. **NOTE:** ***If no obvious reason exists for the low state of charge (i.e., battery age, prolonged storage), proceed to:***	**1.4**

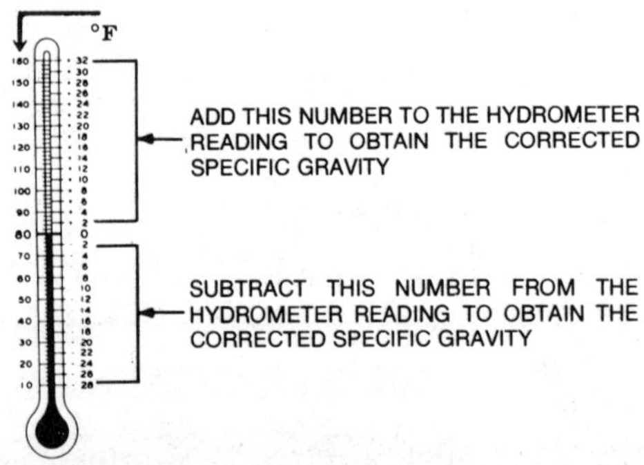

Specific Gravity (@ 80° F.)

Minimum	*Battery Charge*
1.260	100% Charged
1.230	75% Charged
1.200	50% Charged
1.170	25% Charged
1.140	Very Little Power Left
1.110	Completely Discharged

The effects of temperature on battery specific gravity (left) and amount of battery charge in relation to specific gravity (right)

Test and Procedure	Results and Indications	Proceed to
1.4—Visually inspect battery cables for cracking, bad connection to ground, or bad connection to starter.	If necessary, tighten connections or replace the cables:	**2.1**

Section 2—Starting System

See Chapter 3 for service procedures

Test and Procedure	Results and Indications	Proceed to
Note: Tests in Group 2 are performed with coil high tension lead disconnected to prevent accidental starting.		
2.1—Test the starter motor and solenoid: Connect a jumper from the battery post of the solenoid (or relay) to the starter post of the solenoid (or relay).	If starter turns the engine normally:	**2.2**
	If the starter buzzes, or turns the engine very slowly:	**2.4**
	If no response, replace the solenoid (or relay).	**3.1**
	If the starter turns, but the engine doesn't, ensure that the flywheel ring gear is intact. If the gear is undamaged, replace the starter drive.	**3.1**
2.2—Determine whether ignition override switches are functioning properly (clutch start switch, neutral safety switch), by connecting a jumper across the switch(es), and turning the ignition switch to "start".	If starter operates, adjust or replace switch:	**3.1**
	If the starter doesn't operate:	**2.3**
2.3—Check the ignition switch "start" position: Connect a 12V test lamp or voltmeter between the starter post of the solenoid (or relay) and ground. Turn the ignition switch to the "start" position, and jiggle the key.	If the lamp doesn't light or the meter needle doesn't move when the switch is turned, check the ignition switch for loose connections, cracked insulation, or broken wires. Repair or replace as necessary:	**3.1**
	If the lamp flickers or needle moves when the key is jiggled, replace the ignition switch.	**3.3**

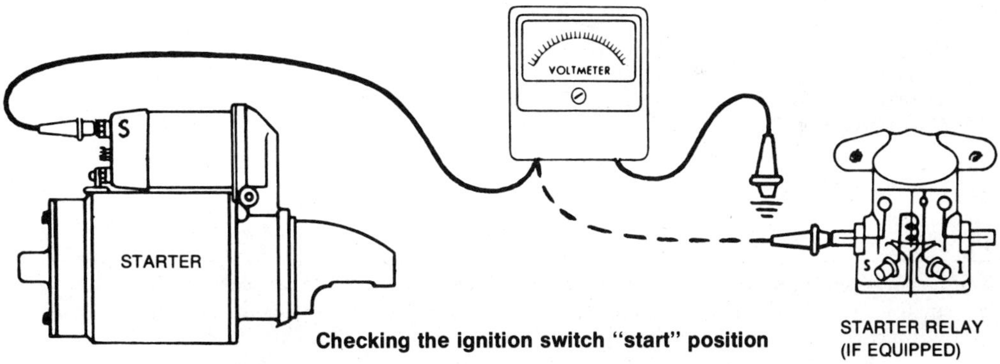

Checking the ignition switch "start" position

Test and Procedure	Results and Indications	Proceed to
2.4—Remove and bench test the starter, according to specifications in the engine electrical section.	If the starter does not meet specifications, repair or replace as needed:	**3.1**
	If the starter is operating properly:	**2.5**
2.5—Determine whether the engine can turn freely: Remove the spark plugs, and check for water in the cylinders. Check for water on the dipstick, or oil in the radiator. Attempt to turn the engine using an 18″ flex drive and socket on the crankshaft pulley nut or bolt.	If the engine will turn freely only with the spark plugs out, and hydrostatic lock (water in the cylinders) is ruled out, check valve timing:	**9.2**
	If engine will not turn freely, and it is known that the clutch and transmission are free, the engine must be disassembled for further evaluation:	**Chapter 3**

Section 3—Primary Electrical System

Test and Procedure	Results and Indications	Proceed to
3.1—Check the ignition switch "on" position: Connect a jumper wire between the distributor side of the coil and ground, and a 12V test lamp between the switch side of the coil and ground. Remove the high tension lead from the coil. Turn the ignition switch on and jiggle the key.	If the lamp lights:	**3.2**
	If the lamp flickers when the key is jiggled, replace the ignition switch:	**3.3**
	If the lamp doesn't light, check for loose or open connections. If none are found, remove the ignition switch and check for continuity. If the switch is faulty, replace it:	**3.3**

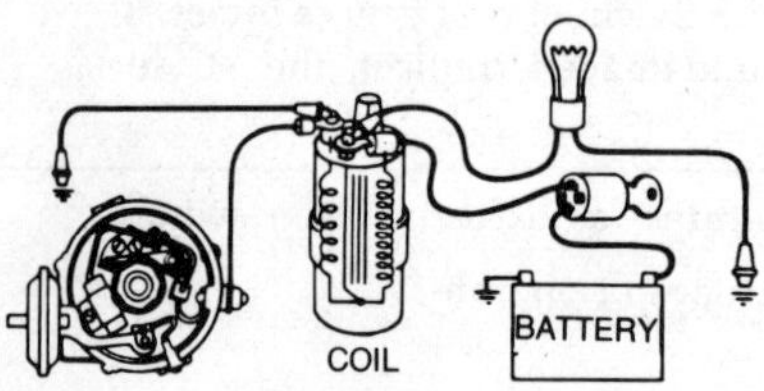

Checking the ignition switch "on" position

Test and Procedure	Results and Indications	Proceed to
3.2—Check the ballast resistor or resistance wire for an open circuit, using an ohmmeter. See Chapter 3 for specific tests.	Replace the resistor or resistance wire if the resistance is zero. **NOTE:** ***Some ignition systems have no ballast resistor.***	**3.3**

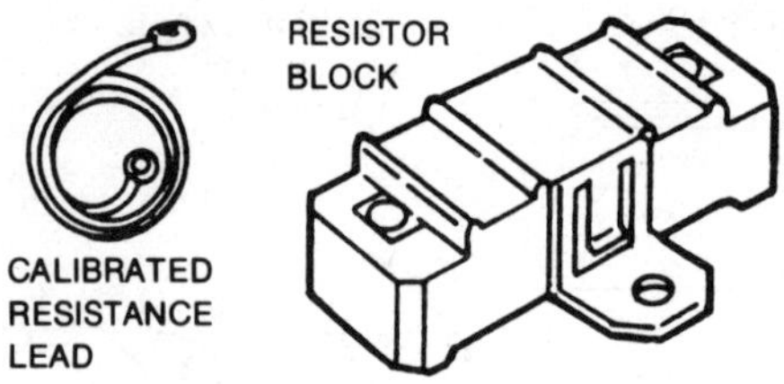

Two types of resistors

Test and Procedure	Results and Indications	Proceed to
3.3—On point-type ignition systems, visually inspect the breaker points for burning, pitting or excessive wear. Gray coloring of the point contact surfaces is normal. Rotate the crankshaft until the contact heel rests on a high point of the distributor cam and adjust the point gap to specifications. On electronic ignition models, remove the distributor cap and visually inspect the armature. Ensure that the armature pin is in place, and that the armature is on tight and rotates when the engine is cranked. Make sure there are no cracks, chips or rounded edges on the armature.	If the breaker points are intact, clean the contact surfaces with fine emery cloth, and adjust the point gap to specifications. If the points are worn, replace them. On electronic systems, replace any parts which appear defective. If condition persists:	**3.4**

Test and Procedure	Results and Indications	Proceed to
3.4—On point-type ignition systems, connect a dwell-meter between the distributor primary lead and ground. Crank the engine and observe the point dwell angle. On electronic ignition systems, conduct a stator (magnetic pickup assembly) test. See Chapter 3.	On point-type systems, adjust the dwell angle if necessary. **NOTE:** ***Increasing the point gap decreases the dwell angle and vice-versa.***	**3.6**
	If the dwell meter shows little or no reading;	**3.5**
	On electronic ignition systems, if the stator is bad, replace the stator. If the stator is good, proceed to the other tests in Chapter 3.	

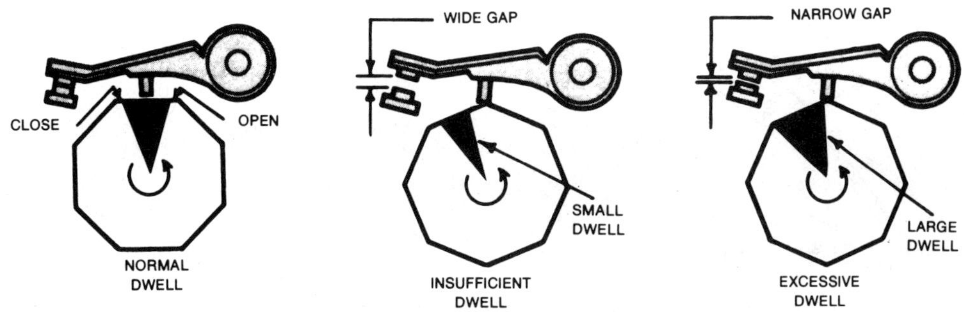

Dwell is a function of point gap

Test and Procedure	Results and Indications	Proceed to
3.5—On the point-type ignition systems, check the condenser for short: connect an ohmeter across the condenser body and the pigtail lead.	If any reading other than infinite is noted, replace the condenser	**3.6**

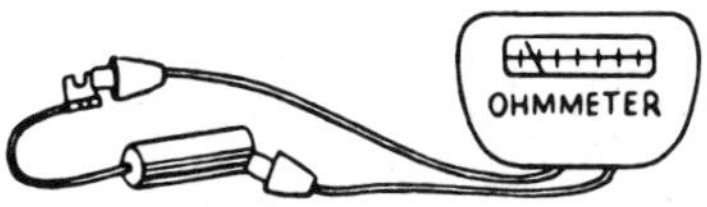

Checking the condenser for short

Test and Procedure	Results and Indications	Proceed to
3.6—Test the coil primary resistance: On point-type ignition systems, connect an ohmmeter across the coil primary terminals, and read the resistance on the low scale. Note whether an external ballast resistor or resistance wire is used. On electronic ignition systems, test the coil primary resistance as in Chapter 3.	Point-type ignition coils utilizing ballast resistors or resistance wires should have approximately 1.0 ohms resistance. Coils with internal resistors should have approximately 4.0 ohms resistance. If values far from the above are noted, replace the coil.	**4.1**

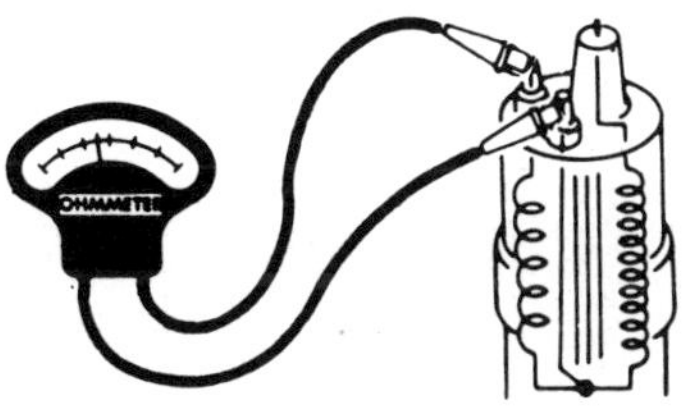

Check the coil primary resistance

Section 4—Secondary Electrical System

See Chapters 2–3 for service procedures

Test and Procedure	Results and Indications	Proceed to
4.1—Check for spark: Hold each spark plug wire approximately ¼″ from ground with gloves or a heavy, dry rag. Crank the engine, and observe the spark.	If no spark is evident:	**4.2**
	If spark is good in some cylinders:	**4.3**
	If spark is good in all cylinders:	**4.6**
4.2—Check for spark at the coil high tension lead: Remove the coil high tension lead from the distributor and position it approximately ¼″ from ground. Crank the engine and observe spark. **CAUTION:** ***This test should not be performed on engines equipped with electronic ignition.***	If the spark is good and consistent:	**4.3**
	If the spark is good but intermittent, test the primary electrical system starting at 3.3:	**3.3**
	If the spark is weak or non-existent, replace the coil high tension lead, clean and tighten all connections and retest. If no improvement is noted:	**4.4**
4.3—Visually inspect the distributor cap and rotor for burned or corroded contacts, cracks, carbon tracks, or moisture. Also check the fit of the rotor on the distributor shaft (where applicable).	If moisture is present, dry thoroughly, and retest per 4.1:	**4.1**
	If burned or excessively corroded contacts, cracks, or carbon tracks are noted, replace the defective part(s) and retest per 4.1:	**4.1**
	If the rotor and cap appear intact, or are only slightly corroded, clean the contacts thoroughly (including the cap towers and spark plug wire ends) and retest per 4.1: If the spark is good in all cases:	**4.6**
	If the spark is poor in all cases:	**4.5**

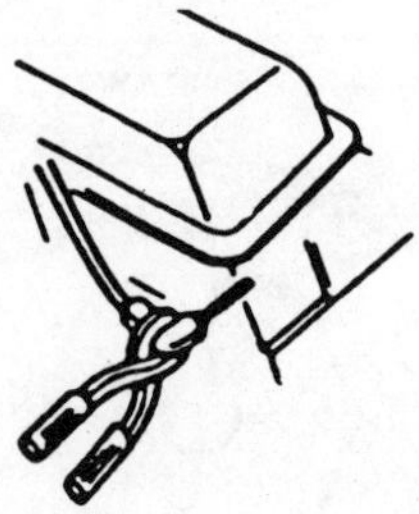

Check for spark at the plugs

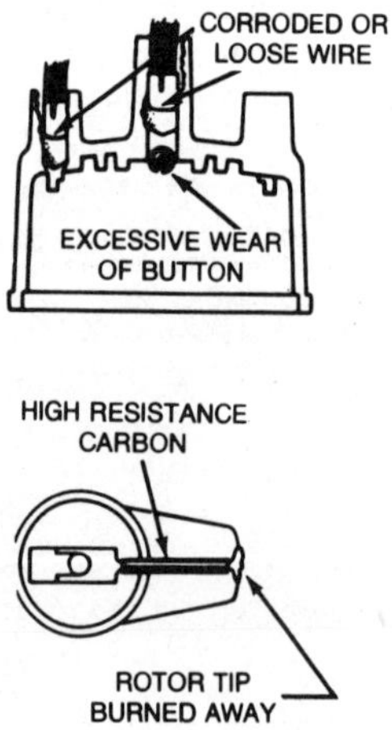

Inspect the distributor cap and rotor

Test and Procedure	Results and Indications	Proceed to
4.4—Check the coil secondary resistance: On point-type systems connect an ohmmeter across the distributor side of the coil and the coil tower. Read the resistance on the high scale of the ohmmeter. On electronic ignition systems, see Chapter 3 for specific tests.	The resistance of a satisfactory coil should be between 4,000 and 10,000 ohms. If resistance is considerably higher (i.e., 40,000 ohms) replace the coil and retest per 4.1. **NOTE:** ***This does not apply to high performance coils.***	

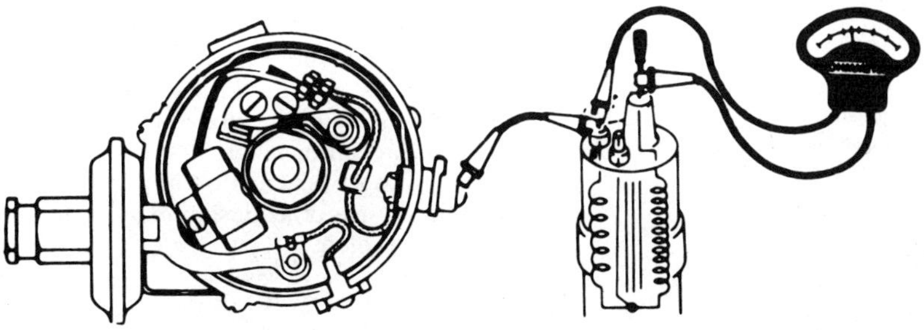

Testing the coil secondary resistance

Test and Procedure	Results and Indications	Proceed to
4.5—Visually inspect the spark plug wires for cracking or brittleness. Ensure that no two wires are positioned so as to cause induction firing (adjacent and parallel). Remove each wire, one by one, and check resistance with an ohmmeter.	Replace any cracked or brittle wires. If any of the wires are defective, replace the entire set. Replace any wires with excessive resistance (over 8000 Ω per foot for suppression wire), and separate any wires that might cause induction firing.	**4.6**

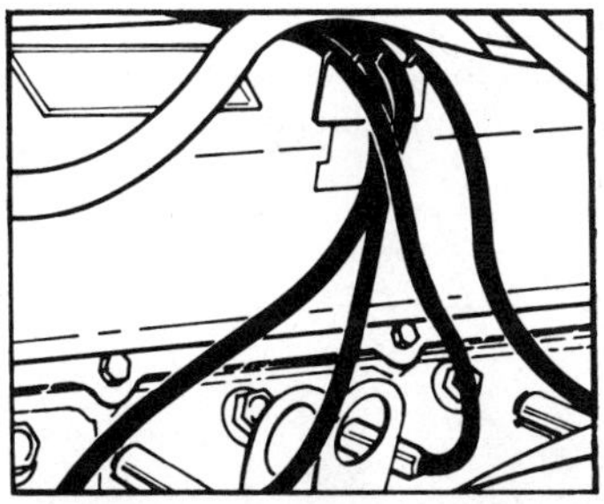

Misfiring can be the result of spark plug leads to adjacent, consecutively firing cylinders running parallel and too close together

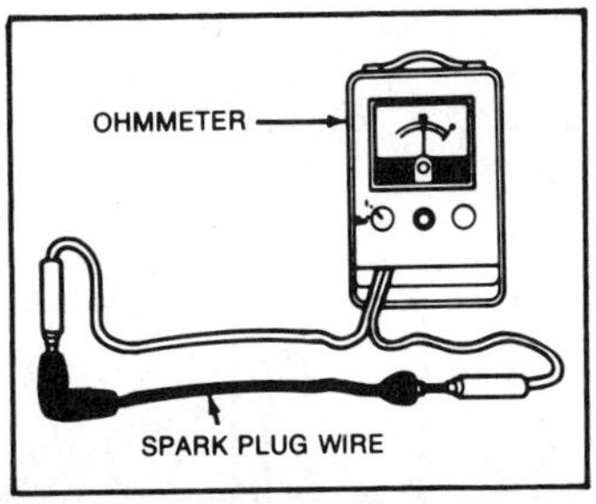

On point-type ignition systems, check the spark plug wires as shown. On electronic ignitions, do not remove the wire from the distributor cap terminal; instead, test through the cap

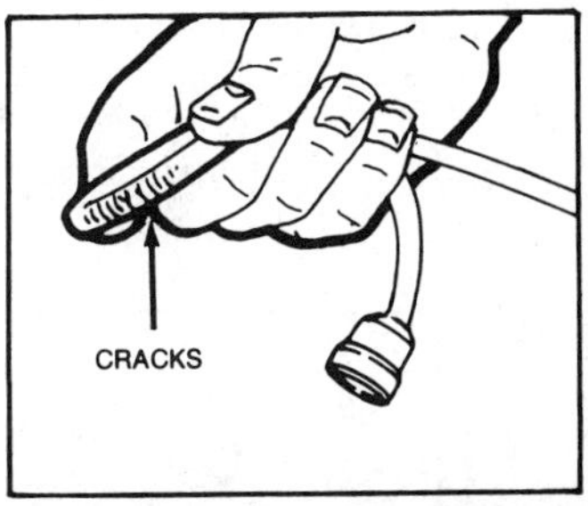

Spark plug wires can be checked visually by bending them in a loop over your finger. This will reveal any cracks, burned or broken insulation. Any wire with cracked insulation should be replaced

Test and Procedure	Results and Indications	Proceed to
4.6—Remove the spark plugs, noting the cylinders from which they were removed, and evaluate according to the color photos in the middle of this book.	See following.	**See following.**

Test and Procedure	Results and Indications	Proceed to
4.7—Examine the location of all the plugs.	The following diagrams illustrate some of the conditions that the location of plugs will reveal.	**4.8**

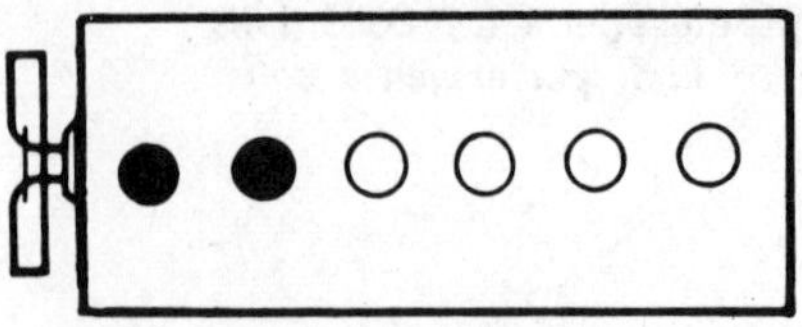

Two adjacent plugs are fouled in a 6-cylinder engine, 4-cylinder engine or either bank of a V-8. This is probably due to a blown head gasket between the two cylinders

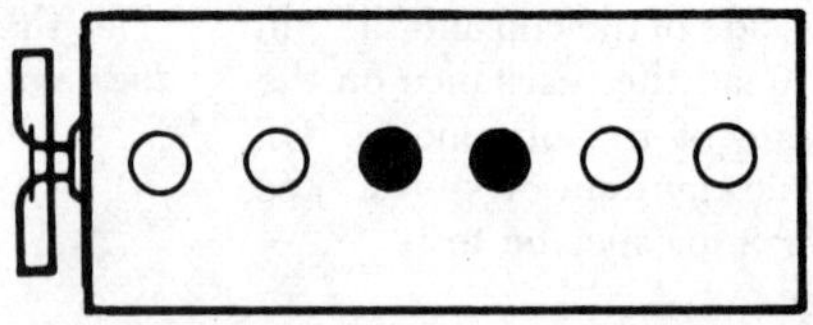

The two center plugs in a 6-cylinder engine are fouled. Raw fuel may be "boiled" out of the carburetor into the intake manifold after the engine is shut-off. Stop-start driving can also foul the center plugs, due to overly rich mixture. Proper float level, a new float needle and seat or use of an insulating spacer may help this problem

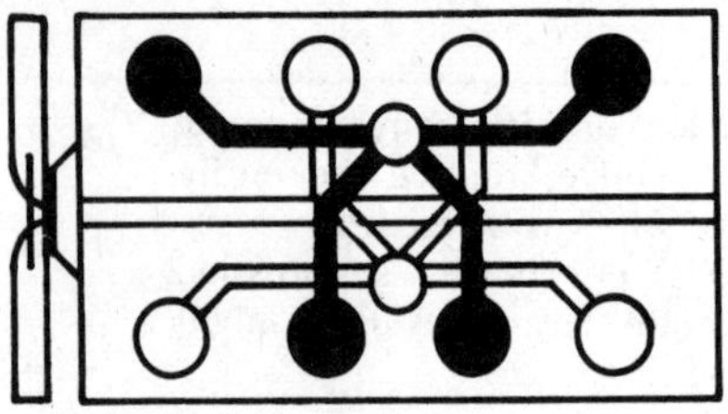

An unbalanced carburetor is indicated. Following the fuel flow on this particular design shows that the cylinders fed by the right-hand barrel are fouled from overly rich mixture, while the cylinders fed by the left-hand barrel are normal

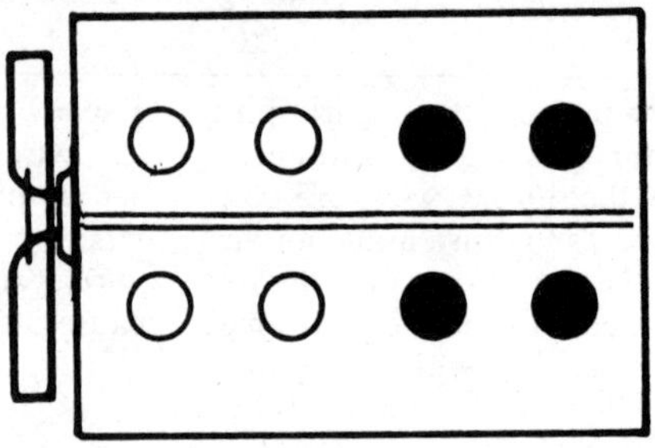

If the four rear plugs are overheated, a cooling system problem is suggested. A thorough cleaning of the cooling system may restore coolant circulation and cure the problem

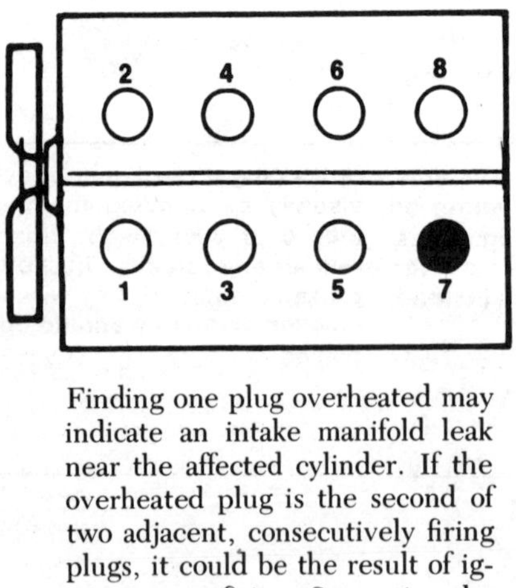

Finding one plug overheated may indicate an intake manifold leak near the affected cylinder. If the overheated plug is the second of two adjacent, consecutively firing plugs, it could be the result of ignition cross-firing. Separating the leads to these two plugs will eliminate cross-fire

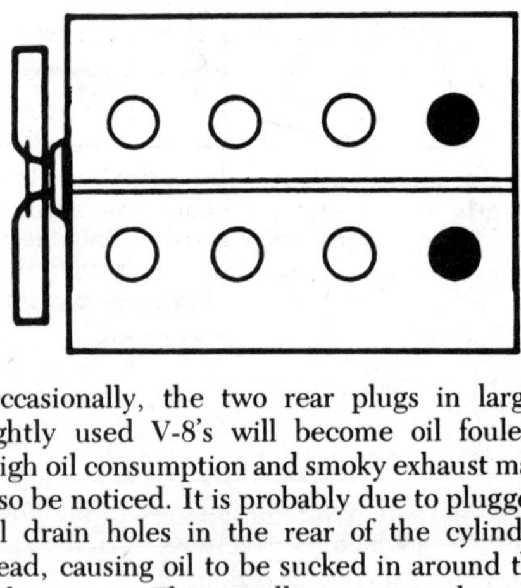

Occasionally, the two rear plugs in large, lightly used V-8's will become oil fouled. High oil consumption and smoky exhaust may also be noticed. It is probably due to plugged oil drain holes in the rear of the cylinder head, causing oil to be sucked in around the valve stems. This usually occurs in the rear cylinders first, because the engine slants that way

Test and Procedure	*Results and Indications*	*Proceed to*
4.8—Determine the static ignition timing. Using the crankshaft pulley timing marks as a guide, locate top dead center on the compression stroke of the number one cylinder.	The rotor should be pointing toward the No. 1 tower in the distributor cap, and, on electronic ignitions, the armature spoke for that cylinder should be lined up with the stator.	**4.8**
4.9—Check coil polarity: Connect a voltmeter negative lead to the coil high tension lead, and the positive lead to ground (**NOTE:** ***Reverse the hook-up for positive ground systems***). Crank the engine momentarily.	If the voltmeter reads up-scale, the polarity is correct:	**5.1**
	If the voltmeter reads down-scale, reverse the coil polarity (switch the primary leads):	**5.1**

Checking coil polarity

Section 5—Fuel System

See Chapter 4 for service procedures

Test and Procedure	*Results and Indications*	*Proceed to*
5.1—Determine that the air filter is functioning efficiently: Hold paper elements up to a strong light, and attempt to see light through the filter.	Clean permanent air filters in solvent (or manufacturer's recommendation), and allow to dry. Replace paper elements through which light cannot be seen:	**5.2**
5.2—Determine whether a flooding condition exists: Flooding is identified by a strong gasoline odor, and excessive gasoline present in the throttle bore(s) of the carburetor.	If flooding is not evident:	**5.3**
	If flooding is evident, permit the gasoline to dry for a few moments and restart.	
	If flooding doesn't recur:	**5.7**
	If flooding is persistent:	**5.5**

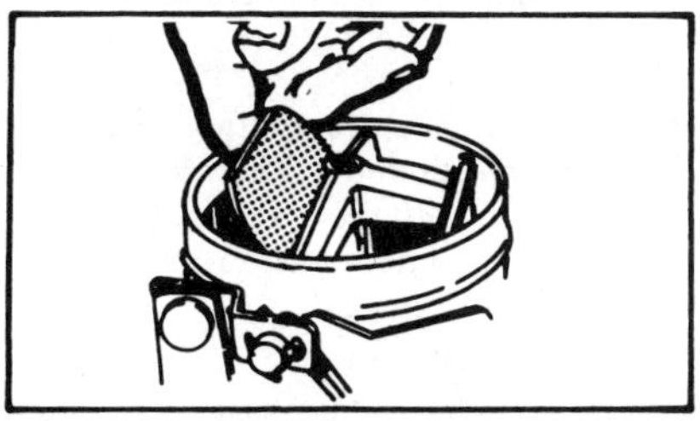

If the engine floods repeatedly, check the choke butterfly flap

Test and Procedure	*Results and Indications*	*Proceed to*
5.3—Check that fuel is reaching the carburetor: Detach the fuel line at the carburetor inlet. Hold the end of the line in a cup (not styrofoam), and crank the engine.	If fuel flows smoothly:	**5.7**
	If fuel doesn't flow (**NOTE:** ***Make sure that there is fuel in the tank***), or flows erratically:	**5.4**

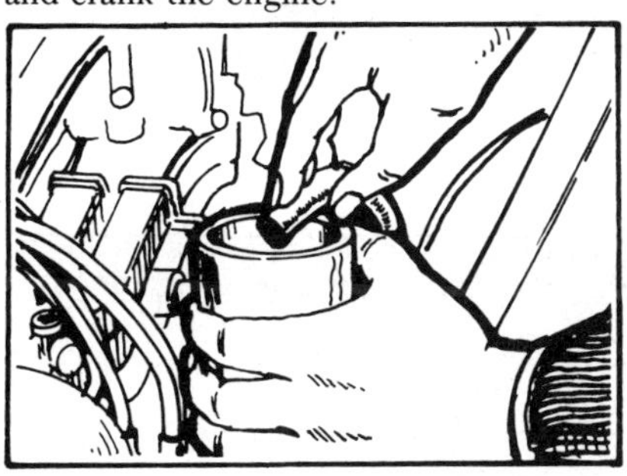

Check the fuel pump by disconnecting the output line (fuel pump-to-carburetor) at the carburetor and operating the starter briefly

Test and Procedure	Results and Indications	Proceed to
5.4—Test the fuel pump: Disconnect all fuel lines from the fuel pump. Hold a finger over the input fitting, crank the engine (with electric pump, turn the ignition or pump on); and feel for suction.	If suction is evident, blow out the fuel line to the tank with low pressure compressed air until bubbling is heard from the fuel filler neck. Also blow out the carburetor fuel line (both ends disconnected):	**5.7**
	If no suction is evident, replace or repair the fuel pump:	**5.7**
	NOTE: ***Repeated oil fouling of the spark plugs, or a no-start condition, could be the result of a ruptured vacuum booster pump diaphragm, through which oil or gasoline is being drawn into the intake manifold (where applicable).***	
5.5—Occasionally, small specks of dirt will clog the small jets and orifices in the carburetor. With the engine cold, hold a flat piece of wood or similar material over the carburetor, where possible, and crank the engine.	If the engine starts, but runs roughly the engine is probably not run enough.	
	If the engine won't start:	**5.9**
5.6—Check the needle and seat: Tap the carburetor in the area of the needle and seat.	If flooding stops, a gasoline additive (e.g., Gumout) will often cure the problem:	**5.7**
	If flooding continues, check the fuel pump for excessive pressure at the carburetor (according to specifications). If the pressure is normal, the needle and seat must be removed and checked, and/or the float level adjusted:	**5.7**
5.7—Test the accelerator pump by looking into the throttle bores while operating the throttle. 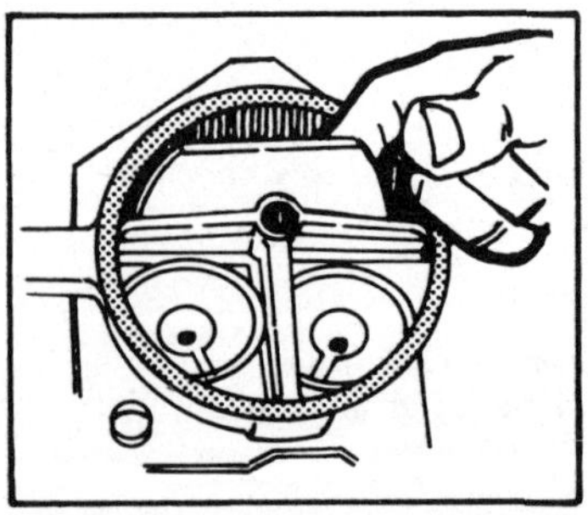 **Check for gas at the carburetor by looking down the carburetor throat while someone moves the accelerator**	If the accelerator pump appears to be operating normally:	**5.8**
	If the accelerator pump is not operating, the pump must be reconditioned. Where possible, service the pump with the carburetor(s) installed on the engine. If necessary, remove the carburetor. Prior to removal:	**5.8**
5.8—Determine whether the carburetor main fuel system is functioning: Spray a commercial starting fluid into the carburetor while attempting to start the engine.	If the engine starts, runs for a few seconds, and dies:	**5.9**
	If the engine doesn't start:	**6.1**

EASY STEP-BY-STEP TIPS FROM PROS

CHILTON'S
AUTO BODY REPAIR TIPS

Tools and Materials • Step-by-Step Illustrated Procedures
How To Repair Dents, Scratches and Rust Holes
Spray Painting and Refinishing Tips

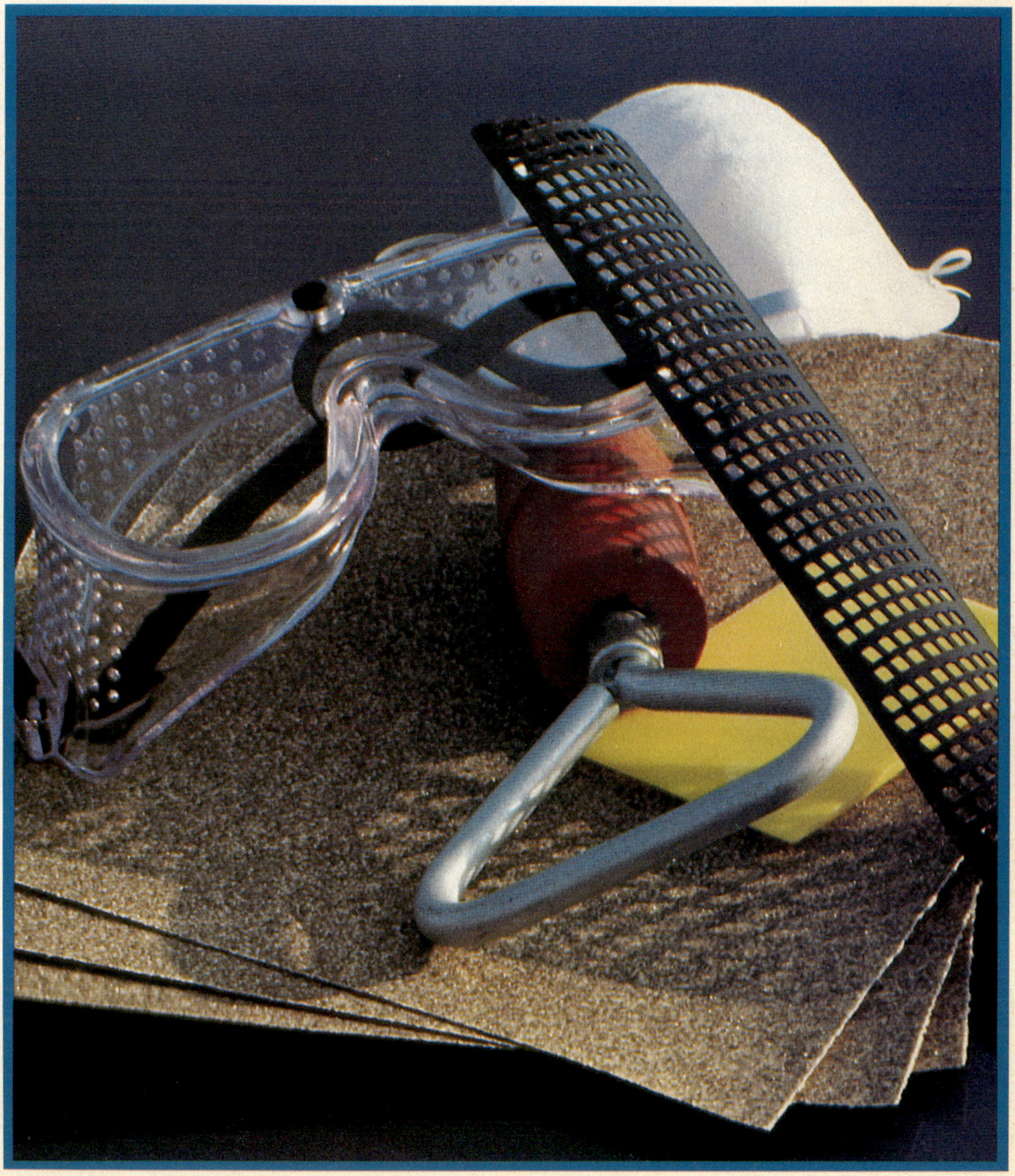

With a little practice, basic body repair procedures can be mastered by any do-it-yourself mechanic. The step-by-step repairs shown here can be applied to almost any type of auto body repair.

TOOLS & MATERIALS

You may already have basic tools, such as hammers and electric drills. Other tools unique to body repair — body hammers, grinding attachments, sanding blocks, dent puller, half-round plastic file and plastic spreaders — are relatively inexpensive and can be obtained wherever auto parts or auto body repair parts are sold. Portable air compressors and paint spray guns can be purchased or rented.

Auto Body Repair Kits

The best and most often used products are available to the do-it-yourselfer in kit form, from major manufacturers of auto body repair products. The same manufacturers also merchandise the individual products for use by pros.

Kits are available to make a wide variety of repairs, including holes, dents and scratches and fiberglass, and offer the advantage of buying the materials you'll need for the job. There is little waste or chance of materials going bad from not being used. Many kits may also contain basic body-working tools such as body files, sanding blocks and spreaders. Check the contents of the kit before buying your tools.

BODY REPAIR TIPS

Safety

Many of the products associated with auto body repair and refinishing contain toxic chemicals. Read all labels before opening containers and store them in a safe place and manner.

• Wear eye protection (safety goggles) when using power tools or when performing any operation that involves the removal of any type of material.

• Wear lung protection (disposabl mask or respirator) when grinding, sand ing or painting.

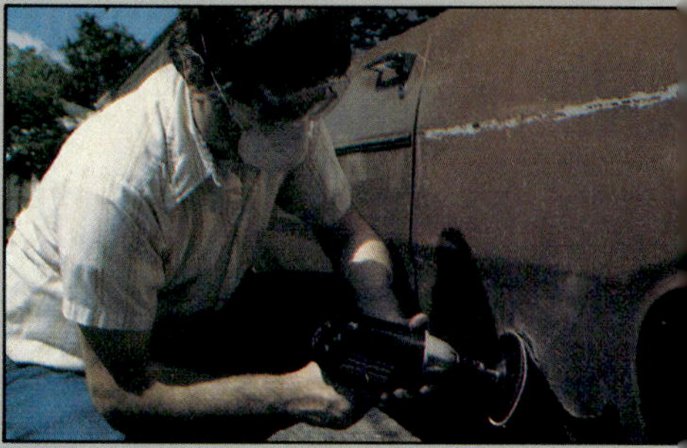

Sanding

1 Sand off paint before using a den puller. When using a non-adhesiv sanding disc, cover the back of the dis with an overlapping layer or two o masking tape and trim the edges. Th disc will last considerably longer.

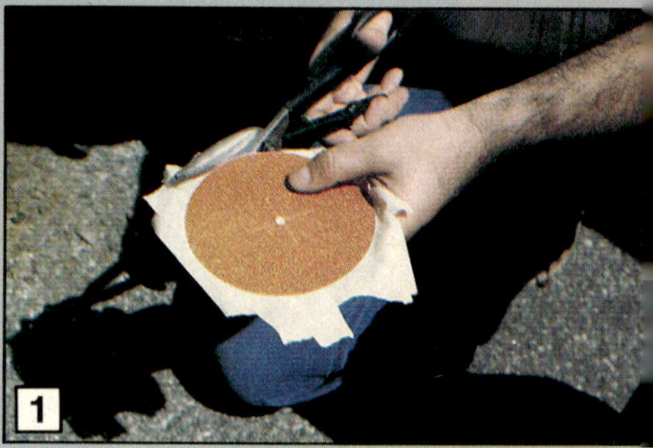

1

2 Use the circular motion of the sand ing disc to grind *into* the edge of th repair. Grinding or sanding away fron the jagged edge will only tear the sand paper.

3 Use the palm of your hand flat on the panel to detec high and low spots. Do not use you fingertips. Slide your hand slowly back and forth.

3

WORKING WITH BODY FILLER

Mixing The Filler

Cleanliness and proper mixing and application are extremely important. Use a clean piece of plastic or glass or a disposable artist's palette to mix body filler.

1 Allow plenty of time and follow directions. No useful purpose will be served by adding more hardener to make it cure (set-up) faster. Less hardener means more curing time, but the mixture dries harder; more hardener means less curing time but a softer mixture.

2

2 Both the hardener and the filler should be thoroughly kneaded or stirred before mixing. Hardener should be a solid paste and dispense like thin toothpaste. Body filler should be smooth, and free of lumps or thick spots.

Getting the proper amount of hardener in the filler is the trickiest part of preparing the filler. Use the same amount of hardener in cold or warm weather. For contour filler (thick coats), a bead of hardener twice the diameter of the filler is about right. There's about a 15% margin on either side, but, if in doubt use less hardener.

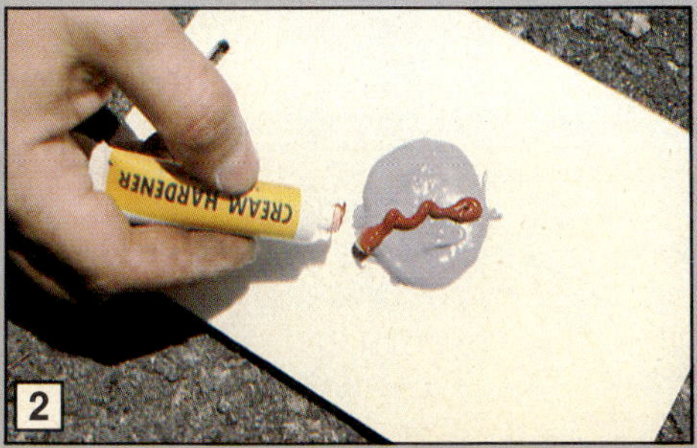

2

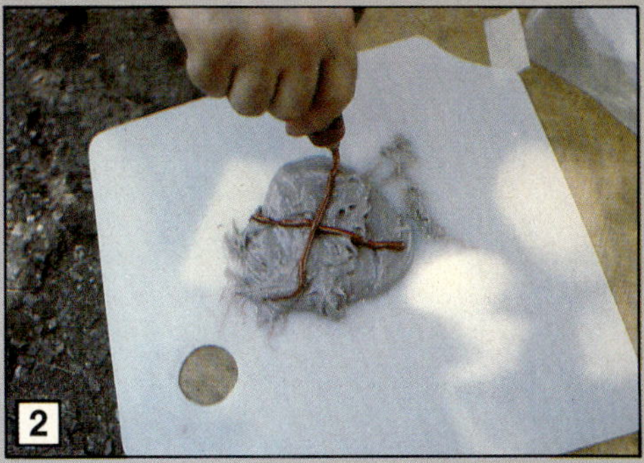

2

3 Mix the body filler and hardener by wiping across the mixing surface, picking the mixture up and wiping it again. Colder weather requires longer mixing times. Do not mix in a circular motion; this will trap air bubbles which will become holes in the cured filler.

3

Applying The Filler

1 For best results, filler should not be applied over 1/4″ thick.

Apply the filler in several coats. Build it up to above the level of the repair surface so that it can be sanded or grated down.

The first coat of filler must be pressed on with a firm wiping motion.

Apply the filler in one direction only. Working the filler back and forth will either pull it off the metal or trap air bubbles.

REPAIRING DENTS

Before you start, take a few minutes to study the damaged area. Try to visualize the shape of the panel before it was damaged. If the damage is on the left fender, look at the right fender and use it as a guide. If there is access to the panel from behind, you can reshape it with a body hammer. If not, you'll have to use a dent puller. Go slowly and work the metal a little at a time. Get the panel as straight as possible before applying filler.

1 This dent is typical of one that can be pulled out or hammered out from behind. Remove the headlight cover, headlight assembly and turn signal housing.

2 Drill a series of holes ½ the size of the end of the dent puller along the stress line. Make some trial pulls and assess the results. If necessary, drill more holes and try again. Do not hurry.

3 If possible, use a body hammer and block to shape the metal back to its original contours. Get the metal back as close to its original shape as possible. Don't depend on body filler to fill dents.

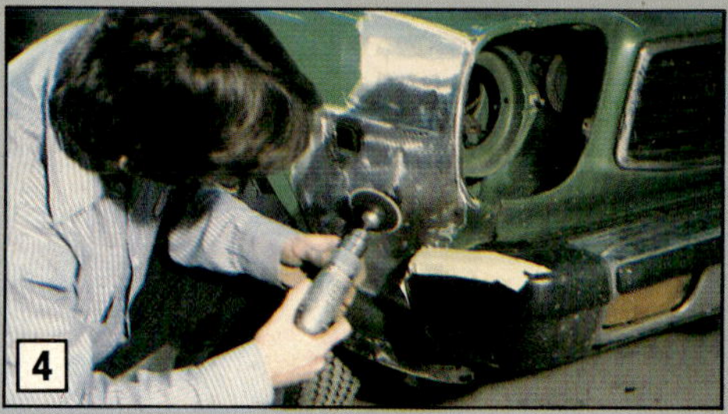

4 Using an 80-grit grinding disc on an electric drill, grind the paint from the surrounding area down to bare metal. Use a new grinding pad to prevent heat buildup that will warp metal.

5 The area should look like this when you're finished grinding. Knock the drill holes in and tape over small openings to keep plastic filler out.

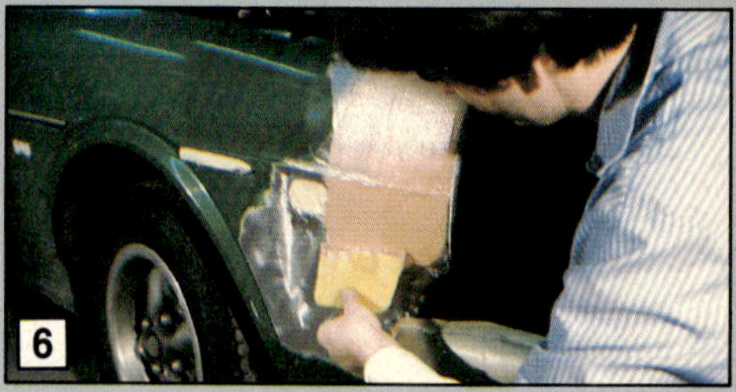

6 Mix the body filler (see Body Repair Tips). Spread the body filler evenly over the entire area (see Body Repair Tips). Be sure to cover the area completely.

7 Let the body filler dry until the surface can just be scratched with your fingernail. Knock the high spots from the body filler with a body file ("Cheese-grater"). Check frequently with the palm of your hand for high and low spots.

8 Check to be sure that trim pieces that will be installed later will fit exactly. Sand the area with 40-grit paper.

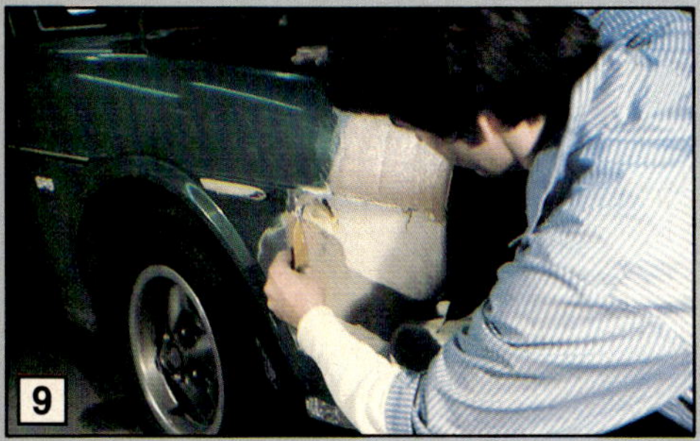

9 If you wind up with low spots, you may have to apply another layer of filler.

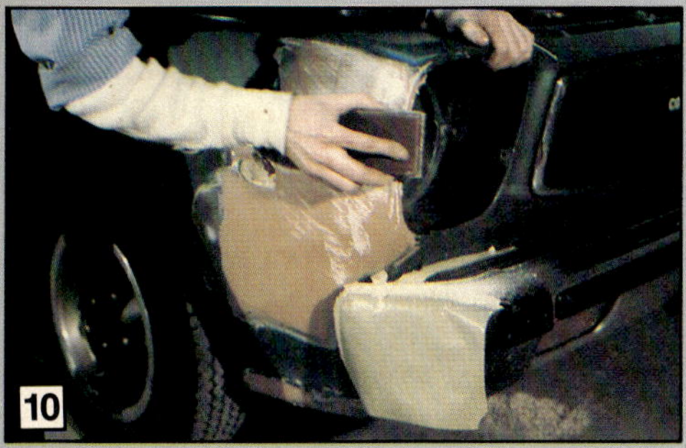

10 Knock the high spots off with 40-grit paper. When you are satisfied with the contours of the repair, apply a thin coat of filler to cover pin holes and scratches.

11 Block sand the area with 40-grit paper to a smooth finish. Pay particular attention to body lines and ridges that must be well-defined.

12 Sand the area with 400 paper and then finish with a scuff pad. The finished repair is ready for priming and painting (see Painting Tips).

Materials and photos courtesy of Ritt Jones Auto Body, Prospect Park, PA.

REPAIRING RUST HOLES

There are many ways to repair rust holes. The fiberglass cloth kit shown here is one of the most cost efficient for the owner because it provides a strong repair that resists cracking and moisture and is relatively easy to use. It can be used on large and small holes (with or without backing) and can be applied over contoured areas. Remember, however, that short of replacing an entire panel, no repair is a guarantee that the rust will not return.

1 Remove any trim that will be in the way. Clean away all loose debris. Cut away all the rusted metal. But be sure to leave enough metal to retain the contour or body shape.

2 Grind away all traces of rust with a 24-grit grinding disc. Be sure to grind back 3-4 inches from the edge of the hole down to bare metal and be sure all traces of paint, primer and rust are removed.

3 Block sand the area with 80 or 100 grit sandpaper to get a clear, shiny surface and feathered paint edge. Tap the edges of the hole inward with a ball peen hammer.

4 If you are going to use release film, cut a piece about 2-3″ larger than the area you have sanded. Place the film over the repair and mark the sanded area on the film. Avoid any unnecessary wrinkling of the film.

5 Cut 2 pieces of fiberglass matte to match the shape of the repair. One piece should be about 1″ smaller than the sanded area and the second piece should be 1″ smaller than the first. Mix enough filler and hardener to saturate the fiberglass material (see Body Repair Tips).

6 Lay the release sheet on a flat surface and spread an even layer of filler, large enough to cover the repair. Lay the smaller piece of fiberglass cloth in the center of the sheet and spread another layer of filler over the fiberglass cloth. Repeat the operation for the larger piece of cloth.

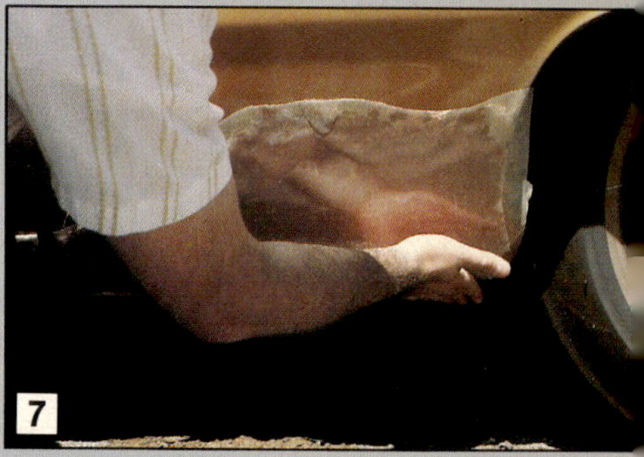

7 Place the repair material over the repair area, with the release film facing outward. Use a spreader and work from the center outward to smooth the material, following the body contours. Be sure to remove all air bubbles.

8 Wait until the repair has dried tack-free and peel off the release sheet. The ideal working temperature is 60°-90° F. Cooler or warmer temperatures or high humidity may require additional curing time. Wait longer, if in doubt.

9

9 Sand and feather-edge the entire area. The initial sanding can be done with a sanding disc on an electric drill if care is used. Finish the sanding with a block sander. Low spots can be filled with body filler; this may require several applications.

10

10 When the filler can just be scratched with a fingernail, knock the high spots down with a body file and smooth the entire area with 80-grit. Feather the filled areas into the surrounding areas.

11

11 When the area is sanded smooth, mix some topcoat and hardener and apply it directly with a spreader. This will give a smooth finish and prevent the glass matte from showing through the paint.

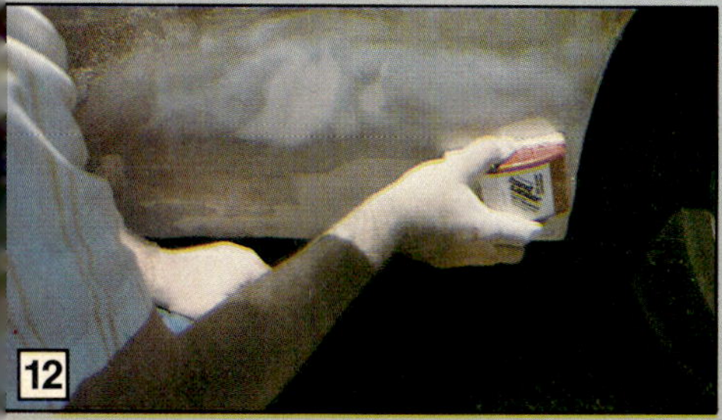

12

12 Block sand the topcoat smooth with finishing sandpaper (200 grit), and 400 grit. The repair is ready for masking, priming and painting (see Painting Tips).

Materials and photos courtesy Marson Corporation, Chelsea, Massachusetts

PAINTING TIPS

Preparation

1 SANDING — Use a 400 or 600 grit wet or dry sandpaper. Wet-sand the area with a 1/4 sheet of sandpaper soaked in clean water. Keep the paper wet while sanding. Sand the area until the repaired area tapers into the original finish.

2 CLEANING — Wash the area to be painted thoroughly with water and a clean rag. Rinse it thoroughly and wipe the surface dry until you're sure it's completely free of dirt, dust, fingerprints, wax, detergent or other foreign matter.

3 MASKING — Protect any areas you don't want to overspray by covering them with masking tape and newspaper. Be careful not get fingerprints on the area to be painted.

4 PRIMING — All exposed metal should be primed before painting. Primer protects the metal and provides an excellent surface for paint adhesion. When the primer is dry, wet-sand the area again with 600 grit wet-sandpaper. Clean the area again after sanding.

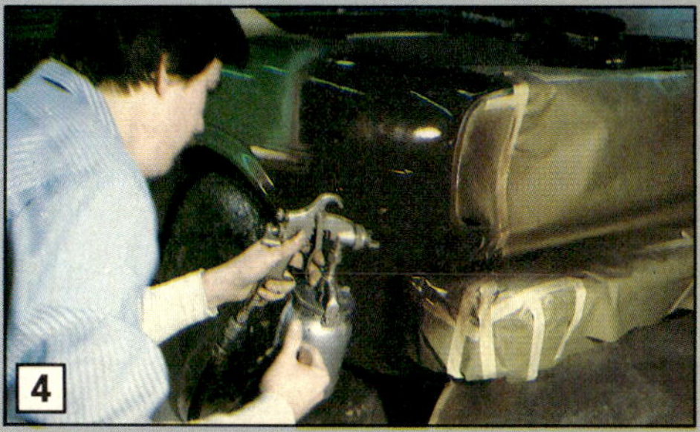

4

Painting Techniques

Paint applied from either a spray gun or a spray can (for small areas) will provide good results. Experiment on an old piece of metal to get the right combination before you begin painting.

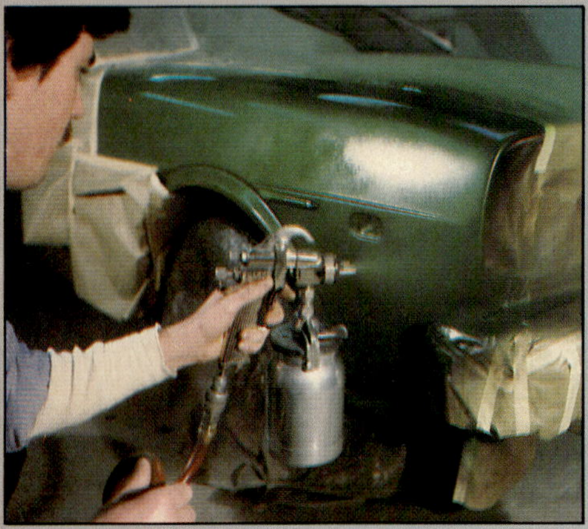

SPRAYING VISCOSITY (SPRAY GUN ONLY) — Paint should be thinned to spraying viscosity according to the directions on the can. Use only the recommended thinner or reducer and the same amount of reduction regardless of temperature.

AIR PRESSURE (SPRAY GUN ONLY) — This is extremely important. Be sure you are using the proper recommended pressure.

TEMPERATURE — The surface to be painted should be approximately the same temperature as the surrounding air. Applying warm paint to a cold surface, or vice versa, will completely upset the paint characteristics.

THICKNESS — Spray with smooth strokes. In general, the thicker the coat of paint, the longer the drying time. Apply several thin coats about 30 seconds apart. The paint should remain wet long enough to flow out and no longer; heavier coats will only produce sags or wrinkles. Spray a light (fog) coat, followed by heavier color coats.

DISTANCE — The ideal spraying distance is 8″-12″ from the gun or can to the surface. Shorter distances will produce ripples, while greater distances will result in orange peel, dry film and poor color match and loss of material due to overspray.

OVERLAPPING — The gun or can should be kept at right angles to the surface at all times. Work to a wet edge at an even speed, using a 50% overlap and direct the center of the spray at the lower or nearest edge of the previous stroke.

RUBBING OUT (BLENDING) FRESH PAINT — Let the paint dry thoroughly. Runs or imperfections can be sanded out, primed and repainted.

Don't be in too big a hurry to remove the masking. This only produces paint ridges. When the finish has dried for at least a week, apply a small amount of fine grade rubbing compound with a clean, wet cloth. Use lots of water and blend the new paint with the surrounding area.

WRONG	CORRECT	WRONG
Thin coat. Stroke too fast, not enough overlap, gun too far away.	*Medium coat. Proper distance, good stroke, proper overlap.*	*Heavy coat. Stroke too slow, too much overlap, gun too close.*

Test and Procedure	Results and Indications	Proceed to
5.9—Uncommon fuel system malfunctions: See below:	If the problem is solved:	**6.1**
	If the problem remains, remove and recondition the carburetor.	

Condition	Indication	Test	Prevailing Weather Conditions	Remedy
Vapor lock	Engine will not restart shortly after running.	Cool the components of the fuel system until the engine starts. Vapor lock can be cured faster by draping a wet cloth over a mechanical fuel pump.	Hot to very hot	Ensure that the exhaust manifold heat control valve is operating. Check with the vehicle manufacturer for the recommended solution to vapor lock on the model in question.
Carburetor icing	Engine will not idle, stalls at low speeds.	Visually inspect the throttle plate area of the throttle bores for frost.	High humidity, 32–40° F.	Ensure that the exhaust manifold heat control valve is operating, and that the intake manifold heat riser is not blocked.
Water in the fuel	Engine sputters and stalls; may not start.	Pump a small amount of fuel into a glass jar. Allow to stand, and inspect for droplets or a layer of water.	High humidity, extreme temperature changes.	For droplets, use one or two cans of commercial gas line anti-freeze. For a layer of water, the tank must be drained, and the fuel lines blown out with compressed air.

Section 6—Engine Compression

See Chapter 3 for service procedures

Test and Procedure	Results and Indications	Proceed to
6.1—Test engine compression: Remove all spark plugs. Block the throttle wide open. Insert a compression gauge into a spark plug port, crank the engine to obtain the maximum reading, and record.	If compression is within limits on all cylinders:	**7.1**
	If gauge reading is extremely low on all cylinders:	**6.2**
	If gauge reading is low on one or two cylinders: (If gauge readings are identical and low on two or more adjacent cylinders, the head gasket must be replaced.)	**6.2**

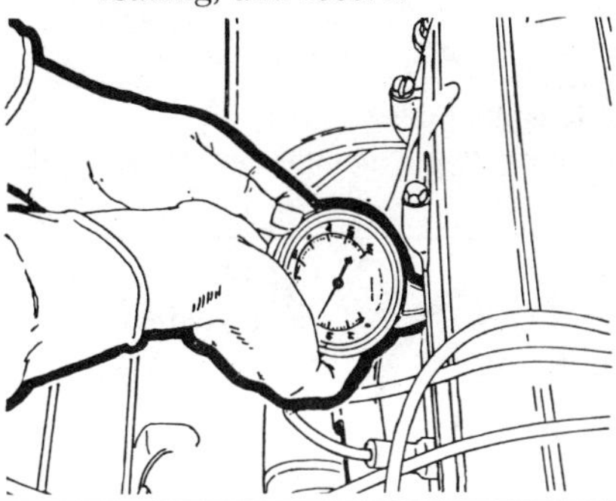

Checking compression

Test and Procedure	Results and Indications	Proceed to
6.2—Test engine compression (wet): Squirt approximately 30 cc. of engine oil into each cylinder, and retest per 6.1.	If the readings improve, worn or cracked rings or broken pistons are indicated:	**See Chapter 3**
	If the readings do not improve, burned or excessively carboned valves or a jumped timing chain are indicated: **NOTE:** ***A jumped timing chain is often indicated by difficult cranking.***	**7.1**

Section 7—Engine Vacuum

See Chapter 3 for service procedures

Test and Procedure	*Results and Indications*	*Proceed to*
7.1—Attach a vacuum gauge to the intake manifold beyond the throttle plate. Start the engine, and observe the action of the needle over the range of engine speeds.	See below.	**See below**

INDICATION: normal engine in good condition

Proceed to: 8.1

Normal engine

Gauge reading: steady, from 17–22 in./Hg.

INDICATION: sticking valves or ignition miss

Proceed to: 9.1, 8.3

Sticking valves

Gauge reading: intermittent fluctuation at idle

INDICATION: late ignition or valve timing, low compression, stuck throttle valve, leaking carburetor or manifold gasket

Proceed to: 6.1

Incorrect valve timing

Gauge reading: low (10–15 in./Hg) but steady

INDICATION: improper carburetor adjustment or minor intake leak.

Proceed to: 7.2

Carburetor requires adjustment

Gauge reading: drifting needle

INDICATION: ignition miss, blown cylinder head gasket, leaking valve or weak valve spring

Proceed to: 8.3, 6.1

Blown head gasket

Gauge reading: needle fluctuates as engine speed increases

INDICATION: burnt valve or faulty valve clearance. Needle will fall when defective valve operates

Proceed to: 9.1

Burnt or leaking valves

Gauge reading: steady needle, but drops regularly

INDICATION: choked muffler, excessive back pressure in system

Proceed to: 10.1

Clogged exhaust system

Gauge reading: gradual drop in reading at idle

INDICATION: worn valve guides

Proceed to: 9.1

Worn valve guides

Gauge reading: needle vibrates excessively at idle, but steadies as engine speed increases

White pointer = steady gauge hand

Black pointer = fluctuating gauge hand

Test and Procedure	Results and Indications	Proceed to
7.2—Attach a vacuum gauge per 7.1, and test for an intake manifold leak. Squirt a small amount of oil around the intake manifold gaskets, carburetor gaskets, plugs and fittings. Observe the action of the vacuum gauge.	If the reading improves, replace the indicated gasket, or seal the indicated fitting or plug:	**8.1**
	If the reading remains low:	**7.3**
7.3—Test all vacuum hoses and accessories for leaks as described in 7.2. Also check the carburetor body (dashpots, automatic choke mechanism, throttle shafts) for leaks in the same manner.	If the reading improves, service or replace the offending part(s):	**8.1**
	If the reading remains low:	**6.1**

Section 8—Secondary Electrical System

See Chapter 2 for service procedures

Test and Procedure	Results and Indications	Proceed to
8.1—Remove the distributor cap and check to make sure that the rotor turns when the engine is cranked. Visually inspect the distributor components.	Clean, tighten or replace any components which appear defective.	**8.2**
8.2—Connect a timing light (per manufacturer's recommendation) and check the dynamic ignition timing. Disconnect and plug the vacuum hose(s) to the distributor if specified, start the engine, and observe the timing marks at the specified engine speed.	If the timing is not correct, adjust to specifications by rotating the distributor in the engine: (Advance timing by rotating distributor opposite normal direction of rotor rotation, retard timing by rotating distributor in same direction as rotor rotation.)	**8.3**
8.3—Check the operation of the distributor advance mechanism(s): To test the mechanical advance, disconnect the vacuum lines from the distributor advance unit and observe the timing marks with a timing light as the engine speed is increased from idle. If the mark moves smoothly, without hesitation, it may be assumed that the mechanical advance is functioning properly. To test vacuum advance and/or retard systems, alternately crimp and release the vacuum line, and observe the timing mark for movement. If movement is noted, the system is operating.	If the systems are functioning:	**8.4**
	If the systems are not functioning, remove the distributor, and test on a distributor tester:	**8.4**
8.4—Locate an ignition miss: With the engine running, remove each spark plug wire, one at a time, until one is found that doesn't cause the engine to roughen and slow down.	When the missing cylinder is identified:	**4.1**

Section 9—Valve Train

See Chapter 3 for service procedures

Test and Procedure	Results and Indications	Proceed to
9.1—Evaluate the valve train: Remove the valve cover, and ensure that the valves are adjusted to specifications. A mechanic's stethoscope may be used to aid in the diagnosis of the valve train. By pushing the probe on or near push rods or rockers, valve noise often can be isolated. A timing light also may be used to diagnose valve problems. Connect the light according to manufacturer's recommendations, and start the engine. Vary the firing moment of the light by increasing the engine speed (and therefore the ignition advance), and moving the trigger from cylinder to cylinder. Observe the movement of each valve.	Sticking valves or erratic valve train motion can be observed with the timing light. The cylinder head must be disassembled for repairs.	**See Chapter 3**
9.2—Check the valve timing: Locate top dead center of the No. 1 piston, and install a degree wheel or tape on the crankshaft pulley or damper with zero corresponding to an index mark on the engine. Rotate the crankshaft in its direction of rotation, and observe the opening of the No. 1 cylinder intake valve. The opening should correspond with the correct mark on the degree wheel according to specifications.	If the timing is not correct, the timing cover must be removed for further investigation.	**See Chapter 3**

Section 10—Exhaust System

Test and Procedure	Results and Indications	Proceed to
10.1—Determine whether the exhaust manifold heat control valve is operating: Operate the valve by hand to determine whether it is free to move. If the valve is free, run the engine to operating temperature and observe the action of the valve, to ensure that it is opening.	If the valve sticks, spray it with a suitable solvent, open and close the valve to free it, and retest.	
	If the valve functions properly:	**10.2**
	If the valve does not free, or does not operate, replace the valve:	**10.2**
10.2—Ensure that there are no exhaust restrictions: Visually inspect the exhaust system for kinks, dents, or crushing. Also note that gases are flowing freely from the tailpipe at all engine speeds, indicating no restriction in the muffler or resonator.	Replace any damaged portion of the system:	**11.1**

Section 11—Cooling System

See Chapter 3 for service procedures

Test and Procedure	Results and Indications	Proceed to
11.1—Visually inspect the fan belt for glazing, cracks, and fraying, and replace if necessary. Tighten the belt so that the longest span has approximately ½″ play at its midpoint under thumb pressure (see Chapter 1).	Replace or tighten the fan belt as necessary:	**11.2**
	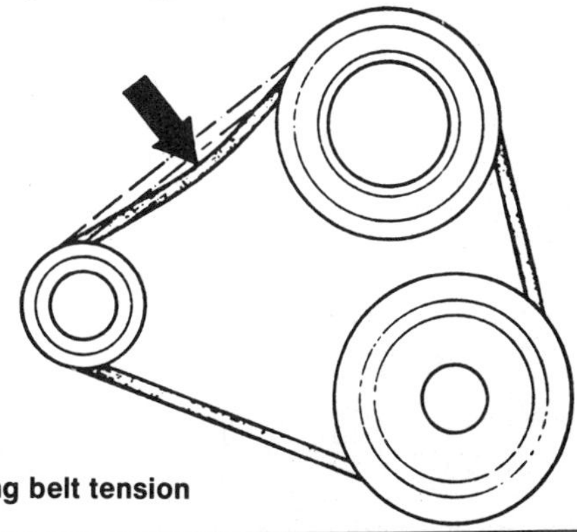 **Checking belt tension**	
11.2—Check the fluid level of the cooling system.	If full or slightly low, fill as necessary:	**11.5**
	If extremely low:	**11.3**
11.3—Visually inspect the external portions of the cooling system (radiator, radiator hoses, thermostat elbow, water pump seals, heater hoses, etc.) for leaks. If none are found, pressurize the cooling system to 14–15 psi.	If cooling system holds the pressure:	**11.5**
	If cooling system loses pressure rapidly, reinspect external parts of the system for leaks under pressure. If none are found, check dipstick for coolant in crankcase. If no coolant is present, but pressure loss continues:	**11.4**
	If coolant is evident in crankcase, remove cylinder head(s), and check gasket(s). If gaskets are intact, block and cylinder head(s) should be checked for cracks or holes.	
	If the gasket(s) is blown, replace, and purge the crankcase of coolant:	**12.6**
	NOTE: ***Occasionally, due to atmospheric and driving conditions, condensation of water can occur in the crankcase. This causes the oil to appear milky white. To remedy, run the engine until hot, and change the oil and oil filter.***	
11.4—Check for combustion leaks into the cooling system: Pressurize the cooling system as above. Start the engine, and observe the pressure gauge. If the needle fluctuates, remove each spark plug wire, one at a time, noting which cylinder(s) reduce or eliminate the fluctuation.	Cylinders which reduce or eliminate the fluctuation, when the spark plug wire is removed, are leaking into the cooling system. Replace the head gasket on the affected cylinder bank(s).	
Pressurizing the cooling system	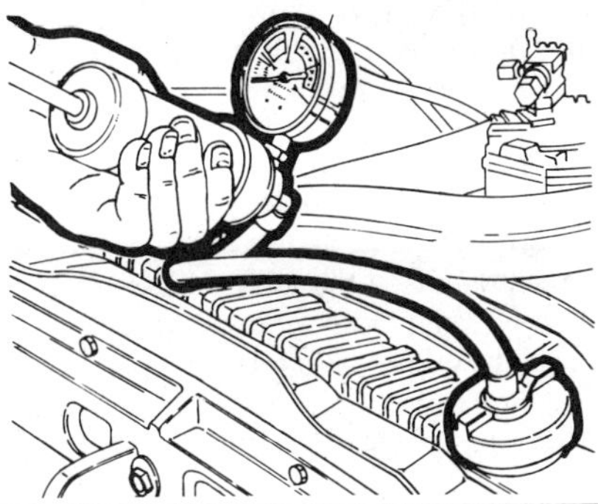	

Test and Procedure	Results and Indications	Proceed to
11.5—Check the radiator pressure cap: Attach a radiator pressure tester to the radiator cap (wet the seal prior to installation). Quickly pump up the pressure, noting the point at which the cap releases.	If the cap releases within ± 1 psi of the specified rating, it is operating properly:	**11.6**
	If the cap releases at more than ± 1 psi of the specified rating, it should be replaced:	**11.6**

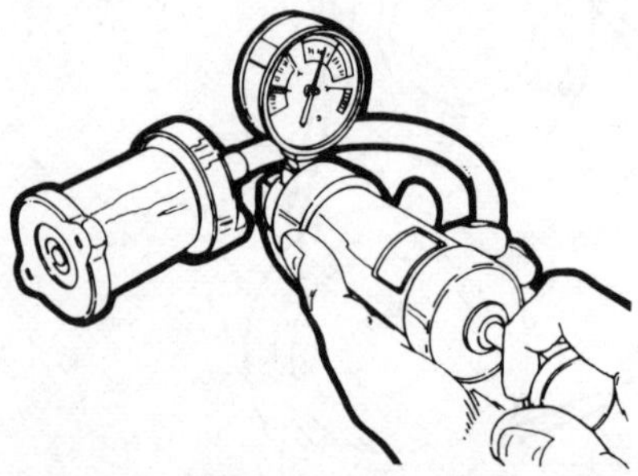

Checking radiator pressure cap

Test and Procedure	Results and Indications	Proceed to
11.6—Test the thermostat: Start the engine cold, remove the radiator cap, and insert a thermometer into the radiator. Allow the engine to idle. After a short while, there will be a sudden, rapid increase in coolant temperature. The temperature at which this sharp rise stops is the thermostat opening temperature.	If the thermostat opens at or about the specified temperature:	**11.7**
	If the temperature doesn't increase: (If the temperature increases slowly and gradually, replace the thermostat.)	**11.7**
11.7—Check the water pump: Remove the thermostat elbow and the thermostat, disconnect the coil high tension lead (to prevent starting), and crank the engine momentarily.	If coolant flows, replace the thermostat and retest per 11.6:	**11.6**
	If coolant doesn't flow, reverse flush the cooling system to alleviate any blockage that might exist. If system is not blocked, and coolant will not flow, replace the water pump.	

Section 12—Lubrication

See Chapter 3 for service procedures

Test and Procedure	Results and Indications	Proceed to
12.1—Check the oil pressure gauge or warning light: If the gauge shows low pressure, or the light is on for no obvious reason, remove the oil pressure sender. Install an accurate oil pressure gauge and run the engine momentarily.	If oil pressure builds normally, run engine for a few moments to determine that it is functioning normally, and replace the sender.	—
	If the pressure remains low:	**12.2**
	If the pressure surges:	**12.3**
	If the oil pressure is zero:	**12.3**
12.2—Visually inspect the oil: If the oil is watery or very thin, milky, or foamy, replace the oil and oil filter.	If the oil is normal:	**12.3**
	If after replacing oil the pressure remains low:	**12.3**
	If after replacing oil the pressure becomes normal:	—

Test and Procedure	Results and Indications	Proceed to
12.3—Inspect the oil pressure relief valve and spring, to ensure that it is not sticking or stuck. Remove and thoroughly clean the valve, spring, and the valve body.	If the oil pressure improves:	—
	If no improvement is noted:	12.4
12.4—Check to ensure that the oil pump is not cavitating (sucking air instead of oil): See that the crankcase is neither over nor underfull, and that the pickup in the sump is in the proper position and free from sludge.	Fill or drain the crankcase to the proper capacity, and clean the pickup screen in solvent if necessary. If no improvement is noted:	12.5
12.5—Inspect the oil pump drive and the oil pump:	If the pump drive or the oil pump appear to be defective, service as necessary and retest per 12.1:	12.1
	If the pump drive and pump appear to be operating normally, the engine should be disassembled to determine where blockage exists:	See Chapter 3
12.6—Purge the engine of ethylene glycol coolant: Completely drain the crankcase and the oil filter. Obtain a commercial butyl cellosolve base solvent, designated for this purpose, and follow the instructions precisely. Following this, install a new oil filter and refill the crankcase with the proper weight oil. The next oil and filter change should follow shortly thereafter (1000 miles).		

TROUBLESHOOTING EMISSION CONTROL SYSTEMS

See Chapter 4 for procedures applicable to individual emission control systems used on specific combinations of engine/transmission/model.

TROUBLESHOOTING THE CARBURETOR

See Chapter 4 for service procedures

Carburetor problems cannot be effectively isolated unless all other engine systems (particularly ignition and emission) are functioning properly and the engine is properly tuned.

Condition	Possible Cause
Engine cranks, but does not start	1. Improper starting procedure 2. No fuel in tank 3. Clogged fuel line or filter 4. Defective fuel pump 5. Choke valve not closing properly 6. Engine flooded 7. Choke valve not unloading 8. Throttle linkage not making full travel 9. Stuck needle or float 10. Leaking float needle or seat 11. Improper float adjustment
Engine stalls	1. Improperly adjusted idle speed or mixture **Engine hot** 2. Improperly adjusted dashpot 3. Defective or improperly adjusted solenoid 4. Incorrect fuel level in fuel bowl 5. Fuel pump pressure too high 6. Leaking float needle seat 7. Secondary throttle valve stuck open 8. Air or fuel leaks 9. Idle air bleeds plugged or missing 10. Idle passages plugged **Engine Cold** 11. Incorrectly adjusted choke 12. Improperly adjusted fast idle speed 13. Air leaks 14. Plugged idle or idle air passages 15. Stuck choke valve or binding linkage 16. Stuck secondary throttle valves 17. Engine flooding—high fuel level 18. Leaking or misaligned float
Engine hesitates on acceleration	1. Clogged fuel filter 2. Leaking fuel pump diaphragm 3. Low fuel pump pressure 4. Secondary throttle valves stuck, bent or misadjusted 5. Sticking or binding air valve 6. Defective accelerator pump 7. Vacuum leaks 8. Clogged air filter 9. Incorrect choke adjustment (engine cold)
Engine feels sluggish or flat on acceleration	1. Improperly adjusted idle speed or mixture 2. Clogged fuel filter 3. Defective accelerator pump 4. Dirty, plugged or incorrect main metering jets 5. Bent or sticking main metering rods 6. Sticking throttle valves 7. Stuck heat riser 8. Binding or stuck air valve 9. Dirty, plugged or incorrect secondary jets 10. Bent or sticking secondary metering rods. 11. Throttle body or manifold heat passages plugged 12. Improperly adjusted choke or choke vacuum break.
Carburetor floods	1. Defective fuel pump. Pressure too high. 2. Stuck choke valve 3. Dirty, worn or damaged float or needle valve/seat 4. Incorrect float/fuel level 5. Leaking float bowl

Condition	Possible Cause
Engine idles roughly and stalls	1. Incorrect idle speed 2. Clogged fuel filter 3. Dirt in fuel system or carburetor 4. Loose carburetor screws or attaching bolts 5. Broken carburetor gaskets 6. Air leaks 7. Dirty carburetor 8. Worn idle mixture needles 9. Throttle valves stuck open 10. Incorrectly adjusted float or fuel level 11. Clogged air filter
Engine runs unevenly or surges	1. Defective fuel pump 2. Dirty or clogged fuel filter 3. Plugged, loose or incorrect main metering jets or rods 4. Air leaks 5. Bent or sticking main metering rods 6. Stuck power piston 7. Incorrect float adjustment 8. Incorrect idle speed or mixture 9. Dirty or plugged idle system passages 10. Hard, brittle or broken gaskets 11. Loose attaching or mounting screws 12. Stuck or misaligned secondary throttle valves
Poor fuel economy	1. Poor driving habits 2. Stuck choke valve 3. Binding choke linkage 4. Stuck heat riser 5. Incorrect idle mixture 6. Defective accelerator pump 7. Air leaks 8. Plugged, loose or incorrect main metering jets 9. Improperly adjusted float or fuel level 10. Bent, misaligned or fuel-clogged float 11. Leaking float needle seat 12. Fuel leak 13. Accelerator pump discharge ball not seating properly 14. Incorrect main jets
Engine lacks high speed performance or power	1. Incorrect throttle linkage adjustment 2. Stuck or binding power piston 3. Defective accelerator pump 4. Air leaks 5. Incorrect float setting or fuel level 6. Dirty, plugged, worn or incorrect main metering jets or rods 7. Binding or sticking air valve 8. Brittle or cracked gaskets 9. Bent, incorrect or improperly adjusted secondary metering rods 10. Clogged fuel filter 11. Clogged air filter 12. Defective fuel pump

TROUBLESHOOTING FUEL INJECTION PROBLEMS

Each fuel injection system has its own unique components and test procedures, for which it is impossible to generalize. Refer to Chapter 4 of this Repair & Tune-Up Guide for specific test and repair procedures, if the vehicle is equipped with fuel injection.

TROUBLESHOOTING ELECTRICAL PROBLEMS

See Chapter 5 for service procedures

For any electrical system to operate, it must make a complete circuit. This simply means that the power flow from the battery must make a complete circle. When an electrical component is operating, power flows from the battery to the component, passes through the component causing it to perform its function (lighting a light bulb), and then returns to the battery through the ground of the circuit. This ground is usually (but not always) the metal part of the car or truck on which the electrical component is mounted.

Perhaps the easiest way to visualize this is to think of connecting a light bulb with two wires attached to it to the battery. If one of the two wires attached to the light bulb were attached to the negative post of the battery and the other were attached to the positive post of the battery, you would have a complete circuit. Current from the battery would flow to the light bulb, causing it to light, and return to the negative post of the battery.

The normal automotive circuit differs from this simple example in two ways. First, instead of having a return wire from the bulb to the battery, the light bulb returns the current to the battery through the chassis of the vehicle. Since the negative battery cable is attached to the chassis and the chassis is made of electrically conductive metal, the chassis of the vehicle can serve as a ground wire to complete the circuit. Secondly, most automotive circuits contain switches to turn components on and off as required.

Every complete circuit from a power source must include a component which is using the power from the power source. If you were to disconnect the light bulb from the wires and touch the two wires together (don't do this) the power supply wire to the component would be grounded before the normal ground connection for the circuit.

Because grounding a wire from a power source makes a complete circuit—less the required component to use the power—this phenomenon is called a short circuit. Common causes are: broken insulation (exposing the metal wire to a metal part of the car or truck), or a shorted switch.

Some electrical components which require a large amount of current to operate also have a relay in their circuit. Since these circuits carry a large amount of current, the thickness of the wire in the circuit (gauge size) is also greater. If this large wire were connected from the component to the control switch on the instrument panel, and then back to the component, a voltage drop would occur in the circuit. To prevent this potential drop in voltage, an electromagnetic switch (relay) is used. The large wires in the circuit are connected from the battery to one side of the relay, and from the opposite side of the relay to the component. The relay is normally open, preventing current from passing through the circuit. An additional, smaller, wire is connected from the relay to the control switch for the circuit. When the control switch is turned on, it grounds the smaller wire from the relay and completes the circuit. This closes the relay and allows current to flow from the battery to the component. The horn, headlight, and starter circuits are three which use relays.

It is possible for larger surges of current to pass through the electrical system of your car or truck. If this surge of current were to reach an electrical component, it could burn it out. To prevent this, fuses, circuit breakers or fusible links are connected into the current supply wires of most of the major electrical systems. When an electrical current of excessive power passes through the component's fuse, the fuse blows out and breaks the circuit, saving the component from destruction.

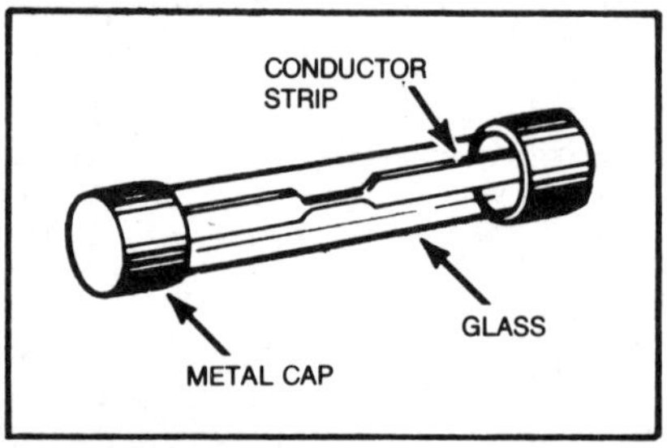

Typical automotive fuse

A circuit breaker is basically a self-repairing fuse. The circuit breaker opens the circuit the same way a fuse does. However, when either the short is removed from the circuit or the surge subsides, the circuit breaker resets itself and does not have to be replaced as a fuse does.

A fuse link is a wire that acts as a fuse. It is normally connected between the starter relay and the main wiring harness. This connection is usually under the hood. The fuse link (if installed) protects all the

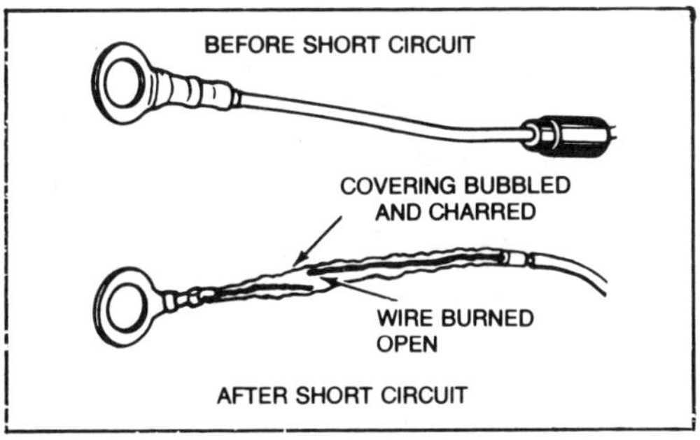

Most fusible links show a charred, melted insulation when they burn out

chassis electrical components, and is the probable cause of trouble when none of the electrical components function, unless the battery is disconnected or dead.

Electrical problems generally fall into one of three areas:

1. The component that is not functioning is not receiving current.
2. The component itself is not functioning.
3. The component is not properly grounded.

The electrical system can be checked with a test light and a jumper wire. A test light is a device that looks like a pointed screwdriver with a wire attached to it and has a light bulb in its handle. A jumper wire is a piece of insulated wire with an alligator clip attached to each end.

If a component is not working, you must follow a systematic plan to determine which of the three causes is the villain.

1. Turn on the switch that controls the inoperable component.
2. Disconnect the power supply wire from the component.
3. Attach the ground wire on the test light to a good metal ground.
4. Touch the probe end of the test light to the end of the power supply wire that was disconnected from the component. If the component is receiving current, the test light will go on.

NOTE: ***Some components work only when the ignition switch is turned on.***

If the test light does not go on, then the problem is in the circuit between the battery and the component. This includes all the switches, fuses, and relays in the system. Follow the wire that runs back to the battery. The problem is an open circuit between the

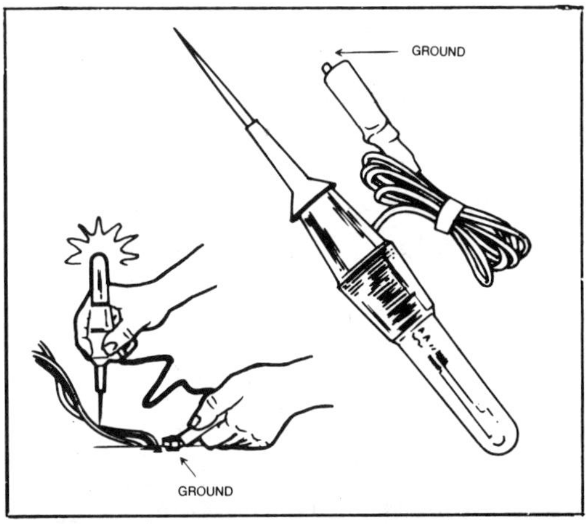

The test light will show the presence of current when touched to a hot wire and grounded at the other end

battery and the component. If the fuse is blown and, when replaced, immediately blows again, there is a short circuit in the system which must be located and repaired. If there is a switch in the system, bypass it with a jumper wire. This is done by connecting one end of the jumper wire to the power supply wire into the switch and the other end of the jumper wire to the wire coming out of the switch. If the test light lights with the jumper wire installed, the switch or whatever was bypassed is defective.

NOTE: ***Never substitute the jumper wire for the component, since it is required to use the power from the power source.***

5. If the bulb in the test light goes on, then the current is getting to the component that is not working. This eliminates the first of the three possible causes. Connect the power supply wire and connect a jumper wire from the component to a good metal ground. Do this with the switch which controls the component turned on, and also the ignition switch turned on if it is required for the component to work. If the component works with the jumper wire installed, then it has a bad ground. This is usually caused by the metal area on which the component mounts to the chassis being coated with some type of foreign matter.
6. If neither test located the source of the trouble, then the component itself is defective. Remember that for any electrical system to work, all connections must be clean and tight.

Troubleshooting Basic Turn Signal and Flasher Problems

See Chapter 5 for service procedures

Most problems in the turn signals or flasher system can be reduced to defective flashers or bulbs, which are easily replaced. Occasionally, the turn signal switch will prove defective.

F = Front R = Rear ● = Lights off ○ = Lights on

Condition		Possible Cause
Turn signals light, but do not flash	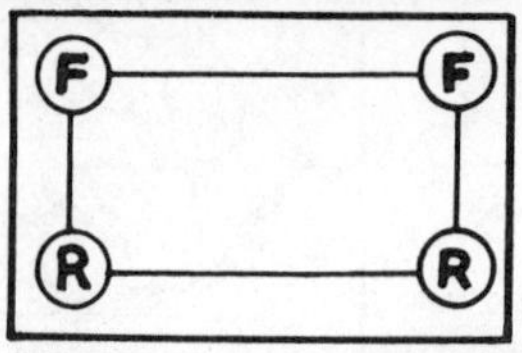	Defective flasher
No turn signals light on either side	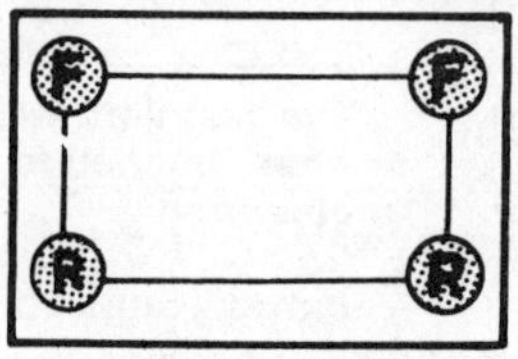	Blown fuse. Replace if defective. Defective flasher. Check by substitution. Open circuit, short circuit or poor ground.
Both turn signals on one side don't work	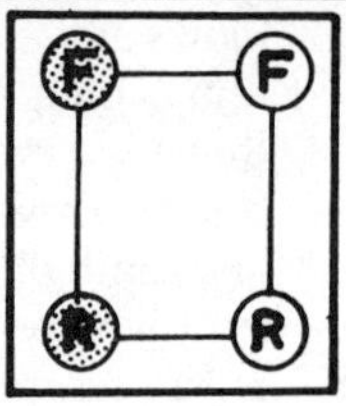	Bad bulbs. Bad ground in both (or either) housings.
One turn signal light on one side doesn't work	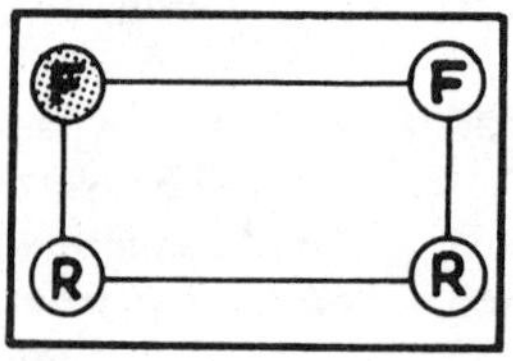	Defective bulb. Corrosion in socket. Clean contacts. Poor ground at socket.
Turn signal flashes too fast or too slowly	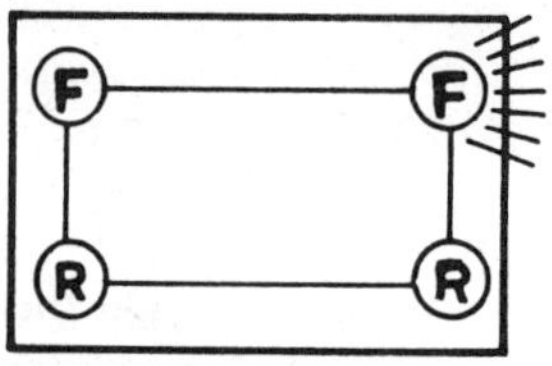	Check any bulb on the side flashing too fast. A heavy-duty bulb is probably installed in place of a regular bulb. Check the bulb flashing too slowly. A standard bulb was probably installed in place of a heavy-duty bulb. Loose connections or corrosion at the bulb socket.
Indicator lights don't work in either direction		Check if the turn signals are working. Check the dash indicator lights. Check the flasher by substitution.
One indicator light doesn't light		On systems with one dash indicator: See if the lights work on the same side. Often the filaments have been reversed in systems combining stoplights with taillights and turn signals. Check the flasher by substitution. On systems with two indicators: Check the bulbs on the same side. Check the indicator light bulb. Check the flasher by substitution.

Troubleshooting Lighting Problems

See Chapter 5 for service procedures

Condition	Possible Cause
One or more lights don't work, but others do	1. Defective bulb(s) 2. Blown fuse(s) 3. Dirty fuse clips or light sockets 4. Poor ground circuit
Lights burn out quickly	1. Incorrect voltage regulator setting or defective regulator 2. Poor battery/alternator connections
Lights go dim	1. Low/discharged battery 2. Alternator not charging 3. Corroded sockets or connections 4. Low voltage output
Lights flicker	1. Loose connection 2. Poor ground. (Run ground wire from light housing to frame) 3. Circuit breaker operating (short circuit)
Lights "flare"—Some flare is normal on acceleration—If excessive, see "Lights Burn Out Quickly"	High voltage setting
Lights glare—approaching drivers are blinded	1. Lights adjusted too high 2. Rear springs or shocks sagging 3. Rear tires soft

Troubleshooting Dash Gauge Problems

Most problems can be traced to a defective sending unit or faulty wiring. Occasionally, the gauge itself is at fault. See Chapter 5 for service procedures.

Condition	Possible Cause
COOLANT TEMPERATURE GAUGE	
Gauge reads erratically or not at all	1. Loose or dirty connections 2. Defective sending unit. 3. Defective gauge. To test a bi-metal gauge, remove the wire from the sending unit. Ground the wire for an instant. If the gauge registers, replace the sending unit. To test a magnetic gauge, disconnect the wire at the sending unit. With ignition ON gauge should register COLD. Ground the wire; gauge should register HOT.
AMMETER GAUGE—TURN HEADLIGHTS ON (DO NOT START ENGINE). NOTE REACTION	
Ammeter shows charge Ammeter shows discharge Ammeter does not move	1. Connections reversed on gauge 2. Ammeter is OK 3. Loose connections or faulty wiring 4. Defective gauge

Condition	Possible Cause
OIL PRESSURE GAUGE	
Gauge does not register or is inaccurate	1. On mechanical gauge, Bourdon tube may be bent or kinked. 2. Low oil pressure. Remove sending unit. Idle the engine briefly. If no oil flows from sending unit hole, problem is in engine. 3. Defective gauge. Remove the wire from the sending unit and ground it for an instant with the ignition ON. A good gauge will go to the top of the scale. 4. Defective wiring. Check the wiring to the gauge. If it's OK and the gauge doesn't register when grounded, replace the gauge. 5. Defective sending unit.
ALL GAUGES	
All gauges do not operate	1. Blown fuse 2. Defective instrument regulator
All gauges read low or erratically	3. Defective or dirty instrument voltage regulator
All gauges pegged	4. Loss of ground between instrument voltage regulator and frame 5. Defective instrument regulator
WARNING LIGHTS	
Light(s) do not come on when ignition is ON, but engine is not started	1. Defective bulb 2. Defective wire 3. Defective sending unit. Disconnect the wire from the sending unit and ground it. Replace the sending unit if the light comes on with the ignition ON.
Light comes on with engine running	4. Problem in individual system 5. Defective sending unit

Troubleshooting Clutch Problems

It is false economy to replace individual clutch components. The pressure plate, clutch plate and throwout bearing should be replaced as a set, and the flywheel face inspected, whenever the clutch is overhauled. See Chapter 6 for service procedures.

Condition	Possible Cause
Clutch chatter	1. Grease on driven plate (disc) facing 2. Binding clutch linkage or cable 3. Loose, damaged facings on driven plate (disc) 4. Engine mounts loose 5. Incorrect height adjustment of pressure plate release levers 6. Clutch housing or housing to transmission adapter misalignment 7. Loose driven plate hub
Clutch grabbing	1. Oil, grease on driven plate (disc) facing 2. Broken pressure plate 3. Warped or binding driven plate. Driven plate binding on clutch shaft
Clutch slips	1. Lack of lubrication in clutch linkage or cable (linkage or cable binds, causes incomplete engagement) 2. Incorrect pedal, or linkage adjustment 3. Broken pressure plate springs 4. Weak pressure plate springs 5. Grease on driven plate facings (disc)

Troubleshooting Clutch Problems (cont.)

Condition	Possible Cause
Incomplete clutch release	1. Incorrect pedal or linkage adjustment or linkage or cable binding 2. Incorrect height adjustment on pressure plate release levers 3. Loose, broken facings on driven plate (disc) 4. Bent, dished, warped driven plate caused by overheating
Grinding, whirring grating noise when pedal is depressed	1. Worn or defective throwout bearing 2. Starter drive teeth contacting flywheel ring gear teeth. Look for milled or polished teeth on ring gear.
Squeal, howl, trumpeting noise when pedal is being released (occurs during first inch to inch and one-half of pedal travel)	Pilot bushing worn or lack of lubricant. If bushing appears OK, polish bushing with emery cloth, soak lube wick in oil, lube bushing with oil, apply film of chassis grease to clutch shaft pilot hub, reassemble. NOTE: Bushing wear may be due to misalignment of clutch housing or housing to transmission adapter
Vibration or clutch pedal pulsation with clutch disengaged (pedal fully depressed)	1. Worn or defective engine transmission mounts 2. Flywheel run out. (Flywheel run out at face not to exceed 0.005″) 3. Damaged or defective clutch components

Troubleshooting Manual Transmission Problems

See Chapter 6 for service procedures

Condition	Possible Cause
Transmission jumps out of gear	1. Misalignment of transmission case or clutch housing. 2. Worn pilot bearing in crankshaft. 3. Bent transmission shaft. 4. Worn high speed sliding gear. 5. Worn teeth or end-play in clutch shaft. 6. Insufficient spring tension on shifter rail plunger. 7. Bent or loose shifter fork. 8. Gears not engaging completely. 9. Loose or worn bearings on clutch shaft or mainshaft. 10. Worn gear teeth. 11. Worn or damaged detent balls.
Transmission sticks in gear	1. Clutch not releasing fully. 2. Burred or battered teeth on clutch shaft, or sliding sleeve. 3. Burred or battered transmission mainshaft. 4. Frozen synchronizing clutch. 5. Stuck shifter rail plunger. 6. Gearshift lever twisting and binding shifter rail. 7. Battered teeth on high speed sliding gear or on sleeve. 8. Improper lubrication, or lack of lubrication. 9. Corroded transmission parts. 10. Defective mainshaft pilot bearing. 11. Locked gear bearings will give same effect as stuck in gear.
Transmission gears will not synchronize	1. Binding pilot bearing on mainshaft, will synchronize in high gear only. 2. Clutch not releasing fully. 3. Detent spring weak or broken. 4. Weak or broken springs under balls in sliding gear sleeve. 5. Binding bearing on clutch shaft, or binding countershaft. 6. Binding pilot bearing in crankshaft. 7. Badly worn gear teeth. 8. Improper lubrication. 9. Constant mesh gear not turning freely on transmission mainshaft. Will synchronize in that gear only.

Condition	Possible Cause
Gears spinning when shifting into gear from neutral	1. Clutch not releasing fully. 2. In some cases an extremely light lubricant in transmission will cause gears to continue to spin for a short time after clutch is released. 3. Binding pilot bearing in crankshaft.
Transmission noisy in all gears	1. Insufficient lubricant, or improper lubricant. 2. Worn countergear bearings. 3. Worn or damaged main drive gear or countergear. 4. Damaged main drive gear or mainshaft bearings. 5. Worn or damaged countergear anti-lash plate.
Transmission noisy in neutral only	1. Damaged main drive gear bearing. 2. Damaged or loose mainshaft pilot bearing. 3. Worn or damaged countergear anti-lash plate. 4. Worn countergear bearings.
Transmission noisy in one gear only	1. Damaged or worn constant mesh gears. 2. Worn or damaged countergear bearings. 3. Damaged or worn synchronizer.
Transmission noisy in reverse only	1. Worn or damaged reverse idler gear or idler bushing. 2. Worn or damaged mainshaft reverse gear. 3. Worn or damaged reverse countergear. 4. Damaged shift mechanism.

TROUBLESHOOTING AUTOMATIC TRANSMISSION PROBLEMS

Keeping alert to changes in the operating characteristics of the transmission (changing shift points, noises, etc.) can prevent small problems from becoming large ones. If the problem cannot be traced to loose bolts, fluid level, misadjusted linkage, clogged filters or similar problems, you should probably seek professional service.

Transmission Fluid Indications

The appearance and odor of the transmission fluid can give valuable clues to the overall condition of the transmission. Always note the appearance of the fluid when you check the fluid level or change the fluid. Rub a small amount of fluid between your fingers to feel for grit and smell the fluid on the dipstick.

If the fluid appears:	It indicates:
Clear and red colored	Normal operation
Discolored (extremely dark red or brownish) or smells burned	Band or clutch pack failure, usually caused by an overheated transmission. Hauling very heavy loads with insufficient power or failure to change the fluid often result in overheating. Do not confuse this appearance with newer fluids that have a darker red color and a strong odor (though not a burned odor).
Foamy or aerated (light in color and full of bubbles)	1. The level is too high (gear train is churning oil) 2. An internal air leak (air is mixing with the fluid). Have the transmission checked professionally.
Solid residue in the fluid	Defective bands, clutch pack or bearings. Bits of band material or metal abrasives are ciinging to the dipstick. Have the transmission checked professionally.
Varnish coating on the dipstick	The transmission fluid is overheating

TROUBLESHOOTING DRIVE AXLE PROBLEMS

First, determine when the noise is most noticeable.

Drive Noise: Produced under vehicle acceleration.

Coast Noise: Produced while coasting with a closed throttle.

Float Noise: Occurs while maintaining constant speed (just enough to keep speed constant) on a level road.

External Noise Elimination

It is advisable to make a thorough road test to determine whether the noise originates in the rear axle or whether it originates from the tires, engine, transmission, wheel bearings or road surface. Noise originating from other places cannot be corrected by servicing the rear axle.

ROAD NOISE

Brick or rough surfaced concrete roads produce noises that seem to come from the rear axle. Road noise is usually identical in Drive or Coast and driving on a different type of road will tell whether the road is the problem.

TIRE NOISE

Tire noise can be mistaken as rear axle noise, even though the tires on the front are at fault. Snow tread and mud tread tires or tires worn unevenly will frequently cause vibrations which seem to originate elsewhere; *temporarily, and for test purposes only,* inflate the tires to 40–50 lbs. This will significantly alter the noise produced by the tires, but will not alter noise from the rear axle. Noises from the rear axle will normally cease at speeds below 30 mph on coast, while tire noise will continue at lower tone as speed is decreased. The rear axle noise will usually change from drive conditions to coast conditions, while tire noise will not. Do not forget to lower the tire pressure to normal after the test is complete.

ENGINE/TRANSMISSION NOISE

Determine at what speed the noise is most pronounced, then stop in a quiet place. With the transmission in Neutral, run the engine through speeds corresponding to road speeds where the noise was noticed. Noises produced with the vehicle standing still are coming from the engine or transmission.

FRONT WHEEL BEARINGS

Front wheel bearing noises, sometimes confused with rear axle noises, will not change when comparing drive and coast conditions. While holding the speed steady, lightly apply the footbrake. This will often cause wheel bearing noise to lessen, as some of the weight is taken off the bearing. Front wheel bearings are easily checked by jacking up the wheels and spinning the wheels. Shaking the wheels will also determine if the wheel bearings are excessively loose.

REAR AXLE NOISES

Eliminating other possible sources can narrow the cause to the rear axle, which normally produces noise from worn gears or bearings. Gear noises tend to peak in a narrow speed range, while bearing noises will usually vary in pitch with engine speeds.

Noise Diagnosis

The Noise Is:	*Most Probably Produced By:*
1. Identical under Drive or Coast	Road surface, tires or front wheel bearings
2. Different depending on road surface	Road surface or tires
3. Lower as speed is lowered	Tires
4. Similar when standing or moving	Engine or transmission
5. A vibration	Unbalanced tires, rear wheel bearing, unbalanced driveshaft or worn U-joint
6. A knock or click about every two tire revolutions	Rear wheel bearing
7. Most pronounced on turns	Damaged differential gears
8. A steady low-pitched whirring or scraping, starting at low speeds	Damaged or worn pinion bearing
9. A chattering vibration on turns	Wrong differential lubricant or worn clutch plates (limited slip rear axle)
10. Noticed only in Drive, Coast or Float conditions	Worn ring gear and/or pinion gear

Troubleshooting Steering & Suspension Problems

Condition	Possible Cause
Hard steering (wheel is hard to turn)	1. Improper tire pressure 2. Loose or glazed pump drive belt 3. Low or incorrect fluid 4. Loose, bent or poorly lubricated front end parts 5. Improper front end alignment (excessive caster) 6. Bind in steering column or linkage 7. Kinked hydraulic hose 8. Air in hydraulic system 9. Low pump output or leaks in system 10. Obstruction in lines 11. Pump valves sticking or out of adjustment 12. Incorrect wheel alignment
Loose steering (too much play in steering wheel)	1. Loose wheel bearings 2. Faulty shocks 3. Worn linkage or suspension components 4. Loose steering gear mounting or linkage points 5. Steering mechanism worn or improperly adjusted 6. Valve spool improperly adjusted 7. Worn ball joints, tie-rod ends, etc.
Veers or wanders (pulls to one side with hands off steering wheel)	1. Improper tire pressure 2. Improper front end alignment 3. Dragging or improperly adjusted brakes 4. Bent frame 5. Improper rear end alignment 6. Faulty shocks or springs 7. Loose or bent front end components 8. Play in Pitman arm 9. Steering gear mountings loose 10. Loose wheel bearings 11. Binding Pitman arm 12. Spool valve sticking or improperly adjusted 13. Worn ball joints
Wheel oscillation or vibration transmitted through steering wheel	1. Low or uneven tire pressure 2. Loose wheel bearings 3. Improper front end alignment 4. Bent spindle 5. Worn, bent or broken front end components 6. Tires out of round or out of balance 7. Excessive lateral runout in disc brake rotor 8. Loose or bent shock absorber or strut
Noises (see also "Troubleshooting Drive Axle Problems")	1. Loose belts 2. Low fluid, air in system 3. Foreign matter in system 4. Improper lubrication 5. Interference or chafing in linkage 6. Steering gear mountings loose 7. Incorrect adjustment or wear in gear box 8. Faulty valves or wear in pump 9. Kinked hydraulic lines 10. Worn wheel bearings
Poor return of steering	1. Over-inflated tires 2. Improperly aligned front end (excessive caster) 3. Binding in steering column 4. No lubrication in front end 5. Steering gear adjusted too tight
Uneven tire wear (see "How To Read Tire Wear")	1. Incorrect tire pressure 2. Improperly aligned front end 3. Tires out-of-balance 4. Bent or worn suspension parts

HOW TO READ TIRE WEAR

The way your tires wear is a good indicator of other parts of the suspension. Abnormal wear patterns are often caused by the need for simple tire maintenance, or for front end alignment.

Excessive wear at the center of the tread indicates that the air pressure in the tire is consistently too high. The tire is riding on the center of the tread and wearing it prematurely. Occasionally, this wear pattern can result from outrageously wide tires on narrow rims. The cure for this is to replace either the tires or the wheels.

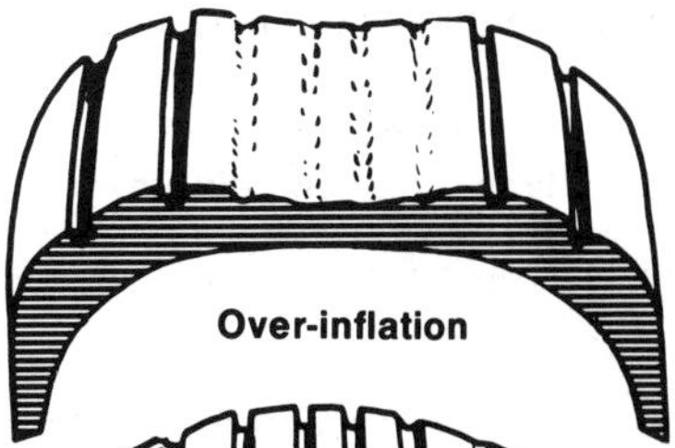

Over-inflation

This type of wear usually results from consistent under-inflation. When a tire is under-inflated, there is too much contact with the road by the outer treads, which wear prematurely. When this type of wear occurs, and the tire pressure is known to be consistently correct, a bent or worn steering component or the need for wheel alignment could be indicated.

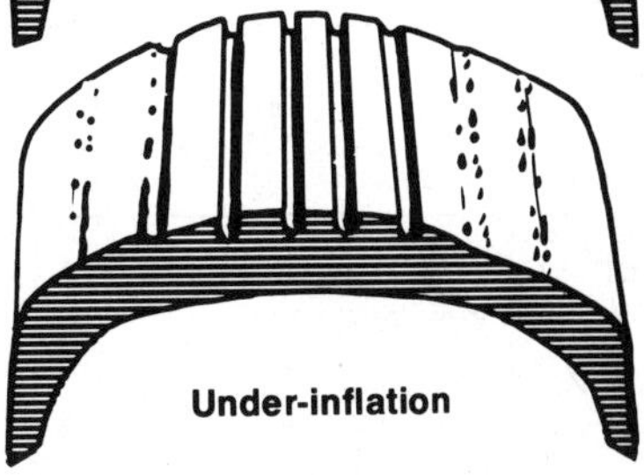

Under-inflation

Feathering is a condition when the edge of each tread rib develops a slightly rounded edge on one side and a sharp edge on the other. By running your hand over the tire, you can usually feel the sharper edges before you'll be able to see them. The most common causes of feathering are incorrect toe-in setting or deteriorated bushings in the front suspension.

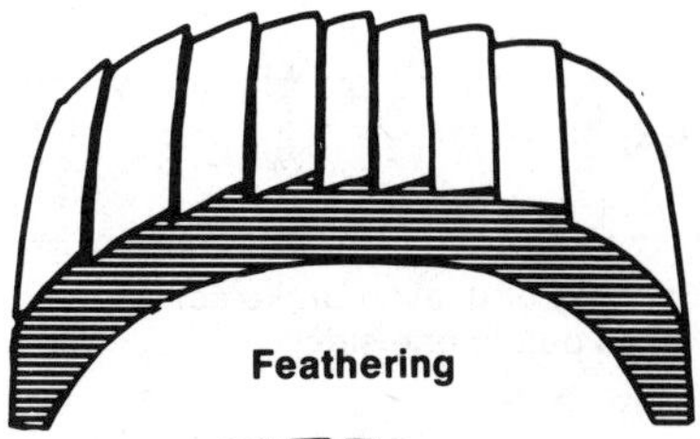

Feathering

When an inner or outer rib wears faster than the rest of the tire, the need for wheel alignment is indicated. There is excessive camber in the front suspension, causing the wheel to lean too much putting excessive load on one side of the tire. Misalignment could also be due to sagging springs, worn ball joints, or worn control arm bushings. Be sure the vehicle is loaded the way it's normally driven when you have the wheels aligned.

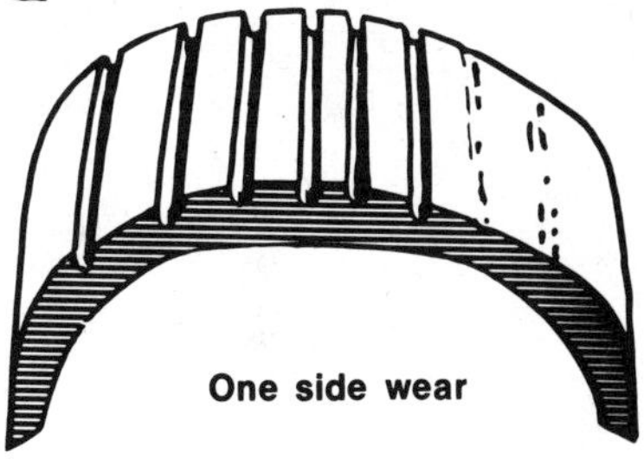

One side wear

Cups or scalloped dips appearing around the edge of the tread almost always indicate worn (sometimes bent) suspension parts. Adjustment of wheel alignment alone will seldom cure the problem. Any worn component that connects the wheel to the suspension can cause this type of wear. Occasionally, wheels that are out of balance will wear like this, but wheel imbalance usually shows up as bald spots between the outside edges and center of the tread.

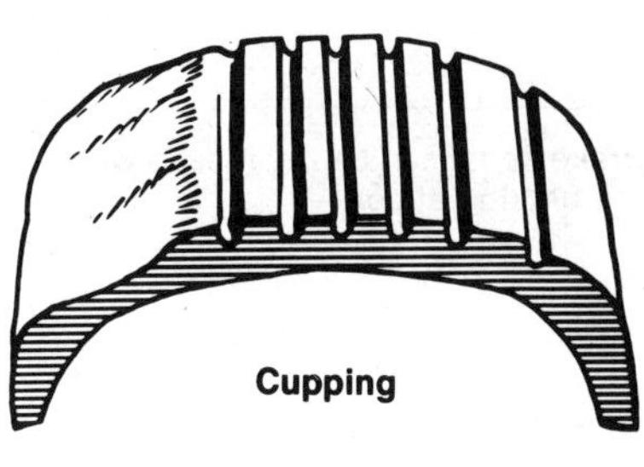

Cupping

Second-rib wear is usually found only in radial tires, and appears where the steel belts end in relation to the tread. It can be kept to a minimum by paying careful attention to tire pressure and frequently rotating the tires. This is often considered normal wear but excessive amounts indicate that the tires are too wide for the wheels.

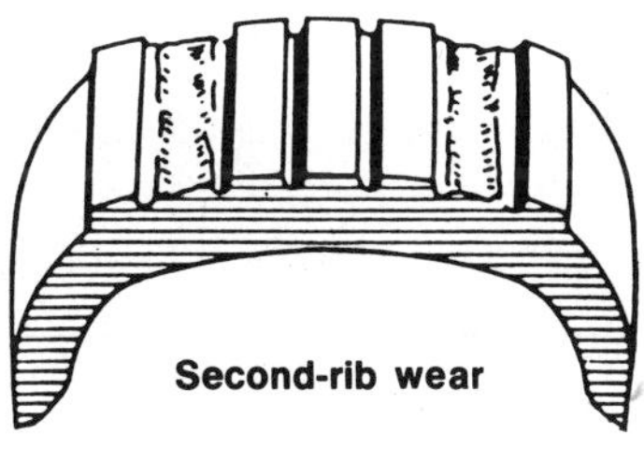

Second-rib wear

Troubleshooting Disc Brake Problems

Condition	*Possible Cause*
Noise—groan—brake noise emanating when slowly releasing brakes (creep-groan)	Not detrimental to function of disc brakes—no corrective action required. (This noise may be eliminated by slightly increasing or decreasing brake pedal efforts.)
Rattle—brake noise or rattle emanating at low speeds on rough roads, (front wheels only).	1. Shoe anti-rattle spring missing or not properly positioned. 2. Excessive clearance between shoe and caliper. 3. Soft or broken caliper seals. 4. Deformed or misaligned disc. 5. Loose caliper.
Scraping	1. Mounting bolts too long. 2. Loose wheel bearings. 3. Bent, loose, or misaligned splash shield.
Front brakes heat up during driving and fail to release	1. Operator riding brake pedal. 2. Stop light switch improperly adjusted. 3. Sticking pedal linkage. 4. Frozen or seized piston. 5. Residual pressure valve in master cylinder. 6. Power brake malfunction. 7. Proportioning valve malfunction.
Leaky brake caliper	1. Damaged or worn caliper piston seal. 2. Scores or corrosion on surface of cylinder bore.
Grabbing or uneven brake action—Brakes pull to one side	1. Causes listed under "Brakes Pull". 2. Power brake malfunction. 3. Low fluid level in master cylinder. 4. Air in hydraulic system. 5. Brake fluid, oil or grease on linings. 6. Unmatched linings. 7. Distorted brake pads. 8. Frozen or seized pistons. 9. Incorrect tire pressure. 10. Front end out of alignment. 11. Broken rear spring. 12. Brake caliper pistons sticking. 13. Restricted hose or line. 14. Caliper not in proper alignment to braking disc. 15. Stuck or malfunctioning metering valve. 16. Soft or broken caliper seals. 17. Loose caliper.
Brake pedal can be depressed without braking effect	1. Air in hydraulic system or improper bleeding procedure. 2. Leak past primary cup in master cylinder. 3. Leak in system. 4. Rear brakes out of adjustment. 5. Bleeder screw open.
Excessive pedal travel	1. Air, leak, or insufficient fluid in system or caliper. 2. Warped or excessively tapered shoe and lining assembly. 3. Excessive disc runout. 4. Rear brake adjustment required. 5. Loose wheel bearing adjustment. 6. Damaged caliper piston seal. 7. Improper brake fluid (boil). 8. Power brake malfunction. 9. Weak or soft hoses.

Troubleshooting Disc Brake Problems (cont.)

Condition	Possible Cause
Brake roughness or chatter (pedal pumping)	1. Excessive thickness variation of braking disc. 2. Excessive lateral runout of braking disc. 3. Rear brake drums out-of-round. 4. Excessive front bearing clearance.
Excessive pedal effort	1. Brake fluid, oil or grease on linings. 2. Incorrect lining. 3. Frozen or seized pistons. 4. Power brake malfunction. 5. Kinked or collapsed hose or line. 6. Stuck metering valve. 7. Scored caliper or master cylinder bore. 8. Seized caliper pistons.
Brake pedal fades (pedal travel increases with foot on brake)	1. Rough master cylinder or caliper bore. 2. Loose or broken hydraulic lines/connections. 3. Air in hydraulic system. 4. Fluid level low. 5. Weak or soft hoses. 6. Inferior quality brake shoes or fluid. 7. Worn master cylinder piston cups or seals.

Troubleshooting Drum Brakes

Condition	Possible Cause
Pedal goes to floor	1. Fluid low in reservoir. 2. Air in hydraulic system. 3. Improperly adjusted brake. 4. Leaking wheel cylinders. 5. Loose or broken brake lines. 6. Leaking or worn master cylinder. 7. Excessively worn brake lining.
Spongy brake pedal	1. Air in hydraulic system. 2. Improper brake fluid (low boiling point). 3. Excessively worn or cracked brake drums. 4. Broken pedal pivot bushing.
Brakes pulling	1. Contaminated lining. 2. Front end out of alignment. 3. Incorrect brake adjustment. 4. Unmatched brake lining. 5. Brake drums out of round. 6. Brake shoes distorted. 7. Restricted brake hose or line. 8. Broken rear spring. 9. Worn brake linings. 10. Uneven lining wear. 11. Glazed brake lining. 12. Excessive brake lining dust. 13. Heat spotted brake drums. 14. Weak brake return springs. 15. Faulty automatic adjusters. 16. Low or incorrect tire pressure.

Condition	Possible Cause
Squealing brakes	1. Glazed brake lining. 2. Saturated brake lining. 3. Weak or broken brake shoe retaining spring. 4. Broken or weak brake shoe return spring. 5. Incorrect brake lining. 6. Distorted brake shoes. 7. Bent support plate. 8. Dust in brakes or scored brake drums. 9. Linings worn below limit. 10. Uneven brake lining wear. 11. Heat spotted brake drums.
Chirping brakes	1. Out of round drum or eccentric axle flange pilot.
Dragging brakes	1. Incorrect wheel or parking brake adjustment. 2. Parking brakes engaged or improperly adjusted. 3. Weak or broken brake shoe return spring. 4. Brake pedal binding. 5. Master cylinder cup sticking. 6. Obstructed master cylinder relief port. 7. Saturated brake lining. 8. Bent or out of round brake drum. 9. Contaminated or improper brake fluid. 10. Sticking wheel cylinder pistons. 11. Driver riding brake pedal. 12. Defective proportioning valve. 13. Insufficient brake shoe lubricant.
Hard pedal	1. Brake booster inoperative. 2. Incorrect brake lining. 3. Restricted brake line or hose. 4. Frozen brake pedal linkage. 5. Stuck wheel cylinder. 6. Binding pedal linkage. 7. Faulty proportioning valve.
Wheel locks	1. Contaminated brake lining. 2. Loose or torn brake lining. 3. Wheel cylinder cups sticking. 4. Incorrect wheel bearing adjustment. 5. Faulty proportioning valve.
Brakes fade (high speed)	1. Incorrect lining. 2. Overheated brake drums. 3. Incorrect brake fluid (low boiling temperature). 4. Saturated brake lining. 5. Leak in hydraulic system. 6. Faulty automatic adjusters.
Pedal pulsates	1. Bent or out of round brake drum.
Brake chatter and shoe knock	1. Out of round brake drum. 2. Loose support plate. 3. Bent support plate. 4. Distorted brake shoes. 5. Machine grooves in contact face of brake drum (Shoe Knock). 6. Contaminated brake lining. 7. Missing or loose components. 8. Incorrect lining material. 9. Out-of-round brake drums. 10. Heat spotted or scored brake drums. 11. Out-of-balance wheels.

Troubleshooting Drum Brakes (cont.)

Condition	Possible Cause
Brakes do not self adjust	1. Adjuster screw frozen in thread. 2. Adjuster screw corroded at thrust washer. 3. Adjuster lever does not engage star wheel. 4. Adjuster installed on wrong wheel.
Brake light glows	1. Leak in the hydraulic system. 2. Air in the system. 3. Improperly adjusted master cylinder pushrod. 4. Uneven lining wear. 5. Failure to center combination valve or proportioning valve.

Mechanic's Data

General Conversion Table

Multiply By	To Convert	To	
	LENGTH		
2.54	Inches	Centimeters	.3937
25.4	Inches	Millimeters	.03937
30.48	Feet	Centimeters	.0328
.304	Feet	Meters	3.28
.914	Yards	Meters	1.094
1.609	Miles	Kilometers	.621
	VOLUME		
.473	Pints	Liters	2.11
.946	Quarts	Liters	1.06
3.785	Gallons	Liters	.264
.016	Cubic inches	Liters	61.02
16.39	Cubic inches	Cubic cms.	.061
28.3	Cubic feet	Liters	.0353
	MASS (Weight)		
28.35	Ounces	Grams	.035
.4536	Pounds	Kilograms	2.20
—	To obtain	From	Multiply by

Multiply By	To Convert	To	
	AREA		
.645	Square inches	Square cms.	.155
.836	Square yds.	Square meters	1.196
	FORCE		
4.448	Pounds	Newtons	.225
.138	Ft./lbs.	Kilogram/meters	7.23
1.36	Ft./lbs.	Newton-meters	.737
.112	In./lbs.	Newton-meters	8.844
	PRESSURE		
.068	Psi	Atmospheres	14.7
6.89	Psi	Kilopascals	.145
	OTHER		
1.104	Horsepower (DIN)	Horsepower (SAE)	.9861
.746	Horsepower (SAE)	Kilowatts (KW)	1.34
1.60	Mph	Km/h	.625
.425	Mpg	Km/1	2.35
—	To obtain	From	Multiply by

Tap Drill Sizes

National Coarse or U.S.S.

Screw & Tap Size	Threads Per Inch	Use Drill Number
No. 5	40	39
No. 6	32	36
No. 8	32	29
No. 10	24	25
No. 12	24	17
1/4	20	8
5/16	18	F
3/8	16	5/16
7/16	14	U
1/2	13	27/64
9/16	12	31/64
5/8	11	17/32
3/4	10	21/32
7/8	9	49/64

National Coarse or U.S.S.

Screw & Tap Size	Threads Per Inch	Use Drill Number
1	8	7/8
1 1/8	7	63/64
1 1/4	7	1 7/64
1 1/2	6	1 11/32

National Fine or S.A.E.

Screw & Tap Size	Threads Per Inch	Use Drill Number
No. 5	44	37
No. 6	40	33
No. 8	36	29
No. 10	32	21

National Fine or S.A.E.

Screw & Tap Size	Threads Per Inch	Use Drill Number
No. 12	28	15
1/4	28	3
6/16	24	1
3/8	24	Q
7/16	20	W
1/2	20	29/64
9/16	18	33/64
5/8	18	37/64
3/4	16	11/16
7/8	14	13/16
1 1/8	12	1 3/64
1 1/4	12	1 11/64
1 1/2	12	1 27/64

Drill Sizes In Decimal Equivalents

Inch	Decimal	Wire	mm
1/64	.0156		.39
	.0157		.4
	.0160	78	
	.0165		.42
	.0173		.44
	.0177		.45
	.0180	77	
	.0181		.46
	.0189		.48
	.0197		.5
	.0200	76	
	.0210	75	
	.0217		.55
	.0225	74	
	.0236		.6
	.0240	73	
	.0250	72	
	.0256		.65
	.0260	71	
	.0276		.7
	.0280	70	
	.0292	69	
	.0295		.75
	.0310	68	
1/32	.0312		.79
	.0315		.8
	.0320	67	
	.0330	66	
	.0335		.85
	.0350	65	
	.0354		.9
	.0360	64	
	.0370	63	
	.0374		.95
	.0380	62	
	.0390	61	
	.0394		1.0
	.0400	60	
	.0410	59	
	.0413		1.05
	.0420	58	
	.0430	57	
	.0433		1.1
	.0453		1.15
	.0465	56	
3/64	.0469		1.19
	.0472		1.2
	.0492		1.25
	.0512		1.3
	.0520	55	
	.0531		1.35
	.0550	54	
	.0551		1.4
	.0571		1.45
	.0591		1.5
	.0595	53	
	.0610		1.55
1/16	.0625		1.59
	.0630		1.6
	.0635	52	
	.0650		1.65
	.0669		1.7
	.0670	51	
	.0689		1.75
	.0700	50	
	.0709		1.8
	.0728		1.85

Inch	Decimal	Wire	mm
	.0730	49	
	.0748		1.9
	.0760	48	
	.0768		1.95
5/64	.0781		1.98
	.0785	47	
	.0787		2.0
	.0807		2.05
	.0810	46	
	.0820	45	
	.0827		2.1
	.0846		2.15
	.0860	44	
	.0866		2.2
	.0886		2.25
	.0890	43	
	.0906		2.3
	.0925		2.35
	.0935	42	
3/32	.0938		2.38
	.0945		2.4
	.0960	41	
	.0965		2.45
	.0980	40	
	.0981		2.5
	.0995	39	
	.1015	38	
	.1024		2.6
	.1040	37	
	.1063		2.7
	.1065	36	
	.1083		2.75
7/64	.1094		2.77
	.1100	35	
	.1102		2.8
	.1110	34	
	.1130	33	
	.1142		2.9
	.1160	32	
	.1181		3.0
	.1200	31	
	.1220		3.1
1/8	.1250		3.17
	.1260		3.2
	.1280		3.25
	.1285	30	
	.1299		3.3
	.1339		3.4
	.1360	29	
	.1378		3.5
	.1405	28	
9/64	.1406		3.57
	.1417		3.6
	.1440	27	
	.1457		3.7
	.1470	26	
	.1476		3.75
	.1495	25	
	.1496		3.8
	.1520	24	
	.1535		3.9
	.1540	23	
5/32	.1562		3.96
	.1570	22	
	.1575		4.0
	.1590	21	
	.1610	20	

Inch	Decimal	Wire & Letter	mm
	.1614		4.1
	.1654		4.2
	.1660	19	
	.1673		4.25
	.1693		4.3
	.1695	18	
11/64	.1719		4.36
	.1730	17	
	.1732		4.4
	.1770	16	
	.1772		4.5
	.1800	15	
	.1811		4.6
	.1820	14	
	.1850	13	
	.1850		4.7
	.1870		4.75
3/16	.1875		4.76
	.1890		4.8
	.1890	12	
	.1910	11	
	.1929		4.9
	.1935	10	
	.1960	9	
	.1969		5.0
	.1990	8	
	.2008		5.1
	.2010	7	
13/64	.2031		5.16
	.2040	6	
	.2047		5.2
	.2055	5	
	.2067		5.25
	.2087		5.3
	.2090	4	
	.2126		5.4
	.2130	3	
	.2165		5.5
7/32	2188		5.55
	.2205		5.6
	.2210	2	
	.2244		5.7
	.2264		5.75
	.2280	1	
	.2283		5.8
	.2323		5.9
	.2340	A	
15/64	.2344		5.95
	.2362		6.0
	.2380	B	
	.2402		6.1
	.2420	C	
	.2441		6.2
	.2460	D	
	.2461		6.25
	.2480		6.3
1/4	.2500	E	6.35
	.2520		6.
	.2559		6.5
	.2570	F	
	.2598		6.6
	.2610	G	
	.2638		6.7
17/64	.2656		6.74
	.2657		6.75
	.2660	H	
	.2677		6.8

Inch	Decimal	Letter	mm
	.2717		6.9
	.2720	I	
	.2756		7.0
	.2770	J	
	.2795		7.1
	.2810	K	
9/32	.2812		7.14
	.2835		7.2
	.2854		7.25
	.2874		7.3
	.2900	L	
	.2913		7.4
	.2950	M	
	.2953		7.5
19/64	.2969		7.54
	.2992		7.6
	.3020	N	
	.3031		7.7
	.3051		7.75
	.3071		7.8
	.3110		7.9
5/16	.3125		7.93
	.3150		8.0
	.3160	O	
	.3189		8.1
	.3228		8.2
	.3230	P	
	.3248		8.25
	.3268		8.3
21/64	.3281		8.33
	.3307		8.4
	.3320	Q	
	.3346		8.5
	.3386		8.6
	.3390	R	
	.3425		8.7
11/32	.3438		8.73
	.3445		8.75
	.3465		8.8
	.3480	S	
	.3504		8.9
	.3543		9.0
	.3580	T	
	.3583		9.1
23/64	.3594		9.12
	.3622		9.2
	.3642		9.25
	.3661		9.3
	.3680	U	
	.3701		9.4
	.3740		9.5
3/8	.3750		9.52
	.3770	V	
	.3780		9.6
	.3819		9.7
	.3839		9.75
	.3858		9.8
	.3860	W	
	.3898		9.9
25/64	.3906		9.92
	.3937		10.0
	.3970	X	
	.4040	Y	
13/32	.4062		10.31
	.4130	Z	
	.4134		10.5
27/64	.4219		10.71

Inch	Decimal	mm
	.4331	11.0
7/16	.4375	11.11
	.4528	11.5
29/64	.4531	11.51
15/32	.4688	11.90
	.4724	12.0
31/64	.4844	12.30
	.4921	12.5
1/2	.5000	12.70
	.5118	13.0
33/64	.5156	13.09
17/32	.5312	13.49
	.5315	13.5
35/64	.5469	13.89
	.5512	14.0
9/16	.5625	14.28
	.5709	14.5
37/64	.5781	14.68
	.5906	15.0
19/32	.5938	15.08
39/64	.6094	15.47
	.6102	15.5
5/8	.6250	15.87
	.6299	16.0
41/64	.6406	16.27
	.6496	16.5
21/32	.6562	16.66
	.6693	17.0
43/64	.6719	17.06
11/16	.6875	17.46
	.6890	17.5
45/64	.7031	17.85
	.7087	18.0
23/32	.7188	18.25
	.7283	18.5
47/64	.7344	18.65
	.7480	19.0
3/4	.7500	19.05
49/64	.7656	19.44
	.7677	19.5
25/32	.7812	19.84
	.7874	20.0
51/64	.7969	20.24
	.8071	20.5
13/16	.8125	20.63
	.8268	21.0
53/64	.8281	21.03
27/32	.8438	21.43
	.8465	21.5
55/64	.8594	21.82
	.8661	22.0
7/8	.8750	22.22
	.8858	22.5
57/64	.8906	22.62
	.9055	23.0
29/32	.9062	23.01
59/64	.9219	23.41
	.9252	23.5
15/16	.9375	23.81
	.9449	24.0
61/64	.9531	24.2
	.9646	24.5
31/64	.9688	24.6
	.9843	25.0
63/64	.9844	25.0
1	1.0000	25.4

Index

Chilton's Repair & Tune-Up Guides

The Complete line covers domestic cars, imports, trucks, vans, RV's and 4-wheel drive vehicles.

RTUG Title	Part No.
AMC 1975-82 Covers all U.S. and Canadian models	7199
Aspen/Volare 1976-80 Covers all U.S. and Canadian models	6637
Audi 1970-73 Covers all U.S. and Canadian models.	5902
Audi 4000/5000 1978-81 Covers all U.S. and Canadian models including turbocharged and diesel engines	7028
Barracuda/Challenger 1965-72 Covers all U.S. and Canadian models	5807
Blazer/Jimmy 1969-82 Covers all U.S. and Canadian 2- and 4-wheel drive models, including diesel engines	6931
BMW 1970-82 Covers U.S. and Canadian models	6844
Buick/Olds/Pontiac 1975-85 Covers all U.S. and Canadian full size rear wheel drive models	7308
Cadillac 1967-84 Covers all U.S. and Canadian rear wheel drive models	7462
Camaro 1967-81 Covers all U.S. and Canadian models	6735
Camaro 1982-85 Covers all U.S. and Canadian models	7317
Capri 1970-77 Covers all U.S. and Canadian models	6695
Caravan/Voyager 1984-85 Covers all U.S. and Canadian models	7482
Century/Regal 1975-85 Covers all U.S. and Canadian rear wheel drive models, including turbocharged engines	7307
Champ/Arrow/Sapporo 1978-83 Covers all U.S. and Canadian models	7041
Chevette/1000 1976-86 Covers all U.S. and Canadian models	6836
Chevrolet 1968-85 Covers all U.S. and Canadian models	7135
Chevrolet 1968-79 Spanish	7082
Chevrolet/GMC Pick-Ups 1970-82 Spanish	7468
Chevrolet/GMC Pick-Ups and Suburban 1970-86 Covers all U.S. and Canadian $^1/_2$, $^3/_4$ and 1 ton models, including 4-wheel drive and diesel engines	6936
Chevrolet LUV 1972-81 Covers all U.S. and Canadian models	6815
Chevrolet Mid-Size 1964-86 Covers all U.S. and Canadian models of 1964-77 Chevelle, Malibu and Malibu SS; 1974-77 Laguna; 1978-85 Malibu; 1970-86 Monte Carlo; 1964-84 El Camino, including diesel engines	6840
Chevrolet Nova 1986 Covers all U.S. and Canadian models	7658
Chevy/GMC Vans 1967-84 Covers all U.S. and Canadian models of $^1/_2$, $^3/_4$, and 1 ton vans, cutaways, and motor home chassis, including diesel engines	6930
Chevy S-10 Blazer/GMC S-15 Jimmy 1982-85 Covers all U.S. and Canadian models	7383
Chevy S-10/GMC S-15 Pick-Ups 1982-85 Covers all U.S. and Canadian models	7310
Chevy II/Nova 1962-79 Covers all U.S. and Canadian models	6841
Chrysler K- and E-Car 1981-85 Covers all U.S. and Canadian front wheel drive models	7163
Colt/Challenger/Vista/Conquest 1971-85 Covers all U.S. and Canadian models	7037
Corolla/Carina/Tercel/Starlet 1970-85 Covers all U.S. and Canadian models	7036
Corona/Cressida/Crown/Mk.II/Camry/Van 1970-84 Covers all U.S. and Canadian models	7044
Corvair 1960-69 Covers all U.S. and Canadian models	6691
Corvette 1953-62 Covers all U.S. and Canadian models	6576
Corvette 1963-84 Covers all U.S. and Canadian models	6843
Cutlass 1970-85 Covers all U.S. and Canadian models	6933
Dart/Demon 1968-76 Covers all U.S. and Canadian models	6324
Datsun 1961-72 Covers all U.S. and Canadian models of Nissan Patrol; 1500, 1600 and 2000 sports cars; Pick-Ups; 410, 411, 510, 1200 and 240Z	5790
Datsun 1973-80 Spanish	7083
Datsun/Nissan F-10, 310, Stanza, Pulsar 1977-86 Covers all U.S. and Canadian models	7196
Datsun/Nissan Pick-Ups 1970-84 Covers all U.S and Canadian models	6816
Datsun/Nissan Z & ZX 1970-86 Covers all U.S. and Canadian models	6932
Datsun/Nissan 1200, 210, Sentra 1973-86 Covers all U.S. and Canadian models	7197
Datsun/Nissan 200SX, 510, 610, 710, 810, Maxima 1973-84 Covers all U.S. and Canadian models	7170
Dodge 1968-77 Covers all U.S. and Canadian models	6554
Dodge Charger 1967-70 Covers all U.S. and Canadian models	6486
Dodge/Plymouth Trucks 1967-84 Covers all $^1/_2$, $^3/_4$, and 1 ton 2- and 4-wheel drive U.S. and Canadian models, including diesel engines	7459
Dodge/Plymouth Vans 1967-84 Covers all $^1/_2$, $^3/_4$, and 1 ton U.S. and Canadian models of vans, cutaways and motor home chassis	6934
D-50/Arrow Pick-Up 1979-81 Covers all U.S. and Canadian models	7032
Fairlane/Torino 1962-75 Covers all U.S. and Canadian models	6320
Fairmont/Zephyr 1978-83 Covers all U.S. and Canadian models	6965
Fiat 1969-81 Covers all U.S. and Canadian models	7042
Fiesta 1978-80 Covers all U.S. and Canadian models	6846
Firebird 1967-81 Covers all U.S. and Canadian models	5996
Firebird 1982-85 Covers all U.S. and Canadian models	7345
Ford 1968-79 Spanish	7084
Ford Bronco 1966-83 Covers all U.S. and Canadian models	7140
Ford Bronco II 1984 Covers all U.S. and Canadian models	7408
Ford Courier 1972-82 Covers all U.S. and Canadian models	6983
Ford/Mercury Front Wheel Drive 1981-85 Covers all U.S. and Canadian models Escort, EXP, Tempo, Lynx, LN-7 and Topaz	7055
Ford/Mercury/Lincoln 1968-85 Covers all U.S. and Canadian models of FORD Country Sedan, Country Squire, Crown Victoria, Custom, Custom 500, Galaxie 500, LTD through 1982, Ranch Wagon, and XL; MERCURY Colony Park, Commuter, Marquis through 1982, Gran Marquis, Monterey and Park Lane; LINCOLN Continental and Towne Car	6842
Ford/Mercury/Lincoln Mid-Size 1971-85 Covers all U.S. and Canadian models of FORD Elite, 1983-85 LTD, 1977-79 LTD II, Ranchero, Torino, Gran Torino, 1977-85 Thunderbird; MERCURY 1972-85 Cougar,	6696

continued on next page

RTUG Title	Part No.
1983-85 Marquis, Montego, 1980-85 XR-7; LINCOLN 1982-85 Continental, 1984-85 Mark VII, 1978-80 Versailles	
Ford Pick-Ups 1965-86 Covers all $^1/_2$, $^3/_4$ and 1 ton, 2- and 4-wheel drive U.S. and Canadian pick-up, chassis cab and camper models, including diesel engines	6913
Ford Pick-Ups 1965-82 Spanish	7469
Ford Ranger 1983-84 Covers all U.S. and Canadian models	7338
Ford Vans 1961-86 Covers all U.S. and Canadian $^1/_2$, $^3/_4$ and 1 ton van and cutaway chassis models, including diesel engines	6849
GM A-Body 1982-85 Covers all front wheel drive U.S. and Canadian models of BUICK Century, CHEVROLET Celebrity, OLDSMOBILE Cutlass Ciera and PONTIAC 6000	7309
GM C-Body 1985 Covers all front wheel drive U.S. and Canadian models of BUICK Electra Park Avenue and Electra T-Type, CADILLAC Fleetwood and deVille, OLDSMOBILE 98 Regency and Regency Brougham	7587
GM J-Car 1982-85 Covers all U.S. and Canadian models of BUICK Skyhawk, CHEVROLET Cavalier, CADILLAC Cimarron, OLDSMOBILE Firenza and PONTIAC 2000 and Sunbird	7059
GM N-Body 1985-86 Covers all U.S. and Canadian models of front wheel drive BUICK Somerset and Skylark, OLDSMOBILE Calais, and PONTIAC Grand Am	7657
GM X-Body 1980-85 Covers all U.S. and Canadian models of BUICK Skylark, CHEVROLET Citation, OLDSMOBILE Omega and PONTIAC Phoenix	7049
GM Subcompact 1971-80 Covers all U.S. and Canadian models of BUICK Skyhawk (1975-80), CHEVROLET Vega and Monza, OLDSMOBILE Starfire, and PONTIAC Astre and 1975-80 Sunbird	6935
Granada/Monarch 1975-82 Covers all U.S. and Canadian models	6937
Honda 1973-84 Covers all U.S. and Canadian models	6980
International Scout 1967-73 Covers all U.S. and Canadian models	5912
Jeep 1945-87 Covers all U.S. and Canadian CJ-2A, CJ-3A, CJ-3B, CJ-5, CJ-6, CJ-7, Scrambler and Wrangler models	6817
Jeep Wagoneer, Commando, Cherokee, Truck 1957-86 Covers all U.S. and Canadian models of Wagoneer, Cherokee, Grand Wagoneer, Jeepster, Jeepster Commando, J-100, J-200, J-300, J-10, J20, FC-150 and FC-170	6739
Laser/Daytona 1984-85 Covers all U.S. and Canadian models	7563
Maverick/Comet 1970-77 Covers all U.S. and Canadian models	6634
Mazda 1971-84 Covers all U.S. and Canadian models of RX-2, RX-3, RX-4, 808, 1300, 1600, Cosmo, GLC and 626	6981
Mazda Pick-Ups 1972-86 Covers all U.S. and Canadian models	7659
Mercedes-Benz 1959-70 Covers all U.S. and Canadian models	6065
Mereceds-Benz 1968-73 Covers all U.S. and Canadian models	5907

RTUG Title	Part No.
Mercedes-Benz 1974-84 Covers all U.S. and Canadian models	6809
Mitsubishi, Cordia, Tredia, Starion, Galant 1983-85 Covers all U.S. and Canadian models	7583
MG 1961-81 Covers all U.S. and Canadian models	6780
Mustang/Capri/Merkur 1979-85 Covers all U.S. and Canadian models	6963
Mustang/Cougar 1965-73 Covers all U.S. and Canadian models	6542
Mustang II 1974-78 Covers all U.S. and Canadian models	6812
Omni/Horizon/Rampage 1978-84 Covers all U.S. and Canadian models of DODGE omni, Miser, 024, Charger 2.2; PLYMOUTH Horizon, Miser, TC3, TC3 Tourismo; Rampage	6845
Opel 1971-75 Covers all U.S. and Canadian models	6575
Peugeot 1970-74 Covers all U.S. and Canadian models	5982
Pinto/Bobcat 1971-80 Covers all U.S. and Canadian models	7027
Plymouth 1968-76 Covers all U.S. and Canadian models	6552
Pontiac Fiero 1984-85 Covers all U.S. and Canadian models	7571
Pontiac Mid-Size 1974-83 Covers all U.S. and Canadian models of Ventura, Grand Am, LeMans, Grand LeMans, GTO, Phoenix, and Grand Prix	7346
Porsche 924/928 1976-81 Covers all U.S. and Canadian models	7048
Renault 1975-85 Covers all U.S. and Canadian models	7165
Roadrunner/Satellite/Belvedere/GTX 1968-73 Covers all U.S. and Canadian models	5821
RX-7 1979-81 Covers all U.S. and Canadian models	7031
SAAB 99 1969-75 Covers all U.S. and Canadian models	5988
SAAB 900 1979-85 Covers all U.S. and Canadian models	7572
Snowmobiles 1976-80 Covers Arctic Cat, John Deere, Kawasaki, Polaris, Ski-Doo and Yamaha	6978
Subaru 1970-84 Covers all U.S. and Canadian models	6982
Tempest/GTO/LeMans 1968-73 Covers all U.S. and Canadian models	5905
Toyota 1966-70 Covers all U.S. and Canadian models of Corona, MkII, Corolla, Crown, Land Cruiser, Stout and Hi-Lux	5795
Toyota 1970-79 Spanish	7467
Toyota Celica/Supra 1971-85 Covers all U.S. and Canadian models	7043
Toyota Trucks 1970-85 Covers all U.S. and Canadian models of pick-ups, Land Cruiser and 4Runner	7035
Valiant/Duster 1968-76 Covers all U.S. and Canadian models	6326
Volvo 1956-69 Covers all U.S. and Canadian models	6529
Volvo 1970-83 Covers all U.S. and Canadian models	7040
VW Front Wheel Drive 1974-85 Covers all U.S. and Canadian models	6962
VW 1949-71 Covers all U.S. and Canadian models	5796
VW 1970-79 Spanish	7081
VW 1970-81 Covers all U.S. and Canadian Beetles, Karmann Ghia, Fastback, Squareback, Vans, 411 and 412	6837

Chilton's Repair & Tune-Up Guides are available at your local retailer or by mailing a check or money order for **$12.50** plus **$2.25** to cover postage and handling to:

Chilton Book Company
Dept. DM
Radnor, PA 19089

NOTE: When ordering be sure to include your name & address, book part No. & title.